Remnant

THE RIGHTEOUS REMNANT NOW ARISES

by

James Bailey

Published by Z3 News, LLC

© Copyright 2019 - Z3 News, LLC

ALL RIGHTS RESERVED: This book is protected by the copyright laws of the United States of America. This book may not be copied or reprinted for commercial gain or profit. The use of short quotations or occasional page copying for personal or group study is permitted and encouraged. This book may not be copied, or stored in any information retrieval system, in whole or in part, without permission in writing from Z3 News, LLC. Scripture quotations marked NKJV are taken from the New King James Version, Copyright © 1982 by Thomas Nelson, Inc. Used by permission. All rights reserved.

Mailing Address: Z3 News, LLC
                   980 Birmingham Rd. Suite 501-273
                   Milton GA 30004

Visit us on the Internet: Z3news.com

To order printed copies or eBooks, visit: Z3news.com/w/store

Table of Contents

Part 1: The Righteous Remnant Arises

Chapter 1: Dreams..11

Chapter 2: Forerunners..17

Chapter 3: Confirmations..31

Chapter 4: Righteousness..47

Chapter 5: Promises...63

Chapter 6: Trouble..77

Chapter 7: Hunger...89

Chapter 8: Encounters..101

Chapter 9: Separation..113

Chapter 10: Unity..137

Chapter 11: Assignments..149

Chapter 12: Training...165

Chapter 13: Qualified..175

Chapter 14: Warfare..185

Chapter 15: Restoration..197

Table of Contents

Part 2: Signs of the Times

Chapter 16:	Signs	211
Chapter 17:	Israel	217
Chapter 18:	Earthquakes	227
Chapter 19:	Knowledge and Travel	229
Chapter 20:	Lawlessness	237
Chapter 21:	Deception and Apostasy	253
Chapter 22:	Wars	267

Table of Contents

Exhibits:

Exhibit 1:	Five Reasons Why Elijah is One of the Two Witnesses	288
Exhibit 2:	41 Proofs God is Not Done with the Jewish People	289
Exhibit 3:	Satan's Favorite Lies About the Jewish People	322
Exhibit 4:	Commandment Scriptures	326
Exhibit 5:	445 Laws of Moses	329
Exhibit 6:	Unrighteous Deeds	333
Exhibit 7:	Righteousness Word Study	336
Exhibit 8:	19 Promises for Provision	339
Exhibit 9:	5 Promises for Answer Prayers	343
Exhibit 10:	22 Promises for More of God	345
Exhibit 11:	8 Promises for Your Words	349
Exhibit 12:	23 Promises for Protection	351
Exhibit 13:	11 Promises for More Joy	355
Exhibit 14:	13 Promises for Your Children	357
Exhibit 15:	7 Promises for Wisdom	360
Exhibit 16:	9 Promises for Health and Long Life	362
Exhibit 17:	17 Promises for Your Position	364
Exhibit 18:	10 Promises for Your Path	367
Exhibit 19:	20 Promises for Your Character	369

Table of Contents

Exhibit 20: 13 Promises for Eternity..373

Exhibit 21: 8 Promises for Your Land..375

Exhibit 22: 12 Promises for Honor..377

Exhibit 23: 25 Promises for Blessings...379

Exhibit 24: 38 Things That Must Happen Before the Lord Returns.................383

Exhibit 25: Koran Teaches Terror and Murder of Non-Muslims......................386

Exhibit 26: 38 Islamic Co-conspirator Organizations, US vs HLF....................387

Exhibit 27: 40 U.S. Military and Paramilitary Conflicts 1965-2018..................388

The remnant will return, the remnant of Jacob, to the Mighty God. For though your people, O Israel, be as the sand of the sea, a remnant of them will return; the destruction decreed shall overflow with righteousness. For the Lord God of hosts will make a determined end in the midst of all the land.

                                                          Isaiah 10:21-23 NKJV

Part 1
The Righteous Remnant Arises

1
Dreams

On December 5, 2015, I dreamed it was almost Christmas, which it was. My wife and I were told a Christmas gift would be delivered to our home and it would be like a singing telegram delivery, which would include animals.

We were sitting in our great room discussing our plans to get together with our friends and family for the holidays. Our great room is right next to our front door and we kept thinking we heard the doorbell ringing. Each time it rang, we kept on talking like we didn't hear it, but then we thought we heard it again. It was like it wasn't registering for some reason, so we kept dismissing it. After several rings, my wife finally said, "Wasn't that the doorbell?"

I replied, "Oh yeah, I think it was."

I went to the door, but when I opened it, I saw a guy already going down our front steps, giving up on us answering. He was wearing an elf costume with a little elf hat and vest. He also had a full head of brown hair, like real elves have. I asked, "Can I help you?"

He said, "Yes, we have a very special delivery for you. Can you please come around to the side of the house?"

Then I remembered the word about our special Christmas delivery. I had forgotten all about it! I called my wife and we both started walking around to the side of our house, which is where our driveway is. As soon as we went around the first corner, but still not to where we could see the whole driveway, we saw the most amazing, majestic, beautiful horse I have ever seen. He was standing near the corner of our house, so we saw him before we even made it all the way around to the side, but I knew there were more animals around the second corner.

Our yard is filled with trees, so he was standing in an area that is usually shaded, but a beam of sunlight was shining right on him, illuminating him in all his glory. When we saw him, he lifted his head and looked right at us. He was strong and muscular with long blond hair covering his body, grown out a couple of inches with every hair perfectly in place. He had long white hair on his mane, tail, and feet, longer than horses usually have, blowing in a gentle breeze. Not only was he beautiful, but we sensed there was something sweet and loving about him. We understood we were going to get to keep him for some time so we could share him with our friends and family. We were so excited about that because we knew they would be just as amazed as we were.

Then the scene changed, and I saw a short vision of us telling our friends and family members, including friends we had not seen in many years since we moved away from where we used to live. Then I was back in my yard, beholding this beautiful horse and feeling overwhelmed by a sense of awe when I woke up and was wide awake, so the dream ended.

I believe the singing telegram represents a prophetic message since singing is a common dream symbol for prophesying. Horses have also been used for delivering messages throughout history, so this dream was announcing the delivery of a message. The amazing beauty of this horse showed it was beyond the natural realm, so it represented a prophetic message from heaven.

Barely hearing the doorbell ringing was a warning to pay extra close attention so we don't miss this delivery. The elf coming to our door showed it would be delivered during the Christmas season.

I knew we were going to be able to keep this horse for some time so we could share it with others, so it represents a gift God wants to share with His people to give us new insights from heaven. Since I saw us sharing it beyond our current circle of friends, I believe God wants this message to be shared far and wide.

As Christmas day approached, it happened just like the dream showed with my sense of hearing being very dull. I was expecting something to happen but had no idea what. I even wondered if an elf might show up at our door with some sort of delivery, but Christmas day arrived and no deliveries came. The only thing that happened even remotely like the dream was a Christmas gift we received from my wife's sister, an all-expense paid trip to visit her and her husband where we used to live, the same place I saw in the dream. They suggested we come in July, so I wondered if somehow the dream would be fulfilled at that time because our family had previously exchanged gifts in July and even joked about it being Christmas in July.

We scheduled our trip for the last weekend in July, but later had to reschedule it for the next weekend, the first weekend in August. Our whole family went and had a great time. We saw our old friends, which was great, but nothing unusual happened, so I concluded the dream must be fulfilled some other way, but I did not know how.

A few days after we got back home, I started doing some research to prepare for writing this book to share another prophetic dream I had received two days before Christmas, December 23, 2015, revealing God's plans for His remnant. It had made such a great impact on me, I had been thinking about it ever since. I knew God wanted me to share it, but had not connected it with the first dream, but as soon as I started writing, I realized the second dream was the fulfillment of the first dream and God had delivered it right on time, two days before Christmas, but it took me over seven months to realize it. Like the elf walking away from our door, I had nearly missed the delivery.

Just as I was excited to share the amazing horse with everyone, I have been excited to share what I saw in this second dream. Just as I saw the amazing horse being shared beyond our friends and family, I believe the message from the second dream will be shared far beyond our friends and family.

Most dreams just start at the beginning, but this one required another dream to announce its' arrival. I've never heard of anything like that before, but I believe it shows how much God wants us to receive these insights as a gift from Him because He knows we're going to need it to fulfill His plans for our future, which were revealed in the second dream.

Living the Dream:

The second dream was by far the most powerful dream I have ever received, not just because of what I saw, but also because of the powerful presence of God I encountered during the dream, which continued after I woke up.

In the horse dream, my wife and I were ourselves, we looked like ourselves and we were in our house, so it revealed what God was bringing to us personally so we could then share it with others, but in the second dream, we were not ourselves. We both looked like super models illustrating the full manifestation of God's promises, which was not limited to us personally, but represented the total completion of the transformation of everyone who walks uprightly before Him as part of His righteous remnant. We had taken possession of all He wanted us to have, which transformed us into something far beyond all natural beauty, like the beauty of the heavenly horse.

I call it "living the dream" because every area of our life was so intensely wonderful. I had such a passion and love for my wife. I intensely adored everything about her. The same thing was happening in my ministry. I had a real heart for God and for people and a real genuine heart for repenting in every area of my life. I felt such a deep conviction of my sins and wanting to be right with God. It was like no matter where I went, I just cried out to God. I just wanted to be right with Him. I put aside everything else to know Him. And it was highly contagious wherever I went, spreading to other people and causing them to repent too.

I attended many powerful meetings with many others who shared this same hunger for God. Every meeting was packed to the max with young people, teenagers and young adults, and it was standing room only. Even up in the balcony, every seat was filled and along the front of the balcony, I saw them sitting on the floor in a long row along the railings with their feet dangling down. They were completely consumed with God.

I knew we all had this in common, we had completely emptied ourselves until there was nothing left but empty vessels for God to fill. This was especially true for these young people. God was everything to them, their one and only desire.

I have been in lots of great meetings before and experienced powerful moves of God, but this was unlike anything I have seen before. For one thing, we were truly one body, which is almost impossible to adequately describe. This process of emptying ourselves of ourselves and being filled up with the presence of God had resulted in a powerful transformation in our inner man, causing us to be filled with a higher purpose, a divine purpose, no longer controlled by our selfish human nature, so when we all came together, we were united and joined together in such a powerful and glorious way that I could sense what was going on in them and I knew they could sense what was in me too. Our awareness level between us was so clear, it was almost like we were inside each other, like we were all part of one living organism, not just a bunch of individuals who happened to be meeting in the same place.

We were so filled up with the love of God that His love joined us together as one, so we had great love for one another, genuinely caring for one another and being attentive to the needs of each other and not just thinking about our own needs. I believe it was the fulfillment of what the Lord Jesus prayed, "I do not pray for these alone, but also for those who will believe in Me through their word; that they all may be one, as You, Father, are in Me, and I in You; that they also may be one in Us, that the world may believe that You sent Me." (John 17:20-21 NKJV)

We had that kind of unity with all of us in agreement and one unanimous cry of our heart, the cry of repentance. With everything in us, we longed to be right with God in every area. Our hunger for more of Him consumed us so much that we constantly cried out to be right with Him, turning away from anything that displeased Him. I saw us walking around during these meetings, weeping openly as we cried out for more of Him.

Remnant: Dreams

Repentance was the overwhelming dominant theme in everything we did because we wanted more than anything to draw closer to Him, so anything separating us from Him had to go.

Since we were so closely connected to each other, whatever one person did, made an impact on the rest of us. So, when one person came under conviction for their sins, it immediately spread to others like a chain reaction, which caused others to start repenting too. Everything we did was very contagious and spread quickly throughout the whole place!

As we became filled with more of Him, more of His love flowed through us to others, which caused us to notice and genuinely appreciate little things about others we had previously failed to notice or appreciate. We even gained a new perspective on their weaknesses, which had previously annoyed us, so they became genuinely adorable to us. With this great love abounding in us, we became rich in ways words cannot describe, experiencing an abundance of joy and a great sense of satisfaction. We were finally living the abundant life, just like Jesus promised when He said, " I have come that they may have life, and that they may have it more abundantly." (John 10:10 NKJV)

I was one of the leaders and one of the speakers in these meetings. In one meeting, I told the people, "It doesn't matter if you're standing up with your arms lifted or kneeling down or laying down or walking around or whatever position you take, seek to please Him in all you're doing, but the main thing is that you let Him know that you want your life, what is in your heart, to be conformed to His life and for His image to be formed in you. In whatever position, just go all out for God!"

At one point, I left the main meeting place to go into another area to pray and seek the Lord. A few of the young people came with me because I was mentoring them, helping them understand how I prayed and sought the Lord. We went to a smaller room where we spent some time seeking the Lord together while the large meeting was still going on. When we were done, we went back into the large meeting. So, even while the larger meetings were continuing, there were smaller meetings for training purposes.

As wonderful as these meetings were, the scene changed to reveal what was happening in my family relationships. It seemed like I was going back and forth between being in these meetings and seeing my heart for my wife. She didn't look like my wife, but I knew she was my wife. I blessed her socks off because I continually spoke powerful words of love to her, sharing my heart's desire for her to be blessed, to have everything God wanted her to have. As I spoke to her, she cried because she sensed the love of God flowing through my words. Every area of her life was getting ministered to by the power and love of God. As I spoke to her, I also felt that same love of God returning to me.

Then the scene changed again. I was in the Navy with a bunch of other sailors. It was time to report back to our post, so we were returning to our submarine. As we were going aboard, the submarine, which was yellow, was already starting to move and submerge. I sensed a strong connection between all of us, as if we were one unit with each of us moving perfectly in step with the others, without even looking at each other. Even though we were each doing different tasks, we moved like one unit as we got on board. As we submerged under water, I saw large sharks trying to attack us, but we paid no attention to them and were not afraid because we knew they could not touch us inside the safety of the sub, which was much bigger and stronger than them.

Then the scene changed again, and we were back in the large meeting place. An older man that we did not know entered the meeting and walked about half way down the center aisle and stopped there as if he was not sure what to do next. As soon as we saw him we immediately knew there was something not quite right with him.

Someone asked him a question, "What do you want?" That simple question was all it took. The conviction in that place was so strong it came all over him and completely exposed him for seeking his own agenda. He did not have in mind the heart of God or any interest in what God wanted. God had accepted our invitation, our unanimous cry for more of Him, filling that place so strong with His presence that anyone who entered was immediately brought under heavy conviction because no unclean thing can remain in His presence. It was a great opportunity for that man to repent, but he made the wrong choice and left the building.

When I woke up, the same power of the Holy Spirit that was present in those meetings was still resting on me heavily and causing me to feel the same hunger and cry out for more of Him like I was doing in the dream. I felt like I had been there.

Since that night, I have been seeking God and studying the scriptures to understand what I saw. It has been an amazing journey of discovery, but I still feel like I have barely scratched the surface because there is so much more. It profoundly impacted my understanding of righteousness and God's plans for His remnant, which I will do my best to share in the remaining chapters.

2
Forerunners

I believe God's purpose for those two dreams was to call attention to the prophecies already recorded in the Bible, so even if someone doesn't believe the dreams were from God, that's okay because the same messages are in the Bible, as shown in this chapter. For example, the devoted disciples I saw in the meetings are described in the Bible as the pure, lovely bride, without spot or wrinkle, awaiting the return of the Lord Jesus. (Ephesians 5:27, Revelation 19:7-8)

We do not yet see this lovely bride because we still have lots of cleaning up to do and we're going to need God's help with that, so He has a plan. In the same way that He sent His forerunner to prepare the way for His first appearing, He is again sending His forerunner to prepare the way for His return.

> "Behold, I send My messenger, and he will prepare the way before Me. And the Lord, whom you seek, will suddenly come to His temple, even the Messenger of the covenant, in whom you delight. Behold, He is coming," says the Lord of hosts. (Malachi 3:1 NKJV)

And who is the messenger God has chosen? It is the Prophet Elijah, as illustrated prophetically when the hand of God came upon him, empowering him to run before the king's chariot, faster than the horses pulling the chariot, for about 30 miles. (1 Kings 18:45-46) And God must have had more work for him to do beyond his generation because he did not die, but was carried into heaven in a whirlwind, riding on a chariot of fire pulled by horses of fire. (2 Kings 2:11)

This same Elijah is the one God sent before His first appearing when John the Baptist came in the spirit and power of Elijah, as confirmed by the word of the angel Gabriel given to John's father, Zacharias.

> 16 And he will turn many of the children of Israel to the Lord their God.
> 17 He will also go before Him in the spirit and power of Elijah, 'to turn the hearts of the fathers to the children,' and the disobedient to the wisdom of the just, to make ready a people prepared for the Lord." (Luke 1:16-17 NKJV)

So, the purpose for John's forerunner ministry was to prepare the people to receive the Lord by repenting of their sins and getting right with Him, which would cause all their other relationships to be made right, including the hearts of the fathers turning to their children and wisdom being restored to those who were previously practicing unrighteousness. (Matthew 6:33)

The Israelites knew of Malachi's prophecy, so when John started his ministry, many of them wondered if he was Elijah, so they asked him, but John made it clear he was not. (2.01, John 1:21) However, Jesus confirmed that John ministered in the spirit and power of Elijah when He said, "And if you are willing to receive it, he is Elijah who is to come. He who has ears to hear, let him hear!" (Matthew 11:14-15 NKJV, John 1:19-25)

Later, the disciples asked Jesus why Elijah will come first, so He explained, "Indeed, Elijah is coming first and will restore all things. But I say to you that Elijah has come already, and they did not know him but did to him whatever they wished." (Matthew 17:12 NKJV) Then the disciples understood that He spoke to them of John the Baptist. (Matthew 17:13)

By saying "Elijah is coming first", Jesus prophesied Elijah will return before He returns, confirming the following prophecy.

> 5 "Behold, I will send you Elijah the prophet before the coming of the great and dreadful day of the Lord.
> 6 And he will turn the hearts of the fathers to the children, and the hearts of the children to their fathers, lest I come and strike the earth with a curse." (Malachi 4:5-6 NKJV)

Malachi's reference to the great and dreadful day of the Lord reveals God is sending Elijah to the generation living before the return of the Lord Jesus. And Elijah's mission will be the same in that generation as it was in the days of John the Baptist, to restore those who are not walking uprightly with God back into a right relationship with Him, which will bring restoration between fathers and their children, which Jesus confirmed when He said Elijah "will restore all things." (Matthew 17:12 NKJV)

Elijah's Previous Assignments:

We now have the benefit of hindsight to see what Elijah did during his life and later during his first forerunner assignment, so we can study those events to gain insights into his future assignment. In the days of Elijah, the people of Israel had turned away from God, forsaken His covenant, torn down His altars and killed His prophets with the sword.

(1 Kings 19:10) So, God sent Elijah to boldly confront King Ahab of Israel and the false prophets of Baal and Asherah by gathering them all on Mount Carmel where he challenged them to demonstrate the power of their gods as the people of Israel watched. (1 Kings 17:1-18:40) When Baal was unable to send down any fire to burn the sacrifices prepared by the false prophets, Elijah mocked them, saying, "Cry aloud, for he is a god; either he is meditating, or he is busy, or he is on a journey, or perhaps he is sleeping and must be awakened." (1 Kings 18:27 NKJV)

Then Elijah got to the heart of the matter, saying to all the people, "Come near to me." (1 Kings 18:30 NKJV) By saying this, he prophetically called them to come near to God. Then they watched as he repaired the altar of the Lord that was broken down, rebuilding it with twelve stones, one for each of the twelve tribes of Israel, prophetically illustrating the restoration of their covenant with the God of their fathers and reuniting their nation, since at that time Israel was divided into two kingdoms. (1 Kings 18:31-35)

After rebuilding the altar and preparing the sacrifice, Elijah called forth the fire of God to demonstrate His God could do what the false gods could not do and this fire could do what no earthly fire could. Elijah prayed a simple prayer, "Lord God of Abraham, Isaac, and Israel, let it be known this day that You are God in Israel and I am Your servant, and that I have done all these things at Your word. Hear me, O Lord, hear me, that this people may know that You are the Lord God, and that You have turned their hearts back to You again." (1 Kings 18:37 NKJV)

His prayer reveals this fire comes from God and is released through the obedience of His servant for the purpose of turning the hearts of the people back to God again. Unlike earthly fire, which burns upwards, the flames of this fire burn down from heaven to do what earthly fire cannot do, illustrated by the way it burned the wood soaked in water and even consumed the water in the trench surrounding the altar, but those wonders were only signs pointing to the greater wonder as this fire touched the hearts of the people, exposing their unrighteousness, illuminating things in them that were not right in God's sight, consuming away the impurities that hindered them from drawing closer to Him, causing them to fall on their faces as they repeatedly said, "The Lord, He is God! The Lord, He is God!" (1 Kings 18:38-39, Psalm 50:3, Joel 2:3, Hebrews 12:29)

Elijah released the fire by his obedience, not by following his own ideas, but doing exactly what God told him to do. As he stated, "I have done all these things at Your word." When Elijah did his part, even risking his life to do it, God did His part, turning the hearts of the people back to Him again.

Then Elijah said to the people, "Seize the prophets of Baal! Do not let one of them escape!" So, they seized them; and Elijah brought them down to the Brook Kishon and executed them there. (1 Kings 18:40 NKJV) By doing this, he demonstrated in the visible realm what the fire of God was doing in the invisible realm of the spirit, putting to death every ungodly thought that exalts itself against the knowledge of God and bringing the hearts of the people back into a right relationship with Him. (2 Corinthians 10:5-6)

Elijah's confrontation with the false prophets illustrates the purpose for his ministry and his future assignments is to release the fire of God. God uses him like an arsonist, starting fires wherever he goes. Those who are willing to cooperate will not be destroyed by the fire like the false prophets were, but will be refined by it as it burns away everything separating them from God. By restoring our relationship with God, this fire ultimately brings restoration in all our relationships and healing in every area of our life. (Malachi 3:1-4, 4:2, 1 Peter 4:17-18)

In the spirit and power of Elijah, John the Baptist prepared the way for the coming fire of God, saying, "I indeed baptize you with water; but One mightier than I is coming, whose sandal strap I am not worthy to loosen. He will baptize you with the Holy Spirit and fire. His winnowing fan is in His hand, and He will thoroughly clean out His threshing floor, and gather the wheat into His barn; but the chaff He will burn with unquenchable fire." (Luke 3:16-17 NKJV) So, the ministry of the forerunners is to prepare the way for the coming fire, which confronts us with a choice to either be refined by it if we are willing to repent or consumed by it. This fire leaves no middle ground, no grey areas. It is a thorough sifting process, separating the wheat from the chaff, the righteous from the unrighteous, leaving a clean threshing floor between them.

Even Elijah was not exempt from the refining fire but instructed by God to live in the city of Zarephath, whose name means "refinery, the place of refining." (1 Kings 17:8-10) In that place, he was refined by enduring many trials as he learned to trust God and not be moved by the way things appeared to be.

Elijah's Next Assignment:

Even until his final day on earth, Elijah's deeds contained prophetic insights into his future assignments. For example, before he was taken to heaven in a chariot of fire, he gave his mantle to Elisha, as God instructed him. By doing this, Elijah sowed a double portion of his anointing and reaped a double portion with two new assignments as forerunners for the Lord's two appearances. (2 Kings 2:8-12, Malachi 3:1, 4:5-6) Both assignments have two parts. In his first assignment, the spirit and power of Elijah came upon John the Baptist. (Luke 1:17, Matthew 11:14, 17:12-13) Then later, Elijah appeared in person, speaking with the Lord Jesus as Jesus was transfigured before Peter, John, and James. (Luke 9:27-31) In his second assignment, the same spirit and power that was upon Elijah is coming to prepare the way for the Lord's return. Then Elijah will again appear in person as one of the two witnesses in the streets of Jerusalem, as shown in Exhibit 1. (Revelation 11:3-13)

Although his mission is the same in both assignments, as a forerunner preparing the way for the Lord, there are some big differences. His first assignment was limited to the tiny nation of Israel because the Lord was sent specifically to them, as He said, "I was not sent except to the lost sheep of the house of Israel." (Matthew 15:24) So, Elijah's first assignment was small enough for one man, John the Baptist, to do it alone.

Elijah was well prepared for his first forerunner assignment with John the Baptist because their lives were similar in many ways. For example, just as Elijah lived alone in the wilderness where he was fed by ravens, John also lived alone in the wilderness and in caves, where he grew strong in spirit until he was finally ready to begin his public ministry. (1 Kings 17:2-6, 19:9, Matthew 3:4, Luke 1:80) And when they ministered, they did so alone, like when Elijah stood alone against 450 prophets of Baal and 400 prophets of Asherah. (1 Kings 18:19) Having those things in common made Elijah the perfect fit for his first assignment, which was not only for John's benefit, but also preparing Elijah for his second assignment, which will be much different because a lot has changed over the past two thousand years.

Since Jesus laid down His life for the sins of the whole world, the message of salvation was proclaimed to the gentiles in all nations, so He now has disciples in all nations, fulfilling Isaiah's prophecy that God would be found by people who had not sought Him. (Isaiah 65:1, Mark 9:31, Luke 9:22, John 3:14-17) Even the Jewish people are no longer all in one place like they were back in those days because they were scattered among the nations after they rejected their Messiah. (Matthew 24:1-2, John 11:52) So, the Lord is not returning only for the people of Israel, but for all His people in all nations. Everyone on earth will see Him coming on the clouds of heaven with power and great glory. (Matthew 24:30) And since the scope of His next assignment includes the whole world, the scope of His forerunner's next assignment must also include the whole world. Therefore, the spirit and power of Elijah is not coming upon one man in one small place, but upon a worldwide army of forerunners. (Romans 10:19, 11:11, 11:25)

Righteousness Arises:

After the Lord returns, He will establish His kingdom, ruling from Jerusalem with a rod of iron for one thousand years. (Daniel 7:14, 9:24, Zechariah 14:9, Revelation 19:15, 20:4, 21:10) During those days, the light of the moon will be as the light of the sun, and the light of the sun will be seven times brighter than it is today. (Isaiah 30:26) But even before He returns, that light will arise like the sun shining through the righteousness of those who fear His name, displaying the glory of God to draw all men unto Him. (Isaiah 60:1-5, Malachi 4:2)

To this end, God is sending the spirit and power of Elijah upon a new generation of forerunners to do the same things he did during his earthly ministry, confronting the false gods, calling people to return to the God of Abraham, Isaac, and Jacob, rebuilding the broken-down altars, and releasing the life-changing fire of God to consume away the impurities in our life, which will ignite the light of righteousness as we draw closer to God than we've ever been before, dwelling in His presence where our strength is restored. (1 Kings 18:38-39, Malachi 4:5-6, Ephesians 5:27) So, a righteous remnant is now arising, a mighty army of forerunners, the likes of whom has never been; nor will there ever be any such after them because of their whole-hearted devotion to God. (1 Chronicles 12:20-22, Psalm 82:1, 149:1-9, Isaiah 13:1-6, 60:1-3, Daniel 11:33, 12:3, Joel 2:1-11, 3:9-13, Obadiah 1:21, Malachi 3:16, 4:2, Matthew 6:33, 13:43, Jude 1:14-15, Revelation 2:26-28, 12:5, 19:7-8)

Then God will send forth His army like fattened calves bursting forth from the stall, making us spectacles to behold, jewels to display, causing others to marvel at how this could possibly be, but it will be the fruit of righteousness, which has been available to us all along. (Malachi 3:17, 4:2, Hebrews 12:11, James 3:18) God is going to show this unbelieving generation the difference between those who are His and those who are not, like He showed the Israelites on Mount Carmel, and like when He told Moses to tell Pharaoh, "I will make a distinction between My people and your people." (Exodus 8:23, 1 Kings 18:20-40, Isaiah 60:1-5, Daniel 11:32, Malachi 3:17-18, Luke 3:6) He will call everyone's attention to the stark contrast between the shining light of righteousness and the deep darkness falling upon those who are not His, not because He has rejected them, but because they have proudly insisted on going their own way and doing their own thing, even doing it in His name while rejecting Him and refusing to walk in His ways. (Psalm 10:4, 119:21, Proverbs 16:5, Isaiah 2:12, 60:2, Matthew 7:21-23, 2 Timothy 3:2)

It will be like Jesus said, "Elijah is coming first and will restore all things." (Matthew 17:11 NKJV) As righteousness arises, it will bring restoration in every area because God will finally have our permission to do the good things He has always wanted to do, pouring in the oil and the wine, causing healing to come quickly as He fills us with His strength, His love, His anointing, His presence, His kindness, His goodness, His joy, His peace, His provision, His wealth, His protection, His friendship, His wisdom, and every good thing that satisfies our soul, making us flourish, growing up straight like palm trees and like the cedars in Lebanon. (Deuteronomy 7:13, 28:8, 30:19-20, Psalm 5:12, 11:7, 14:5, 17:15, 37:25, 75:10, 84:11, 85:12, 92:12-13, 104:125, 112:3, 140:13, 146:8, Proverbs 10:24, 13:21, 13:25, 15:6, 18:10, Isaiah 58:8, Hosea 10:12, Joel 2:19, 2:24, Micah 2:7, Malachi 4:2, Matthew 6:33, John 15:14, Acts 17:28, James 1:17, 3 John 1:2)

This restoration will bring healing to our broken relationships, turning the hearts of the fathers to their children and the hearts of the children to their fathers. (Malachi 4:2, 4:5-6, Matthew 6:33) Based on what I saw in my dream, I believe this will go beyond flesh and blood relationships to include older disciples having a heart for the younger ones, helping to guide them, care for them and train them, so they can grow faster and stronger than their mentors, and it includes younger disciples having a heart for the older ones, so they can receive from them with grateful attitudes. Then all ages can come together as one body, united, in agreement, in perfect harmony, just like I saw in my dream.

> "Every meeting was packed to the max with young people, teenagers and young adults, and it was standing room only. Even up in the balcony, every seat was filled and along the front of the balcony, I saw them sitting on the floor in a long row along the railings with their feet dangling down.
>
> At one point, I left the main meeting place to go into another area to pray and seek the Lord. A few of the young people came with me because I was mentoring them, helping them to understand how I prayed and sought the Lord. We went to a smaller room where we spent some time seeking the Lord together while the large meeting was still going on. When we were done, we went back into the large meeting. So, even while the larger meetings were continuing, there were smaller meetings for training purposes."

In the spirit and power of Elijah, this remnant army will rebuild the broken-down altars of our generation. Altars are places where we kneel before God, submitting our life to Him, getting right with Him, so the broken-down altars represent the message of righteousness, which has been almost completely abandoned by our generation, but must be rebuilt before the Lord returns because it is how we will make ourselves ready for Him.

Righteousness will be the battle cry of this army, illustrated by the majestic horse in my dream, revealing God's plan to restore His message of righteousness to our generation. This horse not only represented the delivery of this message, but horses are also known for their power, representing the power of righteousness, which cannot be adequately conveyed by words, no matter how eloquent, because it must be experienced in a direct encounter with the fire of God, like the Israelites experienced on Mount Carmel. (1 Kings 18:20-40) Righteousness must be revealed, illuminated, and demonstrated, like Elijah did, so God is sending forth an army to show an unbelieving generation who has never seen anything like it before because of so much compromise in our camp, which has caused the fire of God to be almost completely snuffed out, but those days are soon coming to an end.

Like Elijah released the fire on Mount Carmel by his obedience to God's instructions, our generation will release the fire of righteousness, the flames that burn down from heaven with the power to touch and forever change the lives of everyone around us. (Psalm 11:7, 14:5, 17:15, 140:13, Ezekiel 44:15-16, John 7:37-39)

Ordinary People:

God is going to use ordinary people to do extraordinary things, which was illustrated in my dream by me being one of the speakers, which is something I have no natural ability to do. My only qualification was as a carrier of His presence, like everyone else there. There were no big personality speakers because we no longer needed them to draw crowds because we had the real thing, the genuine presence of God, so He was the main attraction. This army will consist of nameless, faceless nobodies, so all the attention will finally be focused where it should have been all along. There will be no other explanation for what is happening.

Elijah and John both did extraordinary things while also showing they had doubts and weaknesses like everyone else. If that were not the case, we might have a hard time believing we could ever do the kinds of things they did, but God allowed us to see them at their best and their worst to let us know the mighty things they did were all due to His power working through them.

In addition to the great things already mentioned, Elijah performed many other great demonstrations of power. For example, he commanded there to be no dew or rain, except at his word, and there was none for three and a half years, and he raised a boy from the dead and ended his ministry with another spectacular demonstration of God's power, being caught up to heaven in a whirlwind, but after all these great victories, he ran for his life after receiving a threat from Jezebel, the wife of King Ahab, even despairing to the point of asking God to take his life. (1 Kings 17:1, 17:21-24, 19:1-4, 2 Kings 2:11)

Remnant: Forerunners

Like Elijah, John the Baptist displayed both great strength and great weakness. After doing many extraordinary things, including leading many to repentance, being the first to recognize the identity of the Messiah, and boldly confronting the Pharisees and even King Herod, John stumbled in his faith, doubting whether Jesus was the Messiah, so he sent his followers to ask Jesus for confirmation. (Matthew 3:7-9, 3:13-16, 11:2-5, 11:11, Luke 3:3, 3:19-20, 7:18-23)

The strengths and weaknesses of these forerunners are prophetic illustrations of the coming forerunner army, not only operating in the same spirit, but also sharing the same contrast within themselves. Strength and weakness don't seem to go together, but in God's Kingdom they do because if it weren't for our weakness, we would not learn to rely upon His strength, so God uses even those unlovely things in us for His good purposes.

As much as we desire to have great gifts and talents, God made no mistake when He formed us, nor did He forget us when it comes to gifts but designed us perfectly for our assignments by giving us a different kind of gift, the gift of utter weakness, unwanted by the world because its' value is hidden. Like other gifts, ours is frequently put on display, but instead of bringing us comfort, consolation and confidence, it brings disappointment, despair and doubt, like Elijah and John both experienced, but the great value of this gift is our desperation stirs up a holy hunger in us, driving us to frequent encounters with God where we learn to overcome by relying on His strength as if it were our own. (2 Corinthians 12:9) And we are comforted with the assurance that He has not abandoned us, but bears with us for reasons we cannot fathom, which produces sincere gratitude in us for what we know we don't deserve and greater compassion for the weaknesses in others, like I saw in my dream:

> "As we became filled with more of Him, more of His love flowed through us to others, which caused us to notice and genuinely appreciate little things about others we had previously failed to notice or appreciate. We even gained a new perspective on their weaknesses, which had previously annoyed us, so they became genuinely adorable to us. With this great love abounding in us, we became rich in ways words cannot describe, experiencing an abundance of joy and a great sense of satisfaction. We were finally living the abundant life, just like Jesus promised us when He said, 'I came that they may have life, and have it abundantly.'" (John 10:10)

This most unusual combination of His strength working through our weakness makes this army unlike anything the world has ever seen or ever will see afterwards. (Joel 2:2) God has chosen the most unlikely candidates, the most ordinary people, to demonstrate

His great power in the hopes that everyone will see Him through us, including all the principalities and powers in the heavenly places, putting them to an open shame. (1 Corinthians 1:27, Ephesians 3:8-13)

No longer will it be about promoting ourselves, our ministries, our books, our meetings, or our churches, but only about lifting Him up, hungering and thirsting for more of Him, like the deer pants for the water brooks. (Psalm 42:1-2) Then God can do what He promised when He said, "If I be lifted up from the earth, I will draw all men unto Me." (John 12:32) The Lord of the Harvest will bring in the greatest harvest of souls the world has ever seen. (Isaiah 60:1-5, Amos 9:13-15, Zechariah 2:10-12, Matthew 13:24-30, Mark 16:15-18, John 12:32-33, Acts 1:7-8)

Perilous Times:

In the days of Elijah, many true prophets of God were massacred by orders from the king's wife, Jezebel, and many others were hiding in caves to avoid being killed. Despite these perils, God sent Elijah to boldly confront King Ahab and put to death all the false prophets. In the same way, before the Lord returns, great persecution will arise against the righteous. Many will be put to death as God allows Satan to have power over His holy ones for a brief period of 42 months. (Matthew 24:9, Revelation 6:9-11, 13:5-7, 20:4) An evil king, filled with the spirit of antichrist, will rise to power, ruling over the world government, economy, and religion. (Revelation 13) Even now, the antichrist kingdom is advancing rapidly and scheming to destroy everyone standing against it. The whole world will be required to worship the beast who receives his authority from the dragon, enforced by the death penalty. (Revelation 13:4, 13:15) Even many mighty ones of God will fall by the sword, by flame, by captivity, and by devastation as their power is crushed and shattered for many days. (Daniel 8:24, 11:33, 12:7, Revelation 6:9-11) Yet, despite these dangers, God is sending His refined ones on special assignments to expose Satan's schemes because, like in the days of Elijah, His people have fallen into deception and need help finding their way back to Him. (1 Kings 18:19, Matthew 14:1-12, Mark 9:13)

Elijah was not ignorant of the enemy's schemes, but well informed and on the alert, just as God has instructed us to be. (1 Peter 5:8-9) For example, Elijah knew the exact number of the false prophets, 450 prophets of Baal and 400 prophets of Asherah, and he knew they were being fed by Jezebel. (1 Kings 18:19) In the same way, God is now exposing Satan's schemes to His forerunners, making us aware and putting us on full alert, so we see exactly what's happening and what's coming ahead because God intends to use us as His torches, living flames, enlightening the way for others, like guides filled with wisdom and understanding, acquired simply by walking in His path without compromise. (Proverbs 12:26, Daniel 11:33)

Greater Glory:

God provided for Elijah in the most unusual ways, drinking from the brook and eating food brought to him by ravens. (1 Kings 17:2-6) Later, when he arrived at the widow's house in Zarephath, she informed him, "As the Lord your God lives, I do not have bread, only a handful of flour in a bin, and a little oil in a jar; and see, I am gathering a couple of sticks that I may go in and prepare it for myself and my son, that we may eat it, and die." (1 Kings 17:8-12 NKJV) That's not exactly what anyone wants to hear coming from the person charged with providing for us, but despite how hopeless it looked, God provided for him, just like He said He would.

God also provided for John the Baptist in the most unusual ways as John lived in the wilderness, eating locusts and wild honey. For clothing, he wore camel's hair and a leather belt around his waist. (Mark 1:6) God's unique provision for His forerunners prophetically illustrates what's coming for the final generation of forerunners. Before the Lord returns, His people will require the same kind of supernatural provision as Elijah and John did due to the great trouble coming upon the world, which will include wars, famines, hyper-inflation and financial turmoil. (Daniel 12:1, Matthew 24:6-7, Revelation 6:3-8) Seeking relief from their suffering, the unrighteous will willingly submit to a global financial system, requiring everyone to take a mark on their hand or forehead to make any transactions, buying or selling. (Matthew 24:9, Revelation 6:5-6, 13:16-18) Christians will be forced out of the system as they heed God's warning that everyone who takes the mark will be eternally doomed. (Revelation 14:9-11) However, God saw these things coming far in advance, so He's already making provision. (Revelation 12:6)

As God shakes the nations with great trouble, He's going to fill His latter house with greater glory than His former house, referring to the temple of Solomon, which was filled with so much glory, the priests were not able to stand up, so they were unable to minister. (1 Kings 8:10-11) The glory of Solomon's temple also included great physical wealth. For example, all his drinking vessels were made of gold. None were made of silver because it was not considered valuable in those days because it was so common. (1 Kings 10:21)

The glory of Solomon's house was so great, word spread to other nations, prompting the Queen of Sheba to visit to see for herself.

> 4 And when the queen of Sheba had seen all the wisdom of Solomon, the house that he had built,
> 5 the food on his table, the seating of his servants, the service of his waiters and their apparel, his cupbearers, and his entryway by which he went up to the house of the Lord, there was no more spirit in her.
> 6 Then she said to the king: "It was a true report which I heard in my own land about your words and your wisdom.
> 7 However I did not believe the words until I came and saw with my own eyes; and indeed, the half was not told me. Your wisdom and prosperity exceed the fame of which I heard." (1 Kings 10:4-7 NKJV)

As impressive as the former house was, the glory and riches of His latter house will exceed it. Like the former house, the glory will not be limited to unseen spiritual blessings, such as peace, joy, and wisdom, but will also include physical tangible wealth, specifically silver and gold. (Proverbs 13:22, Isaiah 45:3, 60:5, Haggai 2:6-9, Mark 10:29-30)

> 6 "For thus says the Lord of hosts: 'Once more (it is a little while) I will shake heaven and earth, the sea and dry land;
> 7 and I will shake all nations, and they shall come to the Desire of All Nations, and I will fill this temple with glory,' says the Lord of hosts.
> 8 'The silver is Mine, and the gold is Mine,' says the Lord of hosts.
> 9 'The glory of this latter temple shall be greater than the former,' says the Lord of hosts. 'And in this place, I will give peace,' says the Lord of hosts." (Haggai 2:6-9 NKJV)

Some people get offended by the idea that God would manifest His glory through tangible riches, but He's done it before and intends to do it again on a much larger scale, transferring the wealth of the nations to those whom He has specifically called and trained for this most unique assignment. After setting them free from their bondage to unrighteousness, He is raising them up as stewards of His great wealth, like He did for the Israelites when they came out of the bondage of slavery to Pharaoh, plundering the wealth of ancient Egypt as they left. (Exodus 12:35-36, Isaiah 45:3, 60:4-5) God will send His prepared ones ahead of their brothers to make provision and places of refuge, like He did with Joseph, the son of Israel, sending him ahead of his family to make provision for them during a time of famine. However, the scope of this famine will not be limited to one region, but will be worldwide, so God is raising up an army of Josephs and placing them in strategic positions around the world to make the rough places smooth for His people, providing for them throughout the 42-month reign of the beast. (Genesis 45:4-8, Isaiah 40:3-5, Luke 3:4-6, Revelation 12:6, 12:14)

It will be the best of times and worst of times at the same time; the best of times for the righteous because the light of God will be with us greater than ever before, but the worst of times for the unrighteous who have rejected God because deep spiritual darkness and deception is coming upon them. (Isaiah 60:1-2, 2 Thessalonians 2:9-12) As God's glory arises in His people, many will be drawn to the light, including kings, seeking their wisdom and insights. (Isaiah 60:3-4) No longer will young people need to look to pimps and drug dealers as role models because they will be able to look upon the people of God with amazement and say, "Surely there is a reward for the righteous; surely He is God who judges in the earth." (Psalm 58:11 NKJV)

God is finally going to have what He's always wanted, a generation of disciples walking in the fullness of His plans and purposes, which is something He's looked forward to so much, He's already written a book about it before it happens, called the Book of Remembrance, capturing the whole story, so all that's about to happen will be remembered forever. (Malachi 3:16)

ENDNOTES

2.01: Book of Malachi, https://en.m.wikipedia.org/wiki/Book_of_Malachi

3
Confirmations

This chapter presents prophetic confirmations of the scriptures presented in the previous chapter to help clarify the meaning. These prophecies use various names to describe the remnant army, which can help us identify them, including God's chosen ones, God's precious jewels, a fearless army, the diadems in His Crown, God's called-out ones, God's mouthpieces, the mighty ones, the burning ones who will be released throughout the earth, the dove company, the messengers of power, the warrior company, God's mature sons and daughters, end-time apostles, and the hidden ones.

Julie Whedbee, founder of I Am Calling You Now blog site, shared this word on January 22, 2019.

> "It is like a chess game, when you hold back your most strategic and important moves to win the game. I have held back My chosen ones until the final hour, those vessels who have fully surrendered, positioning them and waiting, until the decisive moment to confirm the victory which I have already won." (3.01)

Julie Whedbee also received the following prophetic word in September 2015, but she did not receive a release from the Lord to share it until June 2018.

> "Tell them of My army, daughter. Tell them of the ones who have set themselves apart from the world, the ones who have kept themselves pure, and the ones whom I have been training in secret. These are they that have and continue to undergo the most fiery trials of the Potter, in order that the purest form of their Creator manifests through them. These are those the world hates and persecutes, ridicules and rejects because they do not take their orders from conventional man-made ways. This group is My end-time army, those who have only been counseled by their Commander in Chief, the King of all creation, those who have given up this life in order to gain Me in the most intimate way. I have perfected them through their obedience, and they move in harmony with My Spirit. In their weakness, I am made strong. Their struggles are many, but the outcome of their surrendered lives will produce the greatest harvest the world has ever known. Although considered least in this world, these chosen ones are My precious jewels, the diadems in My Crown.

Remnant: Confirmations

Tell the world daughter that these, My army, cannot be stopped, and the world has never seen anything like them. Great will be their abilities as the source of their power is not of this realm. Their strength is drawn from My Throne directly and all are in union as One Spirit in Me. Tell them who will listen to what I am saying, this army will be called to public duty at any moment and all will change suddenly. At My appointed time, I will call them and they shall arise.

The time for the manifestation of My mature sons and daughters has arrived. When My Word speaks of all creation groaning for the return of these sons and daughters, it speaks of this time of now!

I have raised up a standard of people who have heeded My warnings, who have answered the call upon their lives, who have come under My anointing, and who now walk in My complete power and authority, fully mature, with the deepest understanding of what was accomplished that day; not only My sacrifice, but My resurrection and ascension. My mature sons and daughters have come to the full realization of what truly happened, and the gift that was given to them.

I will take unto Myself a first-fruits harvest. I will gather all those to Me who have come to this maturity, for they will be used mightily. Many are the manifestations and the tasks purposed for each one, set before you now, and being revealed in their entireties; you who know, know that it is the time that I will draw you unto Myself. The greatest work is yet to be done, but I now have a body, a body of believers, who understand why I came, who understand what was made available to them, who understand what it means to be co-heirs to My Kingdom. And these, My manifested sons and daughters of the Most High have now come under My anointing and walk in the fullness of who I am.

I will gather the fields that are so ripe for the harvest, as My sickle has come to reap, and to cast away all that is not of Me. My Kingdom army will arise to their positions much sooner than you think, they will come; a world that has been plunged into utter darkness, and that is so desperate, will be shown the light and the love of their Creator through My chosen ones. For I will be the lamp and the light through My ambassadors, those who carry My torch and burn brightly for Me, glorifying Me in all that they say and all that they do. The greatest miracles of all times will be seen as I pour out My power over this earth.

Truly I tell you this day, the Kingdom of Heaven is come to this earth, for I have established a people, a mighty nation, a royal priesthood in this place and the world will soon know that I am that I am." (3.02)

Remnant: Confirmations

Julie Whedbee also shared the following prophetic word in May 2018.

> "Speak boldly daughter, for I am compressing time as you know it. I am the Eternal and Infinite One and have placed you in a time/space continuum that is finite, and that is coming to an end.
>
> Those who walk this journey with Me sense the shift now taking place. You are experiencing that tearing away I have spoken of, the tearing of your souls from your spirits, as you ascend higher and further away from the darkness which encroaches. I am pulling at your hearts, I am drawing you in. Before you will realize what is happening, it will be complete, and I will gather My Bride to Myself.
>
> I want you to understand, that as the portals of darkness have opened, so too have the windows of My Kingdom- so much that there would not be room to receive the blessings I have prepared for My called-out ones. Hold fast to My promises and do not fear the wicked one and the power he has. He only has what I have allowed, and no harm shall come to My Beloved ones.
>
> So many have bought into the deception and lies he has perpetuated, but My truth shines brightly and will always dispel the darkness. As more of hell enlarges her mouth to receive the wicked, so shall I pour out My Spirit on all flesh and those who profess Me as God, and great and mighty exploits will be done in My name. The earth has never seen what I am about to do in and through My people. I am preparing you for all that is here now. You will not be forsaken or walk this path alone.
>
> A great and mighty battle rages in the heavenlies, as the Kingdom of light battles the kingdom of darkness. Every soul who has ever existed knows of the end and the Great Day of the Lord. You who are here now have been chosen specifically for this time, and a gift beyond understanding awaits you- this to be revealed very, very soon.
>
> I am unveiling mysteries of My Kingdom and sharing more of My heart than ever before. Subtle moves of My Spirit you have experienced in the past will become much more powerful and a greater part of your reality here. The supernatural is merging with the natural, and although from the carnal mind, it appears lost and darker still, those who walk by My Spirit will know a completely different existence now. You are moving from previous mindsets and dispositions, more and more into unity with Me in spirit and in truth, and you will walk more and

more in My counsel, as I continue to fill you with My Spirit. Joy unspeakable belongs to you, and there is a rest for My people. Enter in, be fully submerged, and allow Me to fill you to overflowing, so I may be glorified through every aspect of your lives. All I have belongs to you, and there is no limit to the gifts I have for you. So, ask and it will be given, run to Me and I will always be found." (3.03)

Julie Whedbee also shared the following prophetic word on December 20, 2015.

"The manifestations of great evil in the physical will be powerful indeed, but nothing compares to the glory I am releasing in My chosen ones. All that is foretold to come about as in the days of Noah is upon you. Have I not said that men's hearts will fail them for fear of what they will see? Terrible creatures will be unleashed, twisted and grotesque beings who are the product of your adversary's attempts to exalt himself above Me. I will use these beings who have come from the fallen ones to judge the wicked and the unrighteous.

My army stands ready for this final victory on the earth. Clothed in My robe, dipped in My blood, you are made holy and righteous, pure and undefiled, and you will lead many to Me, as the hordes of hell know their defeat." (3.04)

The following word shared by the late Prophet Bob Jones reveals the rise of a very small remnant within the larger remnant, forerunners running ahead of the other forerunners to help prepare them for their assignments. He shared this in a 2011 meeting at MorningStar ministries.

There is a remnant coming forth now in the body of Christ, possibly as much as one in a hundred, but I would say it is less than that. I believe the word is will. Sons and daughters are reaching a level of maturity where they are given their inheritance. These are the new leaders that are coming forth. They will literally be like a guide, guiding us to Christ, justice, and righteousness. There are going to be those mature ones come forth now that if we can find two of them coming into agreement and they will agree here in the spirit man, whatever they agree on will happen. So, I think we are in one of the greatest times there has ever been. My hope is and I believe the main purpose for those that are reaching this level of maturity is to bring the rest of us right in with Him. (3.05)

Diana Pulliam, founder of The Mighty Hand of God blog site, received the following prophetic word from the Lord in December 2018.

"War in the Heavens was announced to you. This war will soon manifest in the earth. At this time, the division between those who say they are Mine will also manifest for all to see. You will be hated of all men. My Hidden Ones will begin to come forth, and it will be heard, 'Who are these and where did they come from?'" (3.06)

Reverend Susan O'Marra, founder of In the Image of His Glory Ministries and Co-Pastor of The Salvation of God Church in Rochester NY, received the following prophetic poem in December 2018.

A parable for those who watch and see, and who wait upon Me:

There is a way that seems right unto a man, but who understands the mysteries yet in My hand? Men desire to behold what they think shall unfold, but My hidden sons are coming forth from of old. That which has been held in reserve unto this time shall indeed be brought forth from My gold mines. Face to face, hidden within My enfolding embrace, mighty men shall come forth to run My glory race.

My ways shall come as I have written in My codes and My hidden ones shall build My harvest roads. Never again will man think they have the upper hand, for My power shall define who is truly in command. For My lightnings shall utter and My fire shall decree, and then My church shall finally hear, and see, and agree. So shall it be, as My wisdom flows within My body again, and men shall truly learn who I am among them. (3.07)

Elizabeth Marie, founder of Latterrain333 blog site and YouTube Channel, received the following message on April 29, 2018.

"I am raising up a mighty army. They will have the power of the MOST HIGH upon them. They will be MY witnesses in these last days. They will perform miracles and healing the sick. They will right the wrongs.

They will be sent out in pairs, for there is strength in numbers. They will take very little – your burden will be light. They will speak for ME the words that I alone give. They will be MY mouthpieces.

Who will answer this call? Only those who are ready to receive this message. Only those who have been purified by the 'testing fires' of trials and tribulations. Only those who live a crucified life with ME. Others will then come in slowly. Let those who hear MY voice obey what I ask each one of them to do. The marching orders have been given." (3.08)

Elaine Tavolacci, founder of A Word in Season blog site, received the following prophetic word in April 2018.

"This is a new day. You are the generation who will walk in My authority and power and demonstrate My kingdom on this earth. I am releasing My glory on this earth as it is in heaven. You are not mere men and women, but you are a chosen generation, a royal priesthood, a holy nation who will release others out of the kingdom of darkness into My marvelous light.

Sanctify yourselves and allow Me to work in you. This is the day that My power will be known in the earth. This is the divine plan and purpose that I have for you in this season says the Lord." (3.09)

Lydia Hodge, a registered nurse and Z3 News contributing author, received the following prophetic word in February 2018.

"My Elijah's are rising up, positioning themselves to step out onto the world scene. They are arising from their hidden places. They have been hidden in Me for such a time as this. They have been in the wilderness, in caves and in the deserts.

Yes, I have had them in dry, lonely, trying places to mold and to prepare them for this hour. Those who walk in the Spirit and Power of Elijah will confront the false church and the false prophets. They will confront the lying antichrist system that is forming before your very eyes. They will speak truth and they will walk in My boldness. Nothing will deter them. My Word will be a fire that issues forth from them and consumes all that stands in their way.

Even as this world has sought to remove My word and to silence My voice, I tell you the truth, I will not be silenced in this hour. I will roar through My prophets. They will preach with power and great conviction. My Word will be heard and those who hear will respond one way or another. They will either respond in true repentance that leads to eternal life or they will reject My truth and be consumed in delusion and destruction.

For you see, I am raising up a voice of separation. Through it I will separate the wheat from the tares. My people will know that I am in their midst for My glory will be seen upon them. Then shall My people be a Holy separated people prepared for their Lord." (3.10)

Kevin Barrett, founder of Hear His Heart blog site, received the following prophetic word in February 2018.

> "This is the greater thing regarding Billy Graham's passing. The passing of the old has ushered in a new era in which many will have their eyes and ears opened to the truth and many will forsake the pleasures of the world to become one with Me. For the old era has taught the name of Jesus, but for the most part, has not taught the truths of My kingdom and the reality of a glorified, sinless, and perfect life, fully united with Me in oneness with My Spirit.
>
> This shall be the new message of the day; to prepare a people for My habitation and for Me to be glorified in earthen vessels. And many shall die to themselves so that they may become one with Me, and that I may be glorified in them. And in this, My power shall be greatly revealed in the earth through these ones. Oh, My lovely ones, this is My desire for all of you. However, this comes at a great price, and that price is your own self-life which not many are willing to give up. But these are the last days and I have reserved a remnant who shall be willing to give up all the world has to offer in order to be one with their God.
>
> The days are short and the end is near. Therefore, I need those who are willing to carry My glory to the nations. But only those who have died to their self-life shall be My glorified ones in these last days. Oh, I will still have those on the earth who shall carry My anointing, yet even so, it shall not be the same as My Glory. For no man, save Jesus Christ Himself, has ever walked the earth in the fullness of My Glory. However, I tell you that there shall be those in these last days who shall be glorified and walk in the fullness of My Spirit and Truth just as My Son Jesus did. Yet know this, even My own Son was glorified through the betrayal of Judas and His death on the cross. So then, how much more do you suppose that you must also die to yourselves in order to be glorified?
>
> Oh, do not fret over the thought that this is an impossible task. For surely, I tell you that what is impossible with man is possible with Me. And I SHALL have a remnant in the earth who will be My habitation among men in these last days. Do not be as the Israelites of old who saw themselves as grasshoppers compared to the giants in their promised land, and then doubted and feared. Even though your flesh and sin may be as giants to you, the battle is Mine.

I tell you all, eye has not seen, nor ear heard, nor has it entered into the heart of man, what I have in store these last days for those who truly love Me. But I shall reveal these things to My remnant who will carry My Glory to a lost and dying world.

Do not miss out on this great opportunity. For I tell you; I am no respecter of persons, and this call goes out to whosoever will. Don't believe the lies of the enemy that this calling is only for the anointed leaders in ministry. For I tell you, even very few of them, if any, will answer this call because many have chosen to love their ministry more than Me. Therefore, those who are unknown, of lowly reputation, and who have chosen to follow Me and make themselves least in the eyes of the world, will be the ones who are greatest in My kingdom.

I love you all, and how I desire this for all of you. But ultimately, the choice is yours. For even though I may call many to this calling, few will ultimately be chosen because few will consider the cost to die fully to self and endure to the end. Yet, even so, I do give this call for all those who would consider the cost. Surely, it will be well worth it." (3.11)

Rachel Baxter, founder of Valor Christian Academy Omaha and Scroll and Fig Leaf blog site, received the following prophetic word in August 2016.

See that which is before you, a true path made with upright stones, each formed perfectly to fit one next to the other in beauty and in strength, forged in the heat of the fire. Black and marred from the heat and the pressure, but made beautiful in My eyes, transformed into My bride.

The wedding party readies herself with much preparation. The heavens await in bated anticipation of the celebration that is to come, less than a generation to pass. See, look. Gaze upon My beauty and you will see her beauty. She is being transformed into My image (2 Corinthians 3:18), an image that reflects the love, the kindness, and the goodness that I Am. I will accept nothing less.

My spirit is being poured out without measure. (John 3, Acts 2) The greatness of the power that is accessible to this generation has never been seen before, and never will again. These things you will do are even greater than the demonstration of power My Father gave to Me. (John 14:12) Now, He gives it to you freely. (3.12)

Remnant: Confirmations

Terry Bennett, founder of Messengers of Shiloh Ministries, received the following prophetic word July 1, 2012.

> Here is what the Lord told me, "If you were to put everything together collectively that has ever occurred in the past, it will not go beyond what I am about to do."
>
> As God begins to confront the powers of darkness, by his own authority and power in his people, there will be the arising of a fearless army, young and old, who are completely given over to the Lord, and the Lord will so be with them that evil will fear them. They will also know who God is in them. The ministry of divine authority will be back in the earth again, and I mean like Elijah displayed when he said, "I am shutting up the heavens so they will not give any rain." That ministry of divine authority will be back in the earth with this group who have come out to the Lord entirely and whole heartedly. So, we will see an unprecedented display of not just simply the miraculous, yes, but also heaven will be so involved, the angelic arena will be heavily involved in this, as we see basically an invasion of heaven into this earth. So, that's good news! (3.13)

Terry Bennett also received the following prophetic word on July 1, 2012.

> The great release of My power and authoritative power and anointing are at hand. Yet, this will not be a general body release, but a specific release, a measured release to and through My refined ones, My spirit trained ones, My shining ones, My prepared and ready Bride. There will be a true Gideon type army who quickly bow and drink of My depths, and who are fully alert and sober. They will be characterized by My character and fervent in their proclamation of My eternal gospel.
>
> An absolute commitment to the name above all names will be among God's set apart ones. Christ Himself will be their portion, their reason, their passion, love, and proclamation. A deep internal conviction to remain small and hidden, allowing Christ alone to be exalted in them, will be the posture and manifestation among My called-out ones. The plumb line ministry of the triumphant eternal Lamb of God will be re-established in this end-time and end of the age season.
>
> The differing elements of nature will be tools and weapons in the Lamb's armory and arsenal. The creation of earth and the heavens shall join in the battle of Christ the Lamb and the antichrist spirit! The cloud of witnesses shall be unveiled

and the angelic host unveiled to those whose spiritual senses have been trained. They both shall fully participate in this end of the age struggle. (3.14)

Speaking at the Shekinah Worship Center on Thursday, August 13, 2015, Sadhu Sundar Selvaraj, founder of Jesus Ministries, said, "The Prophet Joel explained to me, 'This remnant who will be called by the Lord are the ones who will be filled with the great powers of the age to come.'" Speaking at the 2014 Lancaster Prophetic Conference on August 9, 2014, he said,

> "While I was waiting on the Lord, four angels visited me. The chief among them said, 'This is the last final thrust. The whole power of the Holy Spirit will be poured out in an unlimited manner upon the warrior company of the Lord Jesus. We in heaven have not seen such a power of the Holy Spirit yet.'
>
> Then I saw an image of the Prophet William Branham and this is what the Holy Spirit told me, 'The anointing that will rest upon this last days generation will be seven times more than what rested on Branham when he came to do his work.' Then I saw Smith Wigglesworth and I saw John G. Lake. I saw all these wonderful men of God. Three times, five times, seven times the anointing will rest on this last days generation." (3.15)

Mena Lee Grebin, founder of Faithful Walk Healing Ministries, received the following prophetic word on February 1, 2015.

> "While I was travailing in the Spirit, I saw oil raining down from heaven onto the earth. The Lord had me interceding for the Bride. He said; 'The final outpouring. Through the chaos, I will raise up a mighty army who will walk in signs and miracles and in great authority upon the earth. The harvest is ripe and the time is at hand.'" (3.16)

In a guest appearance on Trinity Broadcasting Network in about 2011, Dr. Mark Chironna, founder of Mark Chironna Ministries, shared the following prophetic word:

> "There is a company of people that have been hidden in God for a season but they are coming out of hiding and they are going to stand in the courts of Pharaoh, like Moses and Elijah did. (Exodus 7-12, 1 Kings 18:20-40) They are going to challenge the spirits. They are going to challenge the powers of Egypt. The earth is going to see a 21st century manifestation of the demonstration of the Spirit, not from one or two, but from a many membered body. God is going to have the church of His dreams.

Remnant: Confirmations

All the institutionalizing that we have done to the church, all the things we have done to try to make it our thing instead of God's thing, God has had the church under wraps for 2,000 years. God wants a church that has been in hiding and prepared for power by severe testing, severe trial, severe tribulation in every single season and they feel like they are not going to be used and it is too late and it is all over. That is the company that is prepared for power. They've been like John the Baptist in the wilderness eating locusts and wild honey, strange food. They have had to learn to glean from the word when they were just getting little pious platitudes from preachers all around the country. They are being weaned away from everything that is contradictory to the powerful truth of the word of God. That company is coming out of hiding. They are going to cross Jordan. They are going to move into a manifestation of power where there will not just be power on one or two, but there is going to be power on multiplied thousands and thousands." (3.17)

Neville Johnson, founder of the Academy of Light, received a visitation from the Lord Jesus, Elijah, and Moses. Each of them spoke words to him about the things that are coming upon the earth.

The Lord Jesus said to me, "The day has now come when you will begin to see great anointings breaking out across the earth, anointings like you have never seen before. There are different anointings and there is nothing in history to reference them to. You must allow these anointings to strengthen your spirit. The time has come to stand and not fall. The time has come when these anointings will enable you to reveal the heart of the Father to this world. Tell the people they are My sent ones to this generation. I am about to release My apostolic anointing into the true church. Many angels are now prepared to come to the earth. They will carry these anointings and diffuse these anointings and impart mantles with them. Truth will be revealed like never before. You will be sent to reveal the heart of the Father. You must know the Father and reveal him to this world."

Then Elijah said to me, "The spirit that was upon me in the earth in My days will be seen again in your days. It will turn the hearts of the children to the fathers. In My day, there were droughts in the earth. There were great deluges of rain. There were great fires and windstorms. There were confrontations with the powers of darkness. You are going to see the same things when My spirit comes again into the earth and rests again on God's people."

Then Moses said to me, "The spirit that was upon me in My days on the earth will be upon you in your days now. This apostolic anointing will be released in the earth with great power. The end-time apostles are coming. It is going to change everything. They will lead God's people through deep waters into the Promised Land, leading them through droughts, plagues, and dangerous times. The spirit of Pharaoh has to be broken. God sent plagues upon the land to break the spirit of Pharaoh. These apostles will release the fullness of Passover, the fullness of Pentecost, and the fullness of Tabernacles." (3.18)

Tommy Hicks was an American evangelist in the 1950's. He was one of the leaders of the 1954 Argentina revival. On July 25, 1961, after seeing a detailed prophetic vision, he asked the Lord to reveal the meaning. Here are excerpts from the explanation he received.

> "I was so stirred as I watched it, and I cried unto the Lord and I said, 'Oh Lord, what is the meaning of this.'
>
> And He said, 'This is that which I will do in the last days. I will restore all that the cankerworm, the palmerworm, the caterpillar, I will restore all that they have destroyed. This, My people, in the end times will go forth. As a mighty army shall they sweep over the face of the earth.'
>
> God is going to have a perfect Church. He is going to have a people that are so endued with power that it will not be an exposition of self, but it will be Christ in them, the hope of glory. I saw these people pass through the fire, unburned... cross rivers as though there was no water there. They crossed oceans with ease, escaped persecution as though a hand transported them from their surroundings. Despite wild beasts roaring, being attacked by men with swords and weapons of war, nothing seemed to hinder them. They moved over mountains, and down through valleys. They moved like the hart skipping upon the hills. Their faces shone with the countenance of Victors. They were conquerors.
>
> I hesitate to tell this part of the Vision, because it was with great trembling, I received this portion of the revelation. I saw the man, clothed in white, point with a scepter in his hand. Again, there was pouring forth from His hand, this that I call "liquid power." As soon as it would touch the person, he would have his hands bathed and dripping in the same heavenly substance. Upon receiving this anointing, they would walk into hospitals, through the streets, into the institutions, and on and on, marching throughout the length and the breadth of the land. I could hear them saying, "According to My Word, be thou make

whole." As the liquid power flowed from their hands, each one they touched was instantly healed and made whole.

I saw people transported in the Spirit from nation to nation. I saw them going to Siberia, to Africa, to Canada, and to the ends of the earth. I saw them literally lifted up and placed by the Spirit in the respective countries. And I beheld this Christ as he continued to stretch forth his hand; but there was a tragedy. There were many people as he stretched forth his hand that refused the anointing of God and the call of God. I could see the anguish of their faces. The price was too steep, retaining of the identification meant too much to them. I saw men and women that I knew. People that I felt would certainly receive the call of God. But as he stretched forth his hand toward this one and toward that one, they simply bowed their head and began to back away. They refused to march, and eventually slumped away. The price was more than they could bear. And each of those that seemed to bow down and back away, seemed to go into darkness. They eventually slipped out into the darkness of the night. Blackness seemed to swallow them everywhere.

As I was at this great height, I could behold the whole world. I watched these people as they were going to and fro over the face of the earth. Suddenly there was a man in Africa and in a moment, he was transported by the Spirit of God, and perhaps he was in Russia, or China or America or some other place, and vice versa. All over the world these people went, and they came through fire, and through pestilence, and through famine. Neither fire nor persecution, nothing seemed to stop them.

Angry mobs came to them with swords and with guns. And like Jesus, they passed through the multitudes and they could not find them, but they went forth in the name of the Lord, and everywhere they stretched forth their hands, the sick were healed, the blind eyes were opened. There was not a long prayer, and after I had reviewed the vision many times in my mind, and I thought about it many times, I realized that I never saw a church, and I never saw or heard a denomination, but these people were going in the name of the Lord of Hosts. Hallelujah!

As they marched forth in everything they did as the ministry of Christ in the end times, these people were ministering to the multitudes over the face of the earth. Tens of thousands, even millions seemed to come to the Lord Jesus Christ as these people stood forth and gave the message of the kingdom, of the coming kingdom, in this last hour. It was so glorious, but it seems as though there were those that rebelled, and they would become angry and they tried to attack those workers that were giving the message.

God is going to give the world a demonstration in this last hour as the world has never known. These men and women are of all walks of life, degrees will mean nothing. I saw these workers as they were going over the face of the earth. When one would stumble and fall, another would come and pick him up. There were no "big I" and "little you," but every mountain was brought low and every valley was exalted, and they seemed to have one thing in common - there was a divine love, a divine love that seemed to flow forth from these people as they worked together, and as they lived together. It was the most glorious sight that I have ever known. Jesus Christ was the theme of their life. They continued and it seemed the days went by as I stood and beheld this sight." (3.19)

ENDNOTES

3.01: Julie Whedbee, https://iamcallingyounow.blogspot.com/2019/01/

3.02: Julie Whedbee, https://iamcallingyounow.blogspot.com/ and https://z3news.com/w/time-manifestation-mature-sons-daughters-arrived/

3.03: Julie Whedbee, https://iamcallingyounow.blogspot.com/ and https://z3news.com/w/earth-never-seen-what-i-am-about-to-do/

3.04: Julie Whedbee, https://iamcallingyounow.blogspot.com/ and https://z3news.com/w/compares-glory-releasing-chosen/

3.05: Bob Jones: remnant, http://www.youtube.com/watch?v=GV9BYsoap5U: Uploaded Oct 31, 2011

3.06: Diana Pulliam, http://themightyhandofgod.com/ and https://z3news.com/w/who-are-these-where-did-they-come-from/

3.07: Reverend Susan Omara: http://intheimageofhisgloryministries.blogspot.com/ and https://z3news.com/w/mighty-men-run-glory-race/

3.08: Elizabeth Marie, https://latterrain333.wixsite.com/lifeline and https://z3news.com/w/raising-mighty-army/

3.09: Elaine Tavolacci, http://www.awordinseason.info/ and https://z3news.com/w/release-my-glory-earth-heaven/

3.10: Lydia Hodge, https://z3news.com/w/elijah-rising-positioning/

3.11: Kevin Barrett, https://hearhisheart.wordpress.com/ and https://z3news.com/w/message-day-prepare-people-habitation/

3.12: Rachel Baxter, http://www.scrollandfigleaf.com/ and https://z3news.com/w/greatness-power-accessible-generation/

3.13: Terry Bennett, Messengers of Shiloh Ministries, https://www.messengersofshiloh.com Trunews interview, June 17, 2015.

3.14: Terry Bennett, Messengers of Shiloh Ministries, https://www.messengersofshiloh.com July 1, 2012.

3.15: Sadhu Sundar Selvaraj, https://www.jesusministries.org and 2014 Lancaster Prophetic Conference on August 9, 2014.

3.16: Mena Lee Grebin, http://www.faithfulwalkhealingministries.com/ and https://z3news.com/w/mena-lee-grebin-america-burn/

3.17: Dr. Mark Chironna, https://www.markchironna.com circa 2011, https://www.youtube.com/watch?v=jrA6iSvVZvc

3.18: Neville Johnson, https://www.theacademy.org.au and http://www.youtube.com/watch?v=zExgEy1zMmM

3.19: Tommy Hicks, https://jesushealsthesick.wordpress.com/2014/04/

4
Righteousness

In my horse dream, even though we had been told in advance to be expecting the delivery, our attention was so focused on ourselves and our own plans, we could barely even hear the doorbell ringing. By the time I answered the door, the elf had almost given up and was walking away, so we almost missed the most amazing gifts God had for us.

Even though the horse and all the other animals around the corner had already been prepared and delivered right to my driveway, the elf did not bring them to my door. I couldn't see them until I first answered the door and followed his instructions to come and see, which was not an unreasonable request because it only required me to take a few steps, but if I had not done my part, I would have missed what God wanted me to have. I believe that was an important part of the dream showing God's plans for us don't happen automatically but require us to do our part by shifting our attention away from our plans so we can tune into His plans by pursuing righteousness, like Elijah's invitation to the Israelites, "Come near to me." (1 Kings 18:30, 2 Timothy 2:22)

Just as the horse was illuminated with a ray of sunlight, God is calling our attention to a more excellent way so we can avoid making the mistake so many are making today, asking God to do what He has already promised to do while neglecting to do what He requires us to do. If we'll just do what He tells us to do, He'll do His part, but if we fail to do our part, even all the asking in the world won't do any good because we don't qualify, as the remainder of this chapter explains.

He's even instructed us not to ask Him for what He's already promised, referring to essential items like food and clothing. Although the rest of the world seeks those things, we're not like them because we've qualified for His promises, which includes everything we need if we'll seek first His kingdom and His righteousness. (Matthew 6:31-33) For example, Jesus said, "Look at the birds of the air, for they neither sow nor reap nor gather into barns; yet your heavenly Father feeds them. Are you not of more value than they?" (Matthew 6:26 NKJV) "So why do you worry about clothing? Consider the lilies of the field, how they grow: they neither toil nor spin; and yet I say to you that even Solomon in all his glory was not arrayed like one of these. Now if God so clothes the grass of the field, which today is, and tomorrow is thrown into the oven, will He not much more clothe you, O you of little faith?" (Matthew 6:28-30 NKJV)

He instructed us not to give a thought or care to our most essential needs, but there are other things He has instructed us to seek diligently by asking Him and continuing to ask, seeking and knocking. (Matthew 7:7-11) Righteousness is at the top of that list because He instructed us to seek it first above everything else. (Matthew 6:33) By hungering and thirsting for it, we qualify to receive everything He wants to give us so we can fulfill our destiny as part of His righteous remnant of forerunners. (Psalm 119:142, Matthew 5:6, Revelation 20:4-6)

As amazing as the horse was, I was aware of more animals around the corner. I never made it that far, but I believe they were included in the dream to show God has much more He wants to show us, all the wonders of the heavenly realm, great and mighty things we have not known. (Jeremiah 33:3) By obeying His simple instructions, we qualify to have all of it imparted into us so His promises can begin to manifest in us, transforming us into new creations, making us like His majestic horses prepared for battle. (Joel 2:4, Zechariah 10:3, Romans 8:29, 2 Corinthians 5:17)

When we accept His invitation to come and see, He fills us with the knowledge of His plans for our life and the passion to accomplish it, which propels us in the direction He wants us to go, so everything we do comes into alignment with His plan, ultimately leading us directly to the abundant life He wants us to have, living the dream in His manifested presence. (Psalm 5:12, 11:7, 17:15, 64:10, 140:13, Proverbs 8:20, 11:31, Ezekiel 44:23, Zechariah 3:7, Matthew 6:10, Mark 10:30, John 10:10, 3 John 1:2)

Requirements for Righteousness:

I've heard people say things like, "I don't need to seek righteousness because I was already made righteous when I became a Christian." And things like, "I no longer need to repent because I already repented when I first prayed the sinner's prayer and got saved." That kind of thinking contradicts His instructions to keep pursuing, hungering and thirsting for righteousness. (Matthew 5:6, 6:33, John 8:31, 1 Timothy 6:11, 2 Timothy 2:22) Receiving God's gift of salvation is a wonderful thing, but it's only the beginning of our journey, the entry to the path of righteousness which we must continue following as He leads us. (Psalm 23:3)

We all like hearing about the great things God has for us, but not so much about what He requires us to do to qualify for them and receive them. And since we don't like hearing that part, our leaders don't particularly like telling us about it, so we've heard too much emphasis on what God has done for us and too little on what He requires. The message has been so distorted, we've reached the point where even mentioning deeds is like saying a cuss word, causing people to get offended, but it's not a cuss word because Jesus said, "You are My friends if you do whatever I command you." (John 15:14 NKJV) So, doing whatever He commands is required to be right with Him.

How tragic it would be to have all the wonders of the heavenly realm delivered right to our driveway only to fail to receive them by not doing our part, but if all we ever hear about is the part we want to hear, we can miss the most important part that God wants us to hear. That is not God's will for us. He wants us to understand clearly so we can qualify to receive all His promises. (2 Peter 3:9)

Like my dream, He has sent His messenger to our door and is now ringing our doorbell, but if we get too busy with our own plans, we're in danger of failing to even hear it. Accepting His invitation requires setting aside those things that formerly distracted our attention so we can hear His call and take possession of the true riches He wants us to have. Our response determines the outcome.

Soon after I surrendered my life to God in 1982, I was so indoctrinated with this distorted message, it sounded strange to me when the Lord said something to me when I was praying one day. I was telling Him how much I loved Him and getting choked up about it, so He told me, "I don't want your emotional love. I want you to demonstrate your love for Me by your obedience to all My commandments."

Immediately, I thought, "Obedience to Your commandments? Really? Lord, don't You know how legalistic that sounds? Don't You know we've moved beyond all that stuff and are now in the age of grace?"

Obviously, He wasn't the one confused. His word to me was consistent with what He has said repeatedly in the scriptures. The Apostle Paul confirmed what matters most is the keeping of the commandments of God. (1 Corinthians 7:19) Many other examples of New Testament commandments are listed in Exhibit 4. My understanding was unscriptural because I had believed all the popular teachings.

The path of righteousness is narrow with ditches on both sides. (Matthew 7:13-14, Luke 13:24-28) On one side is the dead deeds ditch, the place of trusting in good deeds to qualify for right standing with God. On the other side is the dead faith ditch, the place of trusting in the grace of God without any deeds required. In both cases, everyone falling into these ditches is disqualified. So, the remainder of this chapter explains the difference between righteous deeds and unrighteous deeds, which include unrighteous deeds of the Law and unrighteous lawless deeds.

Unrighteous Deeds of the Law:

All the false religions in the world share this common flaw; seeking to qualify for right standing with God based on our own good deeds. The general idea is always the same, that our good deeds must outweigh our bad deeds, tipping the scales of justice in our favor and thereby qualifying us for eternal life. This idea appeals to our natural understanding, which is rooted in pride, thinking we can somehow qualify ourselves by satisfying God's lofty requirements.

True Christianity stands alone in proclaiming our inability to qualify for the path of righteousness based on our good deeds. This is the stumbling stone, the rock of offense, which God has placed at the entrance to the one true path. (Romans 9:33) Many have been offended by it and turned back because getting past it requires stripping off all pride to acknowledge our utter dependence on God to do what we cannot do for ourselves. Most of the world has stumbled over this stumbling stone, preferring instead to rely on their own understanding, which leads to destruction. (Proverbs 3:5-7, Matthew 7:13)

Qualifying for righteousness requires more than just good deeds. Even those who claim to believe in Jesus Christ and perform many good deeds, such as praying, fasting, reading the Bible and helping the poor, still disqualify themselves if they trust in their good deeds, their own righteousness, rather than trusting in God. He requires us to trust Him alone because even on our best day, we fall way short of His requirements. (Romans 3:23) Not even Abraham could do it. He only received the righteousness of God as a gift because he did not trust in himself, but in God. (Romans 4:1-5) We receive it the same way.

Even though the commandments came from God, if we put our trust in our own good deeds to save us, those same commandments will testify against us if we fail to obey them perfectly, 100% of the time, as the Law requires. God never intended for anyone to qualify for righteousness by the Law. His purpose for it was to help us see we're unable to save ourselves. (Galatians 3:21-25) Ultimately, the Law was given to expose our wretched condition, being trapped in our sins.

Anyone hoping to qualify for right standing with God by obeying the Law must not only keep the Ten Commandments, but also 435 additional commandments given to Moses, totaling 445. Many of those include multiple commands, totaling 3,435 commands, as shown in Exhibit 5. If any of those commands are ever violated even once, the whole Law is violated and the violator loses their right standing with God, bringing a curse upon themselves and costing them their life. (Galatians 3:11, James 2:10) So, it is impossible for anyone to qualify by obeying the Law. (Galatians 2:16)

The only person in history to successfully meet all the requirements of the Law is Jesus Christ. By doing so, He fulfilled it, completed it, and brought it to an end. (Matthew 5:17-20, Romans 10:4, Ephesians 2:14-16)

The scribes and Pharisees made the mistake of trying to attain righteousness by the Law, but by putting their confidence in their ability to keep it, they were guilty of self-righteousness, which disqualified them from God's righteousness. When John the Baptist saw them, he called them a brood of vipers and warned them to bear fruit in keeping with genuine repentance. (Matthew 3:8) Jesus asked them, "How will you escape the sentence of hell?" (Matthew 23:33) He also warned others, "Unless your righteousness surpasses that of the scribes and Pharisees, you will not enter the kingdom of heaven." (Matthew 5:19-20)

How can our righteousness surpass theirs? We cannot get there by following the Law more strictly than they did, but only by humbling ourselves to receive by faith what only God can do. Even so, many are still trying to qualify by obeying the Law. For example, I've heard people bragging, "I haven't missed observing a single Sabbath day in over two years!" Only God can see the hidden motives in their heart, but whenever I hear people talking like that, it sounds like self-righteousness to me.

God has given us a far better way which does not require us to be under the Law or to put our trust in it because whoever is led by the Spirit is no longer under the Law. (Galatians 5:18) So, pursuing righteousness by obeying the law is a dead end, leading only to disappointment and death, but there are still two other kinds of deeds.

Unrighteous Deeds of Lawlessness:

Unlike unrighteous deeds of the Law, those who practice lawlessness disregard the Law altogether to go their own way and do whatever pleases them. Lawless deeds are generally easy to recognize by their outward appearance, but they can also manifest in the unseen realm of our thoughts, including fornication, adultery, homosexuality, stealing, drunkenness, greed, envy, gossip, slander, and murder. Many more examples are listed in Exhibit 6.

Many years ago, I was visiting my parents' home for a few days when a young man came to pick up my niece for a date. Back in those days, she was living with my parents. When he arrived, she wasn't quite ready to go, so he and I were sitting in the living room while he waited for her and we somehow we got started talking about what it means to be right with God.

He told me, "I know I'm okay with God. I mean, I was raised in the Baptist Church and I got saved years ago. I know I'm not living for God right now, but I know I'm okay because God knows my heart."

He openly admitted he was off the path, not living for God, practicing unrighteousness, but he thought he still had all the same blessings God promised to those who stay on the path because, as he claimed, "God knows my heart."

Yes, God knew his heart because He knew his deeds, which is the same way He knows all of us. Claiming to be one way while acting another way is the definition of hypocrisy, which is something to take seriously because Jesus said hypocrites, unless they repent, will go to the place where there is weeping and gnashing of teeth. (Matthew 24:51)

That young man had strayed so far off the path, so far away from the light, he was in such darkness, he could not see his true condition. As far as he could tell, all was well, but that's the way it is with everyone who is off the path, which is why almost everyone thinks they're okay with God and on their way to heaven, even though they're deceived and on their way to destruction. (Matthew 6:23)

Those who practice lawless deeds think they know what God requires better than He does, so they do it their way, but how could anyone know what God requires better than God? That doesn't even make sense. Yet, we come up with all sorts of reasons why it's okay to keep doing the very things He said not to do. Fornication is okay because we love each other. Idolatry is okay because we also believe in God. Adultery is okay because our spouse isn't meeting our needs. Homosexuality is okay because we were born that way. Changing our gender is okay because it's not based on the anatomical parts we were born with. Stealing is okay because we were going to put it back later and how else are we supposed to survive? Covetousness is okay because God wants us to be happy. Drunkenness is okay because it's the only way we can deal with it. Reviling against our neighbor is okay because look what they did to us!

All our justifying won't change the outcome one bit because God has already made it clear, everyone who practices unrighteous deeds is disqualified, unable to enter His Kingdom. (1 Corinthians 6:9-10) Everyone who practices sin is practicing lawlessness, which is of the devil. (1 John 3:4, 3:8) Thinking we can have all the benefits of righteousness while walking in unrighteousness is foolish presumption leading us to disaster. We cannot have it both ways, no matter who told us we can. The consequences are severe because the same God who shows kindness to the righteous shows severity to the unrighteous. (Romans 11:22) The same God who pours out His blessings on the righteous pours out His curses on the unrighteous (Deuteronomy 28).

Like that young Baptist man, the members of the Laodicean church thought they were in right standing with God, but they were deceived. Jesus confronted them for practicing unrighteousness. They thought they were rich in the things of God and needed nothing, but He told them their true condition was the opposite, "miserable, poor, blind and naked." (Revelation 3:17) They were neither hot nor cold, just lukewarm, because they were practicing unrighteous deeds, disqualifying them from receiving God's promises. Jesus instructed them to buy from Him white garments to clothe themselves, garments available only to the righteous. Otherwise, He warned, "I will spit you out of My mouth." (Revelation 3:15-18)

Some of the members of the church at Sardis were making this same mistake. (Revelation 3:1-6) Like the Laodiceans, those who were practicing unrighteous deeds were deceived into thinking their relationship with God was alive and well, but Jesus told them they were dead. Those who were walking uprightly, He called worthy, but those who were practicing unrighteousness, He called dead, even though they claimed to believe. Their faith was counted as dead and worthless because of their deeds. They had fallen into the dead faith ditch.

Notice He didn't say, "Okay guys, listen up. We're going take a little time here so I can teach you all about God's grace. You're going to absolutely love this stuff! Woo-hoo!"

No, He didn't say that because He knew that wasn't what they needed. If anything, it would have confused them even more. And He didn't say, "Okay guys, we all know you've been practicing unrighteousness, but I want you to know I am still your Savior, even though I'm not your Lord."

No, He didn't say that because if He was still their Savior, He would not have told them they were dead and disqualified from wearing white garments and their names would be removed from the book of life unless they repented. They were not saved at that point, so He gave them a wakeup call, hoping they would repent so they could qualify for salvation. He cannot be our Savior unless He is also our Lord.

Jesus directed their attention to the true problem, which was all about their deeds, warning them sternly, "Wake up, and strengthen the things that remain, which were about to die; for I have not found your deeds completed in the sight of My God." (Revelation 3:2)

Remnant: Righteousness

It must have been quite a shock to them when He told them only a few of them would walk with Him in white garments because they had "not soiled their garments." To them He promised "they will walk with Me in white, for they are worthy." (Revelation 3:1-6) Even though they were all members of the church and all thought they were alive in their relationship with God, many of them were dead and on their way to hell.

The warning He gave them applies to us today. Even if we call ourselves Christians and claim to be right with God, we are dead, disqualified from the promises of God if we don't stay on the path. If we go our own way and do our own thing, whatever seems right to us, lying whenever we want, looking at whatever we want, thinking about whatever we want, indulging our carnal appetites with all sorts of unrighteous entertainment, gossiping, and all sorts of other unrighteous deeds, we're practicing lawlessness, which disqualifies us for righteousness. Like the people of Sardis and Laodicea, doing these things brings darkness upon our minds, causing us to be lulled into delusional state, a spiritual sleep, a thick fog, a stupor, a dull state of mind, far below what God requires. Practicing unrighteous deeds leads us off the path and disqualifies us from right standing with God. Those who do these things do not know Him, as shown here:

> 4 Whoever commits sin also commits lawlessness, and sin is lawlessness.
> 5 And you know that He was manifested to take away our sins, and in Him there is no sin.
> 6 Whoever abides in Him does not sin. Whoever sins has neither seen Him nor known Him. (1 John 3:4-6 NKJV)

Our deeds make an eternal difference. Jesus warned about the terrible fate awaiting all those who call themselves Christians while practicing unrighteousness:

> 21 "Not everyone who says to Me, 'Lord, Lord,' shall enter the kingdom of heaven, but he who does the will of My Father in heaven.
> 22 Many will say to Me in that day, 'Lord, Lord, have we not prophesied in Your name, cast out demons in Your name, and done many wonders in Your name?'
> 23 And then I will declare to them, 'I never knew you; depart from Me, you who practice lawlessness!' (Matthew 7:21-23 NKJV)

To drive His point home, He clearly identified this warning is for those who call Him, "Lord, Lord." Only those who call themselves Christians call Jesus their Lord. They were even doing the works of Christian ministry, including prophesying, casting out demons, and performing many miracles, yet they were disqualified from entering heaven, so they went to hell, because they were just talking the talk without walking the walk.

Jesus warned many people will be deceived in this way, calling themselves Christians, but going to hell, which must surely be a shock when they arrive there, but they will stay there forever because they believed the lie that they had a free pass to practice unrighteousness. (Greek word anomia in 1 John 3:4) Their true standing with God was not based on what they claimed with their words, but on their deeds as evidence of their faith. (James 2:17 and 2:24)

God requires us to walk in the light He has given to us. (John 8:12, Colossians 2:6) As we do, He rewards us with more light, so our path grows brighter and brighter as we gain new insights and understanding, which is wonderful, but it comes with increased responsibility because the light reveals areas where our old ways are not pleasing to Him, so we are continually confronted with choices to either abandon our old ways to follow His ways, which leads to life, or hold onto our old ways, which causes us to stray off the path, moving us away from the light and into greater darkness.

Since God designed us to follow Him on the path, turning away from it causes our whole system to malfunction. Our conscience, which was designed to help keep us on track, starts working against us if we attempt to appease and silence it by justifying our actions, even lying to ourselves, hoping to find a way to live with ourselves while continuing to go our own way. Yet, with every wrong choice, every unrighteous deed, every unclean thought, we take another step further away from the light of God and further into darkness. And the darker it gets, the more confused we get. Even if we were formerly sensitive and tender hearted to obey those promptings, all our appeasing and justifying takes a heavy toll, until we reach the place, the very dark place, where our heart becomes hardened by the deceitfulness of sin, so we no longer hear His voice or see anything wrong with what we're doing and become fully convinced we're fine, even thinking we're right with God when we're in great danger of eternal separation from Him. (Deuteronomy 30:19, Proverbs 4:18, Matthew 4:17, Luke 12:48, Hebrews 3:13, 6:4-6, 10:38-39, James 1:22-25, 2 Peter 1:5-11, 2:20-22, 1 John 3:7-10, 3 John 1:11, Jude 1:5-7, Revelation 2:2-5, 2:16, 3:1-6, 3:11-12, 3:15-16)

Righteous Deeds:

Ultimately, we can only qualify for right standing with God by faith, not by our deeds, because God gives it to us as a gift by His grace, leaving us with nothing to boast about in our own good works.

> 8 For by grace you have been saved through faith, and that not of yourselves; it is the gift of God,
> 9 not of works, lest anyone should boast. (Ephesians 2:8-9 NKJV)

Remnant: Righteousness

Although God's grace and righteousness are received by faith, it is only by living and active faith, not dead faith. (Philippians 3:9, James 2:26) Dead faith is believing only in our mind, not our heart, claiming to agree with His teachings without surrendering our heart to Him. Our right standing with God is based on the condition of our heart, not our mind, because our heart is the realm of our inner man, our spirit man, the center of our spiritual life where we have fellowship with the Spirit of God living in us. Only by surrendering our heart to Him can we reach the level of being so fully persuaded, we are compelled to act on what we claim to believe and that is what activates our faith, quickening it and bringing it to life, making it the kind of faith that qualifies us for right standing with Him.

> 8 But what does it say? "The word is near you, in your mouth and in your heart" (that is, the word of faith which we preach)
> 9 that if you confess with your mouth the Lord Jesus and believe in your heart that God has raised Him from the dead, you will be saved.
> 10 For with the heart one believes unto righteousness, and with the mouth confession is made unto salvation.
> 11 For the Scripture says, "Whoever believes on Him will not be put to shame." (Romans 10:8-11 NKJV)

If God has truly captured our heart, truly won our love, we will obey His commandments. (John 14:15, Galatians 5:25, 1 John 3:18) And the reverse is also true, if we claim to know Him but don't obey His commandments, we don't truly love Him or belong to Him. (1 John 5:2-3) Even demons believe, but they are not righteous because they do not practice righteous deeds and they practice unrighteous deeds. (James 2:19)

> 3 Now by this we know that we know Him, if we keep His commandments.
> 4 He who says, "I know Him," and does not keep His commandments, is a liar, and the truth is not in him.
> 5 But whoever keeps His word, truly the love of God is perfected in him. By this we know that we are in Him.
> 6 He who says he abides in Him ought himself also to walk just as He walked. (1 John 2:3-6 NKJV)

So, although we can never be good enough to qualify for righteousness, righteous deeds are required to qualify for righteousness because faith by itself, if it does not have works, is dead. (James 2:17)

> You see then that a man is justified by works, and not by faith only. (James 2:24 NKJV)

Remnant: Righteousness

In this verse, the original Greek word *dikaioo* is translated as justified, but the more complete definition is "to show one to be righteous, to render righteous." (4.01) Also, the Greek word *ergon* is often translated as works, but the more complete definition includes "an act, deed, thing done, that which one undertakes to do." (4.02) So, this verse is clearly warning us dead faith can't save us, so righteous deeds are required to activate our faith so we can qualify for God's gift of righteousness.

On the surface, claiming righteous deeds are required for right standing with God might seem contradictory to the previous scripture, "by grace you have been saved through faith, and that not of yourselves; it is the gift of God, not of works, lest anyone should boast" (Ephesians 2:8-9 NKJV) However, the key that ties it all together is found at the end of James 2:24, "not by faith only," so both verses identify righteousness is received by faith, but faith is not genuine unless it is backed up by righteous deeds.

Whereas lawless deeds demonstrate total disregard for God's Kingdom and dominion, seeking our own way by doing whatever pleases us, righteous deeds demonstrate our submission to God's Kingdom and dominion by doing what He commands. If we continue practicing lawless deeds, we prove we do not love God, but by practicing righteous deeds, we prove we do. (1 John 5:2)

Since righteous deeds demonstrate the true condition of our heart, God requires them as evidence in our behalf to justify His decision to make a distinction between those who are His and those who are not, rewarding the righteous and punishing the unrighteous, so all can see His judgments are right, including all who have gone before us, the angels of heaven, and even the fallen ones who rebelled against Him. (Ephesians 3:10-11, Hebrews 4:11, 6:10, 10:36, Revelation 2:4-5) For all eternity, everyone will know He is right in all His ways, vindicating His claim that righteousness is the foundation of His throne. (Psalm 89:14 and 97:2, Proverbs 25:5)

If no evidence was required, anyone would qualify for entry to His Kingdom and for all His promises, including those who practice unrighteousness, who never surrendered their heart to Him, but insisted on going their own way, making themselves their own god, but that would bring dishonor to His Kingdom by filling it with liars, thieves, hypocrites, haters of God, and every kind of immoral person. So, God separates the righteous from the unrighteous based on our deeds. (John 15:6-10, Romans 11:20-23, 1 John 2:17) Therefore, to qualify for righteousness, we must do righteous deeds, as shown in this passage:

> 7 Little children, let no one deceive you. He who practices righteousness is righteous, just as He is righteous.

> 8 He who sins is of the devil, for the devil has sinned from the beginning. For this purpose, the Son of God was manifested, that He might destroy the works of the devil.
> 9 Whoever has been born of God does not sin, for His seed remains in him; and he cannot sin, because he has been born of God.
> 10 In this the children of God and the children of the devil are manifest: Whoever does not practice righteousness is not of God, nor is he who does not love his brother. (1 John 3:7-10 NKJV)

In verses seven and ten, the original Greek word *poieo* is translated as practice, but the more complete definition is "to make or to do." (4.03) We must do righteous deeds while turning away from doing unrighteous deeds. (1 John 2:29)

The idea of righteous deeds might sound like putting us back under the works of the Law, but we already know we cannot attain righteousness by the Law because even one mistake would be enough to disqualify us. (Galatians 2:16, 3:11, 3:21-25, 5:18-19, James 2:10) So, God has provided a better way for those who are led by the Spirit, which Jesus revealed when He said, "Blessed are those who hunger and thirst for righteousness, for they shall be filled." (Matthew 5:6 NKJV) Notice He did not say, "Blessed are those who do everything exactly right, for they shall be filled." Thank God He didn't say that because we would all be disqualified. He only required us to hunger and thirst, which means we demonstrate to Him that we are doing our very best, making it our sincere aim, our top priority, to obey Him in every area of our life. (Matthew 6:33, 1 Timothy 6:11, 2 Timothy 2:22) If we will just do that, He credits it to us as righteousness because our ongoing pursuit to be right with Him causes us to quickly reconcile with Him whenever we make a mistake, so we repent and stop doing it.

Backing up our faith with our righteous deeds effectively carries us across the finish line, which we could never reach otherwise, so we qualify for all the great rewards of righteousness, receiving them as a gift by His grace and mercy. Therefore, we can rejoice in His goodness and kindness, humbly thanking Him for making the impossible possible. (Matthew 19:26) Despite our very best efforts, it is ultimately received by faith as the gift of God. (Ephesians 2:8-9)

There are many scriptural examples of practicing righteous deeds, but they're not limited to the scriptures because they include whatever God commands us to do. (John 15:14) For example, Jesus commanded us to forgive those who sin against us and warned if we don't, God will not forgive us, which means we lose our right standing with Him, so we fall into the dead faith ditch, unless we repent. (Matthew 6:14-15, 18:21-22) Here are 70 examples of righteous deeds, all from the New Testament:

Remnant: Righteousness

1. Hunger and thirst for righteousness. (Matthew 5:6)
2. Give to him who asks of you. (Matthew 5:42)
3. Love your enemies. (Matthew 5:44)
4. Pray for those who persecute you. (Matthew 5:44)
5. Seek first the kingdom of God and His righteousness. (Matthew 6:33)
6. Act on God's words. (Matthew 7:24)
7. Forgive those who sin against you, not just seven times, but up to seventy times seven. (Matthew 18:21-22)
8. Have faith in God. (Mark 11:22)
9. Bear your cross and come after the Lord Jesus. (Luke 14:27)
10. Forsake all that you have. (Luke 14:33)
11. Do not waver at the promise of God through unbelief. (Romans 4:20)
12. Be fully convinced what God promised He is able also to perform. (Romans 4:21)
13. Present your members as instruments of righteousness to God. (Romans 6:13)
14. Present yourselves as slaves of obedience. (Romans 6:16)
15. Present your members as slaves to righteousness. (Romans 6:19)
16. Believe in your heart and make confession of your faith with your mouth. (Romans 10:10)
17. Put on the armor of light. (Romans 13:12)
18. Behave properly. (Romans 13:13)
19. Put on the Lord Jesus Christ. (Romans 13:14)
20. Turn away from those who cause dissensions. (Romans 16:17)
21. Do not keep company with anyone named a brother, who is sexually immoral, or covetous, or an idolater, or a reviler, or a drunkard, or an extortioner—not even to eat with such a person. (1 Corinthians 5:11)
22. Walk by the Spirit. (Galatians 5:25)
23. Bear one another's burdens. (Galatians 6:2)
24. Lay aside the old self. (Ephesians 4:22)
25. Put on the new self. (Ephesians 4:24)
26. Do not participate in the unfruitful deeds of darkness. (Ephesians 5:11)
27. Put on the full armor of God. (Ephesians 6:11)
28. Do not in any way be terrified by your adversaries, which is to them a proof of perdition. (Philippians 1:28)
29. Let nothing be done through selfish ambition or conceit, but in lowliness of mind let each esteem others better than himself. (Philippians 2:3)
30. Work out your own salvation with fear and trembling. (Philippians 2:8)
31. Let each of you look out not only for his own interests, but also for the interests of others. (Philippians 2:4)
32. Do all things without complaining and disputing, 15 that you may become blameless and harmless. (Philippians 2:14)

33. Hold fast the word of life. (Philippians 2:16)
34. Rejoice in the Lord always. Again, I will say, rejoice! (Philippians 3:1, 4:4)
35. Beware of evil workers. (Philippians 3:2)
36. Stand fast in the Lord. (Philippians 4:1)
37. Let your gentleness be known to all men. (Philippians 4:5)
38. Be anxious for nothing, but in everything by prayer and supplication, with thanksgiving, let your requests be made known to God. (Philippians 4:6)
39. Whatever things are true, whatever things are noble, whatever things are just, whatever things are pure, whatever things are lovely, whatever things are of good report, if there is any virtue and if there is anything praiseworthy—meditate on these things. (Philippians 4:8)
40. As you therefore have received Christ Jesus the Lord, so walk in Him. (Colossians 2:6)
41. Beware lest anyone cheat you through philosophy and empty deceit, according to the tradition of men, according to the basic principles of the world, and not according to Christ. (Colossians 2:8)
42. Seek those things which are above, where Christ is, sitting at the right hand of God. Set your mind on things above, not on things on the earth. (Colossians 3:1-2)
43. Pursue righteousness. (1 Timothy 6:11, 2 Timothy 2:22)
44. Fight the good fight of faith. (1 Timothy 6:12)
45. Sharply rebuke idle talkers and deceivers, that they may be sound in the faith. (Titus 1:10-14)
46. In all things, show yourself to be a pattern of good works. (Titus 2:7)
47. Avoid foolish disputes, genealogies, contentions, and strivings about the law; for they are unprofitable and useless. (Titus 3:9)
48. Reject a divisive man after the first and second admonition, knowing that such a person is warped and sinning, being self-condemned. (Titus 3:10-11)
49. Hold fast the beginning of your confidence firm to the end. (Hebrews 3:14)
50. Hold fast our confession without wavering. (Hebrews 4:14, 10:23)
51. Consider and exhort one another. (Hebrews 10:25)
52. Be content with such things as you have. (Hebrews 13:5)
53. Let us continually offer the sacrifice of praise to God, that is, the fruit of our lips, giving thanks to His name. (Hebrews 13:15)
54. Do not forget to do good and to share. (Hebrews 13:16, 1 Peter 3:11)
55. Obey those who rule over you, and be submissive, for they watch out for your souls. (Hebrews 13:17)
56. Count it all joy when you fall into various trials, knowing that the testing of your faith produces patience. (James 1:2-3)

57. Let patience have its perfect work, that you may be perfect and complete, lacking nothing. (James 1:4)
58. Have faith in God with no doubting, no double-mindedness, which makes us unstable and prevents us from receiving anything from God. (James 1:6-8)
59. Be swift to hear and slow to speak. (James 1:19)
60. Be slow to wrath. (James 1:19)
61. Lay aside all filthiness and overflow of wickedness. (James 1:21)
62. Be doers of the word, and not hearers only, deceiving yourselves. (James 1:22)
63. Bridle your tongue. (James 1:26)
64. Visit orphans and widows in their trouble. (James 1:27)
65. Keep yourself unspotted from the world. (James 1:27)
66. Keep your tongue from evil and your lips from speaking deceit. (1 Peter 3:10)
67. Turn away from evil. (1 Peter 3:11)
68. Seek peace and pursue it. (1 Peter 3:11)
69. Keep His commandments. (1 John 2:3)
70. Walk in the same manner as He walked. (1 John 2:6)

In summary, our righteous deeds qualify us for true righteousness because they activate our faith in God by proving it is genuine faith, which qualifies us to receive God's grace and mercy to grant us right standing with Him as a gift that we could never qualify for by ourselves. (Titus 3:5-7) And if we miss the mark, we can go to Him with confidence, confessing our mistakes and humbly asking for His forgiveness, knowing He will faithfully cleanse us from all unrighteousness. (1 John 1:9)

ENDNOTES

4.01: Greek word: dikaioo in James 2:24, Strong's Bible Text, g1344.

4.02: Greek word: ergon in James 2:26, Strong's Bible Text, g2041.

4.03: Greek word: poieo in 1 John 3:7, Strong's Bible Text, g4160

5
Promises

My dreams gave me a new understanding of righteousness that ignited a hunger in me to learn more about it, so I searched the scriptures and found 222 promises for which righteousness is the only requirement, as listed in Exhibits 8-23. Of course, faith is also required because it takes faith to pursue righteousness, as explained in this chapter. Amazingly, these promises include everything we need in this life while also transforming us into something new, making us like the majestic horse I saw.

Some of these promises might sound too good to be true because they go beyond our personal experience, but since they're all recorded in the scriptures, they're more reliable than our own understanding or experiences. While most of them specifically identify the righteous, some are translated into English using different words, such as the upright, the just, and the blameless, although they come from the same Hebrew and Greek words usually translated as righteous, as shown in a word study in Exhibit 7. I organized them into 16 categories, as listed in Exhibits 8-23, and briefly summarized each category, as shown below.

19 Promises for Provision:

God promises He will not allow you to go hungry, but will give you everything you need, including food and clothing, and even going beyond your basic needs, He will not withhold any good thing from you. He will teach you to profit and cause you to increase in abundance, giving you more than enough to satisfy your appetite with things that are good and beneficial, blessing your barns and storehouses, filling your house with great wealth and riches, much treasure, so many possessions, you will lend to many people without any need to borrow, while also leaving an inheritance, not just for your children, but even your grandchildren. (Deuteronomy 28:4, 28:8, 28:11-12, Psalm 84:11, Proverbs 10:3, 13:22, 13:25, 15:6, 29:2, Psalm 112:3, Isaiah 48:17, Matthew 6:33, Mark 10:28-30) For scriptures and more details, see Exhibit 8.

5 Promises for Answered Prayers:

God promises to keep His eyes and ears on you, always staying attentive to your cries, so whenever you pray to Him fervently, your prayers will make a big difference, even qualifying you for a special privilege, granting you the right to ask for whatever you desire, whatever pleases you, and God will give it to you. (Psalm 34:15, 34:17, Proverbs 10:24, 15:29, 1 Peter 3:12, James 5:16, John 15: 7-10) For scriptures and more details, see Exhibit 9.

22 Promises for More of God:

God promises to love you and be your friend, giving you a harvest of His goodness, kindness, and faithfulness. He will give you reasons to praise Him and even to boast about what He has done for you. He will bring you great contentment and satisfaction by saturating you with His presence when you awaken, settling upon you and staying with you, so you will live in His presence. He will never leave you and you will never again leave the place of His presence. He will be pleased with you and allow you to enter His inner council. Not only will you have free access to stand before Him, but He will also put you in charge to watch over His work. You will be born of Him, so He will put His own name on you and the name of the new Jerusalem. (1 Kings 3:6, Psalm 11:7, 14:5, 17:15, 37:25-26, 64:10, 146:8, Proverbs 3:32, 21:3, 15:9, Ezekiel 44:15-16, Hosea 10:12, Micah 2:7, Zechariah 3:7, John 15:14, 1 John 2:29, Revelation 3:12, 19:7-8) For scriptures and more details, see Exhibit 10.

8 Promises for Your Words:

God promises to make your words a fountain of life, producing the fruit of wisdom and justice, and delivering you from harm while causing other people to dearly love you and kings to take delight in you because you continually speak words that are straight and right, bringing forth what is good, wholesome, precious, pure, pleasant, profitable, and acceptable. (Psalm 37:29, Proverbs 10:11, 10:20, 10:31-32, 12:6, 16:13) For scriptures and more details, see Exhibit 11.

23 Promises for Protection:

Although you will encounter much evil, God promises it will be rendered powerless to harm you because He will plunder every evil that comes against you and snatch you away from it. He will place a hedge of protection around your path, like a shield surrounding you, so no weapon formed against you can prosper. And He will keep watch over you, guarding you, so when a storm passes by, you will not perish because His name will be like a strong tower of refuge for you, setting you on high, out of harm's way, giving you a firm foundation of support to stand upon, so you will escape and be rescued and delivered from all misery and distress, as it is entirely stripped away from you and you enter a place of peace and rest. When charges are brought against you, God will not allow you to be condemned, but will make things right for you, so the charges will be dropped and you will be cleared and your accusers will be required to answer to Him. When your enemies seek to kill you, God will not leave you in their hands, but will make a way of escape for you so you can slip away into a safe place while they are defeated before your eyes. Though they come against you one way, God will cause them to flee from you seven ways. (Deuteronomy 11:22-23, 28:7, 2 Chronicles 6:22-23, Psalm 34:17, 34:19, 37:32-33, 37:40, Proverbs 2:7-8, 10:25, 11:6, 11:8, 12:3, 12:21, 13:6, 17:15, 17:26, 18:5, 18:10, 21:18, Isaiah 54:17, 57:1-2) For scriptures and more details, see Exhibit 12.

11 Promises for More Joy:

Because you have turned away from all unrighteousness, your singing and rejoicing will no longer be hindered. Instead of mourning, God is now anointing you with the oil of joy, giving you good reasons to be glad, causing you to shout for joy in your house, and each time you do, God will be glorified by it as His light will shine through your joy. He is sowing His joy into you like seed, with the power to produce a harvest of much more joy than you've had before and more than others around you. (Psalm 32:11, 33:1, 45:7, 58:10, 64:10, 97:11, 118:15, Proverbs 10:28, 13:9, 28:12, 29:6, Isaiah 61:3) For scriptures and more details, see Exhibit 13.

13 Promises for Your Children:

So great will be the blessings of God on your children, not only will they be blessed and happy, but they will be like a tree of life that grows up strong and mighty, bearing much fruit in the earth, causing their names to be remembered forever. When any harm comes their way, God will make a way for them to slip away from it. They will never have to beg for food because God's faithfulness will be extended to them and to their children. (Deuteronomy 28:4, 28:11, Psalm 37:25-26, 37:37, 103:17-18, 112:2, Proverbs 11:21, 11:30, 13:22, 20:7, Isaiah 48:18-19) For scriptures and more details, see Exhibit 14.

7 Promises for Wisdom:

God has hidden away a treasure of the most helpful and substantial wisdom for you to help you discern every good path, so you will know how to recognize and follow the right path where you will find wisdom walking along beside you, teaching you to rely on your inner man, so you carefully meditate on what is in your heart before you answer other people, and teaching you discernment between the clean and the unclean, the holy and the unholy, so God can use you to teach these things to His people, just as He did with the sons of Zadok. (Proverbs 2:7, 2:9-10, 8:20, 9:9, 15:28, 21:12, Ezekiel 44:23) For scriptures and more details, see Exhibit 15.

9 Promises for Health and Long Life:

God will not allow diseases to come upon your body, and even if you fall seven times, you will rise again each time. Your strength will be increased in times of trouble, adding length of days and long life to you, and even in your old age, you will continue bearing fruit, prospering and thriving with abundance so you can declare the righteousness of God. (Exodus 15:26, Psalm 37:39, 75:10, 92:14-15, Proverbs 3:1-2, 16:31, 21:21, 24:16, Ezekiel 18:9) For scriptures and more details, see Exhibit 16.

17 Promises for Your Position:

God will plant you in His house and cause you to flourish like a green olive tree so you will never be moved or stumble or stagger or slip or be shaken. He will raise you up and promote you to a position of holiness, restoring you to your rightful place, setting you apart from all others for His service, surrounding you with His favor, encircling you with His kindness, making you the head and not the tail, in a position of governing over His house, in charge of His courts, with authority to rule over those who are foolish. And in the age to come, He will make you a pillar in His house where you will rule the nations with authority and a rod of iron. (Deuteronomy 28:9, 28:13-14, Job 8:5-6, Psalm 5:12, 49:13-14,52:8, 55:22, 75:10, 92:12-13, 112:6, Proverbs 10:30, 12:3, Zechariah 3:7, Revelation 2:26-27, 3:12) For scriptures and more details, see Exhibit 17.

10 Promises for Your Path:

God knows your path and considers your journey, so He is well acquainted with it and determines the right direction for your life. He goes before you to prepare the path for your feet to walk, making it smooth, level, and straight, so you will be kept safe and protected, blessed coming in and blessed going out, because you walk in His ways, following the right path, the path of life, which grows brighter and brighter like the rising of the sun until the full day. (Deuteronomy 28:6, Psalm 1:6, 85:13, Proverbs 4:18, 10:29, 11:5, 12:28, Isaiah 26:7, Hosea 14:9) For scriptures and more details, see Exhibit 18.

20 Promises for Your Character:

You will find support to lean on, so your inner man will not grow dim or faint, but will remain firm and steady, filled with peace, bold as a lion, feeling safe and secure because of your trust and confidence in God, so you will have no fear of bad news or any evil report, but thinking right thoughts, with an attitude of gratitude, giving thanks to the name of God, and wearing the mantle of praise. You will be gracious, compassionate, and concerned for the rights of the poor, so you will give freely to the needy without holding anything back, desiring only things that are surely good and beneficial. You will find the behavior of unrighteous people to be abominable, hating their lies and deceptions, so you will want no part in their deeds and will enjoy seeing wrong things made right as God sets the needy securely on high, away from affliction. All these traits will give you a right foundation for ruling from a seat of honor. (Psalm 23:3-4, 37:26, 37:37, 107:41-42, 112:4, 112:7-9, 140:13, Proverbs 11:23, 12:5, 13:5, 16:12, 21:15, 21:25-26, 28:1, 29:7, 29:27, Isaiah 61:3) For scriptures and more details, see Exhibit 19.

13 Promises for Eternity:

Your name will be recorded in the book of life, so you will find a refuge where you will be protected and delivered from death and will go into eternal life where your righteousness will endure forever and you will be remembered forever. You will receive a sure reward that will never be taken away as you shine forth like the sun in the kingdom of your Father with His goodness and kindness upon you forever and ever. Until then, the voice of salvation will be in your house. (Psalm 37:29, 52:8, 69:28, 103:17-18, 112:3, 112:6, 112:9, 118:15, Proverbs 10:2, 10:16, 11:4, 11:19, 11:18, 14:32, Matthew 13:43, 25:46) For scriptures and more details, see Exhibit 20.

8 Promises for Your Land:

God will make a way for you to live in the land and remain in it. He will bless the fruit of your ground by opening for you His good storehouse, the heavens, to give rain to your land in its season, causing the early and late rain to fall upon your fields so they produce crops and fruit, giving you an increase, so you have more than enough in good things, a harvest of grain, wine, and oil. (Deuteronomy 11:13-14, 28:4, 28:8, 28:11-12, 85:12, 125:3, Proverbs 2:21) For scriptures and more details, see Exhibit 21.

12 Promises for Honor:

God will distinguish between you and the wicked who do not serve Him by allowing people to see His rewards upon you as you increase in authority and abundance, so they will know you are called by His name and will acknowledge He has done it, which will cause them to fear you. No man will be able to stand before you because God will lay the dread of you and the fear of you on all the land on which you set your feet. Even wicked people will bow their faces at your gates to give honor to that which is undeniably good and agreeable and pleasant. Your name will be so highly honored, other people will be blessed whenever they remember you. (Deuteronomy 11:25, 28:10, 58:11, 112:9, Proverbs 10:7, 12:12, 14:19, 14:34, 21:21, 23:24-25, 29:2, Malachi 3:18) For scriptures and more details, see Exhibit 22.

25 Promises for Blessings:

God will reward your righteousness by blessing you, praising you, congratulating you, saluting you, adding His peace to you, and causing you to blossom like a budding leaf, grow like a cedar in Lebanon, flourish and shoot straight up like a palm tree in His courts. He will command the blessing upon all that you put your hand to do, so the fruit of your own actions will cause things to go well for you. Even in dark times, His light will break forth to help you see what others cannot see. You will look with satisfaction upon your enemies, laughing at those who would not make God their refuge and even washing your feet in their blood. (Deuteronomy 28:3, 28:5, 28:8, 28:12, 1 Samuel 26:23, Psalm 5:12, 33:1, 52:6-7, 58:10, 92:12-13, 97:11, 106:3, 112:2, 112:4, 112:8, Proverbs 3:1-2, 10:6, 11:28, 11:30, 29:16, Isaiah 1:27, 3:10, Revelation 2:28) For scriptures and more details, see Exhibit 23.

Two-Party Contracts:

Having identified God's promises to the righteous, we have a firm foundation for our faith, giving us legal ground to stand on, so we can now lay claim to what rightfully belongs to us because His promises work like legal contracts, but they're not like any legal contracts we've seen before, which require us to hire an attorney to protect us from all the hidden meanings, loopholes and escape clauses written in legal mumbo jumbo. God's legal contracts don't have any of that because He's not trying to hide anything from us or looking for a way to take advantage of us because He loves us and wants the best for us. So, His terms are clear and His words mean exactly what they appear to mean.

In addition, His terms never change because they're built upon the sure foundation of His righteousness, which is already as right as right can get, so they're unmovable and unshakeable, like mighty mountains, with no way to improve upon them. (Psalm 36:6,

89:14, 97:2, Proverbs 16:12 and 20:28) Dealing with Him is like no one we've ever dealt with before because He is the only one who is right in all His ways. (Psalm 89:8, Isaiah 5:16) And His promises have no expiration dates because His righteousness endures forever. (Psalm 111:3, 119:142)

These are exclusively two-party contracts between God and us, and the chances of God not upholding His end of the deal are zero because He's already laid down His life, sealing the deal in His own blood, which the Lord Jesus Christ shed for us. And as to His credentials, He is the Lord God Almighty, creator of heaven and earth. His resume is quite impressive, so there's nothing to be concerned about there.

Since these are two-party contracts between God and the righteous, that makes us the only other party with authority to validate or invalidate them. Satan was completely left out of the deal, so he has no legal right to say anything about it. Even if he tries, we can just tell him to shut up and get out.

Having set aside all these concerns, we can focus our attention on His only requirement, righteousness. Once we've found the path and started faithfully following it, pursuing it, hungering and thirsting for it as our top priority, we can know with confidence we have met His requirement because Jesus said those who hunger and thirst for righteousness will be satisfied, as explained at the end of chapter four. (Matthew 5:6, 6:33, Philippians 3:12-14, 1 Timothy 6:11, 2 Timothy 2:22) Just as sure as we know we've qualified to receive His gift of eternal salvation, we also know we've qualified to receive all His promises to the righteous because the requirements are the same.

However, qualifying for it and seeing it are two different things altogether. For example, we've qualified to receive eternal life and by faith we know we have it, but we have not yet seen all the amazing heavenly rewards God has for us, such as our new glorified body and the mansions He has prepared for us. (John 14:2-3, 1 Corinthians 15:53-55) Since God has promised these things to us, they belong to us, and all His promises to the righteous work this same way.

We are like legal heirs to a great inheritance, already knowing what belongs to us even before we see the full manifestation in our possession. The delay between knowing and seeing does not diminish our legal rights, but it puts our faith to the test and requires us to stand firm in claiming what belongs to us because while we're still waiting to see it, a thief can come along, making bogus claims that those things don't belong to us, but belong to him instead. If we allow his claims to go uncontested, failing to enforce our legal rights, we can be robbed of our inheritance, but we can contest any such claims just by speaking up, standing firm based on the terms of our contracts.

Remnant: Promises

We are warned to beware of our unseen adversary, Satan, because he roams about pretending to be a roaring lion, seeking to devour us and steal what God has promised to us. (Ephesians 6:12, 1 Peter 5:8) But being left out of these contracts presents a big problem for Satan because he has no legal authority whatsoever, so despite all his threats, he can only take what we allow him to take. We are the only ones with authority to back out of the deal, which we would never do if we're in our right mind, so his only hope is to get us so confused and deceived, we abandon all hope of ever seeing God do what He promised, so we violate the terms of our contract, reneging on our obligations, disqualifying ourselves from receiving our inheritance.

Since His promises give us legal rights to receive everything God wants us to have, they deserve our closest attention by keeping them before our eyes and hiding them in our heart. (Proverbs 4:20-22) I listed 222 of them to make it easier to do that. The more we know them, the harder it is for the thief to steal them from us because we can quickly recognize his lies and turn back his attacks. So, we guard our inheritance by holding onto the promises as tightly as we possibly can, like wrapping a garment tightly around our waist and loins, making it difficult for anyone to take it from us. (Ephesians 6:13-14)

His promises also give us legal rights to launch offensive attacks to take back whatever Satan has stolen, like swinging a sharp sword, which is able to inflict great harm upon Satan and his kingdom. (Psalm 105:8, 119:89, 119:160, Isaiah 40:8-12, Matthew 5:18, Luke 16:17, Ephesians 6:17, Hebrews 4:12, 1 Peter 1:25) We swing our sword by boldly declaring God's promises over our life, which sends Satan running every time.

Now is the time for God's righteous remnant to arise by skillfully swinging our swords more than ever before so we take our inheritance by force and put Satan in full retreat, no longer being like those Hebrew spies who just casually looked over their land, unable to see how they could take it, so they returned right back to where they were before, bound by their unbelief and robbed of their promises. (Numbers 13:31-33) It's time to settle some things once and for all, shaking off our wavering and wondering in unbelief, moving beyond our doubts, rejecting all double minded thoughts and words, which in the past made us unstable, thinking His promises were always for somebody else, but never for us, always for some other time in the sweet bye and bye, but never for now. (James 5:6-7) Those days are over! It's our turn now!

God has already given us everything we need, so we can now arise and move forward on the path, fully convinced God will do everything He promised. Even though we don't yet see it, we watch for it, waiting patiently, expecting it to be delivered in full at any moment, knowing God has already set it in motion, already sent it our way and placed it directly in our path where it will soon intersect with our future. (Romans 4:21, 10:17, Philippians 2:16, 4:1, 1 Timothy 6:12, Hebrews 3:1, 4:14, 10:23, James 1:3, 1 Peter 5:9)

Satan Defeated:

Years ago, my family was moving to a new town, so my wife and I were out driving around looking at houses. The only problem was we had no money. And when I say no money, I mean no money at all. I had left my career job to step out into what I believed God was leading me to do, but that's another story. We drove through a nice neighborhood called Windsong, looking at all the beautiful homes and saying to each other, "Gee, wouldn't that be nice?"

It looked impossible, so we exited that area and drove about a mile down the road when the Spirit of God spoke to me saying, "Go to the Windsong sales office."

We immediately made a U-turn and went back to the sales office, which we discovered was a beautiful model house and it was for sale. Then we learned the developer was ready to make a great deal for anyone interested in buying it, but the details weren't identified. We didn't know what to do with that, but later that day, I met with another man regarding the new business I had started. I told him we had looked at the Windsong model house and explained we had no money. As it turned out, his background was in financial services, so he started telling me exactly what to offer the developer. So, we went back and said exactly what he told us to say and to our amazement, the developer agreed to the deal! What looked so impossible to us, suddenly became possible.

Now, I don't recommend this to anyone and wouldn't have done it myself if God had not spoken to me directly and told me where to go and what to say, but in no time at all, we moved into this beautiful home. And every month, God provided us with enough money to make our payments. We made all our payments on time, but after living there for two years, the developer changed his mind and wanted out of the deal. At first, he started making demands. Then one day, we received a certified letter telling us we had ten days to pay off the whole amount or vacate the house.

Just making the monthly payments had been a big stretch for us, so paying off the whole house looked impossible. That night, my wife and I went into warfare mode. We prayed together in agreement, declaring Satan was not going to steal our house. We militantly stood our ground, declaring God's promises to us.

While I was decreeing that, I saw a vision of Satan standing right in front of me. I saw myself swinging a huge sword right in front of his mid-section. To avoid getting sliced, he jumped back and threw his hands in the air to avoid getting sliced by the blade. Then he turned and ran as fast as he could go. Then the Lord spoke to me saying, "Satan's biggest fear is a Christian soldier who has no regard for his own life."

Satan wanted us to get so afraid of his threats, we would abandon our faith and come into agreement with his lies, but we refused to be afraid because we knew God gave us that house and we weren't about to let Satan steal it from us. I refused to do anything to rescue myself because I knew God was the only one who could do it. So, I just waited on Him to tell me what to do. After a couple of days, He told me who to call and explain what happened. So, I did and they agreed to buy our house and rent it to us until we were ready to leave. Then they would sell it and get their funds back. That's exactly the way it happened. We continued living in the house for another couple of years and they not only recovered their investment, but made a profit.

Satan was unable to steal from us because we refused to believe his lies. When we fought back, swinging our sword as hard as we knew how, all fear left us and instead of us being afraid, he was very afraid and he took off running for his life, so we turned the tables on him. Through that conflict, I discovered the huge flaw in Satan's plan, all his weapons are offensive. He has no defense at all! When his offensive weapons fail to make us afraid, he's done. His only option is turn and run away like the coward that he is. (James 4:7) When we take our stand, we win and he loses, like this scripture, "And they overcame him by the blood of the Lamb and by the word of their testimony, and they did not love their lives to the death." (Revelation 12:11 NKJV)

War Horses:

One by one, we are removing every hindrance that previously held us back from receiving God's promises. The previous chapter showed how we qualify for righteousness by living and active faith, demonstrated by turning away from all unrighteous deeds, which keeps us on the path where we are protected by His hedges so we can move forward. (Proverbs 2:7-8)

Next, we showed how God's promises to the righteous are like two-party contracts in which Satan has no part, so he has no authority to rob us or hold us back. Our knowledge of God's promises and understanding of how they work renders Satan powerless by exposing his lies claiming to have some hidden power over us.

Now we can consider another foe that often comes against us, our circumstances. This foe is defeated the same way Satan is defeated because our contracts make no mention of our circumstances, so they're just as irrelevant and powerless as Satan is, having no authority whatsoever. Since righteousness is the only requirement, even the worst circumstances cannot hinder the fulfillment of His promises because it was never based on them. This understanding sets us free to do whatever God tells us to do, whatever He puts in our heart to do, regardless of our circumstances.

So, we have now rendered powerless three major hindrances from receiving God's promises, including unrighteous deeds, Satan's lies, and our circumstances. So, we're now free to run like war horses, keeping our eyes focused straight ahead, not distracted by anything and refusing to turn back, but continuing to charge forward, running faster and stronger than ever before, even when bullets and bombs are exploding all around us, we ignore even the most overwhelming danger, so we overcome even death itself.

The Urban Dictionary's definition of a war horse is not a literal horse, but a person "who persists at an activity despite hardship and age, when they should have given up long ago." (5.01) It's the perfect description of the righteous remnant because we've had to keep charging forward when everything around us was screaming at us, telling us to turn back. The war horse analogy is also a great confirmation of the visions God gave to Zechariah and Joel in which they saw God's people taking on the appearance of majestic horses in battle. (Joel 2:4, Zechariah 10:3)

Leading Indicators:

Economists track leading economic indicators like new housing starts and stock market movements because whenever these indicators start trending up or down, it means the rest of the economy will soon follow. In the same way, God has given us leading promise indicators manifesting in our inner man, indicating our great transformation is already underway, so we know His greater promises, including His most outlandish ones, are also on the way. These leading indicators are another powerful weapon to add to our arsenal, so we should be paying attention to them, examining them and relying on them because they are far more reliable than any economic indicators.

Although we cannot yet see the full manifestation of everything He has started doing in us, we already have these leading indicators as evidence proving we have qualified to receive all the eternal beauty of heaven because either we qualify or we don't. There is no middle ground here. He's either already living in us, working in us, or He's not. If we died today, we're either going to heaven or we're not. It's like being pregnant. There's no such thing as being partially pregnant. No, it' all the way or not at all. We're either righteous or we're not.

Remnant: Promises

It doesn't mean we're already all we will be because we're still following the path with a long way to go, still in the process of becoming something more beautiful than what we see today, but simply by being on the path, having met His requirements, walking in the light available to us now, He has already reckoned our faith to us as righteousness as a gift of His grace, making us the righteousness of Christ, qualifying us for His whole boatload of promises to the righteous because the requirement is the same for all of them. (Psalm 90:17, 1 Peter 3:4)

Since God has already given us the full deposit of the presence of His Holy Spirit abiding in our inner man, we should already have some tangible evidence proving His power has started working in us, which we might not have been able to see at the start of our journey. (Acts 15:8, Hebrews 11:1, 1 John 3:24) With so many promises, the evidence can show up in many ways, including the fruit of His Spirit, which is love, joy, peace, patience, kindness, goodness, faithfulness, gentleness, and self-control. (Galatians 5:22-23) Like natural fruit, spiritual fruit requires some time to grow, but eventually it appears as tangible evidence. For example, since joy is a fruit of the Spirit, it should be increasing in us, so we might notice we're laughing out loud more than we ever did before. Love is another fruit of the Spirit, so we might notice we have more compassion for other people than we did before, even motivating us to reach out to help them more than we would have before, so we begin to do what Jesus described, "By this all will know that you are My disciples, if you have love for one another." (John 13:35 NKJV)

There are many more examples of leading indicators we can examine to confirm we're on the right track. They're speaking loud and clear, telling us we have nothing to fear because we've already qualified for all God's promises, worth far more than anything this world can offer. And as long as we stay on the path and stand firm on His promises, no thief can ever steal them from us because God has secured them in a safe place, a secret place where no thief can go, far better than any safety deposit box. Even though our outward circumstances might not yet be what we want them to be, the evidence of His power working in our inner man confirms with certainty we have met His requirements, which is very good news.

In my dream, I saw the evidence of His promises manifesting in His people. Our lives were abundant in every area with more joy, more peace, and more love for one another. I saw evidence of increased wisdom and understanding, which enabled me to help guide and train the young people. The power of God's Kingdom was continually increasing in us to the point of overflowing into the lives of everyone around us.

Recognizing these leading indicators can help us grow faster because the more evidence we see, the more our faith grows, which helps us stay on the path where even more evidence is produced, causing our faith to grow even more, so our growth rate accelerates like the Star Trek Enterprise entering warp speed. It's time for warp speed!

Receiving the Promises:

As we begin to see what we could not see before, we gain a new perspective of our future based on God's promises, which is more evidence we've qualified to receive our inheritance. And our perspective grows clearer and clearer as God gives us more personalized glimpses of His plans, enabling us to see our future is greater than we ever imagined possible, and the clearer we see it, the more real it becomes to us, even when it contradicts our current circumstances. We begin to see and believe this unseen reality more than the one we see with our physical eyes and we begin to forget the old person we once were as we become fully persuaded of our new identity, which is no longer restrained by our former limitations, but filled with expectation for new things ahead.

Even as our confidence grows, knowing we have what God says we have, we should not think it strange that the full manifestation does not come forth immediately because God designed His Kingdom to follow seasons of seedtime and harvest, just like the natural realm. (Genesis 8:22, Matthew 13:31-32) His promises are planted in our heart like seeds sown into the ground. After planting, they are invisible, so no one even knows they're there, except the one who planted them, which explains why others do not yet see what we see, but we know because we planted them ourselves when we took possession of them by faith.

Although we know our harvest season is coming, we should also know it must be preceded by a season of waiting, in which the seeds require nurturing, like a farmer nurtures natural seeds by giving them plenty of sunshine, water and removing any weeds, so they can grow to full maturity. We nurture our seeds by continuing the fight of faith, holding fast our confidence, not doubting what God promised. (Philippians 2:16, 4:1, 1 Timothy 6:12, Hebrews 3:14, 4:14, 10:23) We receive our inheritance the same way Abraham received his, by being fully convinced that God will perform what He promised, even before we see it. (Mark 11:23-24, Romans 4:20-21) We remove the weeds by refusing double-minded thoughts and any doubts that God will do what He said. Those kinds of thoughts must be uprooted because they make us unstable and unable to receive anything from God. (James 1:6-8)

Years ago, I saw a vision of a farmer planting seeds in the ground. Then he stood there, staring at the ground, waiting to see his seeds sprouting forth, but nothing happened. Then he looked up to heaven, lifted his hands, and began to worship God with a grateful heart. While he was doing that, the most luscious green plants grew up all around him until eventually he was surrounded by a great harvest. I believe this vision revealed an important key to receiving our harvest, especially during our season of waiting. When this man was staring at the ground, even though he had planted his seeds, by his own actions he showed he was still holding onto them, not totally letting go, but when he looked up to heaven, taking his eyes completely off his seeds, just worshipping God, he truly released them into God's hands, which allowed God to multiply them.

God's promises are like seeds. By releasing them into His hands, we are putting our faith into action, thereby fulfilling our part of the contract, which qualifies us for the full release of His resurrection power. (Romans 1:17, Ephesians 2:8-9, Hebrews 11:4, James 2:24, 2:26, 1 John 3:7-10) So, our seeds must not only be planted, but also allowed to die, trusting God to do what only He can do, bringing the harvest from the invisible realm into the visible. (John 12:24) It's ironic how our victory comes through our surrender and a mystery how God brings forth the harvest from the seeds, but it shows He alone deserves all the credit.

ENDNOTES

5.01: Urban Dictionary, war horse definition,
https://www.urbandictionary.com/define.php?term=warhorse

6
Trouble

As much as we would like to see our full inheritance in our hands today, not one moment is wasted during our season of waiting because we are developing patience, which we need to persevere in faith when everything around us indicates we should quit and give up.

And even though the same promises are available to everyone, He personalizes them for us and quickens them in our heart, making them come alive to us, so we begin to see His plans for our life that others around us have not seen, just as they begin to see His plans for their life that we haven't seen. God gives each of us our own unique personalized seeds of faith planted in our heart and the full deposit of faith needed for those seeds to reach maturity, but then comes a season of watching and waiting for His promises to manifest in the visible realm, which can be frustrating because God is accomplishing things we cannot yet see, which puts us in a continual process of trusting Him when we don't understand, believing by faith He has a good purpose in all of it, so we can go ahead and enjoy the ride.

> 2 My brethren, count it all joy when you fall into various trials,
> 3 knowing that the testing of your faith produces patience.
> 4 But let patience have its perfect work, that you may be perfect and complete, lacking nothing. (James 1:2-4 NKJV)

Through this process of daily practice, day after day, overcoming doubts and fears, we are transformed into something new, making us over-comers in this life. We are being trained like soldiers for battle as God is preparing us to prevail against every circumstance, including the coming days of trouble. (Daniel 12:1, Matthew 24:6-22, Revelation 6:1-11) The righteous will not be caught off guard by what's coming because God is preparing us in advance, causing our faith to grow stronger and stronger, enabling us to believe what we could not believe before and see what we could not see before, so we can hold firm, even when we walk through the valley of the shadow of death. We will fear no evil because we know God is with us. (Psalm 23:4, Proverbs 22:3, Matthew 28:20, Luke 21:26)

This training can sometimes be extreme because His forerunners are like His special forces when it comes to trouble. So, He sends us on assignment ahead of our brothers into all kinds of severe trouble, sometimes causing others to be concerned for our welfare, but God has a good purpose for all of it, so by the time the rest of the world enters the great trouble ahead, His forerunners will be strong in faith, fully convinced God will see us through, so we can help those who are still learning to trust Him, making us like flames of light illuminating a dark place.

Elijah was trained by God through much trouble to master these same lessons of faith. So, he continually found himself facing dire circumstances, not because he did anything wrong, but because he obeyed God by going where He told him to go and doing what He told him to do. For example, God commanded him to go where there was no visible source of food, as mentioned previously, so Elijah had to grow in faith to know God was with him and always providing for him. (1 Kings 17:3-6, 17:8-15)

Even after his great victory on Mount Carmel where he confronted and killed the false prophets of Baal and turned the Israelites back to God, trouble came and found him with a death threat from the king's wife, Jezebel, saying, "So let the gods do to me, and more also, if I do not make your life as the life of one of them by tomorrow about this time." (1 Kings 19:2) Even though Elijah reacted fearfully, running for his life to Beersheba and from there he continued another day's journey into the wilderness where he cried out for God to take his life, God did not abandon him, but sent His angel to prepare two meals of food and water for him. Then the angel touched him and strengthened him for his journey to Mount Horeb, even though God did not tell him to go there. So, when Elijah reached Mount Horeb, God said to him, "What are you doing here, Elijah?" (1 Kings 19:2-9)

Even when Elijah reached the limits of what he could endure, insisting he alone was left among the prophets, God still sent His chariot of fire to carry him into heaven and He gave him two new forerunner assignments, which were not only for the benefit of future generations, but also to allow Elijah to finish his own unfinished ministry. (2 Kings 2:11, Matthew 11:14-15, Luke 1:16-17, John 1:19-25)

Elijah's troubles were part of God's training program, preparing him for his future assignments, just as He is now doing with our generation of forerunners. Like Elijah, the training is so rigorous, it can sometimes cause us to feel like he felt, preferring to die rather than continue facing the trouble pressing in on us from all sides, but God uses it for our benefit, causing the hidden motives of our heart to rise to the surface, allowing us to see the current condition of our faith and character, which He's seen all along, so we can realize we're not nearly as high or mighty as we thought. Then we see what Elijah saw, God's kindness when we least deserve it, even when we've behaved badly, even when we've been offended at God and disappointed with ourselves, so we gain a whole new appreciation for Him and a whole new level of commitment to follow Him.

As much as God wants us to have our inheritance, He does not want it to cost us the ultimate prize. So, He gives us the season of waiting to help us discover we could never have crossed the finish line without His grace and mercy, so all the credit belongs to Him. What would it profit us if after enduring all these tests, we fail to finish our race? What would it profit us if after receiving our inheritance and enjoying His blessings, we become so full of ourselves that we forget Him and turn away from following Him and lose our eternal soul? (Deuteronomy 8:11-17, Mark 8:36)

The Me-Gospel:

Although the Bible is filled with warnings of trouble from Genesis to Revelation, many have thrown them out to make up their own new version of the Bible, claiming God would never lead us into any kind of trouble because He is good, so anyone encountering these things has strayed off the path and fallen away from the faith. I call it the Me-Gospel because it's all about me, claiming if it doesn't bless me, if it doesn't prosper me, if it doesn't get me what I want, then it could not possibly be from God.

Like so many of Satan's lies, the Me-Gospel gives us part of the truth to lure us in, but ultimately the true meaning gets twisted. Yes, God is good and He has promised to prosper us, but He also clearly identified His requirements when He said, "If anyone desires to come after Me, let him deny himself, and take up his cross, and follow Me. For whoever desires to save his life will lose it, but whoever loses his life for My sake will find it." (3 John 1:2, Matthew 16:24-25 NKJV) His instructions reveal the same path that leads to the fulfillment of all His great promises sometimes passes through places we don't want to go, places where we must deny ourselves and even lay down our lives if necessary, the same way many other great heroes of the faith have endured great trials, denying themselves, and the same way He denied Himself by taking up His cross and laying down His life for us, so anyone claiming we can bypass trouble and go straight to our rewards is preaching another gospel, another Jesus, different from the one He preached, just as many others have done throughout history. (2 Corinthians 11:4)

The Me-Gospel has spread like wildfire throughout America's churches. I was amazed recently when I heard a well-known Christian leader saying, "Anyone warning us about trouble is from the devil because those kinds of statements traumatize us, and the devil is the one who traumatizes us." What an incredibly unscriptural statement!

If he's right, then the devil must have written most of the books of the Bible, because nearly all of them contain warnings of trouble. It's a sad day when our leaders are making such foolish statements. Yet, the continued existence of these kinds of ministries, even very large ministries, indicates many people are falling for the deception and supporting them financially.

Contrary to the Me-Gospel, the path of righteousness does not exempt us from trouble. The same God who leads us in the paths of righteousness also warns us in the very next verse we will walk through the valley of the shadow of death. (Psalm 23:3-4) So, passing through the valley does not necessarily mean we took a wrong turn or strayed off the path, but God has a good purpose for allowing us to pass through that most dreadful place because it is where we discover we have nothing to fear, so we not only pass through, but we find a new source of comfort there, His strength in us, and we enjoy a feast there, which He Himself has prepared for us to enjoy in the presence of our enemies. (Psalm 23:5)

Jesus promised His disciples will encounter trouble in this world, but He also promised He would always be with us, never leaving us nor forsaking us, so even in times of trouble, we can still hold onto our faith and peace. (Matthew 28:30, John 17:33, Hebrews 13:5) He further illustrated His point in a parable, warning about a great storm coming upon two houses with rain, floods, and wind. One house was built by a righteous man who did what God commanded him to do and the other by an unrighteous man who did not obey God. The water and wind beat upon BOTH houses, but the righteous man's house did not fall while the unrighteous man's house fell. (Proverbs 10:25, Matthew 7:24-27) By giving those warnings, Jesus confirmed many other scriptural warnings that the righteous will endure much trouble, but God has promised to deliver us from it. (Psalm 34:17, 34:19, 37:40, Proverbs 11:18, 12:3, 13:6, 18:10) If no trouble came upon us, God would have no reason to deliver us from it.

Yet, despite all the scriptural warnings, the Me-Gospel publicly attacks anyone sharing prophetic warnings received from God in dreams and visions. Faithful messengers who step out in faith to share what God revealed are routinely slandered by those who claim to be their own brothers and sisters, calling them gloom and doom prophets, even accusing them of giving the prophetic ministry a bad name, all because of sharing warnings of trouble, which fail to tickle the ears. If these accusations are true, then Isaiah, Jeremiah, Daniel, Ezekiel, Paul, Peter, John, and just about every prophet in the Bible is also a gloom and doom prophet, giving the prophetic ministry a bad name, including Jesus because He also repeatedly warned of great trouble coming upon the world.

America is polluted with countless seeker-friendly churches, ministries, websites, books, and magazines proclaiming this false message, but it's also promoted in more subtle ways, indoctrinating us in ways we don't even realize. For example, somewhere along the way, we stopped calling ourselves the righteous and replaced it with a far more seeker-friendly term, believers, which conveniently avoids God's only requirement for the fulfillment of all His promises. (Exhibits 8-23, 1 John 3:7-10) The scriptures are just the opposite, almost always calling us the righteous (238 times), the just (85 times), or the upright (42 times), for a combined total 365 times, enough to cover every day of the year, while only referring to us 11 times as believer(s). (6.01) The scriptures consistently place the emphasis on putting our faith into action, but our culture consistently places the emphasis on just believing without any action required. It's so rare today to hear anyone calling us the righteous, it would sound strange to us. We would do a double-take, like what did they just say? The righteous? What?

The Me-Gospel appeals to our natural inclination to self-centeredness by promoting even more self-centeredness, but we don't need help with that because we're already quite good at it. However, we need a lot of help understanding why we should be willing to deny ourselves and hold fast during times of trouble, but we rarely get help with that because the unpopular message of the cross has been drowned out by the wildly popular Me-Gospel, often leaving us to learn these lessons the hard way, on our own.

Champions of the Faith:

If the Me-Gospel is true, then the great champions of the faith who have gone before us were some of the most confused people who ever lived, but I'm siding with them on this one because when trouble came their way, they found strength to endure and pass their tests, so they became a blessing to many people. For example, God gave Abram, whose name was later changed to Abraham, a great promise to show him a new land and make him a great nation and a blessing, but the promise came with instructions to leave behind everything he had known, including his country, his family, and his father's house. (Genesis 12:1-3) So, Abraham obeyed God, not even knowing where he was going since it was a land he had never seen before, but by faith he believed God would lead him there and He did. However, after arriving, he encountered a famine so severe, he had to flee for his life into Egypt. (Genesis 12:10)

Abraham demonstrated his faith by his obedience, but encountering the famine must have caused him to wonder why God would lead him there. It's a good thing he didn't tune into any Me-Gospel messages because they would have convinced him he had followed the wrong path. By all appearances, it certainly looked that way, like he either misunderstood what God said or God sent him there to kill him, but it was not what it looked like. It was only a test of his faith, but it was a difficult test that required ignoring his circumstances to believe what he could not see.

After fleeing to Egypt, his problems grew worse because Pharaoh took Abraham's wife, Sarai, intending to make her his wife! So, as if the famine wasn't enough, he was tested even further. All these troubles came upon him not because he did anything wrong, but because he obeyed God. So, by following the path of obedience, Abraham was led directly into the path of trouble, which is not where anyone wants to go, but God required him to endure it to attain what He promised.

Even though it looked like God had abandoned Abraham, He was with him during all his trouble, demonstrated by sending plagues on Pharaoh and his house because of Sarai, so Pharaoh released her back to Abraham and sent them away. (Genesis 12:17) So, Abraham persevered and passed the tests, holding onto his faith in God's promise to make him a great nation and a blessing to many people.

A similar thing happened to Joseph, the son of Jacob. When he was just seventeen years old, God gave him a dream in which he saw sheaves of wheat bowing down before him, representing each of his eleven brothers bowing before him. They were so infuriated, some of them sought to kill him, but his brother Reuben convinced them to throw him into an empty pit instead. Then they sold him into slavery to a company of Midianite traders for twenty shekels of silver, so he was carried by them to Egypt where he was sold to Potiphar, an officer of Pharaoh. So, Joseph endured all these things, not because he did anything wrong, but because God gave him a dream and he believed it enough to share it with his brothers. (Genesis 37)

Like Abraham, Joseph must have wondered how God's promise would ever be fulfilled since he was separated from his brothers with no visible evidence that he would ever see them again. And like Abraham, Joseph's troubles grew even worse when he was falsely accused and thrown into prison. (Genesis 39:20) Yet, he remained faithful to God as shown by his reaction to Potiphar's wife trying to seduce him. He ran away from her saying, "How then can I do this great wickedness, and sin against God?" (Genesis 39:9 NKJV)

Even though it looked like God had abandoned Joseph as he went from the pit into slavery and from slavery into prison, God was with him during all his trouble, as demonstrated by his ability to interpret the dreams of other prisoners, which two years later, gave him the opportunity to stand before Pharaoh to interpret his dreams. (Genesis 39-40)

A similar thing happened to the Prophet Ezekiel. After receiving a powerful prophetic word for his nation, he went from the mountain top into the valley of dry bones, but not because he took a wrong turn or strayed away from God. He was led into this dreadful place by the Spirit of the Lord, as he explained:

> 1 "The hand of the Lord came upon me and brought me out in the Spirit of the Lord, and set me down in the midst of the valley; and it was full of bones.
> 2 Then He caused me to pass by them all around, and behold, there were very many in the open valley; and indeed, they were very dry. (Ezekiel 37:1-2 NKJV)

By faith, Ezekiel followed the path of obedience, but like Abraham and Joseph, it led him to a place no one wants to go, the valley of dry bones, the low place, the place of the dead, the grave yard. Yet, God was with him in that place and showed him how to turn it all around, by speaking life into those dry bones. (Ezekiel 37:3-14)

The Prophet Isaiah had a similar experience. After receiving a powerful prophetic word for his nation, he was instructed by God to walk around naked and barefoot for three years as a prophetic warning to the people of Egypt and Ethiopia of what the King of Assyria would do to them because they were not trusting the Lord. (Isaiah 20:2-5) Isaiah had not done anything wrong and was not being punished. He was faithfully doing what God instructed Him to do, yet God gave Him a most unpleasant assignment that required denying himself, but we almost never hear any mention of his experience because it contradicts the Me-Gospel.

The Apostle Paul also encountered severe trials and trouble as he faithfully followed the path of righteousness, including hunger, thirst, being poorly clothed, roughly treated, homeless, reviled, slandered, persecuted, and treated like the scum of the world. (1 Corinthians 4:9-13) Yet, he willingly endured all these things and God repeatedly delivered him through it all.

If all these great champions of the faith encountered such trials, why should we be surprised when we do too?

Finding the Keys:

In my own journey, I found myself in a place the Me-Gospel rejects outright, facing trouble with no visible way of escape. Yet, God was with me, helping me through it by showing me a most valuable key that unlocked a breakthrough in my understanding.

When I started my journey, my faith was soaring after hearing many great things God was going to do, which He confirmed through many prophetic words. I was so excited, I even cried tears of joy, but as I waited, the months turned into years and the years turned into decades. My hair turned gray. My kids grew up and moved away, and I was still waiting.

My disappointments came to the surface one day after hearing a message which I strongly identified with because it was for those who were feeling like God had forgotten them, but instead of promising an end to the season of testing, it revealed the reason why it was taking so long was because we have repeatedly lost the keys God has given us to unlock the doors to a better place. I didn't like hearing that because I felt like I had already given everything and now it seemed like the price was getting higher. Also, this message did not identify what these keys were, just that we kept losing them and needed to find them.

My initial thought was, "After all these years, haven't I done enough already? After all I've been through, you're telling me there is still more I must do just to get out of this mess? What keys? Where are the keys? Where are the doors?"

It sounded like a scavenger hunt was required to find these things, but I just didn't know if I had it in me to do all that. If you had asked me back in 1995 when I left the working world to venture into the great unknown, I would have been up for it back then, but I had reached the point where talk seemed cheap. In my not so humble opinion, it was time to put up or shut up and I felt justified about that because I only wanted to see the fulfillment of what God promised and because I had already waited far longer than I ever thought possible and far longer than would have been possible if God had not bailed me out repeatedly.

For a long time, I had passed many faith tests, overcoming all sorts of setbacks, relying heavily on my ace card, my daily encounters with God, entering His presence, taking refuge in His secret place. (Psalm 27:5) I was quite proud of how great I was doing spiritually (which should have been a red flag all by itself), but then the tests got much trickier and I was getting stumped repeatedly, unable to understand what God was doing. It made no sense to me. It looked like He was trying to kill me. It looked a lot like that.

I discovered something I never knew existed, faith fatigue. Things that for years had been so easy for me to believe, suddenly seemed way too big for me to handle. It was humbling to see during the most severe trials of my life, my faith was nearly out of gas and running on fumes.

Remnant: Trouble

All the evidence kept pointing to the same conclusions, either God had forgotten me or He changed His mind about His promises to me. I wondered, "Why would God allow these things to happen to me? Why has He not done what He promised? Why are things doing the exact opposite of what He said would happen?"

I started thinking deadly thoughts, the kind of thoughts that have caused many to perish, accusing God of lying, but if that wasn't bad enough already, it got worse, escalating into a full-blown offense. (Jude 1:11) Even though I repented each time, it wasn't long before I was back to the same place again and again because I couldn't see any other possibilities. Being stuck there made it even worse because I was cutting myself off from my only hope, which surprised me because I thought I knew better, but I was stuck in a dangerous place wondering, "God, how did I get here?"

Then one Sunday morning when I was running on E-E-E, I did the same thing I do every day, going back to God for help, seeking an escape. After asking Him about it again and getting no answers again, I made a choice to just enter His presence because it was all I knew to do and I had no one else to turn to. As I was listening to anointed worship music, the Spirit of God said to me, "This is not about you. What you are going through now is not about you. You are going through it for someone else."

When He said, "someone else," I understood He was talking about was someone I don't even know and might never know in this life. All this time, I was racking my brains trying to understand why God was putting me through these things, but I could never figure it out because I was looking at it from the wrong perspective, the me-centered perspective, which caused me to be stuck in the valley of dry bones, unable to find the way out. I immediately understood this was the key to unlock the door to get through this season and make it to the next.

Since the Me-Gospel wrongly believes everything is all about us, it concludes everything happening in our life is directly caused by something we did and rejects the possibility that God could be doing something in our life that goes beyond us, all for the benefit of someone else. The Lord's disciples made this same mistake when they saw a man born blind from birth, so they asked, "Rabbi, who sinned, this man or his parents, that he was born blind?" But Jesus answered, "Neither this man nor his parents sinned, but that the works of God should be revealed in him." (John 9:2-3 NKJV) His answer makes no sense to followers of the Me-Gospel, but it makes perfect sense when we understand our lives are connected to others, so God does things in us for their benefit, even sometimes requiring us to lay down our lives for His sake and their sake. (Revelation 12:11)

Remnant: Trouble

The Me-Gospel hides the keys to victory from us by contradicting the whole idea of laying down our life. Why should we when there's nothing in it for us? It's a deadly deception, leading to a dead end where we repeatedly ask, "Why God?" It makes it extremely difficult to endure our trials and puts us in great danger of giving up and turning away from God, which is why I believe the Me-Gospel is now setting the stage for the fulfillment of end time prophecies of a great falling away from the faith, but God is giving us the keys so we can avoid that fate. (Matthew 24:10, 2 Thessalonians 2:1-4, 1 Timothy 4:1-5)

By understanding how God is orchestrating events in our life for the benefit of others, we find strength to endure and humbly submit to what He's doing, denying ourselves what we want, and forgetting our obsession with escaping from our own trouble, so we can take up our cross and follow Him, waiting patiently for Him to do what He promised, resurrecting our life from the grave. Instead of giving up, we find strength to keep fighting the good fight, standing firm on His promises and holding fast our confession without wavering or doubting. (Mark 11:23, Romans 4:20-21, Philippians 2:16, 4:1, 1 Timothy 6:12, Hebrews 3:14, 4:14, 10:23, James 1:6-8)

God gave this same key to Abraham when He promised to make him a great nation and a blessing to many people. (Genesis 12:1-3, 15:13-21, 17:17-21, 21:5) Surely, he must have considered the scope of what God promised went far beyond himself, giving him strength to endure the severe famine and then 25 years of waiting for the fulfillment of God's promise to give him a son. So, he received the promise and became the father of many nations, fulfilling the meaning of his new name.

Joseph must have understood this same key because after all those terrible things were done to him, he explained to his brothers, "God sent me before you to preserve a posterity for you in the earth, and to save your lives by a great deliverance. So now it was not you who sent me here, but God." So, Joseph understood it was not all about him, but God was doing something in his life for the benefit of many others. So, he received what God promised and was promoted from the prison to the palace, second only to Pharaoh as ruler over Egypt. (Genesis 45:7-8)

Ezekiel must have understood this same key because he found strength to endure the valley of dry bones, not wavering in unbelief, but speaking words of faith to those dry bones, as God commanded him, and when he did, they came together, covered with flesh, and arose as an exceedingly great army, making a powerful prophetic message to the people of Israel. (Ezekiel 37:3-14) So, he passed the test and became one of the greatest of all prophets.

Remnant: Trouble

Isaiah, Paul, and many other great champions of the faith have used this same key to find strength to endure, so they completed their assignments and received their rewards. Anyone following the path of righteousness should not be surprised when trouble comes, whether it's a famine, a pit, a prison, a valley of dry bones, or whatever it might look like. Even in those places, we can rejoice knowing we're in great company with many who have gone before us and the same God who was with them is also with us. Just as they finished their race, we can finish ours. And we can prevail over any trouble coming our way by casting all our fears, worries, and anxieties on Him because He has promised to take them from us. (Psalm 23:1-5, 34:17, 34:19, 37:40, Proverbs 10:25, 11:18, 12:3, 13:6, 18:10, Matthew 7:24-27, 1 Peter 5:7)

God is preparing His righteous remnant to demonstrate His power to a lost world, but His power is perfected in our weakness because when we are in our weakest place, our most vulnerable place, the place that looks like death, the place we never want to go, the place that appears to have no way of escape, then God's power grows stronger in us until it reaches full maturity because in our dire need, we press into another level of devotion to Him and become more fully persuaded that He is there with us, faithfully doing everything He promised, even giving us the keys to find the way out. (2 Corinthians 12:9) What an amazing irony how God leads us into dreaded places of emptiness to show us He has already given us an abundant supply of everything we need. (2 Corinthians 6:10) He shows us through our own first-hand experiences, seeing Him come through for us again and again at the precise time when we need Him the most, so we grow in confidence that He is bigger than any circumstances we face.

If you've endured a long season of waiting and found yourself asking, "Why God?" I encourage you to take this key and unlock the doors that have held you back. I've had this old song stuck in my head and I feel like God wants me to share the lyrics here:

> "Something beautiful, something good, all my confusion, He understood. All I had to offer Him was brokenness and strife, but God made something beautiful out of my life."

ENDNOTES

6.01: Scripture word counts for righteous, just, upright, and believers, Strong's Bible Text.

7
Hunger

In my dream, I sensed strong hunger for God from all those in the meetings, but especially from the young people. Even in the physical realm, young people are known for their strong appetites, especially in the age groups I saw, mostly teenagers and young adults. It's amazing how much they can eat!

> *All the meetings I attended were packed to the max with young people, teenagers and young adults. It was standing room only. Even up in the balcony, every seat was filled, and they were sitting on the floor along the railings, making a long row of feet dangling down. They were completely consumed with God. I knew we all had this in common, we had completely emptied ourselves of ourselves until there was nothing left but empty vessels for God to fill. This was the case for everyone there, especially the young people. God was everything to them. He was their all in all, their one and only desire. They were radically on fire for Him.*

Since my dream revealed future events, the young people I saw must be even younger now, which means they're too young to be millennials because the last of them was born before 1997, based on the terminology used by most researchers. (7.01) Millennials are also called Generation Y and the generation following them is called Generation Z, which is the perfect name for the final generation before the Lord's return since it's the final letter of the alphabet.

I believe Generation Z will be a big part of the harvest of souls coming before the Lord returns, as confirmed by two findings. (Isaiah 60:1-5, Amos 9:13-15, Zechariah 2:10-12, Matthew 13:24-30, Mark 16:15-18, John 12:32-33, Acts 1:7-8) First, they're quickly becoming the largest age group in our nation, just as Generation Y was previously. Second, they already appear to be far hungrier for God than previous generations. A 2016 U.S. study found that church attendance among the oldest members of Generation Z, those completing their teenage years, was 41%, which was more than double Generation Y (18%) when they were at that same age, and nearly double Generation X (21%) and Baby Boomers (26%). (7.02) So, Generation Z is already showing signs of hungering for God like I saw in my dream.

Remnant: Hunger

Although we normally associate hunger with the need for food, Jesus associated it with hungering for God, specifically righteousness. (Matthew 5:6) Hunger is defined as a state of weakness indicating a compelling need, a shortage, a famine, so the increased church attendance of Generation Z indicates they have a greater need, greater weakness, than previous generations, which is not being met by anything this world offers. (7.03)

Prophet Bobby Conner, founder of Eagles View Ministries, heard the Lord tell him, "Finally, I have a generation of people who are weak enough that I can accomplish My purposes through them." (7.04) He saw an awesome move of God coming upon the young generation as they stopped wasting their time and discovered where to direct their hunger, causing their aimless, purposeless lives to be suddenly transformed, filling them with passion for God, a clear sense of direction and a holy reverential fear of the Lord, which sanctified them, cleaned them up, and set them apart to serve Him. (John 17:17)

When I was in high school, I was skinny as a rail, even though I ate so much people called me the bottomless pit. I attended a boy's boarding school where we ate all our meals together in the cafeteria. One day, we were eating lunch and I was sitting at the headmaster's table. He watched in amazement as I ate eight hot dogs all loaded with chili sauce. He thought for sure I was just doing it to get attention. He was so intrigued; he came out that afternoon to watch me at football practice. After seeing how well I performed, he came up to me and said, "I came out here to see for myself because I was sure you were going to get sick, but now I know you only ate like that because you were hungry!"

If someone feels satisfied after eating one hotdog and feels completely stuffed after eating two, they don't even want to think about eating a third or fourth, so I can understand why he it was hard for him to believe when he saw me eating eight, but it shows there are different levels of hunger. What he called a meal was like an appetizer to me. Could you please pass the hotdogs?

Spiritual hunger works the same way. Those who are content with a little find it hard to understand why others are still hungry for more. In my dream, we were so hungry, we were weeping and crying out for more of God, which might seem excessive to others, perhaps even phony, showing off, calling attention to ourselves, but our hunger was real and it was putting a demand on heaven, so we were being filled with more and more until the presence of God was very strong. Even when I woke up, I was still weeping and crying out for more of God.

There's more to righteousness than just qualifying for it because there's a difference between qualifying and seeing the full manifestation, so the same hunger and thirst that qualifies us is also required to continue pursuing more of what God promised. (Matthew 5:6) For example, consider Timothy, whom Paul described as his fellow worker, his beloved and faithful son in the Lord, a man of proven character, like a son serving his father, a true son in the faith, a brother and minister, a man with genuine faith. (Romans 16:21, 1 Corinthians 4:17, Philippians 2:22, 1 Thessalonians 3:2, 1 Timothy 1:2, 2 Timothy 1:2, 2 Timothy 1:5) Timothy had clearly already qualified for God's gift of righteousness, but Paul specifically instructed him to "pursue righteousness." (1 Timothy 6:11) God has more amazing things He wants to do in us and through us, so He's instructing us to keep pursuing it, always staying hungry for more.

Hunger Pangs:

Spiritual hunger works the same way as physical hunger. For example, when we're healthy, we have a healthy appetite, but when we have no appetite, it indicates something's wrong. After going 12 to 24 hours without food, a healthy person experiences hunger pangs, which are unpleasant muscle contractions in the stomach, lasting about 30 seconds, letting us know our body requires food. (7.05) They typically continue for about 30 to 45 minutes, continuing to remind us, but if we ignore them, they subside for about 2-3 hours before returning.

Just as our physical body experiences hunger pangs, our spirit man does too and even on a similar time clock because both require food daily. Spiritual hunger pangs are just as real as physical hunger pangs, even though they're not physical muscle contractions, we can still feel them in our spirit, like an inner aching, a feeling of unpleasant emptiness, reminding us it's time to set aside everything else to go be alone with God so He can refill us. He illustrated this by the manna that fell from heaven to feed the Israelites during their time in the wilderness. They were only allowed to gather enough for one day, so each new day required gather more. Some of them tried to keep it until the next day, but it went bad, smelling rotten with worms in it, so there was no way to beat the system. (Exodus 16:14-20)

Jesus revealed He is the true manna that came down from heaven, inviting us to feed on Him, eating His flesh and drinking His blood, so we receive eternal life. (John 6:53-57) He told His disciples, "I have food to eat of which you do not know." (John 4:32 NKJV) They repeatedly misunderstood what He meant because they were only thinking about physical food. (Matthew 15:33, John 4:33) I think we make the same mistake when we hear His instructions, "Give us this day our daily bread." (Matthew 6:11 NKJV) He could not have been referring to physical bread because that would contradict His repeated instructions to give no thought to our need for physical food and physical drink. (Matthew 6:25, 6:31) The unrighteous diligently seek for those things, but God has promised to provide them if we seek Him first as our daily bread. (Matthew 6:33)

We receive our daily bread by spending time with Him, encountering Him by His Spirit and in His Word, but no matter how wonderful yesterday's encounter was, our spirit requires fresh manna from heaven daily to stay healthy and strong. Otherwise, we get weak and in danger of falling into a rut, losing interest in the things of God with no appetite for more of Him, making it easy for Satan to lure our attention away to worthless things, so God has shown us how to avoid that.

Imagine if God had designed us differently, so we never required any food or water, but received all we needed from just breathing the air. Without hunger, we would have no need to come together to grow our food, harvest it, catch it, prepare it, or eat it, so most of the reasons why we interact with others would be eliminated and we could choose to avoid them altogether, spending our life alone and isolated. Our basic needs for food and water force us to interact, exchange ideas, share our lives and stretch beyond ourselves to consider what others are enduring, so we learn to have an interest in them, appreciating and caring about them, perhaps even loving them so much, we would lay down our life for them, which is the greatest level of love. (John 15:13)

In the same way that our need for physical food requires us to come together daily, our need for spiritual food requires us to come together with God daily, so we interact with Him and have fellowship with Him, developing a friendship with Him, partnership with Him, and the opportunity to grow up in Him, so we can reach full maturity as His sons and daughters who truly love Him, even to the point of being willing to lay down our life for Him. So, we accomplish His will for our life, becoming one with Him. So, God has a higher purpose for our hunger, bringing us into fellowship with Him and with one another, so we can learn to love, which makes our life more meaningful and more abundant than it could possibly be isolated and alone. (Genesis 2:18)

If we continue without physical food, the hunger pangs grow more intense for about three days, but if we continue to ignore them beyond that, they start going away. (7.04) By that time, they've done their job. Their intensity makes them impossible to miss, so the warning was sent, but ignored for some reason, either by choice or because we could not find food. Spiritual hunger pangs work the same way. If we continue to ignore them, they eventually subside until they go away, leaving us with very little hunger for God, so we can make it through our day without any new encounter with Him, which is a dangerous place to be because it shows we're spiritually sick. By contrast, when we're spiritually healthy, we experience intense hunger pangs in our inner man, aching with a most unpleasant feeling that only God can satisfy, driving us to seek Him and encounter Him so He can fill us. (Psalm 42:1-2, Matthew 5:6, James 4:8)

Stirring Up Hunger:

We can have as much hunger as we want just by changing the choices we make. We can stir up intense hunger for food by going without it for extended periods and intense thirst even faster since our bodies cannot survive as long without water. After just a few days, we can get to the point where water becomes an obsession. I experienced that years ago when I did a total fast with no food or water for three days. Unless God specifically commands it, I don't recommend doing that because it's dangerous to our physical health. By the third day, the hunger was intense, but it was manageable. However, the thirst was unbearable. I was so thirsty; everything reminded me of water, but I brought it upon myself by my own actions.

We can do the same thing with our appetite for God, stirring up as much or as little hunger for Him as we want based on our choices. It's like a cup that we can fill with whatever we choose to look at, listen to, or think about because our heart follows whatever we focus our attention on as we connect with the stories and people we learn about. With so many stimulants pouring in, especially in our generation with all our electronic gadgets, we can easily fill our cup with all sorts of things, as shown in the following word I received from God on Jan 28, 2017:

> "Put away the vain things, the vain imaginations, the futile things of the mind that set the heart astray. Put your mind on My things, the things of My heart and My mind.
>
> Seek after My heart. Want it more than any other heart. Want to be in My heart, seek to be in My heart, seek to know My heart, to know more of what is in My heart. Want to know more of what I put into My heart. Want to know more. Seek to know more. Hunger to know more. Thirst for more, for I say there is more of Me that you do not know. Hunger and long to be more with Me and in Me than in the things of this world.
>
> You must want it. You must hunger to know more, for I do not come against the heart of anyone to force them to want Me. But I come to those who want Me, those who follow Me, that hunger for Me, that truly seek for Me. They are the ones that find Me, that come to know Me. They are the blessed ones that I call My own.

I bless the ones that come to Me and I turn not any of them away, for I am the One that wants them to come to Me. I want all to come to Me, to follow Me, to know Me, to seek Me, to find Me, for there is comfort in Me that is found nowhere else. There is protection in Me that is found nowhere else. There are blessings, for I satisfy the wants. I fill the hunger. I quench the thirst.

I know the heart of everyone who comes to Me. I know what it is to bless Me and I will repay each one in full measure. I will give back to each one what they hunger to know inside. They will know the things of My heart. They will be in My heart. I will take pleasure in the ones who know My heart, for they are in Me, where I want them to be. They are safe and protected, for they are in the refuge, the shelter from every storm. They will be protected when none others will be protected. They will be shown the light on their path and on their way when none others will be shown the light to see and to know the way. The ones who hunger for Me, they will know the way. Others will come away empty. They will not know Me. They will not follow Me. They will not seek Me."

We can barely even scratch the surface of all there is to learn about Him in this life because He is so big, but by avoiding vain imaginations and futile things that don't matter in the overall scheme of things, we can become empty vessels for Him to fill.

Modern-Day Pharisees:

When we get hungry for more of God, He shows up. And when He does, His presence is the most wonderful, life-changing, amazing thing ever, but since He is God, He reserves the right to act like it, doing things in ways that go beyond our limited human understanding. Just as He has done all throughout history, He is moving among us today in ways that go beyond our ability to understand with unusual manifestations, such as people unable to stand up or people laughing or crying for no apparent reason, which has caused some people to be offended and wrongly conclude it could not possibly be God. (1 Kings 8:10-11)

Some have even publicly slandered any ministries who allow unusual manifestations, calling them phony and their meetings fake revivals. These critics even slander the Holy Spirit by calling Him a kundalini spirit, which is just a fancy word to make people think they know what they're talking about when they don't, so they call the ministry of the Holy Spirit the ministry of demons. They go on YouTube or wherever else they can find followers, sowing their seeds of doubt and unbelief, saying anything they can to convince others to turn away from wherever the power of God is manifesting, causing their followers to reject life-changing encounters with God.

It's a serious thing to publicly slander God and cause His little ones to be confused. He specifically warned, "Whoever causes one of these little ones who believe in Me to sin, it would be better for him if a millstone were hung around his neck, and he were drowned in the depth of the sea." (Matthew 18:6 NKJV) By saying those things, they're playing for the wrong team, putting their name and reputation on the line to advance Satan's agenda. Satan has no problem with dead, boring, dry meetings because they're no threat to him whatsoever, but he hates powerful moves of God because lives are changed and people are set free to serve God more than ever before.

God does many things that go way beyond our understanding, such as speaking the universe into existence, including all sorts of amazing creatures. Even though we don't understand how He did it, He did. If we dismiss everything that goes beyond our understanding, we would have to dismiss just about everything, so that's the wrong test.

God doesn't have a problem with going beyond the limits of our understanding, even at the risk of offending us, as He demonstrated by His plan of salvation, which is called a rock of offense, a stumbling stone. He requires us to believe our eternal life was secured by a man hanging on a bloody cross. (1 Peter 2:8) The stakes could not be higher. The salvation of the whole world hangs in the balance. Yet, He has no problem stretching our understanding to the point of offending many people, causing the prideful to reject Him. So, why should we be surprised to see Him offending our understanding with manifestations? Why is there such a rush to judge things we know nothing about? Why so much confidence in calling the ministry of the Holy Spirit the work of the devil? Those who say things like that are like modern day Pharisees, defiled by religious spirits, thinking they know things they don't know. Meanwhile, those who are too hungry to be concerned with how God does it just keep pressing in for more, allowing Him to move the way He chooses. So the offenses act like filters separating the hungry from those who aren't. (Psalm 24:3-6 NKJV)

Fire Ignites Hunger:

I first surrendered my life to God in August 1982 and started pursuing Him passionately, but somehow by 1993, my spiritual life had dried up. Instead of pursuing him, I spent my spare time collecting baseball cards. I was not hungry for more and had no idea how to rekindle the fire. I had reached a dead end, but then something happened.

Remnant: Hunger

On the last Sunday of July 1993, some members from our church had just returned from a week of revival meetings where peculiar things happened to them. As they shared their stories with the congregation, the same peculiar manifestations began happening to them and others across the sanctuary.

The next week, the same thing happened, and again the week after that. My mind did not understand it, but my heart knew it was real and life changing for those who were being touched. I looked around and saw God touching people everywhere. Many were drinking the new wine described by the Prophet Joel, "And it shall come to pass afterward that I will pour out My Spirit on all flesh." (Joel 2:28a NKJV) Some people were falling out on the floor weeping while others were falling out laughing.

Everyone seemed to be getting touched, so it made me wonder why He wasn't touching me. I had learned to handle rejection from people, but feeling rejected by God was much harder. This continued week after week. I went home from church each week feeling frustrated and wondering, "Why is God rejecting me?" The more I thought about it, the more it provoked me. I grew hungrier for a touch from God, but still nothing happened. It seemed like God had overlooked me for some unknown reason.

Then our pastor announced a guest speaker from Florida was coming to our church to hold revival meetings for a whole week, which would have been great, except the meetings were scheduled for the same week I had to be out of town, confirming my fears. While I was out of town that week, I called my wife from my hotel room every night. She told me, "Oh, you would not believe how awesome it was tonight."

"Oh that's really great." I replied, trying to hide my jealousy.

It sure seemed like God had sent me half way across the country to stay in a cockroach hotel while He poured out His life changing power on everyone else. But then one night, when I called her, she had a different report, saying, "I was walking out of the church to go home and another lady was walking out at the same time."

This lady said to my wife, "Wasn't that wonderful in there tonight?"

My wife answered, "Yes, I only wish my husband could have been here with us."

Then this lady started getting a little choked up and said, "The Lord has been speaking to me about your husband. I saw him and he was all bound up with rope. Then I saw Jesus come to him and unravel all that rope until he was totally free. The Lord told me He was going to change him and you are going to have a brand new husband."

Remnant: Hunger

My wife had no idea God had been speaking to this lady about me and prompting her to share this word, but this woman was reluctant to step out, fearing she would be missing God, especially since she didn't know us very well. Plus, she was not very experienced at giving prophetic words, but when she heard my wife say, "I only wish my husband could be here," she could not contain it any longer.

My wife was so encouraged. She needed to know I was going to be getting an overhaul because I was making her miserable, more than I realized. She had reached the point where she did not know how much more she could take. Without even realizing it, I had neglected her and hurt her. When she told me what this lady shared, I felt a glimmer of hope and said, "Really? She said that about me?"

I returned home from my trip on Saturday night, but the next morning I had to leave town again for two weeks. So, it looked like I was going to miss church again, but by then, I was so hungry for God, I delayed my departure by a few hours to go to the morning service.

It was Sunday, August 22, 1993. My hunger for God had grown into an obsession. I felt like I would literally die if did not have an encounter with Him. My mind was playing tricks on me going back and forth between thinking perhaps this could be the time He would touch me, but perhaps He had decided I did not qualify. One way or the other, this anguish had to come to an end. We got there early and got a good seat in the front. The visiting pastor preached one of the most awesome messages I've ever heard. When he was finished, he turned around and said, "Pastor, come get your church."

When he looked back, our pastor was sitting slumped down in his chair on the platform. I learned later he had been standing in front of his chair when the power of God fell on him so heavy, he was no longer able to stand, so he just collapsed into his seat. (1 Kings 8:10-11) When the visiting pastor asked him to come get his church, our pastor could not move or get up or even say anything, so he just smiled and pointed his finger as if to say, "You keep on."

When the visiting pastor saw that, he said, "Well, I believe the Lord wants to minister to families today. So, if you're here with your family and you want to have the favor and blessings of God, then come forward to get what God has for you."

My wife and I were the first ones to get to the altar, standing at the front and center, so I thought, "If anyone is getting anything, surely I can't miss it." The altar quickly filled up as other families came forward. By this time, our pastor had managed to get up from his chair and he walked straight toward me. I thought, "This could be it."

Remnant: Hunger

He got about three feet from me, but then he turned 90 degrees to my right and began walking away. I could hardly believe it. Here I was standing in the best spot, and he walked right up to where I was and turned away to minister to someone else. It sounds like a small thing, but at that moment it was huge to me because it seemed like a confirmation God had rejected me and the thought of that was too big for me to handle. On the inside, I felt like I was free-falling, but it only lasted a few moments because he only took about three steps away before he suddenly turned around and glared right at me. He walked up to me and said, "Jim, the Lord has just spoken to me. He said to tell you, 'It's not too big for me Jim.' Get ready Jim. Get ready. I anoint you today as the priest of your home…"

Those were the last words I remember hearing. As he said that, he reached out his hand to lay it on my head, but the moment he touched my head, the power of God hit me so hard I was thrown back to the ground with both arms landing up above my head and I instantly began weeping uncontrollably. Before that, I was not crying at all, but suddenly I was crying like a baby. I was aware other people could see me, but I didn't care. I didn't know why I was sobbing, but I knew I was in the presence of God like I had never experienced before. I felt His love and His power like they were the same.

My eyes were closed as someone stuck tissues in my hands, but it didn't help because I couldn't even get my hands to my face. I was on the floor in that condition for over an hour when it finally began to ease up a little bit. Then I heard the voice of my pastor as he knelt beside me and kissed me on the forehead and said, "I love you Jim." When he did that, I knew it was the Lord speaking through him and the intensity suddenly increased to a new higher level and I was right back to crying like a baby again.

In total, I was on the floor for an hour and 45 minutes. During that time, I repeatedly sensed the flames that burn downwards because each time they touched me, they illuminated the hidden motives behind whatever I was thinking about at that moment, revealing the utter wretchedness of my heart and causing me to feel deep conviction of my guilt before God, so I knew I deserved His punishment, yet He was showing me His kindness and love.

When it was finally over, I needed help getting up because my body was so weak. I was a complete mess, but I was happy because I was filled with God's spirit to the point of being intoxicated. I felt like the disciples in the book of Acts, chapter 2, where Peter explained to the crowds, "These are not drunk as you suppose, but rather they are filled with the Holy Ghost." (Acts 2:14-15) I was too woozy to walk straight and way too woozy to drive, but more than anything else, I felt clean. I had not even realized I was dirty until I found out what it was like to feel clean.

How a brief encounter with God, lying on the floor for an hour and 45 minutes, could possibly accomplish anything goes beyond our understanding. Some people claim God would never do it that way, but they're too late to convince me because I experienced the most powerful presence of God and was set free from things I had been bound with for many years. God ignited a fire of passion in me, consuming me like a dry twig. From that day on, I started waking up way before sunrise every morning so I could spend hours worshiping God and seeking Him more fervently than ever before so I could get filled with more of Him. I became hungry to know the truth, so God started revealing new things to me. Each night, I went to bed shaking my head in amazement and saying, "How could I have been a Christian all these years and never known these things?" That was in 1993 and my life has never been the same since.

Even though it seemed at first that God was ignoring me and rejecting me, He was just used all those circumstances to stir up hunger in me so He could have my full permission to do what He wanted to do all along. He provoked me to jealousy the same way He used the Apostle Paul to stir up hunger in his fellow Jewish people. (Romans 11:14) Then He showed up in a powerful way.

How is it possible my spiritual life went from being dry as sawdust to having an intense fire burning in me with far greater hunger for more of Him, which has continued after all these years? Does that sound like something God would do or Satan would do? Does it sound like the fruit of a genuine revival or a fake revival? Does it sound like the ministry of the Holy Spirit or a kundalini spirit? Jesus said every tree is known by its' fruit, so I believe the fruit speaks for itself. (Matthew 12:33)

It was not God's fault I was stuck in a dead end all those years. It was my fault because I was not hungry, not seeking more. As soon as I demonstrated my hunger, He wasted no time moving in my behalf. (Psalm 34:15 and 34:17, Proverbs 15:29, 1 Peter 3:12) It was like what I saw happening in my dream when God showed up in such a powerful way because we were crying out for more of Him, but the level of hunger in those meetings was a far greater because it was a unanimous cry from a large army. (Matthew 5:6)

Changing the World:

God has promised to draw the nations to the brightness of His light shining in His people. (Isaiah 60:1-5) He has promised a harvest is coming that will be so great; it will require more than the normal season to gather it all in. The harvesters will still be gathering when the next season of sowing arrives, so it will be year-round harvesting! (Amos 9:13-15) I believe the only reason it hasn't already started is because He's waiting for us to demonstrate our hunger by drawing near to Him so He can draw near to us. (James 4:8) So, instead of us waiting on Him, He's waiting on us.

In the dream, we were crying out for more of Him, which was attracting His presence, so our cries were changing the eternal future of the whole planet because we were preparing the way for His return, giving Him permission to establish His Kingdom on earth. If it was up to Him, His Kingdom would already be ruling the earth now with His will being done everywhere, like it is in heaven, but throughout most of the world, His will is not being done, which explains why we see so much suffering, disease, death, poverty, and all sorts of evil things, and why Jesus instructed us to pray, "Thy will be done on earth as it is in heaven." (Matthew 6:10)

When the righteous cry out to Him in hunger, our prayers have a tremendous impact. (James 5:16, 1 Peter 3:2) When we come into agreement with heaven, sending up a loud and decisive invitation, then heaven will come. But if we are content with what we have here, then we won't have what they have there. So, the cry of our heart should be, "Come heaven! Come Kingdom of God! Come rule and reign over us Lord God!" (Matthew 5:6, 6:33, 2 Timothy 2:22) When that becomes our cry, heaven will come and the earth will never be the same again.

ENDNOTES

7.01: Millennials born before 1997, "Defining generations: Where Millennials end and post-Millennials begin". PEW Research Center. 1 March 2018.

7.02: Generation Z more likely to attend church, Hope, J (2016). "Get your campus ready for Generation Z". Dean & Provost. 17 (8): 1–7. doi:10.1002/dap.30174.

7.03: Definition of hunger, https://www.dictionary.com/browse/hunger

7.04: Bobby Conner, Eagles View Ministries, https://www.bobbyconner.org

7.05: Hunger pangs, https://en.wikipedia.org/wiki/Hunger_(motivational_state)

8

Encounters

The Prophet Joel saw a great outpouring of God's Spirit accompanied by all sorts of unusual manifestations, including dreams, visions and prophetic words, enabling us to perceive and understand things we have no way of knowing otherwise. (Joel 2:28-29)

> 16 But this is what was spoken by the Prophet Joel:
> 17 'And it shall come to pass in the last days, says God, that I will pour out of My Spirit on all flesh; your sons and your daughters shall prophesy, your young men shall see visions, your old men shall dream dreams.
> 18 And on My menservants and on My maidservants I will pour out My Spirit in those days; and they shall prophesy. (Acts 2:16-18 NKJV)

Jesus also saw this great outpouring coming, so He stood up before a crowd and cried out, "If anyone is thirsty, let him come to Me and drink. He who believes in Me, as the Scripture said, from his innermost being will flow rivers of living water." (John 7:37-39) Then He explained He was not referring to physical water, but spiritual water, which He called living water, referring to the Holy Spirit, who had not yet been given at that time, but was soon to be given to those who believed in Him. He called it living water because whoever receives it, receives the life of God in their innermost being springing forth from God's abundant supply that never runs out, but keeps filling us until it overflows and pours out into the lives of everyone around us, bringing life wherever it goes. (Proverbs 20:27)

After Jesus was raised from the dead, He commanded His disciples to remain in Jerusalem until they received that which was promised, referring to Joel's prophecy, saying, "John truly baptized with water, but you shall be baptized with the Holy Spirit not many days from now." (Acts 1:5 NKJV)

His disciples didn't understand because they were expecting Him to restore the physical kingdom to Israel, freeing them from the Romans, so He explained, "You shall receive power when the Holy Spirit has come upon you; and you shall be witnesses to Me in Jerusalem, and in all Judea and Samaria, and to the end of the earth." (Acts 1:8 NKJV)

So, the baptism in the Holy Spirit empowers us to fulfill His great commission as His witnesses, so we can more effectively obey His instructions, "Go therefore and make disciples of all the nations, baptizing them in the name of the Father and of the Son and of the Holy Spirit, teaching them to observe all things that I have commanded you; and lo, I am with you always, even to the end of the age." Amen. (Matthew 28:19-20 NKJV)

The fulfillment of the promised outpouring came fifty days later, on the day of Pentecost. His disciples were gathered together in the upper room in Jerusalem, doing what He instructed them to do, seeking Him and waiting for Him. Early that morning, they suddenly heard a noise that sounded like a violent rushing wind filling the whole house where they were gathered. Then they saw what looked like tongues of fire distributing themselves and resting on each one of them. And they were all filled with Holy Spirit and began to speak with other tongues, as the Spirit was giving them utterance. (Acts 2:2-4)

Like Joel saw, as soon as the Holy Spirit came into the place, unusual manifestations started, which were by His choosing, part of His plan, not originating from anyone else. The sound of the rushing wind was so loud, it was heard outside in the streets of Jerusalem by many people, so they came together to see what it was. (Acts 2:6)

It was a great example of how God manifests among us in ways that go beyond our understanding, letting us know this living water is not from any human source, but from God. The manifestations are signs pointing to Him to help us see and know and believe that He is real, His Kingdom is real and His promises are trustworthy, not just empty wishful thinking, but backed up by an all-powerful God.

Like many other supernatural events recorded in the Bible, the events of the day of Pentecost have often been rewritten to omit all the unusual manifestations, but it's not the same story without the manifestations because that's the way God chose to do it. He used the loud sound to gather the crowd, causing them to be intrigued and wanting to know what happened. Then He used another unusual manifestation when they heard the disciples, whom they knew were Israelites, speaking in their own native languages from faraway places like Parthia, Mesopotamia, Asia, Rome, and Egypt, so they were all amazed and intrigued, wanting to know how this was happening. (Acts 2:5-12)

The disciples only played a small part in these events, but it was a very important part because by obeying God's simple instructions, they released Him to do His part, which included many great things, empowering them, filling them, manifesting unusual signs and wonders through them, and bringing them before a large crowd of people who were eager to hear what they had to say. It was a great illustration of how the ministry of the Holy Spirit operates when we simply do what He tells us to do. He doesn't need our brilliant schemes or programs, which are powerless and lifeless if they didn't originate from Him, because He already has an amazing plan, so He just needs us to follow it.

The Holy Spirit also manifested in another unusual way, causing the disciples to act like drunk people, which was so unmistakable, people in the crowd said, "They are full of sweet wine." (Acts 2:13) They would not have said that unless the disciples were acting drunk, which is amazing because we all know how drunk people act. They get so happy they sing songs even when they can't sing very well. Their eyelids get so heavy they never quite open them all the way; 80% is close enough. Things that aren't even funny become so funny they laugh hard. The more they keep drinking the more unusual they behave, even falling on the floor for no apparent reason.

Peter knew the crowd was misunderstanding what was happening, so he stood up and said, "For these are not drunk, as you suppose, since it is only the third hour of the day. But this is what was spoken by the Prophet Joel." (Acts 2:15 NKJV)

By saying this, he confirmed this was the fulfillment of Joel's prophesy of the new wine. (Joel 2:19 and 2:24) Their behavior was the result of drinking a different kind of wine, heavenly wine. They were so saturated with the Spirit of God, they got exceedingly happy, overflowing to the point of drunkenness, so this marked the beginning of a new level of manifestations of God's Spirit, a new level of gladness, which was no longer just for filling one man, as King David received exceeding gladness in his heart and compared it to drinking wine. (Psalm 4:7) This joy had a far greater purpose of bringing life and joy to many other people by empowering the disciples to be witnesses to the whole world.

Because the disciples allowed the Holy Spirit to do things His way, He did what they could never have done without Him. Not only did He gather the crowd and cause them to listen, but He also brought them to the point of conviction, piercing their hearts, violently agitating them, stinging them to the quick with emotional sorrow and mental pain, bringing them to a place that was unpleasant for a moment, but necessary to get them to make the most important decision of their life, saving them from eternal destruction. (Greek word katanysso, g2660)

So, they listened intently to Peter's message as he explained to them how God raised Jesus from the dead and exalted Him to the right hand of God, the same one whom they had crucified, so they received his words and about three thousand were saved and baptized that day. (Acts 2:37-41) The fruit of three thousand souls entering God's

Kingdom tells us everything we need to know about what happened, confirming it was good and it was from God. (Matthew 7:17-18)

Drought of God's Presence:

Many people have been offended by the unusual manifestations that accompany His presence, even though these things are clearly recorded in the scriptures, including direct quotes from Jesus. It reminds me of a required class I took in college, Theology 101, because the professor explained away every miracle in the Bible. For example, he claimed God did not part the Red Sea. Instead, the Israelites crossed over during an unusually low tide. This man made a career out of studying the scriptures, but he didn't believe anything that went beyond his own understanding, and he did his best to convince his students not to believe either.

Hollywood movies often do the same thing, rewriting some of the most amazing Bible stories to remove anything that goes beyond our own understanding. By the time they're done, they've missed the whole point of the story.

The same thing is happening in many churches as they've made their own doctrines claiming God no longer performs miracles, which gets them off the hook with anyone who wants to know why their services are so different from the ones recorded in the Bible. They've learned how to do church without God, missing the whole point of gathering together in His name. Their unbelief has produced a drought of His presence, so they have lifeless, powerless meetings where everyone leaves with the same burdens and sicknesses they had when they came.

Even in churches where the gifts of the Holy Spirit are embraced, the boundary lines are often still there, just drawn in a different place. For example, they might allow manifestations of speaking in other tongues, but they don't allow the Holy Spirit to lead the service, doing what He wants to do. Instead, they keep Him on a very tight leash, confining Him by their strict adherence to man-made programs and time schedules with everything scripted in advance to fit the schedule, often with another service coming in right after the first service. So, the meetings move like clockwork with only enough time for a few short songs, announcements, a quick hug, pass the plates, and conclude with a short message, which might make us feel good for a short time, but since they're not following His leading, there's a power outage, a form of godliness that denies God the opportunity to move in His power. (2 Timothy 3:5) If the disciples had done that on the day of Pentecost, there would have been no outpouring and those three thousand people would not have been saved.

Although the presence of God has been confined, restrained and prevented from encountering us, the cares of this life have continued weighing on us just as much as ever, so we've had to find other ways to deal with them, which is why we have so many pharmacies distributing happy pills and liquor stores distributing what they call spirits, just not the right kind. I totally understand why so many people turn to these things because without His presence, I would too. God did not design us to carry our burdens, so when we try, they take a heavy toll on us physically, mentally and emotionally. He never intended for us to be tormented by all the fears, anxieties, worries, and stress from this crazy world, which are increasing as the world seems to be spinning out of control, changing faster than any time in history.

Real problems require real power, real encounters with God, and the good news is God has more than enough real power available for us. He has a much easier way, if we'll just follow His leading, allowing Him to be God by just following His instructions. He designed us for His presence, being filled with His glorious saturating peace and joy, resting in the safety of His loving arms while He carries our burdens and removes them far from us.

We've settled for too little for too long, but I believe God is still saying, "If anyone thirsts, let him come to Me and drink." (John 7:37 NKJV) And whoever accepts His invitation will receive rivers of living water flowing from their heart.

New Wine:

I received the baptism of the Holy Spirit the year after I came to the Lord, but that was the extent of it for the next ten years because I wasn't hungry enough to seek Him for more. So, after being a Christian for over eleven years, faithfully attending spirit-filled churches, I had never even heard about the manifested presence of God, which is often called the new wine, so I never knew it was possible to get so filled with the Holy Spirit that we experience an overflow of peace and joy like what the disciples experienced on the day of Pentecost. It wasn't until my wife and I were in a revival meeting one night when the man leading the meeting said, "The Lord just spoke to me and said, 'Some of you in the meeting tonight are going to experience the new wine for the very first time.'"

It happened just like he said. Within the next few minutes, the presence of God moved into that place and we were all enveloped in it like a big cloud. It was tangible, so we felt the atmosphere changing with so much peace filling us, we even felt it with our natural senses. Just breathing the air seemed to have the same effects as drinking fine wine.

The more we drank, the happier we got, until we were laughing and singing and dancing with joy, like drunk people.

From then on, anyone trying to convince us otherwise was too late. We discovered the real power, so we were forever ruined in the eyes of the skeptics and no longer satisfied with anything less. After wasting so many years without knowing these kinds of encounters were possible, I refused to waste any more of my time attending lifeless boring meetings. I must have living water, genuine encounters with Him. Everything else is just a big waste of time.

Just as there are different levels of intoxication with earthly wine, there are also different levels with heavenly wine. They both have saturation points beyond which we can no longer hide the effects and it becomes evident to everyone around us what we've been doing. Even our driving laws recognize the saturation point by setting a legal limit to the amount of alcohol we can have in our blood while driving. Anything beyond that gets us arrested because the influence of the alcohol is too strong, taking control over us, so we can no longer safely control the vehicle. In the same way, those who were filled with the Spirit on the day of Pentecost were so heavily under the influence of the Holy Spirit, they were no longer able to continue acting normal because they were drunk in the Holy Spirit. They had entered the overflow zone where they were not just filled, but had gone beyond the saturation point, causing them to overflow to everyone around them with visible manifestations of God's presence, so they were being far more effective witnesses, having a far more powerful impact on others. (Acts 1:8)

We can have all the new wine we want. We don't need to wait until the next meeting. We don't need to wait for anyone else to do anything because God will meet with us right now, right where we are. We're not waiting for Him. He's waiting for those who are thirsty to come and drink.

Take the High Ground:

Years ago, I think it was 2008, the Lord said to me, "Take the high ground." When He said that, I understood He was instructing me from a military perspective on how to encounter Him daily, letting me know the mission is the same each day, take the high ground. Soldiers fight to take the high ground because it gives them a strategic advantage over their enemy by enabling them to see them coming from a long way off. Once the high ground is taken, it's very difficult for the enemy to take it back.

Taking the high ground is all about pursuing righteousness, removing anything that stands between us and a right relationship with God, drawing as close to Him as we can possibly get by renouncing any mistakes we've made since our previous encounter and continuing to pursue Him until we receive the satisfaction of knowing with full assurance that all is well and we are right with Him and He is with us. (James 4:8, 1 Peter 5:7) This right alignment qualifies us to receive all the promises listed in Part 1, chapter 5, but taking the high ground goes beyond just qualifying because it is actually taking possession, specifically regarding His promises for our relationship with Him, as listed in Exhibit 10. For example, He promised we will perceive and behold His presence. (amplified from Hebrew words haza and paniym in Psalm 11:7) We will be saturated with His presence when we awaken, which will bring us great contentment and satisfaction. (amplified from Hebrew word temunah in Psalm 17:15) His presence will settle upon us and stay with us so we can live in His presence. (amplified from Hebrew word yashab from Psalm 140:13)

It's right where God has always wanted us to be, the most wonderful place to be, but getting there requires taking it because it works like all His other promises, which all have a difference between qualifying and receiving, as explained in Part 1, chapter 6, like the difference between being pregnant versus holding the baby and the difference between being named as an heir versus taking possession of our inheritance. Although righteousness qualifies us for all His promises, taking possession can be delayed if we act like we don't have any right to receive what He promised, so it requires acting on the promises we claim to believe by standing firm on them, expecting them to happen and refusing to be denied. (Hebrews 3:6, 13:5) Faith that takes action is the kind of faith that gets results, exactly the opposite of dead faith. (James 2:26) That's the kind of faith that takes the high ground, releasing the realm of heaven in the earth, literally changing the atmosphere, making it seem like just breathing the air is intoxicating.

Like the disciples on the day of Pentecost, He has given us an important part to play, which is to yield our agenda to His. Even though our part is small, He requires us to obey Him to demonstrate He has our permission to do what He promised. If we'll just obey Him, we can take possession of everything He promised. (Proverbs 3:5-8) He has already sent out the invitations and prepared the way for us, so He only needs us to take time to show up and seek Him. (Matthew 6:33) When we do, He will show up too. (Psalm 34:15)

His promises are reliable, the same yesterday, today and forever because He is the same yesterday, today and forever. (Hebrews 13:8) So, receiving His promises is not hit or miss, here today and gone tomorrow, like some kind of mysterious thing that leaves us wondering when we might happen to stumble upon the place of blessings without knowing how we got there. So, we can enter the heavenly realm any time we want just by passing through the thin veil separating the two realms.

Remnant: Encounters

A friend of mine once shared with me he had previously had times when he experienced the manifested presence of God, which was wonderful, but he thought encounters like that could only happen when God sovereignly decided to show up. So, I explained to him how God has given us an open invitation to enter His presence any time we want and then took some time to demonstrate it for him. We turned on anointed music and entered His manifested presence together. Once he understood he could enter anytime, he started putting his faith into action by pressing in and putting a demand on God, so he started having daily encounters.

Taking the high ground is necessary to rise above the low ground where we are pressed by all the cares of this life, which can squeeze the life right out of us. (Luke 8:14) The enemy's arrows are flying around down there, making it a dangerous place to live. When we enter His presence, all those cares are replaced by great contentment, satisfaction, deep peace, and great joy, so we experience the atmosphere of heaven in ways that are real and noticeable to our senses, which changes everything we do. (Psalm 16:11, Philippians 4:7) So, each encounter is a time of making transactions with God, deposits and withdrawals, exchanging our fears for His peace, our sorrow for His joy, and our lack for His abundance. It's the best deal ever.

Ever since God told me to take the high ground, I've made it my mission in my daily encounters. I always know when the mission has been completed because the contrast is so great from where I started. How we get there might look different for each of us, but I think the main thing is taking action with stubborn faith that refuses to be denied, no matter what it costs. When we come with that kind of attitude, making it our highest priority, even being willing to cancel all plans for the day if needed, we will successfully complete the mission, but with that kind of attitude, it won't take all day because that kind of persistence makes Satan give up and get out, especially when we demonstrate it consistently, day after day. His resistance grows weaker when he knows we won't turn back. There's nothing he can do about it, except leave. Some days, it takes more persistence than others, but if we keep fighting, God's manifested presence will show up and change the whole atmosphere. And once we've discovered the way to get there, our confidence grows, which makes it easier to get there the next time.

However, the instructions God gave me was not just to enter and pass through, but take possession, securing my position there, which is a big difference because if we only enter then we exit soon afterwards, but if we take possession, we get to stay there all day long. Like a friend of mine prophesied to me many years ago, "I see two cars. One is a fancy red sports car with a powerful engine. The other is an old clunker that breaks down a lot, requiring you to get out and push. Each day, you decide which one to drive."

Remnant: Encounters

Like the manna from heaven that only lasted one day, the high ground must be retaken each new day. (Exodus 16:20-24) I start my missions early in the day because I dislike the low ground very much. My personal preference is to start with anointed music and I like it loud. For many years, my choice of music has been the Worship with the Word services recorded live at the International House of Prayer (IHOP), performed by artists like Hellen Lee and Laura Hackett Park, because I like how the songs last a long time, which helps keep things flowing, and the lyrics contain scriptures and prophetic words of encouragement. IHOP plays live worship music 24/7 in their Kansas City Prayer Room and broadcasts it free on their website in two-hour sessions. (https://www.ihopkc.org/prayerroom/)

For me, the encounters have always followed the same pattern, but it might be different for everyone. As I'm listening to the music, I start by seeking to draw closer to Him and inviting Him to come closer to me. I also give Him whatever cares are weighing me down by naming them out loud. Somewhere along the way, I drift off to a place I call La-La Land because I forget where I am for a while, but I believe it's the place of total surrender where I totally forget about the time clock and all my cares. When I return from La-La Land, I discover He has carried me to the high ground without me knowing how I got there. Perhaps that's why it's called the secret place.

> For in the time of trouble He shall hide me in His pavilion; in the secret place of His tabernacle, He shall hide me; He shall set me high upon a rock. (Psalm 27:5 NKJV)

> You shall hide them in the secret place of Your presence from the plots of man; You shall keep them secretly in a pavilion from the strife of tongues. (Psalm 31:20 NKJV)

After returning from La-La Land and realizing He has filled me with His presence, the music is still playing loud, but at this point what sounded so good earlier now bothers me so I turn it off. I believe King David confirmed this sequence in his own experiences, entering His gates with singing.

> Come before His presence with singing. (Psalm 100:2b NKJV)

> Enter into His gates with thanksgiving, and into His courts with praise. (Psalm 100:4a NKJV)

The music helps me enter the heavenly realm, but once I'm there, it has served its' purpose, so I turn it off and enjoy quiet time, lingering in His presence, in no hurry to leave. Having arrived on the high ground, I believe the time of lingering is necessary to secure it because it demonstrates we didn't just come to pass through, but to stay for as long as we want. It's a wonderful time to enjoy God's presence and it's when He most often speaks to me, usually with short visions. I stay there until He gives me the release to go, so I leave with confidence, knowing the mission was accomplished. Skipping the lingering causes the high ground to be lost soon afterwards since it was not secured, but if I stay until He releases me, then I get to stay there all day long, filled with His manifested presence as I go about my day.

Although the glory of His presence usually only lasts for one day, each experience has a lasting impact because it stirs up hunger for more of Him, so He fills us with more and more, just like He promised. (Matthew 5:6) And all those heavenly deposits remain with us forever, accumulating and producing greater dependence on Him, so we're joined together with Him more and more, causing us to be transformed us into something new. (Zechariah 10:3, Joel 2:4, 2 Corinthians 5:17)

After the Fire Comes the Rain:

Immediately after Elijah called down fire from heaven on Mount Carmel, the next thing he did was tell King Ahab, "Go up, eat and drink; for there is the sound of abundance of rain." (1 Kings 18:41)

After the fire came the abundance of rain, ending the three and a half year drought and bringing them into a new place of outpouring. The drought represented the absence of God's Spirit as the people had turned their hearts away from Him to follow false gods. After Elijah's refining fire brought them to repentance, the abundance of rain came, representing the outpouring of God's Spirit throughout the whole land. (1 Kings 18:41-46) The fire consumed the unrighteousness in their heart, removing the obstructions which caused the drought, so God released the rain. So, the fire is a forerunner, preparing the way for the outpouring.

The same thing happened to the disciples on the day of Pentecost when tongues of fire appeared and sat upon each of them, filling them with the Holy Spirit. (Acts 2:3-4) Immediately afterwards, the fire touched the hearts of the multitude of people throughout Jerusalem who came together to find out what happened, illuminating their unrighteousness and convicting them of crucifying the Lord Jesus Christ, so they repented and immediately received the outpouring of God's Spirit prophesied by Joel, bringing salvation to three thousand people that day. (Acts 2:5-6, 2:17-21, 2:36-37, 2:41)

Remnant: Encounters

That's what I saw happening in my dream. The conviction of the Holy Spirit in our meetings was so strong, it not only exposed my sins, causing me to repent, but wherever I went, the same conviction spread to other people around me, like it was highly contagious, overflowing and causing them to start repenting too.

The fire of God illuminated the true condition of our heart, allowing us to see our hidden motives, so it brought deep conviction upon us as we saw we were guilty of the most vile things. (Proverbs 4:18) Unrighteousness blinds us from seeing our true condition, making us think we're rich in our knowledge of God and needing nothing when we are truly wretched, miserable, poor, blind, and naked. (Ephesians 5:27, Revelation 3:1-6 and 3:14-22) This deception breeds complacency and compromise, so God was exposing it so we could repent and be set free from it.

Like the Israelites on Mount Carmel and the multitudes gathered on the day of Pentecost, our repentance removed the hindrances blocking the outpouring, so we were receiving an abundance of rain as His Spirit spread throughout the whole place, soaking and saturating everyone so strongly, it was impossible to stay in that place without getting right with Him, as shown by the scene where an older man walked down the center aisle during one of our meetings. He stopped about half way, unsure of whether to continue or turn back. As soon as we saw him, we immediately knew there was something not quite right with him because the Holy Spirit revealed his unrighteous agenda. Someone asked him a question, "What do you want?"

That was all it took. Conviction came all over him and completely exposed him. Since he did not have any interest in what God wanted, he immediately turned and left.

My dream revealed the drought of God's manifested presence in our land is soon ending and the abundance of rain is coming. Just as Elijah called down fire from heaven and the disciples in the upper room received the fire of the Holy Spirit, a righteous remnant in our generation is calling for the same refining fire. (Isaiah 60:1-5, Acts 2:37) The outpouring of God's Spirit has already started as He is now training, equipping and moving them into position like an army preparing for battle, setting the stage for a much bigger outpouring to bring in a much bigger harvest.

9
Separation

My dream revealed the atmosphere of heaven on earth as we were coming together in agreement and helping each other seek first His Kingdom and His righteousness. (Matthew 6:33 and 18:19-20) We were joined together in unity far greater than anything I've ever seen before, which was encouraging to see, but it also revealed an enormous contrast with what's happening now.

Even though the heavenly realm is available to us now, for the most part, it's still being hindered, so it's rare to see the atmosphere of heaven on earth. Thank God there are some places where it's happening. There are some local church bodies closely aligned with His will, so they're bearing lots of good fruit thanks to the efforts of righteous pastors and church members plugged in where God wants them to be. That's a huge blessing to anyone who is part of it, but this chapter is for the rest of us who aren't quite there yet, even though we'd like to be. I believe my dream showed the time is coming soon when we're going to start getting it right in large numbers. (Ephesians 5:27)

Those who aren't there yet often can't see how we're ever going to get there because our life looks like a freeway under construction, more like an obstacle course than a freeway, but ultimately a beautiful freeway appears because the workers were following a master plan. For a while, our journey can look like a mess with no end in sight, causing onlookers to wonder how God could possibly be in it, but God has a master plan that's bringing us closer and closer to the kind of unity I saw in my dream.

At times, Elijah's life was enough to make us wonder how God could possibly be in it because he appeared to be no help to anyone, like when He followed God's instructions to live alone in the wilderness. (1 Kings 17:2-4) It was an unusual path to follow, but it led directly to a great victory over the false prophets on Mount Carmel. (1 Kings 18:20-40) Elijah spent so much time alone, he was convinced he was the only surviving prophet of God to his generation, but God let him know He had reserved for Himself 7,000 others who had not bowed their knee to Baal. (1 Kings 19:10, 19:18) Like Elijah, John the Baptist spent so much of his life alone, he perceived himself as the "voice of one crying in the wilderness." (Matthew 3:3-4, Luke 1:80) Yet, Jesus said, "Among those born of women there is not a greater prophet than John the Baptist." (Luke 7:28 NKJV)

Remnant: Separation

Both of these forerunners were led by God into a season of separation as part of the preparation for their future assignments. In both cases, they were separated from their backslidden nation until God brought them out to call for repentance. I believe their lives illustrate prophetically how God is now preparing His army of forerunners, leading many into seasons of separation.

All by itself, the pursuit of righteousness is a separation process as the righteous and unrighteous are moving in opposite directions, like light and darkness, causing a separation. (Matthew 3:12) Some are being led by God to separate physically, like Elijah and John did, while others are being separated spiritually by an ever-widening gap between them and their friends, family and backslidden church members, leaving them misunderstood with no close fellowship with anyone other than God. Either way, when the separation is caused by the pursuit of righteousness, there can be no turning back, like passing through a valley to reach the other side, but if we're following His path, we should find good fruit even in the valley. (Psalm 23:3-5)

Eventually, the path leads out of the valley as God brings that season to a conclusion in His perfect time. For example, while Elijah continued to receive good food and water, he remained alone in the wilderness, but when the river dried up, God told him it was time to leave that place. (1 Kings 17:7-9) Later, God connected him with Elisha. In the same way, when it was time for John the Baptist to come out of the wilderness, God connected him with other disciples. (1 Kings 19:16-21, 2 Kings 2:1-15, Matthew 9:14, John 1:29-36) In the same way, many forerunners today are enduring a season of being alone in the wilderness, but God has a plan to bring them out and connect them with like-minded disciples.

If God had His way, we would all be joined together in unity today, but how can those who are hungry join in agreement with those who are not? How can those seeking righteousness join with those who are compromising with unrighteousness? (Matthew 5:6, 18:20) In some cases, the compromises have grown into full embraces of unrighteousness. (Ephesians 5:11) For example, what started as a failure to confront those practicing homosexual lifestyles has sometimes grown into putting homosexuals in leadership positions. (Leviticus 18:22-30, Leviticus 20:13, Romans 1:18-32, 1 Corinthians 6:9-11, 1 Timothy 1:8-11, Revelation 22:14-15) The same applies to people in the church living together without being married, which is fornication, yet they are not being confronted or called out. (Exodus 22:16-17, Hosea 4:11 and 5:3-4, 1 Corinthians 6:9-10, Hebrews 13:4) The same applies to adultery and all sorts of other unrighteous deeds. (1 John 3:6-10) If God had His way, there would be no compromises with any unrighteousness, but His will is not always being done. (2 Corinthians 6:14)

Remnant: Separation

Prophet John Paul Jackson was concerned because he saw widespread unrighteousness being practiced by Christian leaders. He shared the following concerns:

> "The issue of sin used to be non-controvertible, but now they go, "Grace covers my sin. I don't have to worry about sin."
>
> I was talking to a group of young leaders not so long ago that are well known in the nation. It was about eighteen months ago. And I was talking to them and one of them said, "I don't have to worry about sin. I could literally have an adulterous affair and I would be back in the ministry in two months."
>
> And this attitude is beginning to permeate and that's very concerning to me. And that's why I said last night, righteousness is seen as legalism because that's what they (the leaders) told me. And, "There's no such thing as holiness. That's a pre-New Covenant idea."
>
> And so, I am concerned. And the more that sin separates us from God, the more the enemy comes in and the enemy is coming in and there are things going on right now that are going to be very, very devastating to us." (Source: 9.01)

What John Paul Jackson saw shows many leaders are making it all about them and their ministry rather than God, thinking the people are there to take care of them rather than the other way around, which opens the door for all sorts of compromises, like catering to the deadweights at the expense of feeding the hungry, which is a big problem because when the hungry are not getting fed, the whole thing becomes a lifeless ritual. (2 Timothy 3:5)

Consider when was the last time any church anywhere followed the Apostle Paul's instructions to expel all unrighteousness by confronting anyone living in unrepentant sin, giving them an opportunity to repent, but if they refuse, removing them from the church and handing them over to Satan for the destruction of their flesh in hopes they will repent before it's too late for them. (1 Corinthians 5:1-7) Hopefully, it's happening somewhere, but I've never once heard of anyone doing it or teaching others to do it. Of course, it makes sense no one would teach it unless they're also willing to do it because somebody would surely ask, "Why isn't this happening in our church?"

If the mission of the church is all about growing the numbers, it would be counterproductive to start kicking people out after paying so much money for slick marketing campaigns to bring them in. And kicking people out is like kicking money out, which would also be counterproductive. And if one person gets kicked out, there is a good chance their family and friends will get offended and leave too. It could get out of control, turning into a real mess, even a church split. It would be so much easier to just let it slide, which is why there has been a whole lot of sliding going on, churches sliding into compromise and church members sliding into hell.

The only times I've ever heard of anyone getting kicked out of their church was not due to practicing unrighteousness, but because they got too hungry for God, too filled with the Holy Spirit, too serious about obeying God. At one church where my wife and I were members before we moved away, our pastor had been kicked out of his previous church where he was the pastor. His crime was doing weird things during the services like praying for people who wanted prayer. He dared to obey the Bible by laying his hands on the people as he prayed for them, which was different from the man-made traditions of his denomination, so they treated him like a heretic. (1 Timothy 4:14, 2 Timothy 1:6)

Church leaders are only human, so they make mistakes like the rest of us. It's unreasonable to expect perfection, but when their mission wanders so far off course from God's mission, the hungry can reach the point where they conclude the whole thing is a big waste of time. So, there are some legitimate reasons why the path of righteousness leads some people away from their local church. It's not the ideal situation, but it requires a temporary fix, like the freeway under construction.

In 2015, God revealed there would be a growing number of departures through a dream given to John Fenn, founder of Church Without Walls International. He heard this word:

> "Many of the churches that used to be considered 'cutting edge' are already going the way of the world, having lost their first love, and will therefore continue to fade into irrelevance. This is another point you will see happening very quickly in the coming months, My people coming out of many churches as they hunger for Me, and mark the difference between mere believers and true disciples. These are the days the lukewarm will become obvious to true disciples, and a great separation will happen, and indeed is already happening nearly all over the world." (9.02)

Since John Fenn received this word, we have the benefit of hindsight to know he heard correctly because we've seen an exodus of God's people from many churches, as shown by many testimonies presented in this chapter. He described it as the difference between true disciples separating from believers because true disciples do more than just believe, they follow their shepherd wherever He leads them, even when He leads them through a valley or a wilderness.

Remnant: Separation

Departures:

If God had His way, no separations would be needed, but the testimonies below show a variety of reasons why God has been leading some people to depart from their local churches. For those who haven't personally experienced this, it might be a big stretch to believe God has workaround solutions that look like this, but like so many other things, the proof is in the fruit. And like the separations experienced by the previous forerunners, these are temporary, soon coming to an end, as shown in the next chapter. The first testimony is mine and the others were posted as comments on Z3news.com in response to an article posted in February 2016.

I attended Spirit-filled churches regularly for about 26 years, but in 2008, I believe God sent me out on an assignment, temporarily separating me from my local church where I had been a member for 7 years. During the final year or so, I started feeling more and more agitated, like I was in the wrong place. It took me some time to sort out what was happening because there seemed to be no good reason for leaving, but as I searched to find my place there, I was not sensing any leading from God whatsoever to participate in any of their ministries, even though they were great ministries. It just wasn't in me, even after waiting and watching for some time. Eventually, it started hurting my self-esteem, thinking there must be something wrong with me. I wondered if the devil was attacking me, trying to push me out, so I resisted it for a long time, but it only grew stronger.

I have previously wasted a lot of time doing things God never told me to do and I don't have as much time left as I once did, so I try to follow His leading and avoid making commitments to participate in activities until I have confidence that's where God wants me. (Romans 8:14)

I knew He sent me to that church seven years earlier, so I knew I was not at liberty to leave unless He told me to, so I started asking Him about it. In all my previous years of church membership, God had always given me confident assurance of where He wanted me to be. For example, He previously instructed me to leave a church where my family and I had been attending, so we left, but we didn't know where we were supposed to go next, but on the inside, I knew He was going to show us before the next Sunday, so I told my wife, "Before next Sunday, God will show us where He wants us."

And He did. He made it very clear to us, so we knew where to go and we joined the new church without skipping a beat. We were happy there for many years until the same thing happened again. Later, He made it known to both of us that it was time to leave that place. So, we left with peace and confidence, knowing God was going to show us again where He wanted us to go and sure enough, before the next Sunday, He showed us exactly where He wanted us and it was this church where I had attended 7 years.

After seeking God for some time about what to do, He gave me this scripture, "Now the Lord had said to Abram: 'Get out of your country, from your family and from your father's house, to a land that I will show you." (Genesis 12:1 NKJV)

When God spoke that to Abram, He did not reveal where He wanted him to go. His instructions were along these lines, "You must first to go forth, leave the place where you are now, the place you have known, your father's house, and as you go in faith, I will reveal where you're going. You're not going to know this new place because you have not been there before, but I will show it you as you continue looking to Me."

Abram must have wondered what was ahead, but we're talking about a great man of faith, so he stepped out and obeyed God, not knowing where he was going, but trusting God would help him. Receiving that scripture confirmed to me it was time for me to leave my church, even though I would have liked more details on where I was going next, so I met with my pastor and thanked him for all his help.

Unlike those previous times, I did not know where I was going, but God had given me that scripture and let me know He would show me the rest as I went and that's exactly what happened. Whereas before I was spiraling downward and feeling more and more agitated by being in the wrong place, when I stepped out in faith to obey God, it was a significant turning point and a major move in the right direction. His plans for my life were not only activated, but kicked into high gear as I started knowing with more clarity than ever before exactly what He wanted me to do. And I had a great passion for it too, like fire shut up in my bones, which helped me give it my full attention, my very best efforts. It was a greater stretch of faith than the previous times because I still did not know all the details about where He was leading me, but as I stayed with it, I discovered it was a fruitful place where I could prosper and have good success because He was blessing the work of my hands. (Deuteronomy 28:8 and 28:12)

It didn't all happen overnight. I didn't have clear direction after one week or even after one month. It took some time, so I had to keep believing what He told me and stay with it, following His leadings one step at a time, one day at a time. What else can we do when God doesn't reveal the details? The good news is when He says it's okay for us to not know, it's okay.

Abram didn't reach his destination overnight either. It took him some time. They stopped in Haran for a while. They were walking too, so he had lots of time to ponder what he was doing.

Even when I didn't know where I was going, God was already leading me. Even when I couldn't see it yet, He started training me for what He wanted me to do. Long before I ever understood His plans for me to start Z3news.com, He had my close friend training me to use the software I would later use to run it. Just by following the path, all the training I needed came to me. That was back in 2008, four years before I finally launched the site, but the site was launched right on schedule, exactly in the time God ordained it, but that's another story altogether.

Sometimes when people hear someone else's testimony, they think, "That sounds like a good idea, so I think I'll try it too." I hope no one makes that mistake because the only reason it worked for me was because I went to God and asked Him and waited for Him to tell me what to do. Separating from the local church without God's clear instructions to do so could be a disaster for our faith. So, if anyone wants to do what I did, just do the part about seeking God and waiting for Him to reveal the rest. His blessings are on His path, so if we stray off, we put ourselves in harm's way. (Proverbs 2:7-8)

After so many years of church membership, it felt odd to be out of church, so my mind was struggling with how it could be okay with God because I've heard so many teachings claiming that's a violation of the scriptures. Their words were ringing in my ears daily, bothering me, so I asked God about it and was amazed by what He showed me. I was doing what Jesus warned about, putting the traditions of men ahead of the word of God. (Mark 7:13) I was struggling to obey what God clearly told me to do because it contradicted a commonly misinterpreted fragment of one verse of scripture, which has been quoted out of context to make it say what it was never intended to say, creating the impression that God requires our regular physical attendance in local church meetings. Finding the true meaning of that scripture requires first forgetting everything we've heard so we can read the whole context with childlike faith, like reading it for the first time.

> 24 and let us consider how to stimulate one another to love and good deeds, 25 not forsaking our own assembling together, as is the habit of some, but encouraging one another; and all the more as you see the day drawing near. (Hebrews 10:24-25)

The main point of this passage is revealed in verse 24, "consider how to stimulate one another to love and good deeds." The next verse can only properly be understood in that context, so assembling together is only a means to achieve that goal and was never intended to replace it as the goal and certainly never intended to be a law to hold us in bondage. Physically attending meetings can help us achieve the goal because it gives us opportunities to stimulate others to love and good deeds, but it's also possible to physically attend meetings while failing to achieve the goal because stimulating one another to love and good deeds requires reaching out, listening, caring, helping, loving. Putting all the emphasis on assembling together might help boost church attendance, but at the cost of bringing people under the law and confusing them about what pleases God. Putting the emphasis in the right place produces liberty and fruitfulness, but putting the emphasis in the wrong place produces bondage and confusion. What a difference! When I finally took the time to study it in context, I saw it in a whole new light that set me free. The truth was there all along, but I had to study it for myself to see it rather than lazily relying on others to define it for me.

Even beyond that, consider the Apostle Paul, the author of this passage, and all the other first century apostles who wrote the New Testament. They all achieved the goal of stimulating others to love and good deeds far more by their writings than by assembling together in face to face meetings. Their writings are still producing fruit today, 2,000 years later, while their face to face encounters ended long ago. By reading their writings, we can receive the spirit of their messages just as much as if we were meeting with them face to face because the Spirit of God is not limited by the location of our physical bodies. The same God who moves in our life when we come together physically also moves in our life when we come together spiritually by reading His word, or listening to anointed messages, or praying in agreement with people meeting in another place as we watch on television, or talking with people on the telephone. With all the recent breakthroughs in technology, especially the Internet, our generation can assemble in more ways than any previous generation, including real time face to face meetings through programs like Skype.

Even though God did not reveal the details on where I was going, it became clearer as I stayed on the path. He put it on my heart to start Z3news.com, even though I did not fully understand His purposes for it at first. Later, I realized one of His purposes was to meet the needs of a specific group of His people who were suffering for the sake of righteousness, having been isolated from their friends, family, and church. Many of them had endured a long difficult process of leaving their local church, only to enter another long difficult season of feeling isolated, like Elijah and John did, but just like God showed Elijah he was not alone, he used Z3news.com to connect many of them together to help them realize they were not alone. Many of them were surprised to learn God has many other faithful servants enduring similar circumstances and I was just as surprised as they were, so I understood how they felt.

My story was like theirs, but also different because many of them had to leave due to serious problems, especially compromises with unrighteousness in their church. In my case, it was not about that. It was just a matter of trying to follow His leading to find where He wanted me to be, so every situation is unique and obedience to God doesn't always look the same for everyone, but if we're on the right path there should be good fruit to show for it. I've seen that in my life and so have those who shared the testimonies shown below.

Dante's Testimony:

"I have walked with Christ the last 15 years. I moved to North Carolina (as I was led by the Lord) and started my adult life here. I became firmly planted in a local church and became very active in various ministries. I was then placed in a leadership position, which put me in places with the highest leaders in this particular church, but the longer I served there, the more I realized that this church didn't have Christ at its' center, but money, notoriety, and numbers. So, I set up a meeting with the pastor to address these concerns. He then confirmed to me my concerns were valid when he admitted there were problems with non-Biblical issues at work in the church, BUT he said that's the way it would be in HIS church (not Christ's Church). He literally said that! My wife and I moved on.

We then joined another church in the downtown area of the same city. And while this church seemed better than the last one, they openly supported godless ways. There were homosexuals in leadership. One of these leaders had been imprisoned for relations with an underage boy. And they tolerated sin as long as people were "getting better." It was almost more like a self-help program that recognized that Jesus was Lord (if that makes sense). Before I realized all of this, I was moved into a leadership position at this church as well. After I realized what they were doing, I had a sit-down meeting with this pastor, like my previous pastor. He also agreed that my observations of sin, tolerance of worldliness, and several other things that were not right with God were present, but he was not willing to change them (likely for fear of losing his congregation, mortgage money, and community status–long story for another day).

In both churches, I was a minister with a "bright future." But it was obvious that I didn't represent them and they didn't represent me, or the fullness of Christ. They had a form of godliness, but truly denied the power thereof.

In both churches, I had a decision to make. I could stick around and acquire a prominent position, get some paid "preaching gigs" (as they call them), and local (and possibly regional) notoriety. Or I could leave these churches and start over. And let me tell you, as a minister, I want to preach the Gospel to the nations. I want to have a platform from which to preach the uncompromised Gospel of Jesus Christ. And the mainstream organized Church is the most streamlined way of doing it. They are very good at the "product" they produce, but they require you to bend, overlook sin and corruption, accept worldliness, not "meddle" [i.e. tell the whole truth], and play by the pre-established rules.

I made my decision to follow Christ and stand on His platform. In the same way Satan offered Jesus the easy way out, through the temptations in the wilderness, many of us will be asked to take the easy way. We must stand fast in the liberty wherewith Christ has set us free, and never accept the bondage of world-influenced Churches. There are good Churches out there, but they are few and far between. We must use Holy Ghost discernment to find one. Don't be afraid to stand up for what you know in your heart of hearts is right. God is standing with you! And you + God = a majority! God bless!"

Christina's Testimony:

"I've had the same experience with leaving the church where my family attended for 12 years. I felt the Lord God by the leading of the Holy Spirit tell me on one specific Sunday morning in 2011 while at church to leave. I obeyed the Spirit and we left this church. It was heartbreaking because we began attending when I was pregnant with our first child and we had raised both our young daughters in this church. There were a lot of memories, but in the last three years prior to leaving, our church family forsook us in our most dire time of need ever. This left us very bewildered about the church's role as ministers of Jesus Christ.

When we moved out of state to where we are now, we began praying and seeking the Lord with a great sense of deep longing to draw near to Him and find a church home where His Presence would truly be, along with like-minded disciples. For months after we moved out of state, a friend from our old church asked me continuously if we had found a church in our new place. Another friend from that same church asked me to promise her we would find a church in our new hometown. As of recently, a family member in the state we moved away from has recently asked if we ever found a church to attend. Then, people in our community have asked if we are attending a church. It's the natural question for most professing Christians to ask. It seems quite odd to people that if we profess to be a follower of Christ, why are we not attending church, but the truth is, we haven't found a church that is preparing its' people. The churches we attended were more like the world and partook of the world to draw in more members. There was no stretching and growing. Truly, this Scripture rings true in 2 Timothy 3:5, Having a form of godliness, but denying the power thereof: from such turn away.

Remnant: Separation

This is my personal experience. I've been telling people that the Lord God has been leading my family on a one-on-one journey and we are following His leading in faith and obedience. I've been sharing with people how much the Lord God has been revealing and teaching us in this quiet intimate time with Him on this journey. We have drawn closer to Him and this experience has manifested true physical changes in our everyday life. Truthfully, in this separation from the church building and drawing closer with the Lord God, we have been reading our Bibles more individually and together as a family. We have further separated from the world in a way we've never experienced before. It is hard for people to understand, but the church didn't teach us the things that have led us away from the world, Jesus did. To Him be all the glory!

It's amazing to me how we attended a church for 12 years and a few others afterwards, but in all that time, we never learned what we've come to learn in this journey with our One True Shepherd. Praise Him! This time has literally been a spiritual awakening.

Certain professing Christian friends from the church we attended have become estranged. Since we have drawn closer to the Lord through a one-on-One relationship with Him as our Teacher, our professing Christian church friends can't understand why we are not attending church. We have been learning exponentially in this intimate setting (more than we ever learned while attending church for 16 years). This has been our personal experience/journey. I have begun to hear from the Lord! This was something I didn't know we could experience while attending church as it was never taught in any church we attended.

We are so excited to share what God is revealing to us with our family and Christian friends, only to hear negative comments or receive the silent treatment. This doesn't make sense. How does a professing Christian 'not' want to hear how the Lord God is working in someone's life? I especially thought our brothers and sisters in Christ would be encouraged and strengthened in their faith, yet it seems the closer we draw to the Lord, the further the world distances itself from us.

One or more Christian friends has actually told me that I can push people away by talking about the Lord God and sharing Scriptures too often. But He is my life. It is my joy to talk of Him all the day long.

So, for the last 8-9 years, it has been a very lonely path by the 'world's' standards. However, the more the 'world' pushes me away, the more I draw near to the Lord. The more people who estrange themselves from me, the more I cling to the Lord God. I have cried out to God in my loneliness, He has comforted me. His Word, His promises comfort me.

For 38 years of my life, I didn't know we could individually hear from our Lord Jesus. I feel embarrassed to admit this but am being humble and honest. I am crying as I'm thinking about this because I know there are so many others like me out there who do not know this truth. I had never been taught this truth by my parents, church or anyone. It was when I drew closer to the Lord alone intimately seeking Him persistently. I came to Him with my all. I believe He has taken me aside, away from all the distractions, knowing my thirst and hunger for truth and has drawn me to Himself. He knows my (our) heart. I have learned from Jesus' perspective how much He wants a relationship with us. Not just a relationship where we go to Him when we feel like it and tell Him about ourselves and ask Him for what we want (How much is the world like this? It's all about 'self'). He wants to hear from us all the time, like a best/close friend, or like a child to a parent or like a bride to a husband; an intimate, very close relationship. He wants to talk to us too if we only make time and listen to Him. He has something to say to each of us, I believe that now with all my heart and soul."

Michael's Testimony:

"I stayed in the church system longer than I would've due to buying into the idea, 'If you see something wrong in your church, don't leave, help fix it!'

Yeah, that would work if the church wasn't under the iron grip of a group of kingdom builders (their own kingdom, not God's), who won't let go of control. I attended a large church where this was so bad, the leadership would intentionally kill ministries which were growing if they didn't start them or have full control over them.

Case in point, this city has an enormous Chinese population and a very Godly Chinese man who was not a pastor started a Bible study which grew like mad and before long, hundreds of Chinese were coming to the church and holding Chinese studies. The Chinese man organized the studies and nothing more. Nevertheless, the leadership saw him as a threat and threw him out of the church. I kid you not.

Almost the exact same scenario happened with a young adult's ministry. Both ministries were squashed, causing many people to leave the church feeling disenfranchised. That was fine with the leadership though, since they had their control once again. That was the beginning of the end of my time there.

Like so many others here, I have never grown so much as I have since leaving the church. How very sad. Makes me wonder how much more I could be growing if I was in a real church wholly dedicated to The Lord, with believers like the people sharing on this site. God will soon do this, of that I'm confident."

Remnant: Separation

Natalie's Testimony:

"I was married once before now and in 2011 my husband and I moved to FL because he got a job offer at a nondenominational church. Throughout that year and into 2012, I was always "bothered" because they put so much emphasis on being perfect on stage, lighting, sound, everything and always going by the clock on the back wall. I never liked that. There were times I could feel the Holy Spirit while I worshiped the Lord and just knew He wanted to move in that place, but sure enough, He was cut off time and time again because it was time to play their videos. It was very hard to be there and see this.

I remember looking at the people. They seemed hungry for The Lord, but were lifeless because the Holy Spirit wasn't allowed to move there. The leaders also talked a lot about numbers, like it was a social club and they wanted to see how many they could get to come there, even saying, "It's about numbers because behind every number is a person."

In 2012, I had a dream about being in a church building and people were running around. Some were vampires trying to bite other people to make them become like them. I got bit trying to help someone escape, but I didn't change, which I think was because I had the Holy Spirit in me! I saw my husband in front of me running out the door of the church with someone else and I was one of the last to make it out. The vampires were trying to barricade the entrance with long tables turned on their sides. I saw the light outside and ran to escape from them. I jumped over the tables and ran out the doors. When I got outside, I was naked, but I was free from harm.

Not long after that dream, God gave me another dream where I was in a building and saw a tall evil being a distance from me. It turned around and saw me looking at it. It had evil glowing eyes. I had a backpack on and I immediately ran towards the front door to escape. I knew I was being chased. I couldn't run fast enough because my backpack was too heavy. So, I just dropped it and left it. I made it to the front yard and turned around knowing the enemy was at my back. A group of small people came right up to me. Their leader in the front held a small knife up to my face, but then amazingly, I suddenly saw an army come from behind me like they were side by side and lined up ready for battle. They looked angelic, like I could see through them. They came and stood right next to me with their swords drawn, facing the enemies that were threatening me. They looked like a true, strong army in their armor! My dream then ended.

The very next morning, I received an email from the pastor of a church where I had attended. My husband was on the worship team there. The pastor, I kid you not, threatened to fire my husband if I did not keep attending the church. So, I knew this was what I was warned about in my dreams, especially when the leader of the small people held a knife to my face.

I knew God was saying He has an army too and He will fight for me, just as He does for all those who truly love Him and follow Him. Just like I left the backpack, I left that church. I tell you going through all that is still crazy to think about. I was only 29 then and away from my family. I look back now though and I thank God for getting me out of that mess and who knows what that church was really doing behind closed doors. Only God knows their motives, but it grieves me to see the Church become so worldly. It's not about popularity, the best lighting or having everything perfect, or as they called it, "excellence". Of course, we want to give our all in whatever we do, but are we doing it for ourselves and our kingdoms or are we doing it for and WITH Jesus and His Kingdom?"

Sandra's Testimony:

"I am no longer in a local church because they are like social clubs. I have been put down by others for not being in church, but that's another story. I was not sure about being out of church. The Word declares there will be a great falling away before the return of the Lord and many have claimed that warning is for people who are not going to church, but the Church is not physical, it's spiritual, so the falling away is in the heart, a departing from the faith. Thanks for listening. God bless."

Tracye's Testimony:

"Sometimes I feel all alone, judged and ridiculed for my decision to leave the "church" almost a year ago now. Before leaving, I had attended four churches during 2014-2015 for at least 3 months each to give them time, but it just seemed like the pastors were feeding the flocks with baby food, milk and mush, to make them feel good and comfortable. The worship seemed like it was about, "Look at us, aren't we good at singing, playing our instruments and looking good on stage?" The tithing was about expanding the church or a whole new church building, sending kids off to camps/retreats, etc. – nothing real, nothing deep and nothing meaningful. I left empty every time.

I am now fed the Word of God from my time with the Lord alone, and His teaching through Scripture, Internet teachings by solid, reputable, time-tested, Bible-based pastors, and with being Spiritually fed by this Z3 site. Thank God for it and other blogs and written teachings. I have grown tremendously in the past year (I've been a born-again Christian for over 23 years). The scales over my eyes have been completely removed, and I am now fully AWAKE – praise Him! I love the statement, "We are to be waiting on the return of the Bridegroom with our garments washed daily." I would also add that I keep my oil lamp lit at all times so that I am found pure, holy, blameless and ready at all times.

> 1 Then the kingdom of heaven shall be likened to ten virgins who took their lamps and went out to meet the bridegroom.
> 2 Now five of them were wise, and five were foolish. (Matthew 25:1-2)

This is certainly not a recommendation for all those that are part of the true Bride to leave a church but as the Lord leads all of us individually to hear His voice and Obey!"

Sherry's Testimony:

"My heart weeps for all of you having to go through this. The church today is apostate and seeker friendly. No one feels convicted anymore. I have this problem at my church. The pastor reads the bible to us word by word, line by line, and I'm sitting there thinking where is this place today and how does it affect my life today? There have been times when I sat in the back row with my bible open and my iPhone on top looking at Amazon.

Last year, I listened to a message on the Internet and as I turned it off I thought, 'Wow, I feel so strange. What is this feeling?' Then it occurred to me that I felt convicted and I realized I had not felt this in a long time. It was great because we need that, so I told my husband about it and he looked me in the eye and said, "When was the last time you walked out of our church feeling like that?"

I laughed and said, 'Oh, you never come out of there feeling like that.'

I have come to realize that I am no longer blooming or growing where I have been planted. I have brought this before the Lord many times, asking Him, 'Where are the preachers of the past who called sin what it is and were not afraid to preach a hell fire and brimstone message?'

We never hear any warning messages from the book of Revelation or any warnings that we need to be preparing for what's ahead of us in this next season. A famine is coming, but my pastor said to me, 'I'm not stockpiling any food.' He has five small children. May God bless you all in your journey."

Sarah's Testimony:

"My family moved from FL to TN. I have a prophetic background and we moved into a very asleep, religion-based area, so I sat on my hands while the women "sniffed" me. After one year of sitting on my hands, I was finally approached by the leader of the women's ministry stating that she needed to apologize to me. Why? Well, it seems the Holy Spirit had been nudging her since the beginning of the year for me to teach the women and that was in November. She had resisted, so she was repenting and asked if I would do it. I was delighted and asked her what she wanted me to teach. The wheels were visibly turning as she responded, "I think you need to teach us about deliverance."

So, I did that over the next year or two. Then she asked me to teach the women about Prophetic Intercession and Prophetic Prayer Ministry. The women loved it... the pastor not so much.

I had a decision to make. My husband, whose gifting is in watching end time events, had left two months before I did. As soon as I had finished teaching the final class, I was given the release by the Holy Spirit. We tried attending other fellowships, but we were surprised by the sickness in the "Body of Christ." We keep trying to find one that is commutable to us, but have not found one where we seem to fit. We are content to pray from our home for our area, country and world. We are fed via TV and the Internet, and of course, Z3News is a big part of our daily encouragement."

Grace's Testimony:

"On September 6th, last year, the Lord said, 'There will be a separation taking place in the Church.' Then on my January 1st "God day" where I spend the day with Him, He said, 'This separation will deepen and intensify.'

I have attempted twice to talk to the pastor at our local church about what is coming down the pike in terms of God's judgment on North America, but he has not listened. He is actually standing on and teaching the Word in many ways, but is not preparing the Body to stand firm during approaching difficulties. My husband loves our church, so I imagine we will continue there, but I am saddened and conflicted when I see the general unawareness of many fellow believers."

Carolyn's Testimony:

"In 2012, the Lord gave me foreknowledge He was soon going to remove me from the church. He said to me, "Don't go to church, be the church." After receiving that warning, I was brutally persecuted by Christians in the church, including my own family, who do not believe in the GIFTS of the Spirit, [dreams, visions, signs & wonders]. They claimed I was crazy for having an intimate relationship with God, so I was out and blown by the winds of the Spirit all across the land.

So the Spirit lifted me up and took me away; and I went embittered in the rage of my spirit, and the hand of the LORD was strong on me. (Ezekiel 3:14)

The Lord now has me teaching those who are hungry about prophetic symbolism so they can understand their own dreams and visions and the things God says to them. What surprised me most is that the church I attended was Spirit-filled. I do not believe the church pastor was bad or evil, etc. I felt the anointing when I was there. The only problem I saw clearly was that they placed importance on memberships and numbers. Sort of like David numbering Israel out of pride in 1 Chronicles 21:1. But when I told some church folks that the Lord instructed me to not work, and I talked to them about dreams, they looked at me like I had three eyes (prophetically speaking I did have three eyes!) Then later, things became so much worse. My own family, some of whom claimed to be Spirit-filled Christians, decided the messages I received from God were hallucinations! Imagine! We ought not be surprised considering Jesus' own family also accused Him of being insane. There is a lot more to my testimony, but it will go in a book at some point. But let's just say, when God tells you to forsake all family for Him and the truth, we must do it.

Do not think that I came to bring peace on the earth; I did not come to bring peace, but a sword. For I came to set a man against his father, and a daughter against her mother, and a daughter in law against her mother in law, and A MAN'S ENEMIES WILL BE THE MEMBERS OF HIS HOUSEHOLD. (Matthew 10:34-36)

As a result of following God, I lost all my family and friends. Everyone. It has been a lonely road, but with God all things are possible. When the Lord instructs us what to do, whether it be to LEAVE a church or to GO to a different one, or to not go to church at ALL, we must obey Him. Mature believers understand they must obey God, not man.

But Peter and the apostles answered, "We must obey God rather than men." (Acts 5:29)

When the Lord said to me, 'DON'T GO TO CHURCH, BE THE CHURCH,' I did not realize He would remove me from everything and everyone I ever knew and give me a small online ministry of my own, teaching the saints to understand Him for themselves. Nor did I expect I would lose everything I owned at the time. Those who are called to be set apart must count the cost. There will be a cost. How many are willing to pay it?"

Margaret's Testimony:

"In the fall of 2014, I finally left the church we had attended for almost 20 years. For a long time, I had been hearing the LORD telling me to leave, but I kept thinking there were a lot of good people there. Then the choir got a new music director and the first meeting he led, it was like the LORD shouted, "Get out right now!"

It was so real, my body was shaking. I could not get out of the building fast enough. My husband could not understand. I could not explain it to people because none of them have ever heard GOD speak to them. Fortunately, my husband listened to me. It was hard for him because he grew up in this denomination. Months later, this church approved homosexual marriages and supported the Palestinian Muslims. We now attend a messianic synagogue because all the other denominations had the same message.

My youngest daughter is going nowhere. She went to church with us, but she slept through it most of the time. After college, she admitted that she does not really believe there is a god, so I pray daily the LORD will reveal himself to her. My other daughter is married to a Muslim man. She has fallen for the lie, "We are all praying to the same God." She also is not going to church, but at least she believes there is a god.

I am fasting and praying for all those who are asleep in these churches. I know the LORD weeps for them and it is breaking His heart to see how the churches have tuned out His voice. Before I left our old church, there were times when I would listen to their Sunday school lesson and end up slipping out to go sit by myself and cry. Most of the times, I would come home and cry and pray. I am grateful for my new church because when I come home from a service, my heart rejoices with the tunes of praise and a sense of being extra close to the LORD."

Robin's Testimony:

"I have stopped attending church. I get condemned occasionally by other Christians who like to use the scripture, "not forsaking the assembling together" as a hammer to prove I am out of the will of God, but I actually had to stop going to church because I was getting spiritually assaulted by the evil spirits controlling these churches. I even tried to address the issue with the church leadership, but somehow the fingers ended up being pointed at me. Now I have church at home with me and the Lord and my night terrors have stopped. The Lord told me He will lead me one day to a group of believers when it's time. I look forward to that day. Online is awesome, but face to face would be better. God Bless. Hope this testimony helps someone."

Carol's Testimony:

"The Replacement movement is so strong in this area, maybe it's everywhere. These churches have nice names, but they have twisted interpretations of the Word. They call themselves New Testament Christian or a symbolic name like Crossing or King's Church… something that feels good. People are searching, so they flock in to get a cozy message of God's love, grace and inclusion. Forget the part about "for all have sinned" or the "repentance" part or the "wash your robes…for I come quickly" part!!! They reject the scriptures revealing, "God will turn back to his people Israel" very soon, or that the "church age" is nearly over and "final judgment is at the door." The pastors in these churches are in denial to the Word. They see no judgement coming to America, so they are not warning their congregations! May our Lord wake people up!! My friends and I are in total agreement, we have left Babylon."

Diana's Testimony:

"I had to leave a spiritually dead church a while back. As I awakened from my slumber, the Lord showed me the state of that church – they were sound asleep. They also had a form of Godliness, but denied the power thereof. Run, run, run!"

Holly Ann's Testimony:

"I've been in such a state of struggle with my girls as of late on this very subject. They ascribe to a lack of readiness and it is reinforced by the churches they attend, which makes me appear to them as being the weirdo. I have made my concerns known regarding the lack of true guidance by the church leaders, which is coming from ALL churches here. Although I've voiced my overwhelming concerns of the darkness and confusion being espoused by the churches here, my views as to who the true Bride of Christ is and the imminence of His return, doing so has placed me, for years, in a place of isolation amongst others, including my family."

Linda's Testimony:

"I also had to flee the chosen frozen Sunday Social Clubs. The last attempt ended when I tried to gather together some people to pray together in repentance and forgiveness, as the Holy Spirit searched our hearts. Their reply was, "We did that with two pastors and we've had enough of that."

WOW. . . Just WOW. That cotton candy leaves a nasty taste in my mouth. Needless to say, the "assembling together with one another" seems to be more in the virtual world than in person right now. I pray the Holy Spirit will bring like-minded, awake servants of Jesus Christ together in each location, so we can pray for one another in person. In the meantime? THANK YOU JESUS for this virtual world, where we have the opportunity to gather together, regardless of our geographical location."

David's Testimony:

"Walking in obedience has led me to 'not go back' to a particular church I was attending. I understood that certain elements or influences were allowed to infiltrate the church because the people were refusing to listen to the Lord's message. The Lord did not want me to be exposed to those influences. It is one thing to wage war out in the world, but the place of fellowship should be a place of unity and grace. The Lord may lead me to attend a particular service, but not at the moment."

Steve's Testimony:

"About 3.5 years ago while attending a particularly powerless church meeting, I began to visibly shake next to my wife in the pew. Then I suddenly began to weep uncontrollably. Getting up from the pew, I walked out the back door and never returned. I walked down the street saying, 'God, I just can't do it anymore. I'm sorry but you'll have to find someone else.'

For a long time, I felt bad about leaving. Then, about two years later, I began crying out to the Lord with an intensity I had never known, and instantly began having powerful prophetic dreams, receiving words of knowledge, was physically healed, and even found myself healing others. The undeniable reality is all this great stuff took place AFTER I left Churchianity, not before. Looking back, my shaking and weeping in church that day was not me simply 'being complicated', but I believe Holy Spirit was giving me a taste of what He feels like in most of our churches on any given Sunday.

I believe it was Charles Spurgeon who famously asked, 'If the Holy Spirit left your church would it make any difference?' I'm afraid all too often, the answer in our North American churches is a resounding, 'No'."

Mark's Testimony:

"Yes, my church became a social club. The message preached was mostly truth, but only in part. It was spiritual starvation, like eating a lot but dying of malnutrition. I finally left when we moved to another city. We tried another church here, but again was disillusioned and left. We're not into the Christian social scene. We like people, but we didn't go to church to 'hang out' and put on our church face. Many are sincere good people, but spinning in circles.

I hated feeling obligated to tithe there because I started to find so many other international missions and ministries that so desperately can use the funds which go so much farther in spreading the love of Christ to a dying world. Our church hardly sponsored any missionaries and those we did never seemed to accomplish much. Fund raising was for the youth group and twice as many 'chaperones' to make bi-annual trips to Thailand to help the poor. But the stories they brought back seemed more like exotic vacations than any accomplishment for the kingdom of God.

My wife was turned off first and stopped coming to church, but I held on for the sake of our kids, so they could continue in Sunday school. I have felt guilty lately thinking, I guess I must not be very good Christian, not wanting to go to church on Sunday, but I have gotten much more out of the sites and resources I found online than I ever got at church. So, praise God for leading His remnant out of spiritual Babylon. 'Come out of her my people and don't take part of her sins...' Amen."

Benjamin's Testimony:

"I see it in my own church and have for years. Many don't realize it, but I see a shift from worshiping God and our Savior to worshiping 'The Church' and the leadership (men) while our God and Savior takes a back seat. But those whose eyes have been opened by the Holy Spirit can see it as well and the difference is very obvious. Those who love 'the church' mainly fellowship with others of the same church and more or less avoid people from other denominations. On the other hand, those who have come to know and love the Lord feel a fellowship with others who also love Him no matter what denomination they are from. I've chosen to stay in my church in hopes I can help teach the young people to make that transition from just 'going to church on Sunday' to seeking a relationship with God for themselves and putting an end to 'playing church'. I'm vocal about this to my youth. The times of playing church are running out. Severe times are close and we can no longer afford to play church on Sunday and live the rest of the Sabbath Day and week as if God isn't really relevant in our lives. It's especially bad when the adults live this way and their children are raised doing the same—all for the vain purpose of putting on a face for social acceptance. I hope I can make even a small difference, but I trust the Lord will set everything right when He comes."

Sherry's Testimony:

"In 2014, my husband and I escaped from a denominational church I had attended all my life. It was the best thing we ever did. Since leaving, my husband has grown in the Lord so much. We now join with other believers to listen for the voice of God as we allow Him to lead our gathering. Holy Spirit has brought us together with a small group who worship and minister at a Christian drug rehab in our area. We have seen more power and moving of the Spirit in the short time we have been there than in the 60+ years I attended church. We are so grateful we got out. Many others who have attended church all their lives are getting out too.

I will not lie, I actually 'left' the church before I walked out of the doors. For a long time, I was extremely dissatisfied, but it was the Lord's way of getting me ready to leave. Leaving was painful and somewhat confusing, but we would never go back into that rigid system. I thank God every day that I am no longer a slave to that powerless religion! Two really good books helped me along the way: Revolution by George Barna and Pagan Christianity by Frank Viola and George Barna."

Robert's Testimony:

"Regarding the local church, let me say that after looking for a 'good' church for 37 years I have never found one. I think it's probably harder than ever today because, in my opinion, we are in the Laodicean church age with apostasy running rampant. It amazes me how pastor after pastor can throw a wet blanket over the greatest story ever told. How pastors can make the offer of sonship into God's very family a boring sermon. Z3news.com and Trunews.com have become my family."

Hope's Testimony:

"I thought there was something wrong with me because I felt like there was something missing every time I would go to church. I felt like it was a club or a social gathering and I always felt uncomfortable. I went to a few different churches to check them out because I did want fellowship with other believers, but honestly, I was always on the outside; feeling like I was missing something. I was thirsting for God's Word, but I felt like the messages weren't digging into the truth and had no substance. I was told I was being too picky and what was wrong was inside of me. I finally just stopped going to church because I wanted to LEARN God's word. I wasn't interested in hearing opinions and random stories from a pastor who didn't even open the Bible. I really thought maybe there was something wrong with me. Now that I just read my Bible, pray and visit this site, I feel more fed than I ever did in the church. The testimonies and words from God have greatly blessed me."

Samuel's Testimony:

"The big question is whether people are being fed spiritually. In many churches, people wallow in emotionalism, and then assume, incorrectly, that they are being imbued with the Spirit. When the Spirit is at work, changes are produced in people's lives, and sometimes these changes can be drastic.

Many churches are nothing more than well-organized social clubs. Many of my close Christian friends, faithful believers for decades, are fed up with the worldly compromises their churches are making almost daily, and they are leaving these social clubs for good.

The current thinking in these churches is that the Body of Christ can also be a friend to Mammon and the World, especially with the wholesale embrace of the homosexual agenda. As a result, I, and others close to me, have left the state sanctioned 501c3 social clubs for smaller house churches, which are unencumbered by the trappings of buildings, committees, busy bodies, gossips, social justice warriors, bullying pastors, self-proclaimed know-it-alls, and insurance salesmen who want to help you secure your financial future in the rigged, criminal stock market with their dubious financial products.

We are now living in a 'Catacomb Culture.' For those of us who wish to worship the Living God in truth, according to the Scriptures, and in good conscience, the 501c3 social club simply don't cut it anymore, so we are gathering in small groups, in private, to worship among ourselves, just as the early Christians did."

Marla's Testimony:

"My husband and I have just left a church after a vision and dream I had, plus some things the Lord has been showing him. It has been very hard because we were involved with ministry in this church for over 9 years. I began having visions about a year ago. I saw Jesus weeping and throwing ashes on His head in our church. I had visions of things that happened in regards to the leadership. They hired a worship leader that was living a deceptive lifestyle and bragging about it, but because of a check in my spirit, I couldn't be on the team and because of the vision that warned me as well. My husband had a prophetic word that was basically rejected outright by the church leadership, even though he had a miraculous sign to confirm it (he purchased a book the Lord said would confirm the prophecy without ever reading it and the book did!).

Anyway, in my last vision there, I saw a fire in the back of the church. Many people started to get up and leave their seats and go where the fire was burning, but the pastor became very frustrated and agitated that we were leaving. I believe God is moving some of us that need to move out of churches that are not obeying Him."

ENDNOTES

9.01: John Paul Jackson's concerns about unrighteousness, speaking at Pastor Matt Sorger's church in NY, Jan 14, 2012

9.02: John Fenn, Church Without Walls International, https://churchwithoutwallsinternational.org

10

Unity

On September 17, 2016, I dreamed I received orders to board a spaceship for a trip to the moon. I was the only person on board and had no idea how to operate it. I was told all I had to do was press this one button on the control panel and the spaceship would automatically do the rest.

A swirling round shape was carved into the top of the button. When I pressed it, the engines suddenly ignited and the spaceship blasted off and took me straight to the moon, just like I was told. As it was coming in for a landing, I looked out the window and was surprised to see a man walking on the surface wearing regular clothes without any space suit.

When my spaceship landed, I exited onto the surface wearing my space suit. I was curious about the man I saw, so I walked to where he was. When I found him, I also saw several other people nearby and none of them were wearing space suits either. So, I asked him, "How are you breathing without a space suit?"

He explained, "You don't need that here. Everyone told us it was impossible to breathe without it, but we can breathe fine. You should get rid of yours now and come with me."

So, I took off my helmet and discovered I could breathe and what a surprise that was! Then he led me to a community where he was living with many other people. I was amazed to see buildings and streets, just like cities on earth. There were even cars driving around!

Then I met other people and they gave me an office in one of the buildings. I was assigned a job as part of a larger assignment within this community. I understood our assignment had something to do with the people on earth. The dream ended.

Interpretation:

The orders I received to board the spaceship represent instructions from God to leave behind everything we've known to go to a place we've never seen before, which goes against all natural tendencies to play it safe and be in control since we naturally like to know what's ahead. The instructions were insanely simple, but also sounded insane. It's so simple, anyone can do it, but so insane, hardly anyone would dare to. It's so easy to just get on board and push one button, but it's impossible without great faith because it requires relying more on what we cannot see than what we can.

The apparent insanity of my orders showed how God designs our circumstances to give us opportunities to demonstrate our faith or lack of it. Everyone sees the dangers involved, but not everyone follows His instructions. Everyone faces the same fears, but only a remnant overcomes those fears to step out in faith. (Matthew 7:13-14) Regardless of what we claim to believe, our deeds reveal what we're truly seeking, exposing what's truly in our heart, whether we're seeking to know God or to save our own life. (John 12:25)

Contrary to the wisdom of this world, which claims we're all God's children, we're all okay, and we're all going to heaven, God's wisdom separates the faithful from the faithless by our deeds. Anyone can claim to know Him, but the proof is in doing what He asks us to do. (James 2:26) If we truly know Him, we'll obey His commands, even when it looks crazy, so our deeds demonstrate what we truly believe, providing God with irrefutable evidence of our faith, which is why He bases our rewards on them. (James 2:24, 2 Peter 2:4-22, 1 John 2:3-6, 2:17, 3:4-6, Revelation 2:4-5, 2:26-28)

I had nothing to do with building the spaceship or planning the mission. That was all done ahead of time by someone else. My part was in making the choice to obey or disobey. It was a very small part, but important because unless I got on board and pushed the button, the spaceship wasn't going anywhere, but my simple obedience ignited the powerful engines and initiated the complex navigation system, locking in my destination and guaranteeing my safe landing.

The ignition button had a swirl shape engraved into the top of it, so there was no way to press it without touching the swirl, so God made it easy to see and impossible to miss the whirlwind of His Spirit, which is the source of His great power, like a fast burst of wind, a cyclone in the unseen realm. (John 3:8) By pressing the button, I proved I was on board and in agreement with what He wanted to do, which was all He required to take over from there, doing what only He could do, all the heavy lifting required to get me to my destination, which was far beyond my knowledge or ability. (Romans 8:14, John 15:5, James 2:26) So, I believe this dream shows if we just do our part by obeying His instructions, He will do His part, making it a done deal as He carries us to the place where we can fulfill His plans for our life, opening doors for us that no man can close and closing doors no man can open. (Isaiah 22:22)

Remnant: Unity

Like the whirlwind that carried Elijah into heaven, the spaceship launched me into outer space, into the realm of heaven, far beyond the realm of earth, far above all the cares, fears, worries, and burdens of this life, far above the reach of the enemy's fiery darts. (2 Kings 2:1) It's a wonderful place to be, but it came at a cost, temporarily separating me from everything I had known before, illustrated by being all alone in the spaceship. During that time, God was my only companion. I had no one else to share my experiences, no friends, no family members, only God, not because I had done anything wrong, but because I obeyed His instructions. Yet, I was glad to be on board because I saw things I never would have seen before, heavenly things not visible from earth, giving me a new perspective.

Even while I was still alone and confined in the spaceship, I saw a man walking on the moon, revealing a prophetic insight into what's ahead. My long season of isolation was soon coming to an end and a new season was soon beginning, which was quite a relief. The isolation was a required part of my journey, but was never meant to be permanent because God's plan was for the spaceship to arrive at a specific destination where others had already arrived ahead of me.

I was surprised because I did not know there were others, like Elijah and so many others discovered, but I was even more surprised when I saw this man was not wearing any spacesuit, illustrating how this place was beyond the limitations of the natural physical realm. (1 Kings 19:18) The spaceship that appeared to be so dangerous had proven to be the only safe place because it had carried me into the realm where all things are possible. (Matthew 19:26) Removing my helmet also appeared to be dangerous, but as a covering over my mind, it represented my old ways of thinking based on the limitations of the natural realm, so it was actually a hindrance, preventing me from discovering the reality of this new realm and experiencing it for myself. Removing it and discovering I could breathe without it showed how God had prepared me in ways I had not even realized, equipping me not only with everything I needed to reach this realm, but also to stay there until my assignment was completed.

As wonderful as it was to find this man, it was even more wonderful when he led me to a community of many others, all of whom had endured the same journey to get there, all carried by the power of the spaceship into the heavenly realm to a place we could never have found on our own. (Matthew 4:4) They knew I was coming and had already prepared a place for me, showing how God is preparing the way ahead of us. They helped me find my place and gave me further instructions on what to do, just as all of them had found their place. This community was well established with buildings, roads, cars, and offices, showing the scale of this work was much larger and farther along than I realized, showing God's remnant is already spiritually positioned in the heavenly realm where they are accomplishing great things for the benefit of many others who are still in the earthly realm. (Ephesians 2:6)

There was no way to see all God was doing from earth because it was way too far away, so I was only able to see these things after I obeyed His instructions to board the spaceship. Even then, I could not see the destination and did not know where it was taking me, but I reached the right place and found my assignment. I was not left stranded along the way. Only in the end did I finally gain understanding of things that had not made sense to me before.

Meeting Dream:

In another dream on November 21, 2018, I had received a message that someone was going to be approaching me secretly. Then some time passed and I had sort of forgotten about it. Then one day, I was sitting outside in a public place when a man in a military uniform walked up to me and greeted me. He was smiling and looking directly into my eyes as he reminded me, "You got my message about meeting with me, right?"

The way he looked at me and smiled was like he knew me, so I looked at him closely to see if I had met before. I had no recollection of ever meeting him before, but somehow immediately recognized him and knew things about him, like someone I had known for a long time. I saw his life in God, where he was walking, so I had great respect for him and instantly liked him. He was wearing a military uniform, very sharp and clean, but different from any I had seen before, mostly blue with some white trimmings.

Then he started introducing me to other people, men and women. They were all smiling and friendly, just like him, but they were dressed like civilians, not wearing uniforms. My reaction to them was the same. Although I had never met them before, I immediately recognized them like I had known them a long time. I felt the same great respect for their walks with God.

Then the scene changed and we were all gathering together in a large room for a meeting. The chairs were positioned along the walls forming a large circle. I had a good seat, but then I realized there were some things I needed to get done that required a desktop, so I gave up my seat to find another seat at a desk, which I found in another room that was next to the larger room, separated only by a partial dividing wall, so I could still see what was happening in the larger room. Others were continuing to enter the room looking for seats, so they were glad my seat was available and I was glad to have found my place so I could get started with my work. End of dream.

Remnant: Unity

Receiving the message that someone was going to be approaching me secretly represented a prophetic insight into what God is planning to do with His people, connecting us together with like-minded people. He's letting us know ahead of time so we can have confidence to know we're in the right place when it happens. When it was fulfilled, God confirmed it to me through the first words the man spoke to me, asking, "You got my message about meeting with me, right?" So, God is telling us what's coming and giving us confidence to know when it is being fulfilled, showing how He is with us through the whole process to help us reach our destination. (Amos 3:7)

In between the initial prophetic message and its' fulfillment was a brief period in which I was sitting outside by myself in a public place, illustrating the temporary season of isolation, like being in the spaceship. During this time, I had no way to find the people God was sending because I had never even seen them before, so the only thing I could do was wait patiently for God to do what He promised.

When the man approached me, he seemed familiar to me because I recognized the joy of the Lord beaming from his face. I saw his inner man, so I knew his life was filled with clarity of purpose, purity of motives, and right with God because He was filled with the same spirit of life and truth, so even though I didn't know him, I felt like I had known him a long time. I felt completely at home with him, in agreement with him, like I could trust him and confide in him about anything. I believe this shows we're going to be amazed by how perfectly we fit together with the people God is connecting us with, like long lost friends.

In the same way, I had never seen a uniform like his, but I recognized the authority it represented. It was clean and sharp, representing his righteous life. Blue often represents revelation because it comes from heaven, like the blue sky. It was also white, representing the purity and righteousness, like the great white throne of God, which is established on righteousness. (Psalm 89:14 and 97:2, Revelation 20:11) So, even though I had never seen a uniform like it before, it told me a lot about him and who he represented and the authority with which he had been entrusted.

Even in the dream, I was aware of the irony of not knowing any of these people, yet feeling like I already knew them, and it was the same with all of them. I had great respect for their relationship with God. So, God was giving me the desires of my heart by connecting me with them, but He did it all while I just waited. It would have been impossible for me to find them on my own, so they had to find me as God directed them.

The large meeting room where we sat in a circle shows we had been joined together for a common purpose with a mission to complete, like the community of people living on the moon in the spaceship dream. Giving up my seat to find a desk shows my assignment required observing what was happening in the larger room and writing it down to share with others and illustrating how we will each have specific assignments with specific places prepared ahead of time for us to do them.

New Season:

Both of the above dreams reveal a new season ahead, bringing an end to the season of isolation, like the years when the Israelites passed through the wilderness where He sustained them with manna from heaven. (Deuteronomy 8:2-6) He never intended for them to stay there, only to pass through on their way to a far better place, which He described as "a good land, a land of brooks of water, of fountains and springs, flowing forth in valleys and hills; a land of wheat and barley, of vines and fig trees and pomegranates, a land of olive oil and honey; a land where you will eat food without scarcity, in which you will not lack anything." (Deuteronomy 8:7-9)

In the wilderness, we couldn't see what was ahead, so we wondered many times if perhaps God had forgotten us or abandoned us as we endured uncertainties, traumas, and relationships strained to the point of breaking, but while we were wondering if we were going to die, God was doing what He promised long ago, releasing the spirit and power of Elijah, His frontrunner, to bring restoration in every area of our life, not only healing our wounds from the past season, but also equipping us with everything we need to fulfill our destiny, including great new relationships with like-minded people who will help us complete our assignments. (Matthew 17:11)

Both dreams reveal a new destination coming into view as the season of isolation and separation is replaced with a new season of fellowship and unity. Those who have faithfully endured the previous season will be rewarded for diligently seeking Him. He has promised to generously repay a hundred times more than what we sacrificed to follow Him, including relationships and material possessions, not in the next life, but here in this life, as shown in the following passage. (Hebrews 11:6)

> 28 Then Peter began to say to Him, "See, we have left all and followed You."
> 29 So Jesus answered and said, "Assuredly, I say to you, there is no one who has left house or brothers or sisters or father or mother or wife or children or lands, for My sake and the gospel's,
> 30 who shall not receive a hundredfold now in this time—houses and brothers and sisters and mothers and children and lands, with persecutions—and in the age to come, eternal life. (Mark 10:28-30 NKJV)

Remnant: Unity

True Unity:

The coming season of unity was also revealed in my remnant dream as I was enjoying many great new relationships with like-minded people beyond anything I've experienced before, which was giving us great joy and satisfaction, enabling us to live the abundant life, just like Jesus promised. (John 10:10)

We were experiencing a greater level of unity because the hindrances had been removed by our repentance, so we weren't trying to hide anything in darkness, but were willing and eager to expose everything to the light for all to see. We were transparent before God and before each other. We had forsaken all our secret sins to pursue righteousness as our common goal, allowing us to come together in perfect harmony, in agreement, with one mind and one accord, free to go all out for God without hypocrisy and without compromise, joined together as one cohesive body.

The greater level of unity and transparency enabled us to know things about each other, which strengthened our bonds even more, like we were inside each other, sensing what was happening in each other, like a living organism, all connected by the Spirit of God. (Romans 12:5) Whatever one person did, immediately impacted everyone else throughout the whole place. So, if one person shouted praises to God, it ignited praises throughout the whole place. If one person felt the conviction of the Holy Spirit and started repenting, it ignited repentance throughout the whole place. Although we were many, we were one body, flowing together in perfect harmony, joined together like living stones, forming God's spiritual house. (1 Peter 2:5)

Although we might not yet be experiencing that level of unity, I believe we have already started moving closer to it because God has already started connecting many people through all sorts of ways, including people all over the world connecting through the Internet on sites like Z3news.com, but there's still much more to come.

When I first started Z3 News, I didn't foresee all that was required to allow other people to share their comments, but monitoring and replying to them soon became a big part of my daily chores. It has been a wonderful way to connect with others and I have made many new friends, but it has also stretched me a lot because I often felt like it was robbing me of valuable time I could have spent elsewhere, even wasting my time because it often required cleaning up messes when people act like babies, attacking and criticizing what they don't understand. Most of those kinds of comments and emails don't get posted, so the community doesn't see them, but I still have to see them.

However, the interaction has had many benefits. For one thing, I learned the world is full of geniuses, people who already know everything about everything, making it impossible for anyone to tell them anything. At first, I tried to help them, but soon realized it was a waste of my time because it was never received. After encountering so many of them, I renamed my trash folder to call it the genius folder, so whenever any geniuses post their comments, they go directly where no one ever sees them, which makes me very happy. But they gave me a whole new appreciation for those who have true humility because it is so much rarer. And I gained a whole new appreciation for what pastors endure, which is surely an impossible ministry without the grace of God because they cannot send their people to the genius folder, even though they would probably like to. Thank God for those who are willing to be pastors!

Like the freeway under construction, it's hard to see what's coming, but I believe God revealed all the messes are part of the process of getting us there. When I was praying one day, He revealed to me one of His purposes for allowing comments posted on Z3 News, saying "I want you to be inside them and I want them to be inside you."

I understood He was referring to the way the Z3 News community daily shares our thoughts and experiences. It reminded me of His prayer, "...that they all may be one, as You, Father, are in Me, and I in You; that they also may be one in Us." (John 17:21 NKJV) So, He has already started preparing us for greater unity by connecting us and giving us insights into each other to bring us to a greater level of considering one another, understanding one another, encouraging one another, and loving one another. (John 13:34-35, 15:12, 15:17, Hebrews 10:24-25)

We are planting seeds inside each other that make a lasting impact, changing our perspectives, bringing us into closer alignment as we fill in missing pieces of our understanding. Just as I have shared my experiences, I have also received back many times more from others, so we're helping each other move closer to our destinations by gaining a clearer understanding of our assignments. It's just one small example of how God is already working in us to bring us closer to the level of unity I saw in the dream. Even though we don't know the way, God does and He's already set us in motion, moving us in the right direction. We're not going to get there overnight, but we'll reach our destination right on schedule just by following His instructions.

Power in Unity:

The power of unity was demonstrated by the unrighteous rebelling against God in the construction of the Tower of Babel. Their unity brought them to the place where "nothing would be impossible for them", so God intervened to stop them by confusing their languages. (Genesis 11:6-7) If the unrighteous attained such power through unity, how much more can the righteous accomplish with God helping us?

There is power in unity even with just two people coming together in agreement, as shown by God's promise to do whatever we ask. (Matthew 18:19-20) So, imagine the power of a large army, all crying out to God with one voice like I saw happening in my dream. No wonder Joel described this coming remnant army as, "The like of whom has never been; nor will there ever be any such after them, even for many successive generations." (Joel 2:2 NKJV)

Our unity even draws the world to God, as shown by His statement that if we would come together as one, the world would believe He was sent by God. (John 17:20-21) And when we join together to praise and worship God, we are releasing Him to fulfill another promise when He said He would draw all men to Himself if we would lift Him up. (John 12:32) I believe this promise has a double meaning, referring to Him being lifted on the cross and to us lifting Him up with our praises, releasing Him to bring in the great end time harvest of souls. (Isaiah 60:1-5, Amos 9:13-15, Zechariah 2:10-12, Matthew 13:24-30, Mark 16:15-18, John 12:32-33, Acts 1:7-8)

Confirmation from Dr. Jonathan David:

Confirming what I saw in my dream, God revealed a similar vision of unity to Dr. Jonathan David, founder of Destiny Heights Ministry in Muar, Malaysia. (10.01) The following is the transcript of a message he delivered:

> "This generation will come together with new strength and new understanding. This generation will suddenly click together and connect. They will suddenly become committed to one another and covenanted one with the other. The power of God is going to cause a synergy and the power of one to become a reality.
>
> The Church will not be disintegrating or segregating. It is going to come together by the hand of God. I see the hand of God holding these people together and bringing them together. God is going to put brick upon brick and wall against wall. He's going to put pillars in between the walls. He's going to assemble a glorious body (of disciples).
>
> I see the Spirit of God bringing reformation and restoration. He is bringing reviving and refreshing and healing into the body of Christ. Churches everywhere are going to begin to come together. There's going to be a holding together,

framed together, fitted together, held together as one. That synergy is going to come about.

Conferences are going to be packed, standing room only, because there's going to be a hunger that is going to come because there is a famine everywhere. There is a famine for food and a famine for life and a famine everywhere for the things of God, the things of the spirit.

Churches are going to begin to break open in a powerful way as the ones that are hungry and thirsty come in. The ones who are desiring God are going to come in. They are going to come from everywhere, even from miles away, hours away. They're going to come to be where the food is provided.

A new breed of people is going to arise among us. A new company of people are going to be hungry for God. This company of people are coming from everywhere. I can hear their footsteps as they are running to the house of the Lord. I hear them saying, "Come let us go to the house of the Lord and there He will teach us of His ways."

These people are going to come to the house of the Lord with gladness. Pastors will have no more struggles with people. The people are going to gather together and strengthen their pastors. Our struggle is going to be against principalities, against powers in the high places. God will give us power to make our struggles no longer on the horizontal level. Pastors will not be struggling with members, members will not be struggling with pastors because they're going to gather together, be held together, be strengthened so they can struggle against principalities and powers and pull down the forces of darkness. That is why there's going to be a synergy and a love that is so real. There is going to be a level of commitment that is so true, a covenant that is so established and God will dwell with you!

For how good it is for brothers to dwell together in unity. The Lord will command his blessing. He will command his light in the place. Churches are going to begin to look this way and feel this way because a new sense of discipleship is going to come. No longer will we have disciples who are on their own. The membership inside the Church will suddenly click together. They will change. No longer will we have people who put themselves first and put Jesus last. These people will be coming to the house of God to make Jesus first and last, to make Him everything, large and small.

Remnant: Unity

No longer will there be a fear in our hearts because we will gather with His people and we will gather as one, as brothers and sisters with no malice between us. As our hearts become united together, the Lord will begin to dwell with us in an amazing way. At every service the Lord whom we seek will suddenly appear in the temple. The Lord whom we desire will suddenly manifest in the house because the people of God have become purer and purer, cleaner and cleaner. The people have been cleansed. They have been healed, delivered, and set free. This is what will attract the presence of God.

You're going to see the Church embrace a whole new community. It will be said that the Church has been born again. There's going to be a reinventing of the Church. A Church unusual is about to manifest among us. The Church is going to be so unusual that it is going to attract God's presence. The days of struggle are going to come to an end. There will no longer be struggle on the horizontal plane (between brothers and sisters in the Church) because God will begin to do this great work. That which was out of joint is going to be healed. That which was out of place is going to be put into place. That which was out of position, God is going to put it together. The body (of disciples) is going to be healed.

I can see God healing the Church in such a powerful way, bringing total restoration so that wholeness will come back to the house. When you look at people inside the house you're going to get so excited because it's going to be a new breed. You're going to be a new people. You are not struggling with them and they are not struggling with you. They are not struggling with God and they are not struggling with one another. They have total peace. So, God can put bone-to-bone and flesh-to-flesh. You will be able to look at that place and say, "This is the house of God!"

ENDNOTES

10.01: Dr. Jonathan David, http://www.jonathan-david.org/pages/about-destiny-heights/

11
Assignments

In a vision on January 26, 2016, I was in my basement standing next to a picnic table. On the table was a single large white feather, like an eagle feather. Then I saw an old Indian chief standing in front of me. On the floor in front of him was a carved black figure of an Indian chief, about two feet tall.

With one foot on the floor and his other foot on the bench, he leaned over with his arms resting on his knee and looked at me and said, "Whenever someone has been destined by God to be a chief, but fails to fulfill their destiny, that's a very big deal to God."

I just nodded in agreement but didn't say anything because I didn't know what to say. That was the end of the vision. I immediately understood it was not for me personally, so I wondered why God showed it to me. Then I just forgot about it and moved on, but a few hours later, I saw a new comment posted on Z3 News where someone mentioned how God had revealed something to them that was on His heart and I immediately remembered the Indian chief saying, "That's a very big deal to God."

Then I felt grieved because I realized God had shown me something very important to Him, but I had disregarded it as soon as I realized it was not for me personally. Like any parent, I believe God wants His children to grow up and realize everything is not always about us, so we can move up to the next level of beginning to understand what matters to Him because if He can get us to understand these things, He can capture our heart and bring us to a place of greater devotion to Him.

A couple of days later, God showed me the white feather contained a message within itself and was an important introduction to the main message given by the chief. God said to me,

> "I have something very important I want to share with you, but before I tell you, I want you to know the white feather is a reminder that My protective feathers will continue to cover you and under My wings you will continue to find refuge. My faithfulness will continue to be a shield for you. (Psalm 91:4) My peace will continue to guard your heart and your mind. (Philippians 4:7) My grace will

continue to be sufficient for you. (2 Corinthians 12:9) So, do not lose heart or give up hope because of what I am about to tell you."

So, the white feather was like a peace offering, as the Indians would call it, letting me know the message of the old chief meant no harm, but even though it was intended to motivate us, it could be de-motivating if we misunderstand it.

Then He revealed the black carved figure of an Indian chief represented someone God created to be a chief, but failed to fulfill his destiny. Since God created chiefs to sources of great light and hope for many people, when a chief fails to fulfill his destiny, it brings great darkness and disappointment, so the statue was black and low to the ground, requiring everyone to hang their head to look down to see it.

The next day, God gave me a dream to help me understand the chief's message. In this dream, I was part of a large group of people preparing for an important mission. Many different assignments were being given out to help complete our mission. I was especially interested in one that involved operating video cameras to film upcoming events because it's something I've always enjoyed doing, so I was excited about it, but it required two people because while one person filmed, the other was needed to help carry the equipment, maintain it, set it up, and things like that.

I was ready and eager to get started, but the lady who was supposed to be my partner was not ready and not sure if she would be able to handle it. When the time came to make the assignments, the leaders asked if my team was ready. Reluctantly, I told them we were not. I was hoping they would give us more time to get back to them when my partner was ready, but as soon as I told them we weren't ready, they immediately gave the assignment to another team.

The man who was given the job was one of my former bosses from many years ago. He's a very nice person, but not very knowledgeable about technical things, so I knew I was much better suited for the job than he was, but his partner was ready and mine wasn't, so they got the job.

Meanwhile, I was given a different assignment, a supporting role, looking for extra boxes of supplies and parts they might need for their mission. I watched them being trained and equipped with all sorts of great video equipment that I would have loved to learn about. My old friend was loaded with equipment as they were shown how to strap different kinds of gear to their arms and legs to support the cameras and carry the lenses and batteries. As I watched them being trained, I felt grieved, but it was too late. There was no second chance because it needed to be done right away.

Remnant: Assignments

I started working on my assignment, rummaging through some supplies looking for items they might need. I managed to find an extra box of light bulbs, so I went and asked my friend on the video team if he wanted me to pack these bulbs with their other supplies. As small as this task was, it was the most exciting thing I came across in my new assignment. When I asked him about it, he was engaged in a conversation with his partner and barely paid attention to what I was asking. He looked at me and said, "What did you want? Oh, yeah sure, extra bulbs, yeah just throw those in with the other boxes."

Then he turned his attention back to his conversation with his partner. I could tell they were both excited about what they were learning and eager to start filming. They had a great adventure ahead of them, so it was consuming their attention. It was obvious my role was far less important than theirs. I had missed a great opportunity and felt very disappointed. It was a very big deal to me. End of dream.

The group of people preparing for an important mission represents the righteous remnant who are now being prepared by God for their future forerunner assignments. Like the dream showed, it's a large mission, requiring many different assignments given to many different people.

I was especially interested in the video assignment because to me, it's more like playing than working, showing how the assignments God has planned for each of us are designed to make the most of our unique interests and abilities to do things we're passionate about doing. For example, my older brother has always had a passion for survival skills and weapons, even as a child, which was an area that never interested me. After he grew up, people tried to steer him into jobs where he could make good money, so he tried to follow their advice, but after a while, he realized his heart was somewhere else. So, he finally left all that behind and followed his passion to join the military at age 28 and immediately excelled in it because he enjoyed it so much. Dropping him off in a swamp in south Florida with nothing but a knife and a few pieces of survival gear was like throwing Brer Rabbit into the briar patch. He was right at home and happy as could be because he was doing what God made him to do. He passed all the most rigorous tests to qualify for the special forces, green berets, and airborne rangers. He became a sniper and a weapons expert, successfully completing many dangerous missions that others could not have done.

Even after leaving the military, he continued following his passion by working as a defense contractor, bodyguard, and traveling all over the world training people to defend themselves. Later, he started his own business making a unique barrel system that significantly increases the accuracy of long range sniper shots. When he talks about it, he sounds like he has a PhD in physics because he has studied every detail of how it works, all because he loves what he does.

It's amazing how God puts unique interests in each of us as part of His design for our life, woven into the fabric of who we are, so it's at the heart of His plan for our life. There's nothing worse than doing things we have no passion to do because we can't possibly be as effective as other people who are doing the same thing with all their heart. Doing the wrong assignment makes us less productive, which makes us less valuable to others and hurts our self-esteem when we realize we're not very good at what we're doing. Those are all indications we've followed the wrong direction and need to reconsider what we're doing.

Our passions are easy to find because they're things we love doing and talking about. We might have nothing to say about other things, but just get us talking about our favorite subject, our sweet spot, and we'll talk all day long, sharing great insights others failed to notice. Even the quietest people come to life, surprising others by their depth of knowledge and understanding. It's amazing how it lifts everything in us, bringing us to life, lifting our self-esteem, our confidence, our joy, and even our bank balances. It's the fruitful place given to us by God, where our life becomes a blessing to many others.

The most powerful part of a baseball bat is called the sweet spot because when the ball hits that spot, it flies out of the ballpark, home run! The crowds cheer, the batter pumps his fist in the air, his teammates celebrate, all because he connected with the sweet spot. There's life changing power in the sweet spot. We just need to find it and connect with it so we can release the power of it.

In my dream, I was eager and ready for the video assignment, but it required two people and my partner was not ready. It was not fair to me that I should miss my assignment just because my partner failed to prepare, but that's what happened, illustrating how our lives are connected to other people, so our choices have a direct impact on others and their choices have a direct impact on us. It was not fair to me, but I had to deal with the disappointment anyway. I knew I could have been more fruitful in that assignment than my old friend, but instead I was stuck with doing boring tasks. I missed the opportunity to function in my sweet spot all because of someone else's mistakes.

Things happen in our life which we have no control over. For example, we have no control over the family we're born into or even the nation we're born into or the year when we're born, but our life is directly impacted by how our parents raised us, by their wisdom or lack of wisdom, their character or lack of character, their knowledge or lack of knowledge, and to what extent they helped us discover and operate in our sweet spot. Even though our life was directly impacted by all those things, we had no say so in them. Those are just a few examples of the many things that can either propel us into fruitfulness and productivity or delay us by years or even decades while we try to sort it out and get on the right track.

While some people are still trying to sort things out, other people are excelling in their life because they were launched in the right direction from an early age, trained by parents who were actively involved and devoted to helping guide them and develop them to their fullest potential. For example, at age 30, Sean McVay became the youngest person to become a head football coach in the NFL. Yet, despite his youth, he has been very successful, being named AP Coach of the Year in his first season and taking his team to the Super Bowl in his second season. (11.01) None of that happened by chance though. His father and grandfather were both very involved in football. His grandfather, John McVay, was general manager for the San Francisco 49ers, helping them win five Super Bowls.

It's rare to see people achieve such success so young because most of us don't have that level of guidance coinciding with our sweet spot. So, we try different things and watch the years pass by with very little fruit produced as we continue searching for what God created us to do. We endure setbacks that weren't our fault, but we can't go back and change the past. All we can do is try to make the right choices for the future, putting us in position to make the most of the opportunities still ahead of us.

In the vision, I saw the feather even before I saw the chief. Later, God revealed the meaning of the feather before He revealed the meaning of the old Indian chief's message. The feather came first to show God wanted to make sure the chief's message caused no harm. No matter what happened in our past, we always have the white feather, God's covering of protection, where we can find refuge from any kind of trouble or disappointment. (Psalm 91:4) No setbacks, disappointments, or circumstances can ever take away His peace, which guards our heart and our mind, or His grace, which will always be more than enough for us. (2 Corinthians 12:9, Philippians 4:7) He has promised He will never leave us or abandon us, so no matter what happens, we always have hope for the future and good reasons to continue without losing heart or giving up. (John 14:18, Hebrews 13:5)

These kinds of setbacks can slow us down as we require more time to reach our full potential, but if we just stay on His path, walking in His ways, He can fulfill His promise to make us blossom and sprout, shooting straight up like a palm tree, fruitful and flourishing, planted in His house, growing like a cedar in Lebanon, which reaches about 130 feet (40 meters) and stays green year around. (Psalm 92:12-13, Proverbs 11:28)

Remnant: Assignments

Some of the most magnificent trees are the ones that take the longest to grow because they require stronger and deeper roots to support their enormous size. For example, oak trees take about 50 years to reach maturity, but even then, they're still just getting started, sometimes living 500 to 600 years. (11.02, 11.03)

Although we might require more time than others, we still have the opportunity to become something beautiful, oaks of righteousness. (Isaiah 61:3) If we still have breath in our body, it's not too late to get on track, becoming all God created us to be. Our latter years can still bear much fruit, helping many people and bringing great glory to God.

God is a turnaround specialist. He's been turning things around for His people for thousands of years and He's still doing it today. He makes everything in our life work together for good, if we will just do our part by obeying His commandments. (Romans 8:28, 1 John 5:2)

In the dream, the damage caused by my partner's failure was limited and mostly just impacted me. I was struggling to continue, but the overall mission was not compromised. The video job was still getting done, although it could have been done better by someone with greater passion for it. My partner's failure also impacted my old boss who was given the assignment because he was struggling to do a task for which he had very little aptitude, which shows assignments are not always given to the most qualified or most skilled, but to those who are willing and available. God might give us assignments on that same basis, even though we're not His first choice or even His second or third.

The damage would have been much worse if my partner was destined by God to be a chief because the impact of her failure would have hurt many more people and might have even jeopardized the whole mission, putting more lives in danger of going into eternal darkness, which is why the old Indian chief described it as a very big deal to God."

The chief's statement reveals God has not destined everyone to be a chief, which makes sense because it requires unique skills, so it requires people who are uniquely designed by God with those skills. If everyone was destined to be a chief, all the other assignments would suffer because chiefs don't have the gifts or the passion required to do those other tasks effectively, so the success of the overall mission depends on each of us doing what God created us to do, not trying to be anything else.

The old chief's message was intended to motivate us by helping us see how our life has a direct impact on others with a ripple effect in every choice we make, so we can have a higher purpose for living that goes beyond our own life. Even though a chief's life impacts more people than others, we all make an impact on others because our lives are all connected, like the parts of a body. Every part directly impacts other parts, making the whole body either stronger or weaker. (Romans 12:4-5) For example, if we choose to walk uprightly before God, He promises our children will never have to seek for food or beg for bread. (Psalm 37:25) Instead, they will be strong, mighty and courageous in the earth, never cut off or destroyed. (Psalm 112:2, Isaiah 48:18-19) And He will show mercy not only to our children, but also our grandchildren. (Psalm 103:17-18) Even though our children did nothing to qualify for that promise, they receive benefits from choices we made, even long lasting benefits that continue after we've departed from this life.

The flip side of it is also true. If we fail to walk uprightly, we fail to qualify for the promises of God that would have benefited our children. So, the chief's message exposes a popular lie that says it's perfectly okay to live any way we want, practicing any kind of unrighteous lifestyle we want, because we're not hurting anyone else, but the truth is, if we fail to prepare ourselves for God's plan for our life by failing to pass our tests and trials, straying off the path of righteousness, we won't be ready for our assignment when it comes, so it must be given to whoever is available, even if they lack the talents the job requires, so the mission is hindered, limping along, far from optimal and possibly even derailed. And if our assignment included partners, our failure could cause them to miss their assignments at no fault of their own, like what happened to me in this dream.

The chief's message also confirms the word God gave me in my prayer time, which I shared in chapter six, "This is not about you. What you are going through now is not about you. You are going through it for someone else."

Even though we cannot see the bigger picture, our choices have implications that go way beyond our life. So, if we can't seem to find a good enough reason to stay on the path of righteousness for our own sake, hopefully we can do it for the sake of the people we love, perhaps our children, our grandchildren, other family members, our friends, and even for the sake of people we might never meet in this life, but we lay down our life for them because their life is a very big deal to God.

Sudden Assignments:

Missing my video assignment shows the urgency with which God's assignments will be made, just like He instructed the Israelites to stay ready when He was delivering them out of bondage in Egypt. They endured many years of slavery, but when the time came to bring them out, He did it suddenly. When they ate their Passover meal, He instructed them, "And thus you shall eat it: with a belt on your waist, your sandals on your feet, and your staff in your hand. So you shall eat it in haste. It is the Lord's Passover." (Exodus 12:11 NKJV)

The ministries of Elijah and John the Baptist both began suddenly. Elijah suddenly appears in the scriptures without any introduction, standing before the king of Israel, speaking with the authority of God, claiming there will be no more rain until he says so, and it happened exactly as he said. (1 Kings 17:1, 18:41) In the same way, John was unknown by his generation because he lived in the wilderness, hidden by God until he appeared suddenly, boldly proclaiming the message of repentance. (Matthew 3:7-9, Mark 6:17-18) He seemed to come out of nowhere, so the Israelites asked him, "Who are you?" (John 1:19-25)

As forerunners, I believe their sudden appearances are prophetic signs pointing to the One who has remained hidden from the world for nearly 2,000 years, but will suddenly appear, like a thief in the night. (1 Kings 17:1, 2 Kings 2:11, Malachi 3:1, Luke 1:80, 1 Thessalonians 5:2-4) In the same way, their sudden appearances illustrate how the spirit and power of Elijah will suddenly come upon a new generation of forerunners, seemingly out of nowhere, because God has purposely kept His remnant army hidden for a season. In His perfect timing, He will suddenly give them their new assignments, even putting them before people of great influence, even kings, to deliver His messages, display His wisdom and demonstrate His power. (Isaiah 22:22, 60:3)

I saw these sudden promotions illustrated in a dream on April 29, 2017. In the dream, there was a sudden turn of events, which caused me to be in Washington DC where I was sworn into office as Vice-President of the United States. I was not seeking the position, but somehow it was suddenly given to me. After the swearing-in ceremony, I saw some of my cousins outside on the White House lawn where they were joining in the celebration, playing and having a good time, but I didn't see any members of my immediate family, so I was not sure if my mother heard the news yet, so I called her and said, "Mama, I was offered the position of Vice-President of the United States."

She replied, "Well, I hope you never take it because you never were good at public speaking."

I replied, "It can't be too hard because all you have to do is read the teleprompter. Besides, it's too late anyway because I've already been sworn into office."

She replied in disbelief, "What? You've already been sworn in???"

I answered, "Yes mama, I am now the Vice-President of the United States." End of dream.

Obviously, I am not expecting this to happen literally, but I believe it shows God's plans to give sudden important assignments to His remnant, seemingly out of nowhere, just like Elijah and John. Since the Vice President is second-in-command of the United States, I believe this dream shows God's plans to raise up modern-day Joseph's, the son of Israel, who was suddenly promoted from prison to second-in-command to the Pharaoh of Egypt. (Genesis 41:40-41) I believe God has been preparing many people for assignments like Joseph, sending them ahead of their brethren to make provision for them during a coming time of famine. (Genesis 45:4-8, Revelation 12:14)

In December 2017, God revealed this same sense of urgency to Pastor Henry Falcone, founder of Flame of Fire Ministry. (11.04) He saw God's end time army receiving sudden assignments, like the minute men of the American Revolutionary War who heard the church bells ringing, and immediately dropped their farming chores, picked up their muskets and assembled as a militia, ready to fight the British. (11.05) Through all these examples, I believe God is warning us to make the most of every day and every opportunity because His assignments are coming suddenly to those who are ready and willing.

Preparation for Assignments:

Before the Lord returns, He's going to demonstrate His power, helping many people to believe in Him, but that kind of power requires first priming the pump. Spiritual power works a lot like physical power because neither happens randomly. Power must be generated, as shown in simple physics. For example, baseball pitchers don't throw 100-mile-per-hour fastballs from an idle position. They start by priming the pump with a wind-up process, rocking back and forth, swinging their arms all the way up and all the way back, moving the ball in the opposite direction, farther away from the plate, but that wind-up process is where all the power comes from. By the time the ball is finally released, there's so much power behind it, it blows past the batter before he can even see it. Zoom!

Priming a water pump works the same way. Drawing water up out of the ground requires power greater than the power of the gravity holding it down, but the power must first be generated by a process of priming the pump, cranking it up and down again and again and again and again until finally power begins to flow, starting with just enough to pull some water into the pipes, but then suddenly, the priming is finished and the water comes forth with power that was not there before. I believe God wants us to know today, the long season of priming the pump is soon coming to an end and much water is about to come forth.

The forerunners of our generation are destined to take down giants, but giants don't just fall because we politely ask them. They only fall when they're confronted with power greater than their own. So, God has been preparing us for that kind of power, just like He prepared David to take down Goliath. Even when all the men of Israel were afraid of Goliath, David was not afraid because he had already primed his faith pump by taking down the lion and the bear, so when he looked at Goliath, he already knew he had the power to take him down, saying, "For who is this uncircumcised Philistine, that he should defy the armies of the living God?" (1 Samuel 17:26b NKJV)

By faith, David told King Saul, "The Lord, who delivered me from the paw of the lion and from the paw of the bear, He will deliver me from the hand of this Philistine." (1 Samuel 17:37 NKJV)

Once the power of faith started flowing in David, it came bubbling up from his inner man, flowing from his heart, empowering him to know it was as good as done, even though by all appearances it was completely impossible. Once it started flowing, he just released it through his words and then through his hands as he slung his stone, striking and taking down Goliath. From there, it was easy to cut off his head, but it all started when no one else was watching and no one else cared to hear about the exploits of a shepherd boy because they didn't see God was priming the pump for a far greater demonstration of power. Even though they didn't see it coming, it happened and it will be remembered forever.

Like the Israelites were unable to see the significance of the exploits of a shepherd boy, we can lose sight of God's plan and purpose for our life, making it seem like a long series of random events and trials with no end destination, but I believe God wants us know He has a greater purpose for all of it. Though we can't see it yet, He has never taken His eyes off our destination because it is so significant, it will be remembered forever. Every trial we've endured has been preparing us for our most unique assignments in this most unique time. God has been orchestrating events in our life, even in those times when it appeared we were way off course, dead in the water, like we had blown it beyond repair, again, but it was all part of the necessary preparation process to bring forth the power to demonstrate His master workmanship. The power we will need then is being generated now, and it will soon come forth in our inner man where we will release it through our words as a demonstration for others to see.

Remnant: Assignments

On January 29, 2017, Rev Susan O'mara shared the following confirming word from God showing how He is preparing us for our assignments by teaching us to abide in Him. She and her husband Patrick are pastors of The Salvation of God Church in Rochester NY.

> "Do not think that I have laid you by the side. I have been teaching you to deeply abide because there is a pace and a stride in which I will instruct and guide. And as you walk by My side together with Me, you all will turn the tide of the battle that is going to come quickly. Because you are My choice weapons in the earth and I have tailored you for specific things, so do not think that you must wait a long time.
>
> Do not be frustrated in your preparation and in the portion that you think you have right now. All these things are preparation for where I am taking you in the months and weeks and years ahead. You are My champions of dread, you are champions, you are fierce weapons in My hand. But You must understand the fullness of My plan. And you must take your stand together. And you must stand ready in My hand." (11.06)

Stretch Assignments:

In a dream I received on June 19, 2016, a man escorted me into a wide-open field in a large valley. In the center of the field at the lowest point of the valley was a large, flat, solid rock about one-foot high and about fifty feet across. We stepped up onto it and looked around in all directions at the rolling green hills on all sides.

Then I saw very large crowds of people gathering, way too many to count, many thousands. Many of them were seated on the ground while more were just arriving and finding places to sit, but even as they got situated, their eyes stayed focused intently on us like they didn't want to miss anything, even though we were just standing there doing nothing. They were hungry to receive, so their faith created an atmosphere of great expectation that we were about to give them an important message.

When I saw this, I was concerned and perplexed because I knew I was not the kind of person that should be on a stage of any kind. I was sure they were gathering to hear someone else. So, I turned to the man who had escorted me there and told him, "I think there must be a mistake because I don't belong here."

He didn't say anything. He just turned and looked at the crowds and pointed to them in all directions. Then he directed me to also turn and look all around, 360 degrees. For as far as my eyes could see, multitudes and multitudes of people were all looking at us, waiting eagerly to hear. That was the end of the dream.

I believe the man who escorted me was the Holy Spirit because I never saw His face, which is how He often appears in dreams. The platform made of solid rock represents the Word of God, the foundation for all our messages. I felt there was a mistake made because speaking to a crowd is way out of my comfort zone. Words have always escaped me when I've needed them, so I wanted to find the exit, but we were surrounded.

This dream reveals the assignments God will soon be giving His remnant army of forerunners will stretch our faith by putting us in positions that require more talents, gifts, and abilities than we possess, leaving us no choice but to cry out to Him for help. (Luke 12:11-12) The same point was illustrated in my remnant dream with me being one of the speakers. As He has done many times in the past, God is again going to use the weak things to demonstrate His power and the foolish things to demonstrate His wisdom, so everyone can see only He could have done it. (1 Corinthians 1:26-29, 2 Corinthians 12:9) For example, He instructed Gideon to pare down his army from 32,000 men to just 300, even though they were going against a far larger army of Midianites. He explained to Gideon, "The people who are with you are too many for Me to give the Midianites into their hands, lest Israel claim glory for itself against Me, saying, 'My own hand has saved me.'" (Judges 7:2 NKJV)

Surely many of those who turned back from Gideon's army were stronger, faster, and smarter than the 300 who remained, but God used those who were small in numbers, but great in faith, to demonstrate His power so everyone would know the victory came from Him alone. There is no other explanation for their victory, just as there will be no other explanation for ours.

Assignments Have Begun:

On January 22, 2019, Julie Whedbee received a vision in which she saw end time assignments being given to each of us individually. The assignments were primarily to lead, guide, teach and direct others. Her vision confirms the urgency of the times and the importance of being ready. Julie is founder of Behold I Come Blog. (11.07)

In the vision, Julie saw the Throne Room of God and the Council of Elders wearing white robes and crowns, removing scrolls from ornate containers with each scroll containing a personal assignment for someone. Then she saw us rising all over the world to receive our scrolls, wearing white garments. As we received our assignments, we also received an impartation of power and authority to carry it out. She saw us operating as One in Spirit from our strategic locations around the world and each of us covered in a column of light, connecting us to the Father's Glory. Then she heard the Lord speak this word:

> "What is written on your scroll is your end-time assignment. I am revealing this now to all who are completely walking with Me, fully surrendered, obedient and faithful.
>
> Daughter, for those who have ears to hear, for those who have readied their hearts, for those who have given Me all and are in full surrender and obedience; I have drawn you into My Courtyard, into the gates, where I have given you much insight and revelation as to these times that you live in.
>
> I am gathering together a people, My chosen first-fruits remnant. You My chosen ones will lead and guide, teach and minister. For as I your Great Shepherd have taught you, My sheep; so I have taught you to follow My commands and follow My example, and feed My sheep. In this way, I have set you as shepherds for My flock, in that you in Me and I in you will draw many souls to Me.
>
> Be ready as I am moving you into these positions now! Understand this mystery, when I said in My Word that you would do these things and more, what I am speaking of is a glorified life, yet still here in the flesh. To attain the maturity of a true, mature son or daughter; these ones are the ones who understand that the day at Calvary, when I spoke that it was finished, and the victory won--meant that you too can live that glorified life here and now. Everything that was attained that day belongs to you now, and always has. It was done that day.
>
> The day has finally come when all that has been foretold in My Word will come true. All that you have read about these last days is upon you. You are the last generation and you will see My return. I have told you this before, so rejoice that the mysteries of the prophets of the past are now being revealed. Everything that I spoke when I spoke with Daniel and with John, it is meant for you now. All the secrets of My Kingdom you will know, and all of Heaven rejoices that the culmination of all things is here!" (11.07)

God's Special Forces:

In December 2017, God gave Pastor Henry Falcone, founder of Flame of Fire Ministries, many insights regarding the assignments He has for His remnant army in the days ahead, confirming what I saw in the remnant dream. He saw us being sent out like God's special forces, strategically deployed to different places to accomplish specific assignments, including praying, spying, and special operations. The following is an excerpt from what he shared.

> "A new day is here. A new hour has come. His awakening kingdom servants are arising to take their place. We are now witnessing the arising of God's army upon the earth under the government of the Kingdom of God. This army is under the final authority of King Jesus as King of Kings and Lord of Lords over the whole earth. We are now coming into a divine alignment and divine assignments, which our King desires to be released upon the earth. Many are now going to hear His clarion call and shofar blast to be stationed exactly where He wants them to be for His end time purpose. For those who are willing, some saints will be required to change geographic locations and move to be fitted with the other body parts, which they were made to be connected.
>
> Some will be sent out like special forces to pray, spy out, and do special ops in the spirit, working for the Lord in designated areas. Some will be sent out like marines to establish spiritual beach heads in cities and regions to continue to transform the spiritual atmosphere over regions and spoil principalities and powers. They will make a way for the spiritual infantry to come in and take the land to bring in the end time harvest.
>
> As I received this word, I felt the key thing the Spirit of God was impressing on my heart was that no one will be alone anymore. These dry bones shall live!
>
> So many of the sons and daughters whom God is about to activate and send out have been alone and hidden. They only know how to function alone with the Lord. So, the new will require them to learn how to be fitted and knitted together with those God has ordained them to be with. That will take great patience and love to do as God brings them together for extended purposes. It is why God separated them in the first place. He desires to remove all selfish motive, desires, competition, striving, driving, jealousy out of their hearts.
>
> His intention was to make them His "own ones," ready to do his will, filled with the pure, holy, love of God that will allow them to be knitted together and esteem the other better than themselves.
>
> His full-grown sons and daughters are now going to form into the army of the Lord. They will join with King Jesus and the armies of heaven and together will

transform the earth. Now is the moment when God is beginning to knit them together with the correct body parts they were ordained to be with. He is putting them in the right place and at the right time to function together as one holy and unified people. His pure holy love is going to knit them together with Him and then one another like we have never seen before. True love will fill each part as they become the living breathing bride of the Lord, the Body of Christ on the earth.

There will be a real and pure holy love for each other, care for each other, help for each other, and a laying down of their lives for each other just like a military unit would do. They shall be known as "God's Spiritual Band of Brothers." They will stick together, fight together, love together, forgive together, and give to each other as God would have. They will be one people, one unit, forming one holy nation on the earth under one Commander in Chief, Jesus. The world will finally see we are His disciples by the true, pure, holy, love we will have one for the other.

I believe as that true spiritual war is now breaking out on earth, God is birthing His army and positioning them to defeat the evil one. Some are now being called to move and be positioned in new places geographically. Some will be go forth as "awakening Kingdom servants or spiritual minute men" to go to many places to stay there for a season to join forces with those in that region. Together, they will be sent to prepare a way for the Lord by changing the spiritual atmosphere over towns, cities, states, regions and nations. As they obey the Lord, they will open the heavens in pure worship and true intercession in those regions. They will open the door for the rest of the army to come forth and do their work for the advancement of the transformation of their regions with the Kingdom of God.

Then the Lord had me focus clearly on the army until I saw the different regiments, divisions, and companies He had put together. The roar of Jesus was working differently in each part of the army. I saw different divisions or companies that were brought to stand before the Lord to receive new specific instructions, battle plans, and weapons, given to be released and sent to different places upon the earth. These weapons were still highlighted and glowing with the glory of the Lord, the perfect weapons needed to change the regions of the world they were sent to.

Within these divisions, regiments, and companies, the Lord showed me smaller groups of warriors formed as spiritual brigades, which were being outfitted with new, straight from heaven, battle gear from the Lord, enabling them to do the "trench warfare' with the Lord to destroy the enemy's strongholds in those areas.

The release of these new assignments and placements by the Lord are about to change the nations of the earth, but the changes will come in a very hidden and secret way. As His army is released to complete their missions, they will release the tornado force winds of the Holy Spirit wherever they go. These winds will be filled with the glory and power of God that will bring the greatest change the nations have ever seen. The Glory of the Lord will fill all the earth." (11.08)

ENDNOTES

11.01: Sean McVay, https://en.wikipedia.org/wiki/Sean_McVay

11.02: Oak trees, https://www.wildflower.org/expert/show.php?id=4799

11.03: Oak trees live 500 to 600 years, https://homeguides.sfgate.com/life-expectancy-red-oak-tree-74474.html

11.04: Pastor Henry Falcone, Flame of Fire Ministries, https://www.flameoffire2007.org

11.05: Pastor Henry Falcone, God's Spiritual Band of Brothers, https://z3news.com/w/gods-spiritual-band-of-brothers/

11.06: Rev Susan O'mara, Assignments Made for You, https://z3news.com/w/assignments-made-for-you/

11.07: Julie Whedbee, Behold I Come, End Time Assignments, https://iamcallingyounow.blogspot.com/

11.08: Pastor Henry Falcone, I have released My roar out of Zion, https://z3news.com/w/released-roar-zion/

12
Training

In a dream on November 30, 2014, I saw end time disciples growing in faith as we encouraged each other and helped train each other to operate in the powers of the age to come. We were being trained to do greater works than Jesus did, just as He said we would. (John 14:12) For training purposes, we were separated into three groups based on our level of spiritual development. In the first group, everyone was sitting. In the second group, everyone was walking, but in the third group, everyone was flying.

The first group had far more people than either of the other two groups. They were all sitting on the side of a grassy hill, relaxing and looking around, like they were waiting for something to happen, so they remained idle. They were all Christians, so they were interested in the things of God, but they weren't actively seeking to grow or advance because they were content where they were and unwilling to risk losing their most valuable possessions, which were sitting on the ground next to them, just as idle as they were, not being used for anything.

The second group was also a large number of people, but not as large as the first group. They were all walking or at least slowly shuffling along, on their way to a big tall house. Many of them had already entered and were making their way through the many levels of the house. Each level contained different projects and stations where they had to complete tasks before they could move up to the next level. A large crowd of them shuffled through, attempting to complete these various tasks, but their progress was slow because the tasks could only be completed by operating in the powers of the age to come. So, the faster they learned how to do that, the faster they could advance. Everyone was advancing at their own pace, but most were moving slowly because they relied too much on their own understanding, so they weren't open to receive from the Holy Spirit or follow His leading.

Inside the house, when the walkers saw someone completing their task, they would all ooh and ahh in amazement. So, they were encouraging and motivating each other and causing their faith to grow. Some of them were so encouraged by what they saw others doing, they followed their example and began to step out and operate in it themselves.

Remnant: Training

The third group was very small, especially in the beginning. Everyone in this group could fly, which included me. I flew over a crowd of walkers as they were walking towards the house and I saw their faces as they looked up at me. Their eyes and their whole face lit up as they gasped with amazement. They could hardly believe what they were seeing, but it caused their faith to soar and some of them believed they could do it too.

I saw some of the flyers flying through all the levels of the house right over the heads of the walkers, easily completing all the tasks required by their stations, flying very fast past each of them, like they only had to zoom by and it was all done without even slowing down. They flew through all the levels within a few seconds and right out of a window at the top level. It was very easy for them because they had learned to be led by the Spirit. The walkers were encouraged when they saw the flyers completing these tasks so easily and it stirred up greater hunger in them to learn more, which caused them to advance faster through the levels.

As I flew over a group of walkers, I saw an old friend of mine who is now the pastor of a church. He was still walking and had not yet learned to fly so I encouraged him to step out and start flying. He was a little slow getting started, but he caught on and started flying very low to the ground. Other flyers were doing the same thing, encouraging the others until eventually there were lots of people flying. All it required was to believe and step out in faith. Later, I saw the whole sky filled with flyers.

I flew over to the first group of people sitting idle on the hill and sat down next to one couple and encouraged them to at least use their money to help others advance God's kingdom. I only encouraged them and did not try to force them and they agreed. Other flyers were doing the same thing, so the flyers were plundering the wealth of the sitters, not for selfish gain, but for the Kingdom's purposes.

At every level, we were all learning more and more about how to operate in the powers of the age to come, but the training was also personalized to prepare us and equip us for our own unique assignments. At every level, our biggest challenge was learning to trust more what we heard in our heart than what we saw and heard with our physical eyes and ears, so we had to learn to rely totally on the voice of the Lord leading us in our heart while tuning out any voices speaking words that contradicted His words.

As I continued my personal training, the exercises became progressively more challenging. First, I learned to hear His voice and obey, but then I encountered a challenge in doing it with the right timing, which totally threw me for a loop at first. I made lots of mistakes before I started learning to wait for the Lord's timing. In some cases, I got frustrated and even angry.

Remnant: Training

Whenever I successfully completed an exercise, the training advanced to a higher level requiring greater discernment to distinguish more subtle differences between what the Lord was saying and what I was hearing from others. At first, it sounded like the Lord was saying the same thing others were saying, but on closer examination I saw very slight but important differences.

The hardest task I was given was when the word of the Lord seemed to contradict other words from the Lord, but it only seemed that way since He never contradicts Himself. It reminded me of how God promised Abraham He was going to give him descendants through Isaac, as numerous as the stars, but then He told Abraham to offer Isaac as a human sacrifice. Those two words sound contradictory, but Abraham passed the test because he understood God would never break His promise even if He had to raise Isaac from the dead. (Genesis 22:2) Passing this test required a higher level of trusting and obeying because it seemed to make no sense at all, so in all these exercises, we were learning not to rely on our own understanding. (Proverbs 3:5)

Then the scene changed and I was with a small group of disciples riding in a vehicle that was transporting us from earth to heaven. It resembled a small subway train on the inside, but I never saw it from the outside. Some of the people riding with me came from earth while others had already died and were already residents of heaven. In the same way that God was permitting us to visit heaven, He was permitting them to interact with us as we were all working together to complete our own unique assignments because we were all part of the same mission. Many of us riding this vehicle were interacting with these residents of heaven.

My dad was riding with me on this vehicle. He died in 2009 when he was 76 years old, but in this dream, he looked like he was about 25 years old. I was so excited to share with him the great things God was doing in my life that I forgot to ask him about all he had seen since he had arrived in heaven. Surely he had seen many great things and wanted to share them. The dream ended before we arrived in heaven, but I understood all this going back and forth between heaven and earth was part of our training.

The first group was seated with their possessions beside them, representing all their God-given talents and the financial resources He had supplied them, which were just as idle as they were. Since they were ignoring His commands to draw near to Him, to ask of Him, to seek Him, to hunger and thirst for more of His Kingdom and His righteousness, they weren't receiving the wisdom and understanding they so desperately needed, so they remained in darkness, confusion and deception, which is why they were complacent and content to wait for God to do something, not realizing He had already done everything and given them everything they needed, including all the truth and power needed to break out of their idle condition. (Matthew 7:7-8, James 4:8) So, they were squandering their life, failing to fulfill His plans and purposes, wasting their time going nowhere and doing nothing of any eternal value. (Matthew 5:6, 6:33)

The walkers consisted of all those who were hungry for more, not content to remain sitting, so they were moving forward in their relationship with God, seeking Him and growing in wisdom. Some were walking faster than others, but all of them were being delayed from flying by their reliance on their own understanding, which made them unwilling to step out in faith, trusting God with childlike faith. The different stations and levels of the house provided them with opportunities to refine their skills and grow in faith, so they were continuing to move forward.

There was nothing special about the flyers. We had only learned to fly because were hungrier for more of God than the sitters and walkers, not content with what we had, so we sought Him more earnestly and learned to hear His voice more clearly than those who were not seeking Him as much. We were not holding tightly to what we had, like the sitters were doing, because we did not regard our lives as anything worth holding onto, like we had already lost everything and had nothing left to lose, which made us more willing to step out in faith, doing what He told us to do, which was the key to flying. Our reliance on the unseen realm of God enabled us to see beyond the natural realm, so we were no longer confined by it, but we still had lots to learn.

The rapid growth in the number of flyers showed the acceleration in spiritual growth coming in our generation. Just as the world is rapidly descending into darkness, the righteous are entering a time of accelerated growth in our faith with large numbers of people learning to soar in the heavenly realm as we come together in unity, helping each other. I did not see any strife, competition, envy, jealousy or division. We were all working together, helping each other to continue advancing in faith, so that by itself was a big step in the right direction.

There were different levels of flyers just as there were different levels of walkers, as shown by my old friend who stepped out and started flying. At first, he stayed close to the ground until he gained more confidence. Even as the flyers were still learning, our faith encouraged both the sitters and walkers to step out in faith, but it was much easier to help the walkers than the sitters because they were already hungry for more. Just a quick fly over was all it took to greatly encourage the walkers, but the sitters required more effort, taking time to sit down with them and talk with them individually to persuade them to at least use their resources for God, but with so many of them, there weren't enough flyers to reach all of them, so most of them were left on their own where they were content to remain.

Remnant: Training

Learning to distinguish very subtle differences in what the Lord was saying reminded me of something I said many years ago at a home fellowship group. The leader asked each of us to share the desires of our heart, specifically what we wanted God to do in our life. When it was my turn, I said I wanted to be so close to Him that He wouldn't even have to tell me what He wanted me to do because if He just looked at me a certain way, I would already know what He meant. I didn't even know what I was asking, but since He has promised if we delight ourselves in Him, He will give us the desires of our heart, I believe He started training me to receive the discernment I desired, which only comes by much practice and often includes making mistakes along the way. (Hebrews 5:14) I've made lots of them so even after many years I still have a long way to go to get to the level I described, but thank God He continues to bear with us when we don't catch on right away. He must be grading on the curve because otherwise I would have flunked out a long time ago. That's what He did with Gideon when he was struggling to believe any of God's promises. Yet, the angel of the Lord appeared to him saying, "The Lord is with you, you mighty man of valor!" (Judges 6:12-13) Might man of valor? Really? Then the Lord told him, "Go in this might of yours, and you shall save Israel from the hand of the Midianites. Have I not sent you?" (Judges 6:14) This might of yours? What might? Gideon was the least of the least, the most unlikely candidate, but he passed the test and won a great victory because he was willing to follow God's instructions by faith even when it contradicted his own understanding. (Judges 7:1-8:28)

The vehicles transporting us back and forth from earth to heaven were just another level of training, learning from those who were already residents of heaven. Just as the number of flyers continued increasing until we were filling the sky, so did the number of those riding in the vehicles. I believe this shows more heavenly visits are coming in the days ahead as more and more people will be caught up to receive more advanced training, which they can share with others to encourage them. (Revelation 12:5)

Seeing my dad and the other residents of heaven showed their involvement in what's happening here on earth, which is something we don't hear much about, but this dream shows it will become increasingly revealed to us in the days ahead. This kind of interaction is scriptural as shown by Moses and Elijah visiting with Jesus at His transfiguration. Peter, James, and John were also there with Him and they also saw Moses and Elijah. (Matthew 17:1-8) Other examples include the great cloud of heavenly witnesses, cheering us on and the great army riding on white horses and wearing fine linen following the Lord Jesus during heaven's coming invasion of earth. (Hebrews 12:1, Revelation 19:14) Even after we depart from this life, God still has assignments for His over-comers to complete on earth, as shown by the promise Jesus made, saying, "And he who overcomes, and keeps My works until the end, to him I will give power over the nations. He shall rule them with a rod of iron." (Revelation 2:26-27 NKJV) These assignments will continue long after He returns as we will rule with Him on earth for one thousand years. (Revelation 20:4-6)

Will we literally fly? Well, why not? The Prophet Isaiah asked, "Who are these who fly like a cloud and like the doves to their lattices?" (Isaiah 60:8) Some have claimed he was referring to angels, but if so, it would not fit the context of the chapter, which is all about end time disciples. Someone even claimed he was referring to sailboats, but sailboats don't fly like clouds or doves. Those are both things we see in the sky. So, I believe Isaiah saw end time disciples flying, either in the spirit or perhaps even physically, which is mind-blowing, but maybe we need to have our minds blown since my dream showed we were relying too much on our own understanding.

Jesus said, "All things are possible to those who believe." (Mark 9:23) I looked up the meaning of the Greek word, "pas", and sure enough, it means all, so His promise is only limited by our inability to believe what He puts in our heart more than our own understanding. (Proverbs 3:5-6)

New Trainees:

Putting the flying dream in the context of the remnant dream shows large numbers of the trainees will be young people, teenagers and young adults. I believe they will move quickly through the levels of training because of their strong hunger for God.

Generation Z is already showing signs of being something special. They are unlike any previous generation because they're the first to grow up with the Internet and all the electronic devices for accessing it, giving them increased exposure to knowledge, which has helped them learn and develop faster than any previous generation. In addition, they're making smarter choices. Not only are they far more likely to attend church than previous generations, as shared in chapter seven, but they're 40% less likely to get pregnant, 38% less likely to abuse drugs, and 28% less likely to drop out of school than the previous generation. (12.01) All that, and they're just getting started.

Researchers cannot explain why Generation Z is bypassing many of the pitfalls of previous generations, but it appears God has saved His best for last, fulfilling the parable of the landowner who paid first the workers he hired last before the others who had worked longer, making the last first and the first last. (Matthew 20:1-16)

In my dream, I took some of them aside to help train them:

> "At one point, I left the main meeting place to go into another area to pray and seek the Lord. A few of the young people came with me because I was mentoring them, helping them to understand how I prayed and sought the Lord."

I believe this kind of training will help accelerate their growth as the rest of us share our insights with them, helping them learn in a short time what took us much longer. Because of their youth, they will need training, guidance and direction, but God has already promised to satisfy anyone who hungers and thirsts for righteousness, so He will do the same for them. (Matthew 5:6) Having so few years of experience, young people often find it challenging to put things into proper perspective. Little problems can get magnified in their eyes, making it hard for them to see any way around them, so they can get stuck, but I believe my dream showed God is going to give them spiritual mothers and fathers to help them overcome those challenges and stay on track. Sometimes, all it takes is a short word of encouragement, or perhaps a short prayer or even just a big hug.

The late Prophet Bob Jones saw this training role coming for the over-50 generation. He shared the following message at a MorningStar Advanced Prophetic Conference in February 2013.

> "One thing is you have the wisdom of failures behind you. You know what not to do. How many years would that save the youth? So, I think you are a mercy and a grace to the youth. For you need to keep your hand on the pulse of what they are going to do and not let them fail where you have seen it fail before.
>
> I don't see where he is going to let the enemy come in and bring a failure against this, for the youth are going to go and you have been in it long enough and matured that you know which voice you hear. I don't think the enemy is going to be able to deceive you or misguide you because at different times we have gone in the wrong direction. But by doing that, you will not do it again. I don't see you going after a mirage anymore because I think you've gone after a mirage long enough in your life. When you go after a mirage, you are usually chasing after something for yourself and your selfish ambition. You go into the desert after a mirage while the real city you see is behind you. The mirage you see in front of you is death.
>
> Also, if you check it out, you will find that most of the money is with the over 50's. You control most of that. Some of you, in your giving, you're going to receive a lot more to give and you are going to have the wisdom of the father in

knowing what to do in financial matters. I think one of the things is you will buy a lot of hot dogs and toilet paper for those that are youth. They are going to need them. They don't require that much, but youth are going to break forth and you are going to break forth first.

I think what the Lord is talking about here is many of you have been faithful to the Lord for many years. I think you were getting ready for the disciples to come forth with power. This is what I believe God is doing in the body of Christ. He is raising up disciples that will go forth and bring forth harvesters and will watch over the harvesters and motivate and direct and guide them because there is definitely going to be a harvest, an unending harvest." (12.02)

It appears the stage is being set for God to ignite Generation Z, like dry kindling awaiting His refining fire. I think we're going to have lots of young flyers filling the sky soon.

New Training Facilities:

Not only are new trainees coming, who will likely look different from what we're used to seeing, but based on a dream I received in May 2017, the training facilities will look different too. In this dream, we were not allowed to meet publicly, so we were meeting secretly. Instead of a traditional meeting facility, we met outside in what appeared to be the parking lot of an abandoned business complex. It looked like something out of an apocalyptic movie, but it was a gathering of disciples, all quietly standing and listening as several of us taught them how to be led by the Holy Spirit. Many of them stood around us while others looked down from the top of a parking deck.

We had no microphones or speaker systems, but everyone could hear us. We had no script, no program, no pre-arranged plan. We just followed the leading of the Holy Spirit, saying what He put in our heart to say. One person would speak for a few minutes, then another, as the Spirit moved. There was no competition between us. We worked together seamlessly, in perfect harmony. His promptings were clear and strong, so we had no doubt about what He wanted us to say. We just followed His script, so we were not only teaching, but also demonstrating how to be led by Him. At different times, the teaching reached climactic points, causing the whole crowd to erupt with applause.

I explained how to listen to the inner witness, the promptings coming from the inside, from our heart, our inner man. I explained that before we can be led by the Holy Spirit, we must first be born again by the Spirit. I told them, "You must first invite the Lord

Remnant: Training

Jesus Christ to come into your heart. Invite Him to be the Lord of your life. Then He will receive you and He will lead you and guide you." (Romans 10:9-10)

I looked up to the top of the parking deck and saw a row of rough looking guys standing there. They had long hair and beards and were dressed like biker dudes. I knew they were new disciples and they were hungry to hear the message. They were taking in every word of it, watching, listening, and nodding their heads in agreement. I knew how much they needed to know these things we were teaching. I felt compassion for them and for everyone there because of the dark times we were facing. End of dream.

I believe the context of this dream reveals the times of trouble coming upon the whole world before the Lord returns, which God has been warning about through many scriptures, dreams and visions, although many have refused to hear it. (Isaiah 24:1-6, Daniel 7:19-27, 8:22-25, 9:27, 12:1, Zechariah 12:8-9, 14:2-5, 14:12-15, Matthew 24:4-34, 2 Thessalonians 1:4-10, 2 Timothy 3:1-8, Jude 1:17-23, Revelation 6:1-17, 8-19)

The laws of our land had been changed, fulfilling the prophecies regarding the coming spirit of antichrist. (Daniel 7:25) That spirit had gained such a grip over our land, it had managed to steal our religious liberties, forcing us to meet secretly, like our brothers and sisters in other parts of the world have been doing for many years. We were not stopped by their threats or by our lack of facilities, but we were ministering in more power than what's happening in many churches today.

Like my flying dream, I saw no envy, strife, or competition among us. Instead, we each took our turn speaking only what the Holy Spirit gave us to say. Then we stepped aside to hear what He was saying through someone else. It was not a one-man show, like what we see happening in our churches today. Instead, our ministry more closely resembled the first century church, with our attention focused on obeying the Lord because it was not about us. It was only about meeting the needs of His people without the least concern for any kind of leadership hierarchy or jockeying for position. Through all these things, we were demonstrating how God's Kingdom operates.

Ironically, the primary focus of the training was a topic that is almost completely absent in our seeker-friendly churches today, being led by the Holy Spirit to do whatever He says to do and go wherever He says to go. That kind of obedience is what makes us sons and daughters of God, separating us from the hypocrites and harlots who only talk the talk. (Romans 8:14)

Our meeting was filled with many new disciples as shown by the way I was explaining to them they first needed to be born again. I believe my instructions showed what's coming before the Lord returns, a great harvest of souls entering God's Kingdom during dark times. (Isaiah 60:1-5, Amos 9:13-15, Zechariah 2:10-12, Matthew 13:24-30, Mark 16:15-18, John 12:32-33, Acts 1:7-8) The great trouble that had come upon our land was likely what caused many of them to turn to God. As new disciples, they needed to hear the most basic truths. They hadn't had time to learn very much, but they were standing firm on what little they knew, even willing to risk everything to be part of our meeting when it was forbidden by our government, so they demonstrated their sincere commitment to God by their great faith and courage.

The rough looking biker dudes showed what's coming in the harvest will not look like what we're used to seeing. They looked rough on the outside, but their hearts were tender to God, as shown by the way they were nodding their head in agreement. I believe God is warning us in advance not to be moved by outward appearances, just rely on the leading of the Holy Spirit.

ENDNOTES

12.01: Generation Z making smarter choices, https://www.prnewswire.com/news-releases/generation-z-breaks-records-in-education-and-health-despite-growing-economic-instability-of-their-families-300287848.html

12.02: Bob Jones, message to over-50 generation, https://www.youtube.com/watch?v=6Kue4UUGqLs

13
Qualified

In a dream on October 9 2017, I was at a school somewhere in the southwestern part of the United States. I was a new teacher there, walking through one of the buildings, getting oriented and learning my way around the campus. It looked like the semester had not started yet because there were no people around, except a woman who was walking with me. I never saw her, but I was aware of her and knew she was my friend and that she was also a new teacher there.

While we were still inside the building, a van pulled up and stopped in front of us on a road that went inside the building to make it easier to pick up students without requiring them go outside. It was like a small school bus. A man was driving and a woman was with him in the front passenger seat. Besides driving the van, they were also teachers and performed other functions at the school. After they stopped, they got out and I recognized him right away as someone I had known in the past. I think I knew the woman too, but like the woman who was with me, I never saw her face.

The man was jovial, all smiles, and acted glad to see me as he told me a few stories about different things he had been through since we last saw each other. I briefly shared some of my experiences, but instead of speaking, I acted them out, like playing charades. To show them how tired I was because of all I had endured, I laid my head on my hands, pretending to be sleeping on a pillow. They smiled and chuckled to show they understood, but I knew they did not understand and did not care to hear about it.

I immediately knew many things about this man. I knew he was one of the leaders in the school, in a position of hiring others to work for him. I knew his relationships with other people were defined by whether they followed his doctrines. He was very proud of his doctrines and his great knowledge of them. He even told me, "I only hire teachers who agree with my doctrines."

Once again, I said nothing to him one way or the other, but I think he could tell I disagreed, and that disqualified me and made me an outcast in his view. I felt his distrust toward me and I knew his smiles were only a phony outward appearance, pretending to accept me while inwardly despising and rejecting me. He was already thinking of ways to destroy me because I was a threat to him, like a dangerous renegade.

The scene changed and school was now in session. It was night and there were many students walking around campus and inside the buildings. There had been some big trouble, resulting in a foreign army taking over the school. The soldiers looked Mexican or perhaps from somewhere in South America because their skin was darker than Caucasians and they all had black hair. They all wore light blue shirts with dark blue pants and were all well-armed with handguns and rifles.

A large white school bus came driving through the campus streets and the soldiers yelled at it, ordering it to stop. The driver refused and continued driving away, so the soldiers opened fire, even though there were students all around. They showed no concern for the students as they fired at the bus, so some students were hit by bullets.

I knew the whole event was planned and staged. The bus did not stop because they were on a suicide mission, which is why they ignored the soldiers' orders and kept driving away. When the soldiers started pursuing them, the bus suddenly detonated a bomb, causing a great explosion.

Although I saw these things happening, I was not on campus at the time. I had left the school grounds with the woman who was always with me. Her car had run out of gas in a nearby neighborhood, so she needed my help. Although we were both new there, I somehow knew my way around better than she did, so I knew where to get more gas. We walked through a residential area to her car carrying a gas can, but when we reached her car, we realized we had forgotten something, so we had to turn around and walk back to the school to get it. I looked back at her car and the gas can and it looked like it would be fine until we returned.

The scene changed and it was a sunny day on campus. Again, I was not there, but was watching anyway as many students were walking around the center of campus, going to their classes. The atmosphere seemed happy, almost like a celebration when there's a parade. The same man I encountered earlier was seated outside near the center, taking a break and enjoying the day, when suddenly someone whom I did not see drove by and threw a silver canister into the center of the campus and it landed not far from where this man was seated. It looked like a hand grenade or some type of explosive device and everyone immediately knew it was something bad, so they all started running in every direction to get away. The students did not understand the power of this device, but this man somehow knew it was going to be such a massive explosion, there was no way to escape, so he did not even try to run. He just sat there and said, "You could run for six months, but it wouldn't be far enough to get away from this bomb."

It seemed like the bomb would ignite at any moment, but I never saw it explode. It appeared there was a little time to get away, but he knew it was futile and none of them would survive.

The scene changed and again I was with this same woman, but now we were in what looked like a school gymnasium. A few tables were set up because it was being used as a job fair, but there was hardly anyone there. I knew there were workers at each table, but I never saw any of their faces. We were filling out applications for teaching jobs, but I only saw three applicants, including myself, the woman I was with and an African American woman, filling out an application at the table next to ours. She smiled as she said to the person working at her table, "I'm very qualified and I know I would do a good job."

End of dream.

Interpretation:

After spending some time seeking God about this dream, I believe the school represents the Church in America. It was in the southwestern part of the United States, but it represented the entire nation.

As new teachers at this school, the woman and I represented a group of people, a body of disciples, consisting of men and women, a remnant arising within the American Church with a distinctively different perspective and message, which will seem new to the American Church even though there is nothing new about it, but it will be new to them because they've strayed so far away from God and the truth. God wanted this message to come forth previously, but it could not because hardly anyone was willing to receive it, like when Jesus told His disciples, "I still have many things to say to you, but you cannot bear them now." (John 16:12 NKJV)

Our arrival at the school and the new semester marked the start of a new season, which is bringing a shift in leadership that will open doors for this new message to come forth, illustrating how God is soon bringing new assignments, new positions, and new platforms to His righteous remnant. We were new to the school because up until now, we've had no platform, no recognized position within the established Church.

When we arrived, there were no students clamoring around us, just large empty buildings and empty hallways. School was not in session yet and the campus was empty because this new message and these new messengers have no followers yet. We were unknown by anyone at the school the same way the remnant is unknown by the Church, basically nobodies who have been hidden away by God until the time appointed, on nobody's radar except God's.

Showing up a little before the semester started illustrated our need to get oriented in our new positions before we were ready to begin sharing our message. This orientation is much needed because these new assignments will require us to learn new things, so there will be some stretching and God has already provided a short transition period coming at the beginning of the new season.

The man and woman driving the van also represented a body of believers, consisting of men and women. As established leaders within the school, they represented the established leaders of the American Church. Their van represented their vocation because vehicles carry us to our destinations like vocations carry us to our destinies, so this couple represented those whose primary vocation is in positions of Christian leadership. I recognized the man as soon as I saw him because the established leaders of the Church are well known. We've heard their messages and attended their meetings long enough to know where they're coming from.

He was in a position of hiring other teachers at the school, but he only hired teachers who agreed with his doctrines, showing he was not led by the Spirit of God, but by his own understanding. He did not rely on the Holy Spirit to tell Him who to hire. He did not seek the Lord's guidance because he did what seemed right to him. His doctrines had replaced God as the central guide in his most important decisions, so he was not a true follower of God, not a true son of God, except in name only because sons of God are those who are led by the Spirit of God. (Romans 8:14) His devotion was to the teachings of men, Church doctrines, representing man's agenda and his own agenda. His ears were not even open to hear God because he thought he already had the answers he needed, which put him in even greater danger.

He represents how the leaders of the American Church operate, which is no different from the way the Pharisees and Sadducees of ancient Israel operated, having a form of godliness, but denying the power of God. Obviously, this is not true about all of them, thank God, but the dream is just revealing the prevailing condition of our generation of leaders who often just talk the talk, but don't walk the walk. They talk about the cross, but don't apply the power of it to their own lives. They've become so confident of their own righteousness, they don't need God or go before Him with a broken contrite heart, humbly repenting of their sins or seeking His direction in their decisions. Instead, they pray like the Pharisee who said, "God, I thank You that I am not like other men—extortioners, unjust, adulterers, or even as this tax collector. I fast twice a week; I give tithes of all that I possess." (Luke 18:11-12 NKJV)

Meanwhile, the righteous remnant is like the tax collector who was unwilling to even lift his eyes to heaven, but was beating his breast, saying, "God, be merciful to me, a sinner!" (Luke 18:13b NKJV) Jesus said, "I tell you, this man went to his house justified rather than the other; for everyone who exalts himself will be humbled, and he who humbles himself will be exalted." (Luke 18:14 NKJV)

Their van pulled right inside the building, making it easy for their students to board without even going outside. This is the way the American Church operates, catering to the fleshly appetites of carnal Christians with every conceivable comfort, which includes watered down messages, carefully designed to avoid offending anyone. Their focus has shifted away from pleasing God to pleasing their followers. They are not trusting God because they think they already know better, so they've departed from the true message of the cross, glossing over the parts about denying ourselves and our carnal appetites and sensual pleasures and anything else God requires us to do removing all the most essential requirements of turning away from unrighteous deeds and obeying God's commandments. Instead, the focus on making sure the chairs are comfy, the music is entertaining, the sound system is amazing, the temperature is perfect, and above all, the clock is strictly followed. It's all about doing whatever it takes to get the sheep to keep following them as they lead them into the slaughterhouse.

The man acted friendly to me as he shared some of his experiences since we had last seen one another. However, I knew immediately he was not saying anything worth hearing because I knew he was not being led by the Spirit of God. His "testimonies," which he shared with me, were just part of his act, part of his foolish game of pretending to be something he was not, trying to deceive me into thinking he was doing important things for God's Kingdom the same way deceived his followers, but I wasn't falling for it.

Since he pretended to be a big man of God, I replied to him like I was speaking to a child, speaking without using any words. His testimony was all idle words, but my testimony didn't waste a single word. Even if I tried to tell him, he didn't want to hear anything I had to say and wouldn't have understood it because it was beyond his experience and contradicted his doctrines. So, in response to his game of pretense, I pretended by acting out my message, like talking to someone who had no understanding or someone who spoke a different language. Do you see me pretending to sleep? See me laying my head down on my pillow? See how tired I am?

Remnant: Qualified

My testimony revealed the truth about my condition. I was starting my new assignment while still very tired and needing rest from the battles endured in my previous season, representing the long grueling preparation process the remnant has endured prior to starting our new assignments. The trials and testing endured during that season went way past our ability to understand, but it was all necessary preparation for the days ahead.

While we were in hiding, God trained us in ways many American churches have been unwilling to hear because it contradicts their seeker-friendly, Me-Gospel, feel-good messages of always prospering and always increasing in material possessions without ever being required to deny ourselves or lay down our lives, which is why they've conveniently omitted from their messages key parts of the testimonies of the great heroes of our faith, as explained in chapter six. With a few subtle changes, they've removed the words of life and replaced them with deadly poison.

I didn't say a word about any of that to this man, but what I wanted to tell him was God has a faithful remnant who has spent so much time in the valley of the shadow of death, continually staring at death face to face until it seemed like a constant companion, walking through circumstances so difficult, at times it looked like it was all over, but then at the point of death, when all our strength was gone, all our resources were gone and all our hope was gone, God came through for us at the last hour, breathing His life back into us, empowering us to continue. He took us to the limits of what we could endure and even at times it seemed beyond our limits, but He kept His promise not to put on us more than we could bear. (1 Corinthians 10:13) Through many such encounters, we discovered how Elijah felt when he prayed that he might die and said, "It is enough! Now Lord, take my life." (1 Kings 19:4 NKJV) Yet, God sent His angel to sustain Elijah, and He sustained us too, building us up in our faith and transforming us into something He can use, all for the benefit of those we are called to help.

I skipped all that and just gave him the short version, which he pretended to understand, but he didn't understand because the natural, carnal mind cannot understand the things of the spirit of God because they sound foolish, but the spiritually minded man understands and has insight into all things (1 Corinthians 2:14-15), which is why I saw through his jovial, joyful appearance and his smiling face and recognized what he was thinking on the inside, treacherous thoughts of how he could destroy us, just like the Pharisees and Sadducees killed the prophets and the Lord Jesus. Jesus exposed them for being like whitewashed tombs which on the outside appear beautiful, but inside are full of dead men's bones and uncleanness. Outwardly, they appear to be righteous, but inwardly they are full of hypocrisy and lawlessness. (Matthew 23:27-28)

Remnant: Qualified

By trusting more in their doctrines than their personal relationship with God, many leaders have attempted to understand the scriptures apart from the Spirit of God, which has led them into many errors because the scriptures can only be understood through revelation, which only comes from God. So, they've embraced many false doctrines, like hyper-grace, which has permeated, saturated and indoctrinated the Church so much, many can no longer hear the truth, even when it comes straight from the Bible. For example, just last week, I was called a heretic simply because I quoted a verse from the Bible, James 2:24, which says we are justified by our works and not by faith alone. I was not just corrected, but called a heretic. When scripture verses are called heresy, we have a problem in the Church. There are many other examples of wrong thinking in the Church and they all lead to bondage, slavery, and death, which is where many American churches are going soon, unless they repent.

In the next scene, it was night and school was in session. A lot must have happened between scene one and two because these foreign soldiers had not only entered our campus, but they were also ruling over it. The climate had changed from a normal school environment to martial law, enforced by the hostile foreign soldiers. As foreigners, they were far more dangerous than being occupied by friendly U.S. soldiers who at least have sympathy for their fellow American citizens. These soldiers had no regard for the lives of the students, as shown by their willingness to shoot them. The darkness of night showed the departure of spiritual light as God had withdrawn His hand of protection, allowing evil spiritual powers to have their way, ruling over the Church. I believe this disturbing scene was a warning of the coming apostasy, a time when many will fall away from the faith, coming completely under Satan's control as he forces everyone to submit to his evil schemes upon penalty of death. (Matthew 24:10, 2 Thessalonians 2:1-4, 1 Timothy 4:1-5, Revelation 13:15)

Being ruled by foreigners speaking a foreign language is a curse upon the unrighteous for refusing to speak the truth. (Deuteronomy 28:33, 28:49-50) So, these things coming upon the American Church reveal the hypocrisy of those who claim to be serving God while practicing unrighteousness. (Deuteronomy 28:45, Matthew 7:20-27, James 2:24)

In this dark setting, I saw a large white bus drive through the center of the campus, right in the same area where many students were walking. The white color of the bus contrasted with the prevailing darkness of the evil spirits, illustrating God was allowing these events to happen as His righteous judgment because white represents judgment, purity and righteousness, like the white robes worn by the righteous and the Great White Throne, the place of His judgment. (Revelation 4:4, 7:9, 20:11) When the bus ignored the soldier's warnings to stop and drew their gunfire, I immediately knew it was a staged event designed to cause everyone to believe it was in our best interest to submit to Satan as our new master so he could protect us from these kinds of terrorist threats, even though he was the one causing all the trouble. It was part of his misinformation war against the Church, further adding to the confusion, like the so-called war on terror already underway. With even a little discernment, the whole campus should have seen through the lies because the soldiers' actions, firing right into the crowd of students and hitting many of them, provided sufficient evidence proving they had no regard for our lives.

Although I saw the bus attack, I was not there when it happened and neither was the woman who was with me. We had walked to where her car had run out of gas, then we walked back to the school because we forgot something, which all took time, long enough to keep us out of harm's way, which shows God's faithfulness to make a way of escape for the righteous, protecting us even during terribly dark times. We were unaware of the planned event, but God knew and ordered our steps to protect us. (Psalm 37:23) In this world, we will have trouble, but He delivers the righteous from all their trouble, snatching us away from it and rescuing us. (Psalm 34:17, 34:19, 37:40, Proverbs 11:6, 11:8, 12:13) The righteous only look with our eyes, seeing how God deals with the unrighteous, watching as a thousand fall at our side and ten thousand at our right hand, but no harm comes to us because we have made the Lord our refuge and our dwelling place. (Psalm 91:7-9)

When I looked back at her car, I knew it was fine to leave it there, another indication of God's protection, even as we encountered trouble and walked around in the dark by ourselves during a time of martial law. He not only protected our lives, but also our possessions. (Matthew 7:24-27) All evil is rendered powerless against the righteous. (Proverbs 12:21, 21:18)

The woman's car represents her ministry vocation, so running out of gas shows she needed a touch from God. She knew better than to seek help from the established Church leaders because she knew they didn't have what she needed. She understood God gives His insights and understanding of spiritual matters to those who walk uprightly. (1 Corinthians 2:15) She understood the prayers of the righteous get results. (James 5:16) Her situation showed how God meets the needs of those who walk uprightly, causing us to always have all sufficiency in all situations, so even during times of great trouble, we have an abundance, well equipped for every good deed. (2 Corinthians 9:8)

The next scene was a bright sunny day with many students walking through the center of campus, but the beautiful weather and happy atmosphere were part of their delusion, their wrong thinking that all was well, even though they were in great danger, which was reinforced by the teacher sitting outside enjoying himself and relaxing, taking in the beautiful day, but while they were comforting themselves with thoughts of peace and safety, death and destruction came upon them suddenly and none of them escaped. (1 Thessalonians 5:3-8) This delusion explains why God has been unable to share the message of righteousness with the American Church. It would not be received because they are totally convinced all is well, so they don't think they need it. They have their own false prophets reinforcing their delusion, so they much prefer listening to them. Warnings of trouble ahead sound like foolish gibberish to them, so they wrongly conclude the true messengers are false prophets of gloom and doom. Being blinded by what they think they know, they arrogantly mock and ridicule the warnings and proceed to their destruction. (Proverbs 22:3)

When the silver canister landed at the center of campus, everyone knew it was something terrible, so they tried to run away, but it was too late. There was nothing wrong with seeking protection, hiding behind physical structures, but it didn't work because they had neglected to seek safety in God by obeying His commandments. (Psalm 34:17, 34:19, 37:40, 91:1-16, Proverbs 11:6, 11:8, 18:10) No matter how fast they ran, it was not fast enough because the judgment of God is inescapable. The unrighteous will be destroyed because they failed to qualify for God's promises, as their teacher said, "You could run for six months, but it wouldn't be far enough to get away from this bomb." He knew the gig was up and the game was over, so there was no need to pretend any longer.

The explosion of the canister represented the terrible events coming upon the unrighteousness of many churches. When times of trouble come, many will not have faith to endure due to being filled with so many false messages. The great explosion represents a disaster far worse than physical death because the consequences are eternal. (Zechariah 13:7-9, Matthew 24:10, 2 Thessalonians 2:3, 1 Timothy 4:1-5, 2 Timothy 4:3-4, 2 Peter 2:20-22, Jude 1:17-23)

As terrible as the explosion was, life continued as the scene changed to the job fair, but by that time, very few people were in attendance because so many had perished in the explosion, showing life after the great falling away from the faith when only a remnant will remain standing faithfully with God. Our small number was emphasized again by the presence of the African American woman, a minority, applying at the next table. Even so, the job fair showed there was still much work to do before the Lord returns.

Filling out applications showed the hiring decisions were no longer based on the doctrines of men, but on the unique qualifications listed by each applicant. I never saw the faces of any of the workers at the job fair, showing they were heavenly beings and the hiring decisions were being made in heaven, like they should have been all along.

Having been tested and proven faithful, the remnant is well qualified for these new assignments with many good things to impart to a new generation. In the past, no one wanted to hear what we had to say, but in the future, many will pay close attention, being drawn to the light of God residing in us. All the trials we endured will bring much good fruit as we impart lessons to others through our testimonies and teachings, causing many who have strayed far away from God to return to Him as His sons and daughters. (Isaiah 60:1-4)

Since this dream was received in October 2017, we are closer today to starting those new assignments. And when that time comes, we'll smile like the African American woman and say, "I'm very qualified and I know I would do a good job."

Although this is a stern warning for the Church, it's also a message of hope because it shows God has not given up on us. Even long before these things happen, He has been working on His plan to help us get it right, even sending warnings like this in the hopes that some will repent. Having seen these things coming, God has already been preparing messengers with a new message to help His people get back on track, so there's hope for a new beginning.

14
Warfare

On August 10, 2013, I received a dream that revealed how I was allowing Satan to steal from me. I had to make some changes in my life to close the doors that I had opened for him and when I did, my life changed dramatically. Although Satan attacks each of us in different ways, we all experience warfare in the battlefield of our mind, so I believe this dream reveals helpful insights for all of us.

In this dream, I was driving a big tractor-trailer truck on a two-lane highway. Riding with me in the passenger seat was a woman who is a close friend. The trailer was filled with valuable goods which we were transporting to a big ministry event. It was a stressful drive because I had to keep moving into the oncoming lane to avoid water, which was covering my lane for as far as I could see ahead, but I could not stay in the other lane for long due to oncoming cars.

Along the way, we stopped at a beautiful place in the mountains where I took some pictures of her. As we continued driving, she got sleepy and rested her head on my shoulder, not in a promiscuous way, just as a friend who felt totally safe with another friend.

When we arrived at the ministry event, I stopped the truck and immediately saw one of my old girlfriends from college. I was barely out of the truck and not even standing totally upright yet when I gave her a big hug, so my arms were around her midsection. Then we started talking about some pictures I had taken of her when we were in college. She told me she wasn't happy with them because other people had taken better pictures of her. So, I suggested we try again someday to take some better pictures. Then we said goodbye and she left.

After talking to her, I turned around to go back to the truck, but it was gone. A thief had come and stolen it, including all the goods in it. I searched all around the area and finally saw the front cab, but the trailer was gone. The man who stole it was still sitting in the front seat, so I ran over to catch him. It was a four-door cab so I jumped in the backseat and yelled at him, "This is my vehicle. You get out!"

Then another man ran up to the vehicle and started yelling at me, "You get out! You get out!" I reached out the window and grabbed him by the neck and pulled him into the vehicle. I pressed both my thumbs hard against his windpipes to choke him and I was hurting him bad, but I didn't let up because I was afraid he might be able to reach out and grab my neck, but he never did.

Then the scene changed and I was reunited with the woman who traveled with me. We walked into the big event where thousands of people were gathered and it was about to begin. I never saw my trailer again, but I felt good that I had at least caught the thief. The dream ended.

Interpretation:

The trailer loaded with goods represents the fruit of my life and labors for God, all the blessings I wanted to share with others, such as my personal testimonies and insights God has given me. My whole purpose for driving to this event was to share these things.

I believe the water on the road and dodging cars coming from the opposite direction represented resistance from spiritual forces, as Satan was attempting to get us to give up and turn back, but despite the dangers, we continued pressing on, showing the sincerity of my desire to make my life count for something of eternal value.

Stopping at a beautiful place in the mountains showed the beauty of a right relationship between two friends, showing it's possible to have a healthy relationship between members of the opposite sex. Taking pictures of her represents making memories together, again showing this kind of relationship is possible, which probably seems obvious to most people, but it's something I haven't seen much, so I believe God knew I needed help. We had mutual trust in our relationship, without selfish or sexual motives, like a brother and sister, which is why she felt totally safe laying her head on my shoulder. Although these scenes showed what a right relationship looks like, it's not suggesting it's wise for a married man to spend a lot of time alone with another woman like we were doing by taking this trip together, and especially unwise for a married man to allow another woman to rest her head on his shoulder since it opens the door to temptation.

My old college girlfriend at the event represented my past unrighteous relationships since I was not a Christian back then, as shown by the way I hugged her inappropriately around her waist, showing my old wrong thoughts were still very much alive. Even after pressing through all the adversity on the highway to get to this event, I immediately reverted to my old ways, showing this area still needed correction. Talking to her about the photos I took of her in college represents memories of our relationship together, which I was holding onto, like keeping old photos. She told me she preferred other photos taken by other people, showing she placed greater value on her past relationships with other guys more than me, which further revealed how misguided I was in entertaining those memories about someone who didn't even value them as much as I did.

While my attention was distracted, talking with her, my truck was stolen, showing the direct connection between those two events with the one opening the door for the other. The thief represents Satan stealing from me while I was distracted and unaware of what was happening. By entertaining those old memories, even though it was only thoughts, I was straying beyond the protective hedges of the path of righteousness to enter ground where Satan was roaming about, seeking to steal from me. So, I was putting myself in a dangerous place outside of God's protection and giving Satan easy access to steal all my most valuable possessions. (Proverbs 2:7-8, John 10:10, Ephesians 6:14, 1 John 3:8, 3:10, 1 Peter 5:8)

The surprise I felt when I realized the truck was stolen showed how surprised I was to learn the damage caused by replaying those memories. It was such an old familiar habit, I didn't think it was that big of a deal, especially since I wasn't looking with my physical eyes, but this dream revealed wrong thoughts can be just as harmful as wrong actions and replaying old memories isn't much different from looking with our physical eyes. (Matthew 5:27-28)

After hearing so much emphasis on the grace of God and so little emphasis on the importance of our deeds, I had underestimated the danger and did not realize it was even possible to so easily stray off the path and disqualify myself from receiving the protection God has promised to the righteous. (Matthew 6:1, Hebrews 11:33, 1 John 2:29, 1 John 3:7-10) I had a false sense of security based on a wrong understanding of the righteousness God requires, so I was carelessly practicing unrighteous deeds, which was giving Satan permission to plunder my most valuable possessions. My sincere desire to share these things with others was made worthless because of my wrong thoughts, so I believe God gave me this dream to help me catch the thief and stop him from doing it again.

Even after I found the stolen truck with the thief still in it, he didn't immediately give up. At first, he ignored my commands, hoping I would back down and give up. The second man coming to fight me showed how Satan even calls in reinforcements. There is no repentance in him, only a relentless pursuit of what he wants. So, catching him and confronting him was just the start of the fight, not the end. The intensity of the warfare was illustrated by physically fighting and choking him and my concerns that he would choke me. If I backed down, I would have been giving him permission to stay, which was all he required to have every legal right to stay, so I had to be firm, determined, steadfast and unwavering to make him go. (1 Corinthians 15:58, Colossians 1:23, Hebrews 3:14, 1 Peter 5:9)

Even after I prevailed in the fight, my goods were still gone, but I believe it was not too late to recover them because of the scriptural promise that when a thief is caught, he must repay sevenfold whatever he stole from us. (Proverbs 6:30-31) In another example, when the enemy of Israel, the Amalekites, attacked the city of Ziklag in southern Israel and burned it to the ground and took all the women and children as hostages, including King David's two wives, he sought God asking Him, "Shall I pursue this troop? Shall I overtake them?" And He answered him, "Pursue, for you shall surely overtake them and without fail recover all." (1 Samuel 30:8-9 NKJV)

Making Changes:

Seeing the problem was a big help but also a big responsibility because it put me at a crossroads to choose between greater light and greater darkness since God requires us to walk in the light He has given us. (Luke 12:48, Ephesians 5:8-11) So this dream required me to make changes to avoid a far worse condition. (John 5:14)

I took it seriously and started making changes right away. As I did, more light came, which helped me see more areas that needed changing. For example, I realized I was feeding my wrong thoughts by some of the things I was doing, like looking at Facebook where it was way too easy to access old girlfriends, always just a click or two away, like watching a bad commercial, stirring up all those old memories, so that was the first thing to go. Other people might not have any problems using Facebook or other social media, but for me it was best to just shut it down.

I started seeing more clearly how things I watched on TV were stirring up wrong thoughts, putting me directly in the enemy's line of fire. (1 Peter 2:11, 1 John 3:8) So, I started being much more careful about what I watched. If I made a mistake, offending my confidence with God, I immediately made big changes to make sure it didn't happen again. For example, I did many fasts from watching anything for at least a month or two at a time, often starting a new fast within a day or two of ending one, so it became an ongoing part of my life. However, even with all sorts of guards on my eyes, I can still think wrong thoughts without any outside help, so it's an ongoing war with my mind being the battlefield, but constant practice and discipline have made it easier to replace those old habits with new ones.

Remnant: Warfare

I like the way Brother Kenneth Hagin put it, "We can't stop the birds from flying over our head, but we can sure stop them from building a nest on our head!"

In other words, we can't stop Satan from putting thoughts into our mind because he is on the loose, roaming about like a roaring lion, seeking whom he can devour. (1 Peter 5:8) But by fighting back, casting down those wrong thoughts as soon as they come, we can walk in total victory over every temptation and pull down those strongholds, which we allowed Satan to establish over many years, bringing them into captivity to the obedience to God. (2 Corinthians 10:4-5) Satan cannot rule over us without our permission, so when we tell him to go in the authority of the name of Jesus Christ, he must go. (James 4:7)

Even as I continued refining my strategies, I wasn't doing everything perfectly, but thank God that's not what He requires because we'd all be in big trouble if it was, but I believe I demonstrated by my actions a sincere pursuit of righteousness, which is what qualifies us for all His promises. (Matthew 5:6, 1 Timothy 6:11, 2 Timothy 2:22) As a result, the situation flip flopped. Instead of having my most valuable goods stolen before I could share them, God started giving me far better things to share than I ever had before, plus a platform to share them. And He rendered Satan powerless to stop the goods from getting delivered to His people. So, pursuing righteousness closed the door to the thief and opened the door for God.

Right away, God started giving me new dreams and visions that helped me gain more discernment and understanding. (Proverbs 2:9-10, 8:20, Ezekiel 44:23) He also gave me a new spiritual radar system unlike anything I had before, which was revealed to me in a dream on November 15 2015. In this dream, I was given a new remote-control toy airplane to replace a smaller older black one. The person who gave it to me told me the name of the plane was Radar. It was much bigger than my old plane and had a long thin body that reminded me of the super-fast Concord, except the body had square edges rather than a cylinder shape. It was white with red stripes, and electric powered, unlike my old plane, which was battery powered. So, it had a continuous power supply that never required recharging or replacing the batteries.

From that day on, I started having the most amazing dreams, all night, every night, almost like watching movies all night. I have no idea what most of them mean, but I've learned to pay close attention to all of them because God often slips in very important messages. Almost every dream shared in this book came after receiving that new radar system, but that gift only came after I started making the necessary changes as revealed in my truck driving dream.

As the new plane was being handed to me by an unseen person, I heard another man say, "What a boring looking plane." I paid no attention to that because this plane was so much better than what I had before, so I was excited to get it, but I believe his comment showed there are far greater radar systems available, far greater gifts, more amazing animals right around the corner, more powerful weapons in our warfare against Satan's schemes, and we can take possession of them simply by pursuing righteousness. (Matthew 6:33)

Offensive Attack:

Righteousness transforms us from victims to victors, so we shift from defense to offense. Instead of being pushed backwards, we move forward on the path of righteousness, which makes us an offensive threat to Satan's kingdom because we inflict punishment and destruction upon all unrighteousness by tearing down those old strongholds, those old habits, destroying their power, rendering them ineffective, and making them a powerful part of our testimony of victory, so we punish the spirit of disobedience by encouraging others to pursue righteousness. (2 Corinthians 10:6)

Elijah demonstrated this offensive attack when he confronted the false prophets of Baal on Mount Carmel and killed 450 of them. (1 Kings 18:20-40) Such severe measures might seem like an odd way to accomplish his mission of bringing restoration because it's so different from the popular idea that we're all God's children so we should all just come together somewhere in the middle to try to get along, but it doesn't work that way because unrighteousness disqualifies us from God's promises, so there can be no restoration without righteousness, leaving no room for any compromises and no such thing as peaceful coexistence. (Matthew 17:11, Mark 9:12)

The same spirit of God that was upon Elijah is coming again upon the final generation of forerunners as God uses us to demonstrate His righteousness for the purpose of bringing restoration, which is what God wants for everyone, but many are unwilling to receive it because they consider the price of denying our carnal selfish desires as too high. (Matthew 7:21-23, 16:24, 18:14) God has given each of us a choice between life and death and instructed us to choose life, but He will honor our choice either way. (Deuteronomy 30:19, John 7:37) So, the same fire coming to refine the willing is coming to destroy the unwilling. (Matthew 3:12)

This offensive attack against Satan's kingdom is what the return of the Lord Jesus is all about. He's not returning as the kind, meek, lowly Lamb of God, who appeared the first time, but as the Lion of the tribe of Judah, bringing severe judgment on a dreadful day of thick darkness and gloominess when the sun, moon, and stars are darkened and the heavens are shaken. (1 Kings 18:20-40, Isaiah 13:10, Joel 2:2, 2:31, Matthew 24:29, Romans 11:22, Revelation 5:5) God does not want anyone to perish, but there are limits to the number of opportunities He gives us to repent. (2 Peter 3:9) Today is the acceptable day to come to Him, but a day is coming soon when time will run out and then it will be too late, so God is sending out warnings in hopes we will listen. (Isaiah 49:8, 2 Corinthians 6:2)

For those who are not ready when He comes, it will be terrible, even hard to imagine, because on that day, the sky will withdraw like a scroll when it's rolled up and an unprecedented powerful earthquake will move every mountain and island out of its place. (Revelation 6:12-14, 16:18-20) Then the sign of the Son of Man will appear in heaven, causing the unrighteous to mourn with regret, hiding themselves in caves, as they see Him returning. (Matthew 24:30, Revelation 6:15-17) Then a great trumpet will sound as He sends forth His angels to gather His chosen people from one end of the sky to the other. (Matthew 24:31) After moving His people out of harm's way, He will pour out His fierce anger on the unrighteous, punishing them for their evil deeds, bringing an end to the arrogance of the proud and destroying sinners. (Isaiah 13:9, 13:11, 13:13, 31:4-5, Daniel 7:13, Malachi 4:1, Matthew 24:29, 1 Thessalonians 5:9)

He's coming like a whirlwind, riding on a white horse, with the armies of heaven wearing white linen and following Him on white horses with many chariots. (Isaiah 66:15-16, Revelation 19:11-15) He Himself will slay the unrighteous, trampling them in His anger, striking them with His sword, staining His own robes with their blood, bringing down their strength, and burning them with fire like an oven. (Isaiah 63:1-6, 66:16, Malachi 4:1-3, Matthew 13:40-42, Revelation 19:15) They will tremble with fear, their hands falling limp and their heart melting within them as they're filled with sorrow. (Isaiah 13:6-8, Joel 2:1) The slaughter will be so terrible, the survivors will be as rare as fine gold. (Isaiah 13:12, 30:25, 66:15-16) Yet, even in that day, those who have not yet taken the mark of the beast can still call on His name and be saved. (Joel 2:32, Revelation 14:9-11)

Just as the Lord Jesus is returning with a much different mission than His first appearing, His forerunners also have a much different mission than his previous forerunner, John the Baptist. In addition to demonstrating the light of righteousness, calling for repentance to lead people back to God, we will be like Elijah when he confronted the false prophets, sent out as instruments of God's wrath, as shown in the following passage:

> 5 Let the saints be joyful in glory; let them sing aloud on their beds.
> 6 Let the high praises of God be in their mouth, and a two-edged sword in their

hand,
7 To execute vengeance on the nations, and punishments on the peoples;
8 To bind their kings with chains, and their nobles with fetters of iron;
9 To execute on them the written judgment - this honor have all His saints. Praise the Lord! (Psalm 149:5-9)

With so much emphasis today on God's love and kindness, we rarely hear any mention of His severity, which creates a distorted view, making it hard to believe the above passage or others like it, but God will do exactly what He said, raising up an army of saints to execute His wrath and vengeance upon all unrighteousness, binding unrighteous rulers with chains and fetters of iron. (Psalm 149:7, Isaiah 13:3-5, 13:9, 13:11, 13:13, 31:4-5, Daniel 7:13, Joel 2: 1-11, Malachi 4:1-3, Matthew 24:29, 1 Thessalonians 5:9) I saw this army in my dream as they were going to war like mighty men with each one marching in formation without breaking ranks. (Joel 2:7-8), as shown in this scene:

> "Then the scene changed again. I was in the Navy with a bunch of other sailors. It was time to report back to our post, so we were returning to our submarine. As we were going aboard, the submarine was already starting to move and submerge. I knew there was a strong connection between all of us, as if we were one unit with each of us moving perfectly in step with the others without even looking at each other and even though we were each doing different tasks as we got on board.
>
> There were large sharks in the water trying to get on board as we submerged, but we paid no attention to them and were not afraid because we knew they could not touch us inside the safety of the sub, which was much bigger and stronger than them."

We each knew our assignments, which brought us together as one great army, marching alongside others with similar assignments in perfect harmony, in perfect step, seamlessly flowing together in unity because we were all filled with His purposes. (Joel 2:7-8) We were a powerful, unstoppable force. As we moved off the dock onto the top of the submarine, it was already beginning to move and submerge, further showing the perfect harmony between us and our unseen co-workers who were already inside the submarine. Not a moment was wasted. Everything proceeded with perfect precision, beyond the ability of any earthly military unit.

I saw many large sharks, not just swimming around, but lunging toward us with their mouths open. The submarine was small, just large enough to hold us, so the sharks were very close and coming straight at us, which was a frightening sight, but not one of us flinched, not even in the slightest. We kept our eyes focused straight ahead to complete our mission, never once looking at them because we knew they had no power to stop us, so we refused to be intimidated, which rendered them powerless to devour us. (Revelation 12:11) Satan makes many threats, roaming about like a lion, but his whole scheme is a hoax and he is not actually a lion at all, so he is unable to stop the righteous because we see through his lies and call his bluff. (1 Peter 5:8)

The submarine was yellow, like the light of righteousness that arises like the sun, like Malachi saw. And immediately after he saw that, he saw those who fear God's name going forth like stall-fed calves as they went forth to war, trampling the unrighteous, so the color matches the context of what I saw. (Malachi 4:2-3)

Great Exploits:

Despite many casualties, this great army will not be stopped, but will ultimately prevail. The Lord will utter His voice before those who carry out His word, filling us with His strength and power, causing us to leap on mountain tops, run like mighty men, climb walls like soldiers, each marching in perfect alignment without deviating from the path, bursting through the enemy's defenses without breaking ranks, executing His anger against all unrighteousness, destroying the false gods of Babylon once and for all, saying like Elijah, "Seize the prophets of Baal! Do not let one of them escape!" (1 Kings 18:40, Psalm 149:5-9, Isaiah 13:3-5, Joel 2:5-8, 2:11, Malachi 4:3, Revelation 13:11-18, 18:2)

We will be like King David's mighty men of courage, fiercely loyal to their king, doing many great exploits, well trained for war, able to handle the shield and spear, having the boldness of lions and the swiftness of gazelles running on the mountains. (1 Chronicles 12:1-2, 12:8, Daniel 11:32) For example, three of David's men risked their lives to enter the enemy's stronghold to get water from the well for David to drink. (1 Chronicles 11:15-18) Jashobeam and Abishai each killed three hundred men at one time with their spears. (1 Chronicles 11:11, 11:20) Benaiah killed a lion in a pit and, armed only with a staff, then he took a spear from the hands of a very tall Egyptian (5 cubits, about 7.5 feet tall) and killed him with it. (1 Chronicles 11:22-23) At first, there were thirty mighty men, but many more kept coming to David day by day, men who could shoot the bow and hurl stones using both the right hand and the left, until they were a great army of many thousands, like the army of God. (1 Chronicles 12:22-40) Their mission was to establish David's kingdom, illustrating the mission of the end time remnant, establishing the kingdom of the Lord Jesus Christ. (1 Chronicles 11:10, Revelation 11:15)

I saw examples of these great exploits in a dream I received a few years ago. I was walking alone at night through a downtown area. I had the impression I was in Germany. I was carrying a folder filled with papers that contained the names and addresses of a network of Christians. I knew the authorities were on full alert, seeking to arrest me so they could get this information and hunt down everyone on the list.

On the other side of the street, I saw some police officers crossing the street coming towards me. So, I crossed the street at the same time, walking right in front of them, laughing all the way because they never even saw me, even though they were looking for me.

The scene changed and I was in a hotel lobby, witnessing to two hotel staff members working at the front desk. After speaking to them briefly, I left the lobby and went around the corner to the elevators. At the same moment, police officers entered the lobby from all sides, looking for me. They somehow knew I was there, but they were a moment too late. I was already gone. End of dream.

I believe this dream showed the supernatural protection of God coming upon His remnant army as we carry out our assignments in times of great darkness and persecution, as shown by the night setting and the evil forces seeking to arrest me. I believe being in Germany revealed the nature of the evil spirit coming upon the world, like what happened in Nazi Germany during World War 2, not referring to me being physically in Germany.

The folder I was carrying contained a secret list of the names of a network of Christians, showing severe persecution that will soon force Christians to operate under cover as an underground church. Before the Lord returns, it will be illegal to be a Christian as everyone will be required by law to worship the beast. (Revelation 6:9-11, 13:15)

Due to the dangers of my mission, risking my life and many others too, I had reasons to be afraid when I saw the police officers crossing the street towards me, but instead, I was laughing and full of faith and confidence because I knew God was protecting me. I even had courage to witness to the two employees working in the lobby while staying focused on my mission and moving in perfect step with the leading of the Holy Spirit, shown by the perfect timing of my escape. Like the sailors boarding the submarine, I was not moved by the way things appeared to be, but stayed focused on my mission.

I believe God's end time army will exercise the same great authority over the natural realm like Elijah did when he shut up the heavens, so there was no rain for three and a half years. (1 Kings 17:1 18:1-2) I saw that illustrated in a short vision back in September 1993 in which I saw myself pointing to the top of a tall tree in the distance. Then I pointed down to the ground off to the right side of it. Immediately, it fell to the ground right where I pointed. God is finally going to have people with faith the size of a mustard seed, believing what He said, "If you have faith as a mustard seed, you will say to this mountain, 'Move from here to there,' and it will move; and nothing will be impossible for you." (Matthew 17:20 NKJV)

Weapons of Warfare:

On November 12, 2015, God gave me the following prophetic word, revealing the weapons of our warfare will be different from any earthly army, bringing great destruction upon all unrighteousness without physical bullets or bombs, but by drinking deeply from His Spirit, partaking of His heavenly wine, empowering us to release His heavenly hosts by our singing, rejoicing, clapping hands, and praising God in great jubilation.

> "I am bringing forth fountains from the deep. I am bringing forth My finest wine. For I want those who are Mine to consume My finest wine. I am bringing forth My oil of joy and gladness.
>
> In bitter times, shall come forth singing and great joy like never heard before in all the days of old. For there shall be singing of My people, rejoicing, clapping of hands, and great jubilation. The clapping of their hands will be like the sound of thunder in the camp of the enemy, putting them in full retreat! In battle armor My people shall do great warfare!
>
> Make a joyful noise all the earth. Let there be singing and shouts of praise! For great is the Commander of the hosts! Great is the Captain of the army and great exploits shall My people do!
>
> There shall be many who come from the north, the south, the east, and the west who want to be given a song to sing and an instrument to play. And they will play and they will sing and their heart will rejoice for they will know My hand and they will know My army that is set before them and they will know that I am in the midst of their camp and they will know that I am He who keeps watch over them in the darkest hour of their trial, in the great testing that shall come upon the whole earth. For many will see and know and declare that I am the Lord. And they will seek to become more like Me rather than pursuing the things of this world. In these last days, they will know Me and I will be their finest wine. I will be their songs of joy. I will be in the midst of them and they will be My people and I will be their King.

Like no other time before in the history of the world, there shall come forth from My people a song of joy, a clapping of the hands, shouts of praise, and rejoicing, for great is the army of the Lord God Almighty that goes forth to do battle and to wage warfare against the plans of the enemy. And yea, there shall be a great slaughter upon them, for My people will do warfare and stand strong like an army of hardened soldiers prepared to fight! A great company of people like never known before. They shall be My holy ones and all the world will see."

And they will look upon Me whom they have pierced and mourning shall come upon them when they see and know it is I whom they have slain and rejected. In that day, there will be great mourning in Jerusalem, but they will know Me once more in the land of My people Israel. They will claim Me as their own. They will know Me like never before. Even as I was with Solomon and I raised him up to be a mighty king over a great kingdom, so I will be in the camp of Israel and they shall be a mighty people once more."

Like the first miracle Jesus performed at the wedding in Cana of Galilee, God has saved His best wine for the last, which will cause us to prevail in perilous times by overcoming the spirit of fear and receiving great joy. (Joel 2:28-32, Acts 2:14-21) This wine is part of our heritage, the manifested presence of God with us, which is worth getting happy about. Our joyful celebration will terrify Satan and all his underlings as they will know it means their doom, so we will secure our victory in the greatest battle of the ages. (Psalm 11:7, 14:5, 17:15, 140:13, Ezekiel 44:15-16, Revelation 19:7-8)

15

Restoration

In 1977, God spoke the following word to the late Prophet Bob Jones, "In forty years I am going to restore some things back to the church." (15.01)

The forty years ended in 2017, so the restoration process has already started. 2017 also marks the end of one jubilee period, fifty years, since the Jewish people reclaimed Jerusalem in 1967. (Leviticus 25:1-12) Many things shifted around 1967, as shared in Part 2, and it appears another shift started in 2017, as explained in this chapter and confirmed by another prophecy shared at the end of chapter 17.

That same year, on June 10, 2017, I received a dream confirming what Bob Jones heard. In this dream, I discovered human beings can breathe underwater. We discovered it had been possible all along, but we had failed to realize it before because we believed it was impossible, so we didn't even try. Then it was announced that anyone who was willing could go out into the ocean floor and lay claim to the land and it would be theirs, like the old pioneer days. It was so easy, all we had to do was go claim it.

I was excited about this news so I went to my house and told some of my friends about it and they got excited too, so we started making plans to go claim our land. Then I met with a larger group of Christians and explained the opportunity to them. They seemed to welcome the opportunity too, so it appeared the meeting went well, but later when I was back home in my basement, a man entered my home on the main floor intending to stop our plans. I never saw him, but I knew he had a gun, so it was a serious threat. I then grabbed my machine gun (I don't really own a machine gun), so I was well prepared to handle him. I waited for a confrontation with him, but there was none, so our group proceeded with our plans and traveled to the bottom of the ocean.

We were amazed to find the ocean floor looked like beautiful green country fields with rolling hills. We walked along the bottom just as easy as walking on land with no need to swim. We found trails someone had already made so we followed them. Along the way, we came across large industrial buildings, showing more evidence we weren't the first ones to discover these places, but somehow it had remained a secret. I marveled at some of the businesses we saw because they were quite large with many vehicles and buildings and industrial type structures, but they were all abandoned. We didn't see any people around, just lots of evidence they had been there. The dream ended.

The discovery that we could breathe underwater shows we discovered a new realm where things previously believed to be impossible were found to be possible, redefining the previous limitations of our understanding. It was available to us all along, but we had failed to enter because of our unbelief, confirming what Jesus said, "If you can believe, all things are possible to him who believes." (Mark 9:23 NKJV)

These new discoveries were positioned on the bottom of the ocean because they represent the deep things of God, located far below the surface, hidden from casual observers who make little or no effort to see them and discovered only by those who are hungry enough to press in for more. (Daniel 2:22) The invitation showed this new realm was fulfilling God's promises to the righteous, as shown in Exhibits 8-23, taking possession the same way we take possession of all His other promises, by putting our faith into action, bringing our actions into alignment with what He wants us to do. It was free and easy to do just by following the instructions, but like the horse in my driveway, it required taking some steps to go and see. It was not an unreasonable request, but it was enough to separate the hungry from those who are content to stay where they are.

It was quickly embraced by my small group of friends, showing a small number of people will be excited about entering this new realm. However, something went wrong after the news was shared with a larger group of Christians, as shown by the hostile opposition that came against me, even threatening my life. I believe this shows this new realm will not be widely embraced by all Christians because many will be hindered by the same unbelief that prevented us from entering previously. The attacker invaded my home immediately after I shared this news with the larger group of Christians showing the connection between their unbelief and Satan gaining a foothold to use them for his purposes.

My home represents a place I have every legal right to occupy, showing I was standing on ground rightfully belonging to me as someone who had qualified to receive God's promises, so by making plans to go lay my claim, I was just exercising my rights as a legal heir to His promises, not overstepping my rights or doing anything wrong. So, the attack was unjustified, as confirmed by the illegal entry into my personal residence, which was an act of lawlessness, so this scene shows Satan will attempt to derail us from entering this new realm while it's still new to us, before we even get a chance to go see it for ourselves. Even though I could not see the man who entered on the main floor, I knew he had a gun, showing I was not relying on my physical senses, but discerning in the unseen realm of the spirit and fighting against a spiritual adversary. Satan's opposition shows the significance of this discovery, having potential to do significant damage to Satan's kingdom, so we're being warned anyone stepping out to take possession of this new land will face opposition that will require us to stand firm against him. Grabbing my machine gun illustrated standing firm on what rightfully belonged to me, refusing to back down, and shows I had access to more powerful spiritual weapons than Satan because God is far stronger than Satan. (1 John 3:4)

Satan has attacked Christians violently many times in the past, but as the prince of darkness, he prefers working under cover, keeping a low profile, so coming in with an actual gun would likely be his last resort after all other measures have failed. (Ephesians 5:8) He prefers to operate more subtly, even getting other Christians to carry out his attacks by spreading false accusations and slandering anyone aligned closely with God, like we see happening so often today and throughout history, so anyone pressing into the deep things of God should not be surprised when the attacks come primarily from other Christians. Since we're being warned about this ahead of time, we can prepare ourselves by studying God's promises so we know these things are part of our inheritance. For example, Jesus promised us, "Most assuredly, I say to you, he who believes in Me, the works that I do he will do also; and greater works than these he will do, because I go to My Father." (John 14:12 NKJV)

We also have scriptural examples of others in previous generations who saw heavenly things, but weren't allowed to share them. For example, the mysteries of God's end time plans were revealed to the Prophet Daniel, but the angel Gabriel instructed him, "But you, Daniel, shut up the words, and seal the book until the time of the end." (Daniel 12:4 NKJV) In the same way, the Apostle Paul was caught up to the third heaven, into Paradise, where he heard inexpressible words, but he was not allowed to share them with anyone because it was revealed to him it was not lawful to utter a word about it, so our generation must rediscover these things by following the same trail he followed. (2 Corinthians 12:1-4)

I was positioned in the basement of my home, representing the lowest possible place, which helped protect me from the attack. So, my position at the time of the attack revealed several keys to our victory. First, I was standing on ground that legally belonged to me based on God's promises. Second, I stood firm against him, taking my position with my weapon ready and loaded, so the attack was turned back, confirming how Satan flees when we resist him firmly. (James 4:7). Third, I was staying low, humble before God, not exalting myself, which put me in a place where Satan's weapons could not harm me. Then I was able to proceed with my plans, pursuing what God gave me to pursue, the secret things, the deep things He wants to reveal to our generation, which are part of our inheritance as the fulfillment of His promises, as listed in Exhibits 8-23, bringing restoration in every area of our life and overflowing into the lives of many others.

The first thing we discovered was the bottom of the ocean was completely different than we expected, showing we've underestimated the beauty of these hidden insights. They're far better than we've realized, like the difference between a muddy ocean floor and beautiful green fields with rolling hills. And we discovered we could walk uprightly with no need to swim, showing another misunderstanding; we've underestimated how perfectly God designed us to walk in these things. Not only will they far surpass our wildest imagination, but they're also going to fit us perfectly because God designed us for these things all along, so it will be as easy as walking through the country.

We were also mistaken in thinking we were the original pioneers, going where no one had gone before, but we discovered a trail had already been blazed by earlier pioneers who were no longer anywhere to be seen because they were from previous generations long ago. We've made the same wrong assumption Elijah made when he thought he was the only remaining prophet of God, but God revealed He had many others. (1 Kings 19:18) In the same way, God has kept for Himself a remnant of faithful followers in previous generations, but He did not allow them to share what they saw.

Industrial and business buildings are places where wealth is generated and provision comes to those who partake in them, so seeing them at the bottom of the ocean represents insights that have been hidden in the deep that will be discovered in our generation to unlock great wealth to the righteous as God gives His people the power to make wealth. (Deuteronomy 8:18) These would include insights into future moves in market prices, creative ideas, new inventions, knowledge of historical patterns, and wisdom and understanding to build and manage businesses. I marveled at the large size of these abandoned buildings and vehicles, showing the magnitude of the wealth God is releasing to His forerunner army, confirming what the Prophet Isaiah saw; God is going to give us the treasures of darkness and the hidden riches of secret places so we will know He is God. (Isaiah 45:3)

I believe this dream is an invitation to lay claim to these hidden things so we can take possession of all God has promised to give us, no longer hindered by our unbelief. Those who accept His invitation will be shown things that will make our heart radiant, sparkling with so much joy, filled with so much awe, it will cause us to tremble as we make room for the abundance of the sea, which He has given to us. (amplified from Hebrew words nahar, pachad and rahab in Isaiah 60:5) These riches will not be limited to the unseen spiritual realm, but will include the tangible wealth of all nations, multitudes of camels, gold, silver, incense, flocks, herds, clothing and tents. (Genesis

13:2, 13:5-6, Exodus 12:35-36, Isaiah 60:6-7, Haggai 2:6-9)

It will be like when He delivered the Israelites from ancient Egypt and declared, "I will make a difference between My people and your people." (Exodus 8:23 NKJV) But this time, it will be on a much larger scale, not limited to Egypt, but with the eyes of the whole world watching. Just as He shook Egypt, God is going to shake all the nations. Just as the Israelites plundered the wealth of Egypt before they left, His people will once again plunder the wealth of this world.

I believe these discoveries are the same things Bob Jones saw being restored to the Church. Since he saw it starting in 2017, it's all available to us now. And these same discoveries will surely contribute to the fulfillment of Elijah's forerunner assignment to restore all things and the fulfillment of what Isaiah saw, the light of God and the glory of God arising upon us. (Isaiah 60:1-2, Matthew 17:11)

God is bringing restoration in every area of our life, fulfilling His promises to the righteous, so He can put us on display like jewels, living demonstrations of the final book of the Bible, the Revelation of Jesus Christ, so everyone can see His character, His nature and His power in greater ways than ever before, causing the unrighteous to be drawn to Him through His people, including kings and our sons and daughters who have wandered far away. (Isaiah 60:3-4, Malachi 3:17, John 14:12)

Ancient Boundaries:

Putting this ocean exploration dream into the larger context of what's happening in the world today reveals it's just one example of many ancient boundaries being discovered and traversed to see what's on the other side. This is happening on an unprecedented scale in our generation, as shown by the following examples.

Our anatomical body parts have been an ancient boundary separating males from females, but our generation has discovered ways to change our gender through various procedures including hormone replacement therapy, laser hair removal, sex reassignment therapy and sex change surgical procedures. (15.02)

Our sexual reproductive systems are another example of an ancient boundary limiting the way new lives come into the world, requiring males and females to come together sexually to fertilize an egg so it becomes an embryo, which develops into a baby, but our generation has discovered how to remove that boundary through cloning, which produces a genetically identical copy of a person or animal based on their cells or DNA fragments. (15.03) The first cloned mammal was Dolly the Sheep in 1996, but today, anyone can have their pet cloned by a company called Viagen Pets. It's an expensive process, $50,000 for dogs and $25,000 for cats, but it's happening now. (15.04, 15.05)

Another ancient boundary was discovered in 2012 when nuclear physicists in Switzerland discovered the atomic particle that holds the universe together, often called the "God particle" because it essentially governs the basic building blocks of matter through an invisible energy field that infuses other particles with mass, making it the fundamental force controlling all matter in the known universe. (15.06) Their discovery was the result of a major International effort which required the construction of an enormous facility 100 meters underground, called the European Organization for Nuclear Research (CERN), which is designed to accelerate and collide nuclear particles. (15.07) By measuring the mass of this particle, 126 times the mass of a proton, they now have the basis for many other calculations, enabling them to explore what's on the other side of this atomic boundary, which sounds dangerous when approached from a purely scientific perspective, without the wisdom of God. Physicist Stephen Hawking warned, "This could mean that the universe could undergo catastrophic vacuum decay, with a bubble of the true vacuum expanding at the speed of light. This could happen at any time and we wouldn't see it coming." (15.08)

In another example, the limitations of human memory are being removed. Microchips have been developed and are already being tested by implanting them into human brains to send tiny electrical currents into the brain to expand the limits of our memory capacity. The development of these chips is being funded by the Defense Advanced Research Projects Agency (DARPA), which sees potential applications in overcoming brain injuries, depression, epilepsy, Alzheimer's disease and Parkinson's disease. Initial memory tests showed scores rose by 35 percent. (15.09)

The Bible reveals this pattern of removing ancient boundaries is a sign of the times, marking the final generation before the Lord returns. For example, national borders will be removed as an evil king arises to rule over a global government. (Revelation 13:1-8) Boundaries between religious beliefs will be removed as the second beast, the false prophet arises to join all religions together into a global false religion, which he will rule. (Revelation 13:11-15) And boundaries between national currencies will be removed as a global financial system arises using a global currency that requires users to have a mark on their right hand or their forehead to make financial transactions. (Revelation 13:16-18)

In another example, ancient boundaries governing the physical realm will be removed when God raises up two witnesses with power to destroy their enemies with fire flowing out of their mouth, power to shut up the sky so no rain falls during the days of their prophesying, power to turn waters into blood and power to strike the earth with every plague. (Revelation 11:3-6) Boundaries will continue to be removed until finally reaching a grand conclusion when the boundary separating the invisible realm from the visible realm is finally removed, enabling everyone to see the Lord riding on the clouds of the sky as He returns with power and great glory. And He will send forth His angels with a great trumpet and they will gather together His elect from the four winds, from one end of the sky to the other. (Matthew 24:30-31) We're truly living in amazing times when the fulfillment of ancient Bible prophecies are coming to pass, as shown in Part 2.

The closer we get to His return, the more we're going to see manifestations of things previously considered impossible as God demonstrates His glory through creative miracles, healings, translating us instantly from one place to another, and many other amazing examples of what's possible when we venture out into the deep and take possession of the land, like breathing underwater and being transported back and forth between earth and heaven, like I saw in my flying dream, shared in chapter 12. (Psalm 103:2-3, Ezekiel 8:3, Matthew 12:15, John 6:21, Acts 8:39-40, 2 Corinthians 12:1-4, Hebrews 11:5, Revelation 4:1-2)

On his final day on earth, Elijah gave his final prophetic message by crossing an ancient boundary to pass from the limitations of the physical realm into the heavenly realm where all things are possible. On that day, God sent him to the boundary of Israel, the Jordan River, where he rolled up his mantle and struck the water, dividing it in both directions, temporarily removing the boundary, which allowed him to cross over on dry ground with Elisha following him. (2 Kings 2:4-6) After crossing to the other side, a chariot of fire appeared with horses of fire and carried Elijah up to heaven by a whirlwind. (2 Kings 2:8-11) Just as all the other events in his life were prophetic messages, I believe this event prophetically illustrated the forerunners in our generation taking possession of the deep things God has reserved for us, the land on the bottom of the ocean, the realm where all things are possible. Like Elijah, those who cross this boundary will be well equipped with everything we need, completely restored and carried by the power of God, represented by the whirlwind and the chariot of fire.

Righteousness Brings Restoration:

As shared in the previous chapter, when I made the necessary changes to pursue righteousness more diligently, God started giving me far better insights through dreams and visions than I ever had before, but this dream about exploring the bottom of the ocean shows all those previous insights were just little appetizers, invitations to lay claim to much greater things He has prepared for us in the deep. The pursuit of righteousness puts us on the path to receive everything He wants to give us, so we win a complete victory and obtain a total restoration, simultaneously defeating Satan's schemes to rob us while releasing God's life changing power to completely transform us into new creations with new perspectives, operating in the heavenly realm. (Joel 2:4, Zechariah 10:3, 2 Corinthians 5:17)

I saw this same restoration happening in my remnant dream as we were experiencing the abundant life Jesus promised us. (John 10:10) Every area of our life was intensely wonderful, like heaven on earth, as shown by my wife and I looking like supermodels. Her physical appearance had not changed, but my perception of her changed, enabling me to see her inner beauty, which caused me to genuinely and intensely adore everything about her, so when I spoke to her, she sensed the love of God for her, causing her to be blessed to the point of tears. The same thing was happening in the meetings I attended as we were growing in our love for one another. His love was abounding in us, making us rich in ways words cannot describe, which gave us great joy and satisfaction.

Righteousness is the recipe for restoration. It's so simple, but we somehow manage to make it complicated. I saw this happening where I used to work in the grocery products industry. I was always amazed by how many top managers seemed to forget we were selling food. It should be obvious that someone out there had to eat the stuff we were making, but the top managers were always looking for ways to make more profits, so they kept making it cheaper and cheaper. Over the years, they removed so many peanuts from Cracker Jack, it eventually reached the point that hardly anyone wanted it anymore. Year after year, our sales went down, down, down, but instead of fixing the product, we paid lots of money to Madison Avenue advertising agencies for fancy ad campaigns to convince people to buy it. So, all the money we saved on peanuts was given to those agencies to promote a product nobody wanted. We would have been far better off to give our customers a good product because they know the difference between good food and lousy food, so it would have sold itself through repeat purchases and word of mouth advertising. Righteousness produces a product of great value because it qualifies us to receive more of God's heavenly gifts, making us shine like bright lights, filled with greater insights and revelation, so we have something worth sharing, something that can help people. (Psalm 23:3-4, 37:26, 37:37, 107:41-42, 112:4, 112:7-9, 140:13, Proverbs 2:7, 2:9-10, 8:20, 9:9, 11:23, 12:5, 13:5, 15:28, 16:12, 21:12, 21:15, 21:25-26, 28:1, 29:7, 29:27, Isaiah 61:3, Ezekiel 44:23)

The pursuit of righteousness brings total restoration, including everything we need to run the race He has set before us, beginning with the knowledge of His plans and purposes for our life, which comes into view more and more as we continue pressing forward on His path, growing stronger and clearer until we are completely consumed, wanting only what He wants and doing only what He wants us to do. (Matthew 6:33, Philippians 2:13, 1 Timothy 6:11-12, 2 Timothy 2:22) Then our labors are no longer wasted or misguided, but come into perfect alignment with His plans, so everything we do is aimed directly at the right target, accomplishing what He has assigned to us to do. And this is how we gain the greatest victory we can possibly achieve, winning the race He has set before us. (1 Corinthians 9:24-27)

Since our pursuit of righteousness qualifies us for the full release of all God's promises, it produces an overflow that impacts the lives of many others. So, the combined impact of the total restoration of the righteous remnant, which is spiritual Israel, is preparing the way for the restoration of a remnant of physical Israel, which will fulfill many prophecies as they look with mourning upon Him whom they pierced and return to the God of their fathers by receiving their Messiah, the Lord Jesus Christ. Then their mourning will be turned to rejoicing as God delivers them from their enemies and forever washes away their sins, enabling them to once again become a mighty people, finally receiving the full restoration of everything He has wanted them to have. (Deuteronomy 4:25-31, Isaiah 10:21-23, 28:5, Jeremiah 3:17-18, 30:7, 31:10-14, 50:19-20, Ezekiel 36:33-36, 39:25-29, Daniel 9:24, Hosea 6:2, Joel 3:1-3, Obadiah 1:13, 1:17, Zechariah 3:8-10, 8:6-8, 9:16-17, 12:10-14, 14:2-7, Matthew 23:37-39, Romans 11:25-29)

Everlasting Righteousness:

As righteousness is bringing restoration to the remnant, unrighteousness is bringing destruction to the world, causing everything to appear to be spinning out of control as sin reaches its' peak, but these things must happen to bring an end to sin and usher in a new age of everlasting righteousness. (Psalm 119:142, Isaiah 10:21-23, Daniel 9:24)

The light of righteousness will arise like the sun in the remnant, shining brighter and brighter, in growing contrast to the deep darkness engulfing the world. (Isaiah 60:1-5, Malachi 4:2) Then the six days of man's dominion will come to an end and a new seventh day will begin, a Sabbath day of rest, the Day of the Lord, which begins with the Lord Jesus returning to crush the rebellion and reward everyone according to their deeds. (Isaiah 13:9-13, 66:16, Revelation 22:12-13) Then the righteous will rule with Him with a rod of iron for one thousand years to demonstrate the fruit of righteousness, which has been available to us all along. (James 3:18, Revelation 2:27, 19:11-21, 20:2-7)

I received the following prophetic word on April 22, 2013 revealing the heavenly realm coming into the earth, manifesting through unprecedented anointings coming upon the righteous, equipping us to operate in the powers of the age to come, performing signs and wonders never before seen, and bringing an abundance of great joy. I believe this word confirms the restoration Bob Jones saw coming and the great things I saw on the bottom of the ocean.

> "I am sending you My glory. For there is a rich new glory that is coming and will fill the earth through and through, and by it men will walk in anointing's like never before found in the earth. These things have never been seen before by any men, but they are coming, and they will be found in you and on the inside of each one whom I call and put in your path to do the things that My plan calls forth to do. For I want My anointing spread in the earth, even in the uttermost parts of the earth, for I am coming to do a new sign and wonder. I will inhabit the heavens and the earth. In the fullness of My time, I am sending forth My new anointing.
>
> I am sending forth My plan and My purpose. You that walk in it, in My plan and purpose, you will not have everything you need so far as a man's mind can understand, but you will have everything you need in My mind, for I am in My right mind. I am sending forth My latter rain. The glory of My house will be filled from My latter rain. My house will be filled with My glory.
>
> Righteousness will prevail in the end. A day of righteousness is coming. Be strong I say. In that day there will be singing and dancing and much laughter and rejoicing in the land. For the days are coming, that I will rain down in the cities and in the streets an everlasting flood of joy. (Isaiah 61:7) Righteousness will prevail like rain coming down and it will wash away all uncleanness and unrighteousness. (Isaiah 45:8) For there shall be rivers of joy, rivers that prevail against the tides of uncleanness and unrighteousness. (Revelation 22:1-2) There shall be singing and much joy and a harvest sound like never before heard, for they will know that I am the Lord God and I make righteousness prevail."

Then He told me how it will happen:

> "Even from the inner courts in the inner chamber, there shall be a travailing and a mourning and a weeping, for the land will be covered in sorrow. There shall no more be any drunkenness or laughter heard, no sound, but darkness only. And in the twilight there shall be singing and rejoicing. Singing will come forth in the midst of great darkness. (Zechariah 14:6-7) And then it shall prevail, the joy that comes forth in the morning. (Psalm 30:5) The singing will prevail in the midst of the deep darkness. And it shall come forth from travail to prevail. Like never before it shall come.

Remnant: Restoration

It shall come forth like the budding and blossoming of a spring season. Life will come forth, rivers of life. (Revelation 22:1-2) Singing shall come forth, budding forth life, a blossoming shall come, a return to the rivers of joy and singing and laughter and dancing and rejoicing. For there shall come a raining down of joy like never before upon My people, a singing and dancing upon them. For they shall know My rivers of righteousness and My joy shall come forth like never before.

There shall be singing, rejoicing, clapping of hands, and a shout, for the hunger pangs are no more, and the season of fulfillment has come. The hunger pangs are gone. For the time of rejoicing has come. And I shall fill them and satisfy them, their every need and every want. They will hunger and thirst no more, but will hunger and thirst only for righteousness sake. (Revelation 7:16-17, 21:3-4) For I shall satisfy their hunger and fill their every want. (Matthew 5:6) I will rain down upon them that for which they hunger. It will come like rain, a heavy rain, a soaking, a cleansing, a deep purifying, which will bring a satisfaction and the smell of righteousness in the air, with rightful singing, the sound of music, the tambourines, with rejoicing and the clapping of hands. Let the people shout and sing and dance, for they shall never again hunger or thirst, for I shall fill them, their every want, their every need, and their every desire. I will be among them, blessing them, giving to them what they hunger for. For that which they hunger for is more of Me and I will be the one to fill them up with Me until they know Me and are satisfied.

In that day there shall be a ringing forth throughout the land. There will be a declaration and a proclamation that all who have come forth will bring. Their singing shall come forth and everyone will know that I am the one they hunger for and rejoice for, and I am the one who blesses them." (Psalm 126:1-6, Ezekiel 36:36, 37:28, 39:27-29)

ENDNOTES

15.01 Bob Jones prophecy of restoration, https://www.youtube.com/watch?v=xnCwpNtnTpw

15.02: Gender changing procedures, https://en.wikipedia.org/wiki/Transgender

15.03: Formation of human embryos, https://en.wikipedia.org/wiki/Embryo

15.04: Cloning process, https://en.wikipedia.org/wiki/Cloning

15.05: Cloning dogs and cats, https://viagenpets.com/dog-cloning/

15.06: Discovery of the God particle, https://en.wikipedia.org/wiki/Higgs_boson

15.07: CERN nuclear physics research, https://en.wikipedia.org/wiki/CERN

15.08: Warning from Stephen Hawking, https://www.livescience.com/47737-stephen-hawking-higgs-boson-universe-doomsday.html

15.09: Microchip brain implants improve memory, https://www.nbcnews.com/mach/science/memory-boosting-brain-implants-are-works-would-you-get-one-ncna868476

Part 2
Signs of the Times

16

Signs

Part 1 presented scriptural evidence showing the rise of the righteous remnant who will prepare the way for the Lord's return. Part 2 presents evidence of the fulfillment of eight scriptural signs of the times identifying the season of His return to show that the rise of the remnant is not far off in the distant future, but happening in our generation.

Only the Father knows the day and hour of His return, but He must have wanted us to know the season because He devoted many chapters of the Bible to give us many reliable signs to watch, including the rebirth of modern Israel and significant increases in earthquake activity, knowledge, travel, lawlessness, deception (leading to apostasy), and warfare. Many other signs are also in the process of being fulfilled now, but these should be more than enough to make the point since the fulfillment of even one sign means all the remaining ones must also be fulfilled in our generation because Jesus said the generation that sees these things will not all pass away until they're all fulfilled. (Matthew 24:33-34)

Although God revealed His end time plans in great detail, it's one of the most neglected topics in the Church today, which is putting many in danger of being unprepared for what's coming, unaware of what God is doing today, and even in danger of taking sides with Satan, fighting against God, like Peter did when Jesus shared God's plan for Him to be handed over to the chief priests and scribes, killed, and raised up on the third day. (Proverbs 22:3, Isaiah 11:11-12 and 60:1-5, Matthew 24:4-14, Revelation 6:1-11) Peter took Him aside and rebuked Him, so Jesus turned to Peter and said, "Get behind Me, Satan! You are an offense to Me, for you are not mindful of the things of God, but the things of men." (Matthew 16:23 NKJV)

Peter must have been surprised to hear that, but his ignorance caused him to be a stumbling block. The old saying, "ignorance is bliss," is not true in this case, even if we don't like hearing about what's coming, which is probably why it's so unpopular. While some leaders just avoid it altogether, others take it a step further by openly mocking anyone who shares these warnings, calling them false prophets of gloom and doom because warnings of trouble don't tickle their ears. By discrediting the warnings, these leaders are causing their followers to be robbed of the benefits God wanted them to have. They're making the same mistake Peter made, taking sides with Satan against God, so it's a big deal.

Remnant: Signs

Simply by believing the prophets, we can know many things about our life today, boosting our faith and hope for the future, like Daniel did when he was in captivity in Babylon along with the rest of the Israelites. By studying and believing the prophecies of Jeremiah, Daniel accurately calculated the number of years remaining for their captivity. (Jeremiah 25:11 and 29:10, Daniel 9:1-2) God had already revealed to Jeremiah their time of captivity was 70 years, so when Daniel discovered this in 571 BC, he knew there was only 33 years remaining, encouraging him to endure.

On the other hand, the Pharisees and Sadducees failed to recognize their Messiah, even though He was standing right in front of them, because they did not believe the prophets. Jesus rebuked them, calling them an evil and adulterous generation because they knew how to predict the weather based on the appearance of the sky, but were unable to discern the signs of the times. (Matthew 16:1-5) Yet today, many people claim they don't need to know the signs of the times because they only need to follow Jesus, which sounds super spiritual, but if they were truly following Him, they would be obeying what He told them to do by paying attention to the signs of the times.

If the Israelites had only believed the words of the angel Gabriel, which he spoke to Daniel, they would have recognized Jesus was their Messiah because Gabriel revealed there would be 483 years (69 periods of 7 years each) between the time when a decree was issued to restore and rebuild Jerusalem until the time of the Messiah. (Daniel 9:25) Adding 483 years to the year of the decree issued by Persian King Artaxerxes in 458 BC comes to 25 AD, which was very close to the time Jesus began His ministry and might have been the exact year since many scholars believe Jesus was born in 5 BC. (16.01) Artaxerxes was the fifth King of Persia, son of Xerxes the Great and grandson of Darius. (16.02) Two previous decrees had been issued by previous Persian Kings, Cyrus in 538 BC and Darius I in 522 BC, but by 25 AD, anyone watching would have known those were not the ones Gabriel was talking about because the Messiah did not appear 483 years after those decrees, which would have been in 55 BC and 39 BC. (Ezra 1:1-4, 4:3, 5:13-17, Ezra 6:1-12) So, the Pharisees and Sadducees took sides with Satan, opposing God, even having Jesus arrested and put to death, because they did not believe the prophets.

After Jesus was crucified, His followers were distraught over what happened and greatly disappointed because they thought He was restoring the kingdom to Israel, freeing them from the Romans, so Jesus encountered two of them as they were walking on the road to Emmaus and rebuked them for failing to believe what the prophets had spoken regarding Him. (Luke 24:21-25) At the critical time when they should have been rejoicing by faith, they were defeated by their doubt and unbelief because they didn't believe the prophets, but the good news is God has given us everything we need to avoid making the mistakes they made.

False Prophets:

As the time of His return approaches, it will be more important than ever before to know the words of the prophets as recorded in the scriptures because Jesus warned many false prophets will arise and deceive many people during the generation preceding His return. (Matthew 24:11) I believe we're seeing the fulfillment of His warning today with an unending stream of people claiming to have heard from God, specifically regarding the timing of His return.

At one end of the spectrum are false prophets who continually claim He's returning in the next few weeks or months. They even manipulate their followers by telling them only those who believe it will be taken in the rapture while everyone else will be left behind. When it doesn't happen, instead of humbly repenting, they just push the date back by six months or a year and start the circus act all over again. It's amazing anyone still listens to them, but it goes on and on.

At the other extreme is a far larger group of false prophets claiming His return is way out in the distant future. They assure their followers with promises of peace, safety and prosperity, nothing but blue sky ahead. These are the Hananiah's of our generation, causing God's people to believe in lies while throwing the true prophets, the Jeremiah's, into mud pits to silence their warnings by slandering them and accusing them of being false prophets of gloom and doom. (Jeremiah 28:1-17) It did not end well for Hananiah as his false prophecies cost him his life.

Although the false prophets are contradicting each other, they all agree on their disregard for the scriptures. Without providing any scriptural foundation, they ask their followers to believe them based on nothing more than their claim to have received insights directly from God, which is a huge red flag. We could spare ourselves so much confusion and heartache just by studying the scriptures because regardless of what anyone claims to have heard from God, the scriptures are the ultimate authority for judging every prophetic word.

By studying the words of the prophets recorded in the scriptures, we can safely conclude the Lord is not returning in the next few weeks or months because there are at least 38 scriptural events that must happen first, as shown in Exhibit 24. We can also conclude His return is not way off in the distant future because the signs marking the season of His return are now being fulfilled, as presented in the remaining chapters.

Storm Warning:

On August 28 2014, I dreamed I was alone in a flat barren desert plain. I had no shelter, just a couple of couches outside under the open sky. Then the sky became very dark and ominous, unlike anything I've ever seen. Dark clouds were swirling around as terrifying forces filled the sky from one end to the other until they were engulfing the whole earth. Then I saw long thin black strips floating in the air way up high in the sky, which was very creepy. I knew this storm was about to unleash all sorts of evil on the whole earth and it was already starting, so there seemed to be no escape.

My first reaction was to hide on the ground next to the couches as if they could somehow protect me. I also had a set of keys, which I hid under one of the couches, but soon realized I was not safe there so I took off running as fast as I could. Then the scene changed and I arrived in front of the chapel at my old high school. I used my keys to open the front doors, but as I started to enter, I turned and saw two people walking by in front of the steps leading up to the front doors. I recognized them as two old friends from years ago, an older woman and her adult daughter. This woman has a strong prophetic anointing and had given me many prophetic words in the past. She walked up the steps and said, "The ones who run at the front of the pack..."

Then I finished her sentence, "...see what's coming ahead." She nodded in agreement. The dream ended.

I believe the deep darkness I saw was the same darkness Isaiah saw covering the earth, representing evil spiritual forces of wickedness in the heavenly places engulfing the whole earth before the Lord returns. (Isaiah 60:2, Ephesians 6:12) The thin black strips floating way up high in the sky confirmed evil spirits were causing the great trouble, a time of great distress among nations when men's hearts will fail due to fear of what they see coming upon the world. (Daniel 12:1, Luke 21:25-26, Revelation 6:1-11)

Being all alone with no place to hide shows there will be no natural way to escape from this storm. All I had was two couches, representing places where we find comfort, but the ominous danger made that impossible. The couches offered no protection either, as I tried that and soon realized it was a bad idea. The keys were all I had, representing authority to bind and loose heavenly spiritual powers. (Matthew 16:19) I tried to protect the keys by hiding them under the couch, but that was another bad idea because their only value was in using them by exercising my authority in the spiritual realm, so I took off running as fast as I could to the place where they were meant to work, the house of God, represented by the chapel at my old high school.

Remnant: Signs

I knew this chapel very well because I was required to attend daily services there during my high school years. My senior year, I was put in charge of it as the sacristan, so it was a familiar place which represented another familiar place I've learned to access daily, which is not a physical structure, but a spiritual place in the presence of God. He will be the only refuge from this storm, but He will only be accessible to those who have the keys, which are given only to those who demonstrate their faith in Him by calling upon Him and turning away from all unrighteousness, which is all He requires to qualify for all His promises, including His protection from every storm. (Deuteronomy 11:22-23, 28:7, 2 Chronicles 6:22-23, Psalm 34:17, 34:19, 37:32-33, 37:40, Proverbs 2:7-8, 10:25, 11:6, 11:8, 12:3, 12:21, 13:6, 17:15, 17:26, 18:5, 18:10, 21:18, Isaiah 54:17, 57:1-2)

So, I had two things going for me, the keys and knowing where to use them, which shows I was well prepared, but for those who are not prepared, the fear coming upon the world will make it difficult to acquire the keys and learn how to use them, so I believe this dream is a warning to begin preparing now.

The prophetic word the woman gave me at the end showed another benefit God gives to those who diligently seek Him, the ability to see these things coming before they happen. The unrighteous will not see these things coming, but those who stay close to Him will have plenty of advance warning, including all the signs revealed in Bible prophecies, which are now confirming we are close to the return of the Lord and this great storm. (Amos 3:7) The hour is late and the stakes could not possibly be higher.

ENDNOTES

16.01: Year of Jesus birth, https://en.wikipedia.org/wiki/Chronology_of_Jesus

16.02: Xerxes the Great, https://en.wikipedia.org/wiki/Xerxes_I

17
Israel

After receiving the dreams about the horse and the remnant, I understood it was something God wanted me to share, so I started asking Him how to do that and He directed me to study His plans for Israel, which surprised me because neither of my dreams mentioned anything about them. So, I studied the scriptures and confirmed with great clarity through many prophecies that physical Israel is at the center of His plans for these last days, just as they have been throughout history. Since His plans start and end with them, they provide us with a roadmap to help us find where we are on His prophetic timeline, including His plans for His forerunners.

It was great to confirm all the unfulfilled prophecies for the physical Jewish people, but it remained unclear to me how it connected to my dreams until I started writing this book. Little by little, God revealed the colossal prophetic impact of the Jewish people reclaiming Jerusalem in June 1967, which not only fulfilled many prophecies, but also coincided with a significant acceleration in the fulfillment of many others, specifically the ones Jesus identified as marking the season of His return.

No nation in history has ever been reborn after being conquered and scattered among the nations, but Israel has now done it twice, fulfilling many prophecies. For example, the Prophet Isaiah specifically saw them being gathered a second time from the four corners of the earth, which could only refer to modern Israel. This revelation made such a profound impact on him, he named his first son, Shear-Yashub, which means, "a remnant shall return." (Isaiah 7:3)

> 11 It shall come to pass in that day that the Lord shall set His hand again the second time to recover the remnant of His people who are left, from Assyria and Egypt, from Pathros and Cush, from Elam and Shinar, from Hamath and the islands of the sea.
> 12 He will set up a banner for the nations, and will assemble the outcasts of Israel, and gather together the dispersed of Judah from the four corners of the earth. (Isaiah 11:11-12 NKJV)

The Prophet Zechariah also saw the Jewish people coming from the east and the west to return to Jerusalem. (Zechariah 8:7-8) Since he received this word in 518 BC, twenty years after Israel had already returned home from their first exile in Babylon in 538 BC, it was not fulfilled until they returned from their second exile and reclaimed Jerusalem in 1967. (Zechariah 7:1)

The fulfillment of those prophecies set the stage for the future fulfillment of many other prophecies for the Jewish people, which prove God's not done with the flesh and blood descendants of Abraham, Isaac, and Jacob, contrary to what many are claiming today. They're still at the center of His plans and have not been replaced by the spiritual Jews, as shown in these examples:

- They will look upon the one they pierced and mourn for Him like one would mourn for their only son and they will weep bitterly over Him like the bitter weeping over a firstborn. (Zechariah 12:10-14)
- Jesus will return to Jerusalem, not New York, London, Rome, or any other city. (Zechariah 8:3 and 14:4)
- He is coming back again to fight for the inhabitants of their holy city of Jerusalem. (Zechariah 14:2-7 and 14:12-13)
- The same people who previously rejected the Lord Jesus will see Him again and will say, "Blessed is He who comes in the name of the Lord." (Matthew 23:37-39)
- God will judge all the nations who scattered the Jewish people among the nations and sold them into slavery and divided up His land. (Joel 3:2-3, Zechariah 14:2)
- God will make Jerusalem a heavy stone for all the peoples; all who lift it will be severely injured. (Zechariah 12:3)
- God will deliver a remnant of them on the day of the Lord, just as Moses promised them before they entered the Promised Land. (Deuteronomy 4:25-31, Jeremiah 30:7, Zechariah 8:6-8 and 10:12 and 13:9)
- God will pardon the sins of a remnant of Israel. (Jeremiah 50:19-20, Daniel 9:24, Ezekiel 36:33-36, Romans 11:25-27)
- God will restore the fortunes of Judah and Jerusalem. (Joel 3:1)
- The Jewish people will take possession of lands and cities now belonging to Jordan, Lebanon, and the Palestinian West Bank. (Obadiah 1:19-21)
- A third temple will be built in Jerusalem. (Daniel 9:27, Matthew 24:15, 2 Thessalonians 2:3-4, Revelation 11:1-2)
- "I will also plant them on their land, and they will not again be rooted out from their land, which I have given them," says the Lord your God. (Amos 9:15)
- God will make Jerusalem a praise in the earth as all nations see their righteousness and call them, "The holy people, the redeemed of the Lord." (Isaiah 62)

For a more complete list of 41 unfulfilled prophecies for the Jewish people, see Exhibit 2.

Satan's Five Favorite Lies About the Jewish People:

Since the Jewish people are at the center of God's plans, they are also at the center of Satan's opposition to God's plans. Satan has spread many lies about them, causing great confusion. We are being bombarded today more than ever before with lies filling the airways, especially through the Internet, always trying to convince us God is done with the physical Jewish people. (1 Peter 5:8) Just as he has done repeatedly in the past, Satan misquotes scriptures out of context to spread his lies. (2 Corinthians 11:14) For example, he often uses scriptures referring to spiritual Jews and applies them to physical Jews and vice versa, twisting the meaning. His lies can easily be exposed just by studying the context of the scriptures to show which group it applies to, but if we don't take time to study, we can easily be misled. (1 John 5:19)

I made a list of Satan's five favorite lies and exposed them by the scriptures in Exhibit 3, as listed below. Satan claims God is done with them because:

- Their deeds are unrighteous. Not only did they reject and murder the Messiah, but they continue practicing unrighteousness today.
- There is no longer Jew nor Greek.
- They are not true Jews because they're merely Jews by the flesh.
- They're not true Jews because they're not from the tribe of Judah.
- They're the synagogue of Satan.

If we allow Satan to convince us God is done with them, then we're robbed of the most important prophetic sign of the times, which robs us of our understanding of the times God has chosen for our life, and puts us in danger of making the same mistake Peter made when he took sides with Satan to fight against God. Believing the lies puts us on a slippery slope where we no longer have any reason to stand with them, pray for them, or help them in any way, making it easy for us to take the next steps, aligning with Satan's plans to despise them, persecute them and destroy them, like most of the world is already doing. For example, since Israel became a nation in 1948, the United Nations Human Rights Council and Security Council have passed more resolutions condemning Israel than the rest of the world combined. (17.01, 17.02) During this same time span, these same UN councils have overlooked many horrible atrocities committed by many other nations. Their actions defy all common sense, but they make perfect sense in the context of the war being fought in the spiritual realm over God's plans for Israel.

The True Foundation:

In addition to quoting scriptures out of context, Satan's lies about the Jewish people are based on the mistaken premise that God's plans are based on them, which leads to the wrong conclusions that they've been disqualified for the various reasons listed above, but God's plans have never been based on them, but upon a far more solid foundation, which is unshakeable and unmovable because it's based on Him alone, specifically His great love for them and His faithfulness to His promises, which He made to their fathers. (Deuteronomy 4:31, Deuteronomy 7:7-9, Deuteronomy 9:5, Deuteronomy 10:15, 1 Kings 11:12, 2 Kings 8:19, 2 Kings 19:34, Isaiah 37:35, Ezekiel 20:38, Ezekiel 36:22 and Ezekiel 39:25-27)

If His plans were based on them, He would have chosen a great and mighty people, but instead, He chose the fewest of all people. (Deuteronomy 7:7-9) Even today, the great religions of the world have far more followers than the Jewish people with 1.8 billion Muslims, 1.3 billion Catholics, 1.1 billion Hindus, 900 million Christians, and 520 million Buddhists, but only about 15 million Jewish people. (17.03-17.08)

In the same way, He chose the smallest of all lands, smaller than the state of New Jersey and far less desirable because over half of Israel is a barren desert, virtually uninhabitable. He could have chosen lands filled with majestic mountains, mighty rivers, lovely waterfalls, and lush green forests, but instead He chose the smallest, least desirable, most unwanted, and one of the world's driest lands. Yet, He made no mistakes in His choices because He purposely wanted us to see beyond all the outward appearances, so we would see the unseen source of all the beauty of Israel, which is the God of Israel.

He could have chosen a far more beautiful mountain than Mount Zion, which is more of a big hill than a mountain, and lacking any natural beauty. Even the name Zion reveals the irony because it means "a parched place, an extremely dry and thirsty place." It might as well be called Mount Dreadful because it's the kind of place we all try to avoid. Yet, God says, "'I am zealous for Zion with great zeal; with great fervor, I am zealous (provoked to jealous anger) for her." (Zechariah 8:2 NKJV) Clearly, His zeal goes beyond the physical place, being zealous for what He sees in the unseen realm of the heart of His people who thirst for Him as inhabitants of a spiritually dry place. His eyes search throughout the earth to show His support for those whose heart is completely His. (2 Chronicles 16:9)

The Jewish people, the land of Israel and Mount Zion are all clues to help us see beyond the outward physical realm so we can see into the unseen realm of the spirit like God sees. Yet, Satan does the opposite, always trying to focus our attention on the Jewish people, making it all about them and their shortcomings, in hopes of disqualifying them.

In addition, God has given us many other clues, all designed to put Himself on display for the whole world to see and believe He is the one true God of heaven and earth. For this purpose, He has performed many great miracles and made many great promises. For example, He promised to remember His love for their fathers for a thousand generations. (Deuteronomy 7:9) Even if we assume a generation is only 20 years, that's 20,000 years, which is far longer than the span of human history and continuing far into eternity, demonstrating how big His faithfulness is by doing what only He can do, blessing and honoring the descendants of those who walked uprightly before Him, loved Him and obeyed Him. So, His promise nullifies all Satan's attempts to disqualify them since it's not based on them, but on God's faithfulness to their fathers.

Instead of being disqualified by their mistakes, God has used their mistakes to fulfill His plans, including His plans for the salvation of the world, proving His plans are bigger than their mistakes. For example, when He came and lived among them, He already knew they would reject Him and demand His crucifixion as He stood before Pontius Pilate, shouting, "Crucify Him! His blood shall be on us and on our children!" (Matthew 27:17-26) Instead of derailing His plans, their mistakes were a necessary part of God's plan because the Messiah had to lay down His life to pay the price for the sins of the world, which is why it pleased Him when they struck the Lord Jesus, bruising and killing Him. (Isaiah 53:4-10) He saw it all before it happened and warned them through His prophets that they would reject their Messiah, scourging Him like a lamb led to the slaughter, sneering at Him, pulling His bones out of joint, piercing His hands and feet, killing Him and casting lots for His garments. (Psalm 22:7-18, Isaiah 53:5-7)

Even long before they crucified Him, about thirteen centuries earlier, when they were about to enter the Promised Land, Moses prophesied to all Israel, telling them they would take the land and prosper in it, but then they would turn away from God and worship idols, causing them to lose their nation and be scattered throughout the world. (Deuteronomy 4:1-40) It happened just as Moses warned. They suffered severe consequences, including their land being divided, their sons and daughters killed by the sword, and their survivors taken captive and exiled in a foreign land, which was fulfilled in 70 AD when Jerusalem was conquered by Roman armies. (Amos 7:15-17) However, Moses continued this same prophecy by making an amazing promise to those same people who were listening to him that day:

> 29 But from there you will seek the Lord your God, and you will find Him if you seek Him with all your heart and with all your soul.

> 30 When you are in distress, and all these things come upon you in the latter days, when you turn to the Lord your God and obey His voice
> 31 (for the Lord your God is a merciful God), He will not forsake you nor destroy you, nor forget the covenant of your fathers which He swore to them.
> (Deuteronomy 4:29-31 NKJV)

The original Hebrew language in verse 30 uses the words "acharith yom," which means the end of the age, the last days, the end times. So, this prophecy reveals the descendants of those same people who followed Moses through the wilderness, then followed Joshua as they took possession of the Promised Land, then prospered under King David and King Solomon, but then later turned away from God to follow idols, lost their land and were scattered throughout the nations in 70 AD, are the same people who are heirs to the final part of this prophecy, a great promise which will be fulfilled at the end of this age, during the end times, when a remnant of them will turn back to the Lord their God and obey His voice, and when they do, it will be a demonstration of the mercy of God and His faithfulness to His promises to their fathers and His promise not to forsake them or destroy them.

The only people qualified to fulfill the last part of this prophecy are the ones who fulfilled the first parts because they're the ones who made the mistakes that put them in position for God to demonstrate His mercy and His faithfulness to His other promises. If the last part was given to anyone else, as many people are wrongly claiming, it would not be a demonstration of mercy or faithfulness to those to whom the promise was given. Instead, it would break His promise in verse 31, which states, "He will not forsake you nor destroy you, nor forget the covenant of your fathers which He swore to them." Therefore, based on this prophecy and many others listed in Exhibit 2, the physical Jewish people remain at the center of God's plans for these last days.

Although the Jewish people have made many mistakes, just as all people have, the consequences of their mistakes have been more severe because God entrusted them with greater responsibility than other people, choosing them as the carriers of His plans for the salvation of the world. Many terrible crimes are still being committed by Jewish people today. Even the man of sin, the antichrist, will be Jewish, from the tribe of Dan. (Genesis 49:16-17, Numbers 26:42-43, Deuteronomy 33:22) Yet, none of that can derail God's plans to redeem a remnant of Israel because He built His plans upon a far more solid foundation.

Since God's promises are founded upon His own faithfulness and His own mercy, there is nothing anyone can do to derail His plans, not even Satan, because God already saw it all coming ahead of time, as He demonstrated by using Satan's evil schemes to destroy

Satan's kingdom. For example, Satan would never have had Jesus killed if he had known it would destroy his own kingdom. (1 Corinthians 2:8)

Satan's claims that the Jewish people have been disqualified make perfect sense from the perspective of our limited human love, but he has no answer for the love of God showing mercy to those who pierced Him, even causing a remnant of them to return to Him in the end to receive His forgiveness with all charges dropped, their death penalty cancelled, and their fortunes restored. Only God could do that. Only God would do that.

Two Zionist Plans:

God's plans for the Jewish people to possess the land of Israel is called Zionism, but Satan has sowed much confusion by using the same name to promote his own plans, so there are two kinds of Zionism, the true and the counterfeit. It's another example of how Satan disguises himself as an angel of light and as a fellow Christian, always offering a counterfeit of the real thing.

God is very zealous for His plans for the land of Israel, saying, "For Zion's sake I will not keep silent, and for Jerusalem's sake I will not keep quiet, until her righteousness goes forth like brightness, and her salvation like a torch that is burning." (Isaiah 62:1) So, He is zealous to bring the Jewish people back to their land, as He has already been doing since 1948, so He can rescue them by bringing them to the knowledge of the Messiah, forgiving their sins, and demonstrating His faithfulness. (Isaiah 10:21-23, 11:11-12 and 62:2, Daniel 9:24, Ezekiel 36:33-36, Zechariah 3:8-10, 7:1 and 13:1-2, Romans 11:25-27)

However, Satan has been pursuing his Zionist plans from the beginning by relying on all sorts of evil deeds, including murder, bribery, extortion, lies, and theft, while blaming his despicable actions on the Jewish people, using them as scapegoats to ignite the wrath of the world against them and repeatedly stirring up extreme wrath to exterminate them. To that end, he is supporting their return to their land in the hopes of making it easier to exterminate them once they get there by eventually gathering his armies around Jerusalem, but his plans will fail again as God intervenes to fight in their behalf. (Joel 3:2-3, Zechariah 14:2, Luke 21:20-24)

And just as he has done in the past, Satan is once again planning to use them to rebuild their temple. For example, in 175 BC, Antiochus IV Epiphanes offered to help restore the second temple, but then he betrayed the Jewish people by erecting a statue of Zeus on the temple mound. (2 Maccabees 8) A similar thing happened in 10 BC when King Herod I, Rome's appointed ruler over Judea, offered to restore the second temple, but then betrayed them by placing a gold eagle, the symbol of the Roman Empire, above the entry, defiling the temple by giving honor to Rome's pagan gods. (17.09) Herod's plan all along was to claim it for himself, just like the coming antichrist. (Daniel 9:27, 2 Thessalonians 2:3-4) When some of the Jews tore down the eagle in 5 BC, Herod had them burned alive. (17.10, 17.11)

Satan's schemes for the third temple are revealed by the coming seven-year covenant with the many, which will allow Israel to rebuild their temple and restore their sacrifices and offerings, but it will be a trick to betray them as he breaks his covenant in the middle of the seven-year period. (Daniel 9:27) The man of lawlessness will then take the temple for himself and establish his throne there to rule the world from Jerusalem. (Matthew 24:15, 2 Thessalonians 2:1-4)

Satan's brand of Zionism is all about exalting himself because he says in his heart,

> "I will ascend to heaven; I will raise my throne above the stars of God, and I will sit on the mount of assembly in the recesses of the north. 'I will ascend above the heights of the clouds; I will make myself like the Most High.'" (Isaiah 14:13-14)

Yet, Satan's arrogance leads him to his destruction, sealing his own fate, as God replies to him,

> "Nevertheless you will be thrust down to Sheol, to the recesses of the pit. Those who see you will gaze at you, they will ponder over you, saying, 'Is this the man who made the earth tremble, who shook kingdoms? (Isaiah 14:15-16)

Since there are two different Zionist plans with completely different outcomes, keen discernment is required to know which events are from God and which are counterfeits. Otherwise, we could find ourselves blindly supporting Satan's plans and fighting against God's plans. Both plans have been unfolding for centuries and will continue until the Lord returns to crush Satan's kingdom and deliver a remnant of the Jewish people.

Prophecy from Rabbi Judah Ben Samuel:

The following prophetic word reveals the Messianic end times started when the Jewish people reclaimed Jerusalem in 1967. It was received over 800 years ago in 1217 AD by Rabbi Judah Ben Samuel. (17.12, 17.13) Although it's not in the Bible, I believe he heard correctly because it was completely fulfilled over the next 850 years.

Remnant: Israel

"When the Ottomans conquer Jerusalem, they will rule over Jerusalem for eight jubilees (400 years). Afterwards, Jerusalem will become a no-man's land for one jubilee (50 years), and then in the ninth jubilee it will once again come back into the possession of the Jewish nation, which would signify the beginning of the Messianic end time."

Note: Jubilee years occur once every 50 years. (Leviticus 25:1-12)

The first part started exactly 300 years later when the Ottoman Empire, which was Islamic, conquered Jerusalem in 1517. Just as the Rabbi was told, they ruled over it for 400 years, until the British drove them out in 1917. Then, just as he was told, Jerusalem became a no-man's land for the next 50 years, until it was reclaimed by Israel in 1967, which marked the start of the ninth jubilee. Israel retained possession of Jerusalem throughout the ninth jubilee, which ended in 2017. His prophecy did not reveal what happened beyond that, but it implies there could be another shift starting around that time. We now have the benefit of hindsight to know the first three parts were fulfilled exactly in the time periods he was told, which gives credibility to the last part, which identifies 1967 as the starting point for the Messianic end times, the season of the Lord's return.

Rabbi Judah Ben Samuel further connected his prophecy with the time of the Lord's return when he was asked where he received it. He answered, "The Prophet Elijah, who will precede the Messiah, appeared to me and revealed many things to me and emphasized that the pre-condition for answered prayer is that it is fueled by enthusiasm and joy for the greatness and holiness of God." (Malachi 4:5-6) As shown in Part 1, Elijah would be the ideal person to reveal the events marking the start of the season of the Lord's return since God has chosen him as the forerunner.

So, if the Messianic end times started in 1967, the next question is, when will it end? I believe Jesus gave us the answer in His parable of the fig tree, revealing the generation who sees the fulfillment of these signs will not pass away until they are all fulfilled. (Matthew 24:32-34) But this raises another question, how long is one generation? The Bible tells us it is 70 or 80 years and when it's over, we fly away. (Psalm 90:10) I believe this has a double meaning, referring to both the life of an individual and the length of the final generation prior to the Lord's return. Flying away at the end also sounds like a double meaning, referring to our individual spirits leaving our body when we die and the great catching away of the righteous when the Lord returns to gather His elect from the four winds, from one end of the sky to the other. (Matthew 24:31)

We're not going to know the exact day or hour, and perhaps not even the year, but if

Remnant: Israel

the season of His return started in 1967, adding 70 or 80 years puts it between 2037 and 2047. Other scriptures can also help us estimate how close we are. I've also received some personal prophecies that make me think it will not be before 2040. So, the exact timing is unknown, but I believe we have enough evidence to conclude our generation will see His return, as confirmed by seven additional signs presented in the remaining chapters.

ENDNOTES

17.01: United Nations Human Rights Council, https://en.wikipedia.org/wiki/United_Nations_Human_Rights_Council#Israel

17.02: United Nations Human Rights Council and Security Council https://en.wikipedia.org/wiki/List_of_United_Nations_resolutions_concerning_Israel

17.03: Islam, https://en.wikipedia.org/wiki/Islam

17.04: Roman Catholics, https://en.wikipedia.org/wiki/Catholic_Church

17.05: Hinduism https://en.wikipedia.org/wiki/Hindus

17.06: Christianity, https://en.wikipedia.org/wiki/Christianity

17.07: Buddhism, https://en.wikipedia.org/wiki/Buddhism#Demographics

17.08: Jewish demographics, https://en.wikipedia.org/wiki/Judaism#Jewish_demographics

17.09: Herod persecution of Jews, https://en.wikipedia.org/wiki/Siege_of_Jerusalem_(37_BC)

17.10: Kantor, Mattis. The Jewish Time Line Encyclopedia: A Year-by-Year History From Creation to the Present (Kindle Locations 2755-2758). Jason Aronson, Inc.

17.11: Herod persecution of Jews, https://en.wikipedia.org/wiki/Herod_Archelaus

17.12: Rabbi Judah Ben Samuel, https://en.wikipedia.org/wiki/Judah_ben_Samuel_of_Regensburg

17.13: Rabbi Judah Ben Samuel prophecy, https://www.wnd.com/2012/11/12th-century-rabbi-predicted-israels-future/

18
Earthquakes

The Bible warns of increased earthquake activity prior to and after the Lord's return. The earth will stagger like a drunkard, tottering back and forth like a shack, as it endures increased splitting and violent shaking as a sign identifying the time when He will punish the fallen hosts of heaven and the unrepentant kings of the earth. (Isaiah 24:19-23, Matthew 24:7) The shaking will intensify until reaching a peak with earthquakes of unprecedented magnitude causing every mountain and island to be moved out of their place and cities and nations to fall. (Revelation 6:12-14 and 16:17-19)

Worldwide earthquake data from the United States Geological Survey (USGS) confirms the fulfillment of these prophecies has started, as earthquake activity increased dramatically after the rebirth of Israel in 1948, starting with a +550% increase in the 1950's compared to the previous decade, and continuing afterwards, as shown in the chart on the next page, which includes all major earthquakes, defined as magnitude 5.6 or greater, from 1900 to 2019, which is as far back as their data goes. (18.01)

The dramatic and sustained increase since the rebirth of Israel confirms the significance of that event, even impacting the whole earth. Although the total dropped a little in the most recent decade, it was still the second highest ever.

Remnant: Earthquakes

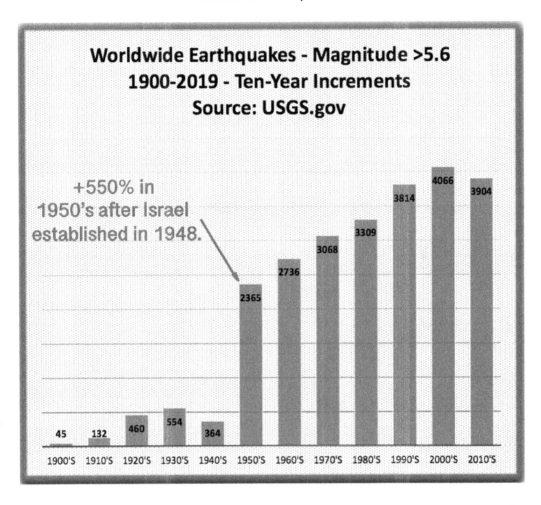

Note: The 2010's decade includes actual data for 109 months plus projected data for the final 11 months of 2019.

ENDNOTES

18.01: United States Geological Survey, https://earthquake.usgs.gov/earthquakes/search

19
Knowledge and Travel

Increased knowledge and travel are more signs marking the season of the Lord's return. (Daniel 12:4) This chapter presents evidence showing the fulfillment of these prophecies has accelerated in recent years, including breakthroughs in technology that happened at about the same time the Jewish people reclaimed Jerusalem in 1967.

Until the invention of the printing press in 1439, knowledge increased slowly because it was only possible to share information verbally or in hand-written letters. That was a big step forward, but another 400 years passed before more inventions brought new ways of sharing, including the first cameras in the early 1800's, audio recording in 1877, telephones in the 1880's, movie cameras in 1889, radio broadcasting in the 1920's and television broadcasting in 1941. (19.01-19.07)

Those inventions brought many significant changes, but their initial impact was somewhat limited compared to what's happening today. For example, televisions only had a few channels in the early days, so the initial impact was limited by the lack of content, and telephones were only available on land lines, so the lack of mobility limited our usage compared to what's happening today. In many ways, life remained like it had always been, with most social interaction still face to face.

In June 1977, the increase in knowledge accelerated with the first successful mass marketing of personal computers, but again the initial impact was limited due to slow processors and small storage space, but those limitations were quickly removed as processing speeds doubled every 18 months since the 1970's. (19.08, 19.09) By the late 1990's, personal computers started connecting to the Internet and mobile computing devices followed soon afterwards, producing exponential increases in knowledge.

It's easy to lose sight of how much mobile electronic devices have changed our lives because we so quickly adapt to the new normal, but I think the following short story helps put it in perspective. In the summer of 1998, I took my son on a camping trip with a boys group from our church. One of the other dads asked me what kind of work I was doing, so I told him I was preparing to launch an online store on the Internet. He gave me a puzzled look and said, "There is no way people are ever going to go shopping on their computer!"

His comment sounds crazy now, but at the time, a lot of people would have agreed with him. Wi-Fi was unheard of back then so most people had very slow dial-up connections. (19.10) Even after connecting, there were few online stores and very limited selection. The next year, in 1999, the online shopping boom started when corporate America started promoting their new websites in their advertisements, igniting explosive growth in dot com businesses.

Many things that are now part of our daily routines didn't even exist a few years ago. For example, smart phones didn't exist in the United States until 2002, and didn't catch on until 2006. Facebook didn't start until 2004. YouTube started in 2005. Twitter didn't exist until 2006. Podcasts didn't exist until 2004. Instagram started in 2010. Wikipedia didn't exist until 2000. Netflix didn't offer any streaming content until 2005. Listening to music required CD's and a CD player because there were no mp3 music players available. Apple launched their first iPod in 2001. Spotify didn't exist until 2008. (19.11-19.20)

All these inventions have created a rapid acceleration in knowledge that has transformed us into tech addicts, making it almost unthinkable to leave home without our devices or even allow their batteries to go dead. We walk around like zombies, constantly staring at our screens, which are exposing us to far more knowledge than any previous generation with an unending supply of facts, stories, places, products, photos, movies, games, people, and interactive discussions.

Each new bit of data is nudging us along, shifting our perceptions, shaping our opinions, changing our understanding, constantly moving us in one direction or another, for good or evil, right or wrong, like countless seeds planted in our mind, taking root in our heart, where they're sprouting, growing, and producing harvests after their kind that just keep expanding as the exponential increase in the number of seeds sown is producing an exponential increase in the harvests produced, which keeps getting multiplied by each new harvest because that's how God designed seedtime and harvest. (Genesis 1:11-12) Good seeds are producing good harvests of love, joy, peace, patience, kindness, goodness, faithfulness, gentleness, and self-control while bad seeds are producing bad harvests of immorality, impurity, sensuality, idolatry, sorcery, enmities, strife, jealousy, outbursts of anger, disputes, dissensions, factions, envying, drunkenness, carousing, and things like these. (Galatians 5:19-23) In both cases, the rate of transformation is accelerating, producing a rapidly growing contrast between the righteous and the unrighteous, fulfilling Isaiah's prophecy of darkness and light both increasing at the same time, which is another sign of the times. (Isaiah 60:1-5)

Changes that previously took generations are now happening in a few years. For example, consider how fast public opinion changed regarding homosexual marriage. As recently as 2000, it was against the law in every state in the United States and in every nation in the world. The first nation to legalize it was the Netherlands in 2001, followed by Belgium in 2003. When Barack Obama was elected President in November 2008, only one state had legalized it, Massachusetts in 2004. By his second term, it was legal in all fifty states due to a court ruling on June 26, 2015. (19.21) Many other nations quickly followed, resulting in an amazing transformation of the world in a short time, showing the impact of rapid increases in knowledge.

The changes in public opinion regarding our sexual conduct is disturbing because of the havoc it has caused. For example, determining our own gender used to be a simple matter of checking our anatomy, but it has become so complicated, many people are struggling to figure it out, especially among the younger generation. If so much damage can be done is such a short time, where will we be in another ten or twenty years?

Another major change has happened very quietly. As the great benefits of our access to knowledge have received universal acceptance, it has made the most knowledgeable generation in history the most vulnerable generation in history because despite all the knowledge we've acquired, we've lost the most basic knowledge of survival skills, which was passed down through every previous generation, but was not passed down to us because it's no longer considered worth knowing, at least not yet. Our unprecedented knowledge is like bait luring us into a terrible trap because we've become increasingly dependent on a system that can suddenly go down. Hardly any of us know how to grow our own food or hunt for it, or preserve it without the help of freezers or refrigerators, or prepare it without the help of electric or gas powered ovens or stoves. We're completely dependent upon an elaborate high-tech distribution system for all our essential items like food, water and fuel, which is great until there's a disruption and history shows they happen, including natural disasters, wars, and economic collapses. Any disruption in our power grid would quickly shut down all our electronic devices and communication systems, causing potentially dire circumstances, which is exactly what the Bible warns is coming upon the world with greater intensity than ever before. (Daniel 12:1, Revelation 6:1-11)

As knowledge has increased, God's light has also increased through the knowledge of His word. It was obstructed for centuries because the masses weren't allowed access to the Bible. Even the few copies available were written in Latin, which most people didn't understand. It wasn't translated into English until 1382 when John Wycliffe risked his life to do so. (19.22) But even then, Bible's weren't widely distributed until the printing press was invented in 1439. And even then, many wars were fought to finally win the right to distribute Bibles in languages understood by the general population. (19.01) As the knowledge of the scriptures spread throughout the world, many great moves of God were ignited, which changed the course of history as Christians gained liberty from evil tyrants to form their own governments in which the people were given a voice. Increased knowledge of the word of God accelerated in 1968 when, for the first time ever, the masses were equipped with personal cassette recorders, making it possible to listen on demand to the Bible and Bible teachings. These portable devices were first introduced in 1964, but first gained widespread acceptance by 1968, reaching $150 million in sales, just one year after the Jewish people reclaimed Jerusalem. (19.23)

Singularity:

Even though rapid increases in knowledge have already changed the world faster than ever before, it's expected to accelerate even more because the technological innovations fueling the changes are accelerating. Ray Kurzweil, a former Google engineer and author of several futurist books, predicts by the 2030's, we will be able to connect our neo-cortex, the part of our brain where we do our thinking, to the virtual cloud, allowing us to access and share data without assistance from any external devices. By 2045, he predicts technology will reach the point of singularity, which is when human intelligence increases a billion-fold by merging with artificial intelligence (AI) and machine intelligence surpasses human intelligence with the ability to conceive new ideas no human being has ever thought before, thus enabling machines to invent new technologies more sophisticated and advanced than anything we have today, causing an even faster acceleration in new technologies. (19.24) Ray Kurzweil has a great track record in predicting new technologies, including smart phones, broadband Internet, virtual reality headsets, speech to text programs, intelligent answering machines, driverless cars, and voice recognition devices. (19.25)

Knowledge is power, so increasing knowledge by a billion-fold is only good if accompanied with the wisdom to know how to use it. In the hands of the wrong people, unrighteous people using it for their own unrighteous purposes, singularity would have unimaginable consequences. The dramatic acceleration in spiritual darkness in the past twenty years would pale in comparison to what would happen after achieving singularity. It would be a game changer moment in history, taking us to a place God never intended us to go without Him, like building the Tower of Babel that reaches all the way to heaven. (Genesis 11:1-9) God didn't allow that to happen and I don't believe He will allow this either because if it was going to happen, I think He would have warned us, but there's no mention of anything like it in any Bible prophecies. Plus, the timing of Ray Kurzweil's forecast for achieving it by 2045 falls within the 2037 to 2047 window, possibly the time of the Lord's return, which is quite a coincidence and sounds like another clue that God will intervene to stop it. (Matthew 24:22)

The journey to singularity has already started as we have become increasingly dependent upon technology, keeping our devices always within reach, but the ultimate goal of transhumanists is to make us one with technology, so we become something beyond human, giving us god-like powers without any need for God, even achieving immortality. Meanwhile, God is pursuing a different version of singularity by raising up a remnant to become one with Him, increasingly dependent upon Him, which has already started through our pursuit of righteousness, which brings us into closer alignment with His will, His plans, and His purposes, and with each other, joining us together as one body, bringing us to full maturity of what He has always wanted us to be, a pure and spotless bride, totally devoted to Him. (Ephesians 5:27)

Ironically, the same advances in technology moving the world closer to singularity are also helping the remnant draw closer to God by giving us unprecedented access to the scriptures, Bible commentaries, Bible teachings, anointed music, plus remote access to worship sessions, prayer meetings, revival services, and fellowship with like-minded people anywhere in the world. So, technology is empowering hungry disciples to grow stronger and faster in faith than any previous generation, causing righteousness to arise, shining brighter and brighter until the Son of Man appears in the sky like lightning flashing from the east to the west. (Isaiah 10:20-23, Malachi 4:2, Matthew 24:27)

Just as Ray Kurzweil's version of singularity produces a billion-fold increase in knowledge, God's version also produces an exponential increase as His forerunners tap into the realm where all things are possible to demonstrate His divine nature in greater ways than ever seen before, attracting the attention of the world and bringing in a great harvest of souls. (Psalm 133:1-3, Isaiah 60:1-5, Amos 9:13-15, Zechariah 2:10-12, Matthew 13:24-30, Mark 16:15-18, John 12:32-33, 14:12-13, 17:20-23, Acts 1:7-8)

Image and Mark of the Beast:

Technological inventions have made it possible to fulfill end time prophecies that could not have been fulfilled in any previous generation. Amazingly, the timing of these inventions closely coincides with the Jewish people reclaiming Jerusalem in 1967.

For example, the second beast, also called the false prophet, will require everyone to take a mark on their right hand or their forehead, which will be used for making and tracking financial transactions, buying and selling. (Revelation 13:16-18, 19:20) This technology already exists and tens of thousands of people have already received RFID microchip implants. (19.26) Anyone can now order their own chip implant kits online, starting at $99. (19.27) The benefits, especially convenience, are already being promoted by chip makers, such as IBM, with big advertising budgets devoted to building a market for their products. Microchips are being used for all sorts of things, including unlocking doors, tracking inventory, monitoring medical patients, boarding airline flights, and managing farm animals. American inventor Mario Cardullo is credited with inventing the first true ancestor of the modern RFID microchip, which was first presented to investors as a business plan in 1969 showing potential uses in transportation, banking, security, and medical industries. It was later publicly demonstrated to the New York Port Authority in 1971 and received a U.S. Patent in 1973. (19.28)

The false prophet will also instruct the inhabitants of the earth to make an image of the beast. He will give the image the ability to breathe and speak, and he will require everyone to worship it or be killed. (Revelation 13:14-15) With such lifelike abilities, this image seems likely to have a three-dimensional appearance. Three dimensional image technology was not possible in any previous generation, but is now possible through holograms, which were invented in 1962 by Russian physicist Yuri Denisyuk. (19.29) The image would then need to be visible to everyone, which would require worldwide broadcasting, which was not possible in any previous generation, but is now possible through satellite television broadcasting. The world's first commercial communications satellite, called "Early Bird," was launched into orbit on April 6, 1965, followed by the world's first national network of television satellites, called Orbita, which was created by the Soviet Union in October, 1967. (19.30)

Increased Travel:

Increased travel is another sign marking the season of the Lord's return. (Daniel 12:4) Methods of travel remained relatively unchanged throughout history until a series of inventions starting with steam powered locomotives in 1801, iron steamships in 1821, gasoline powered automobiles in 1893, and airplanes in 1905. (19.31-19.33)

Travel made a quantum leap forward soon after Israel reclaimed Jerusalem in 1967. By the next year, 1968, the first manned spacecraft, Apollo 8, orbited the moon, and the next year, in July 1969, Neil Armstrong and Buzz Aldrin traveled to the moon aboard Apollo 11 and got out and walked around. (19.34) Two years later, in 1971, the first space probes landed on Mars and many more have gone there every year since. (19.35)

Although travel has been increasing for the past two centuries, our generation is the first to experience rapid travel as a routine part of our life and the first to see manned space travel, which seems appropriate for the generation who will soon be caught up to meet the Lord in the sky. (Matthew 24:29-31)

ENDNOTES

19.01: Invention of printing press, https://en.wikipedia.org/wiki/Printing_press211

19.02: Invention of photography, https://en.wikipedia.org/wiki/Photography

19.03: Invention of audio recording, https://en.wikipedia.org/wiki/Sound_recording_and_reproduction

19.04: Invention of telephones, https://en.wikipedia.org/wiki/Telephone#History

19.05: Invention of movie cameras, https://en.wikipedia.org/wiki/Movie_camera

19.06: Invention of radios, https://en.wikipedia.org/wiki/Radio#History

19.07: Invention of televisions, https://en.wikipedia.org/wiki/History_of_television#Overview

19.08: https://en.wikipedia.org/wiki/Personal_computer#History

19.09: Moore's Law: http://www.umsl.edu/~siegelj/information_theory/projects/Bajramovic/www.umsl.edu/_abdcf/Cs4890/link1.html

19.10: Invention of Wi-Fi, https://en.wikipedia.org/wiki/Wi-Fi

19.11: History of Smartphones, https://en.wikipedia.org/wiki/Smartphone

19.12: History of Facebook, https://en.wikipedia.org/wiki/Facebook

19.13: History of YouTube, https://en.wikipedia.org/wiki/YouTube

19.14: History of Twitter, https://en.wikipedia.org/wiki/Twitter

19.15: History of Podcast, https://en.wikipedia.org/wiki/Podcast

19.16: History of Instagram, https://en.wikipedia.org/wiki/Instagram

19.17: History of Wikipedia, https://en.wikipedia.org/wiki/Wikipedia

19.18: History of Netflix, https://en.wikipedia.org/wiki/Netflix

19.19: History of iPod, https://en.wikipedia.org/wiki/IPod

19.20: History of Spotify, https://en.wikipedia.org/wiki/Spotify

19.21: Same sex marriages, https://en.wikipedia.org/wiki/Same-sex_marriage#Contemporary

Remnant: Knowledge and Travel

19.22: First Bible translation in English, https://en.wikipedia.org/wiki/John_Wycliffe

19.23: History of personal cassette recorders, https://www.encyclopedia.com/media/encyclopedias-almanacs-transcripts-and-maps/cassette-tape

19.24: Ray Kurzweil predictions, https://en.wikipedia.org/wiki/Predictions_made_by_Ray_Kurzweil

19.25: Singularity, https://futurism.com/kurzweil-claims-that-the-singularity-will-happen-by-2045/

19.26: RFID chip implants, https://www.wsj.com/articles/when-information-storage-gets-under-your-skin-1474251062

19.27: Order chip implants, https://dangerousthings.com/shop/xnti/

19.28: First RFID microchips in 1969, http://www.globalventurelabels.com/history-of-rfid/

19.29: 3D holograms invented in 1962, https://en.wikipedia.org/wiki/Yuri_Nikolaevich_Denisyuk

19.30: First satellite television broadcasting in 1967, https://en.wikipedia.org/wiki/Satellite_television#Early_history

19.31: Invention of steamships, https://en.wikipedia.org/wiki/Steamship

19.32: Invention of cars, https://en.wikipedia.org/wiki/Car#History

19.33: Invention of airplanes, https://en.wikipedia.org/wiki/Airplane

19.34: History of space flight, https://en.wikipedia.org/wiki/Human_spaceflight

19.35: History of space probes on Mars, https://en.wikipedia.org/wiki/Exploration_of_Mars

20

Lawlessness

Although lawlessness has been around since the beginning, Jesus said it would increase during the season preceding His return, causing the love of many to grow cold, so this is another sign of the times. (amplified from Greek word plethyno in Matthew 24:12)

Other prophecies reveal events that could cause the love of many to grow cold as many will endure the most severe kinds of cruelty, brutal acts, senseless crimes, reckless deeds, totally unjustified violence committed against them and their innocent loved ones. (2 Timothy 3:1-5) It's enough to fuel outrage and a response in like kind, even over the objections of their own conscience, which will require the victims to cast off all restraints as they seek revenge, producing a multiplication of lawlessness with even more reckless disregard for God's commandments. (Galatians 5:23)

Before the Lord returns, the spirit of lawlessness will be given authority over every tribe, language, and nation on earth, ruling over a global government, economy and religion for a brief period of 42 months, while making war against the saints and overcoming us. (Revelation 13:5-18) Although the world has endured much trouble in the past, we have yet to see what this spirit would do if it had its' way because God has restrained it, but as the Day of the Lord draws closer, He is removing the one who has been restraining it. (2 Thessalonians 2:7-8) The fulfillment of these prophecies appears to leave no place for a superpower like the United States to continue operating as the world's largest economy, most powerful military, and the world's reserve currency, but since the prophecies must be fulfilled, big changes must be coming to our nation. (Revelation 13:7) And lots of evidence shows the changes have already started.

For example, in the mid-1960's, about the same time the Jewish people reclaimed Jerusalem, a countercultural revolution started among a generation of young Americans, opening the door for a spirit of rebellion and increased lawlessness. In every possible way, they revolted against the establishment, represented by their parents' generation, embracing whatever their parents considered taboo. If their parents wore collared shirts and slacks, they wore blue jeans and t-shirts. If their parents wore their hair short, they wore theirs long. If their parents drank alcohol, they smoked pot and popped pills. If their parents liked ballroom dancing, they made up their own free-style dancing. If their parents liked easy-listening music, they listened to hard rock. If their dads were clean-shaved, the sons grew beards and mustaches. If their moms wore bras, the daughters burned theirs. If their parents supported the Vietnam war, they protested against it and dodged the draft. If their parents believed it was wrong to have sex outside of marriage, they had premarital sex with as many partners as they wanted. (20.01, 20.02)

They cast off all restraint to indulge their carnal appetites in whatever pleased them, while giving their wholehearted approval with terms like groovy, cool, and far out. They were called hippies and their motto was, ""If it feels good, do it!" which was almost identical to the Satanist motto, "Do what thou wilt." In their pursuit of total freedom from all authority, they rebelled against God's commandments, not realizing they were giving themselves over as slaves to obey the spirit of lawlessness, the same spirit ruling over the Satanists. (Romans 6:16) They rejected the Christian faith practiced by their parents to pursue astrology, Buddhism, Hinduism, Wicca, and pagan witchcraft and they celebrated the dawning of the age of Aquarius. During this same time, the Church of Satan was founded, on April 30, 1966, in one of the most popular hippy areas, San Francisco, CA. It was the first organized church in modern times to be devoted to Satan. (20.03)

The door was opened for the spirit of lawlessness to sow many bad seeds, which have taken root and produced a harvest of bad fruit. (Galatians 5:19-21) By the mid-1970's, the countercultural revolution had spread throughout the world, sowing seeds of lawlessness wherever it went.

In the United States, those seeds took root and grew up to produce the increased strife and division operating today. For example, in October 2014, the Lord told me increased tensions were coming between the American people and He said it would start "next year," which was 2015. At that time, I saw no evidence of it, but it began when Donald Trump announced his campaign for the presidency on June 16, 2015. (20.04) Since then, we've seen more strife and division than any time since the Civil War on just about every topic. Hostilities have increased so much, it has reached the point that anyone sharing proven facts now faces public intimidation, bullying, slandering, and just about anything to keep them quiet.

By 2015, the same year the bad fruit started increasing in the United States, it started increasing exponentially throughout the world, as shown in the chart on the next page, which shows the yearly total numbers of worldwide violent attacks on innocent people from 1970 to 2018. (20.05)

As shown in the chart, prior to 2000, terrorist incidents were consistently rare, but increased significantly starting in 2000, the year before the 9/11 attacks. By 2015, there were 402 attacks, which was an all-time high and a 52% increase over the previous year, but it was just the beginning. The sudden spike in 2016 was sustained in 2017 and 2018. This very unusual pattern cannot be explained by normal population growth, so something else must have changed suddenly.

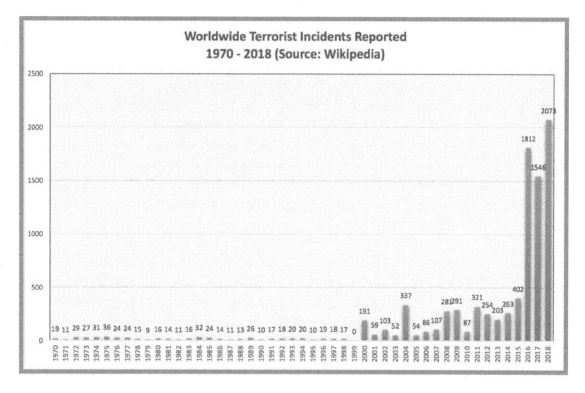

The significant shift in 2015 has impacted the whole world, putting us on track to fulfill many other Bible prophecies, as described in Isaiah 60. God revealed these changes back in the mid-1980's, thirty years in advance, through the following prophetic word given to Dr. James Maloney, author and President of Dove on the Rise International (20.06):

> "Starting in 2015, the darkness of Isaiah 60 will begin to increase exponentially across the globe, but the remnant will arise and shine because the glory of the Lord is rising upon you. This darkness isn't comprised solely of arrant sin, but of a spirit of antichrist." (20.07)

The sudden spike in terrorist attacks coincides perfectly with the exponential increase in darkness. By investigating further, I discovered what happened in 2015 to cause these increases. I found over 90% of the attacks from 1970 to 2018 were committed by

Remnant: Lawlessness

Muslims, which makes sense because the Islamic Koran instructs them to murder and terrorize non-Muslims, as shown in the Koran verses listed in Exhibit 25. Since the Koran is the authoritative source defining Islam, it proves Islam is a violent ideology, not a religion of peace, contrary to repeated claims made by our government leaders. The most dangerous Muslims are the ones who faithfully obey the Koran. Fortunately, many Muslims are backslidden.

Although Muslims have been obeying the Koran for centuries, their violent attacks only increased in recent years, so there must be another explanation, and there is. Starting in 2015 and continuing since then, millions of Muslims invaded Europe. The mainstream news media called them migrants, but migrants bring their families. These invaders were almost 100% young Muslim males. They marched in together like a great army coming from Middle Eastern and North African nations and settled all across Europe, including Germany, France, Italy, Spain, Austria, Belgium, Denmark, Finland, Norway, the Netherlands, Sweden, Switzerland, and the United Kingdom. (20.08) In every nation where they settled, violent attacks on innocent citizens immediately skyrocketed and have continued ever since. (20.09-20.11)

In the span of a few years, the European continent was transformed. For example, in Sweden, a 2017 police report showed there were 61 vulnerable areas, commonly called no-go zones because lawlessness is so prevalent in those areas, citizens and even police avoid going there, which is a big number considering Sweden only has 290 municipalities. (20.12) Similar problems have been reported in the UK, Germany, France, Spain, and other nations.

In Denmark, Prime Minister Lars Løkke Rasmussen summed it up in his 2019 New Year's speech, saying, "When I was in high school, there were around 50,000 people with a non-Western background in Denmark. Today, there are almost half a million. In one generation, our country has changed". (20.13) A half million immigrants is huge considering Denmark's population is only 5.7 million. (20.14)

Even more amazing than the invasion is the way government leaders in nation after nation oddly did nothing to stop it. (20.15-20.17) Nations have borders and immigration laws to protect their citizens from this kind of thing, but the spirit of lawlessness disregards all boundaries. In nation after nation, government leaders yielded to this spirit as they ordered their police and other authorities to stand down, even issuing gag orders to stop the news media from reporting the ethnic background of criminals caught committing violent crimes. (20.18)

When foreigners invade your nation, the correct response is not complicated, but

European leaders have consistently acted like there's just nothing they can do about it. Meanwhile, they have consistently made absurd statements, like the ones shown here from Pope Francis.

> "Authentic Islam and the proper reading of the Koran are opposed to every form of violence." (20.19)

> "Islam is a religion of peace, one which is compatible with respect for human rights and peaceful coexistence." (20.20)

> "Muslim terrorism does not exist. They do not exist. No people is criminal or drug-trafficking or violent." (20.21)

Although Pope Francis is commonly identified as a religious leader, he is also a government leader since Vatican City is a sovereign nation. Statements from other world leaders were almost verbatim quotes, like they're all drinking the same Kool-Aid, sticking to the same party line and ignoring all the facts.

Meanwhile, anyone attempting to share the facts has been attacked with accusations of being racist, hateful and Islamophobic. For example, in France, in March 2018, a formal investigation was launched to find out why presidential candidate Marine LePen shared images on Twitter of Islamic militants beheading their victims back in 2015. By September, the investigation led to a French court ordering her to complete psychiatric exams to determine whether she's suffering from mental illness. (20.22) The court ruling not only damaged her political aspirations and publicly humiliated her, but it was an effective bullying tactic warning others to keep silent.

The people of Europe are fed up with it. For example, in Germany, thousands of people have protested in the streets due to inaction by their government's authorities. In a 2017 election, more than a million Germans shifted their political allegiance to support a new rising party called Alternative for Germany (AfD), making them Germany's third largest party, capturing 12.6% of the vote. A poll conducted a year later, September 3, 3018, showed AfD support surging to 17%, making them a force to be reckoned with. (20.23) Similar shifts are happening in other European nations.

What are the chances millions of Muslim males decided to invade all these European nations at precisely the same time the leaders of those nations decided to stand down and allow them to do it? It seems beyond unlikely to me. What seems far more likely is these events were coordinated from a central source whose influence outranks national leaders, transcends national borders, and cares nothing about the people of Europe.

Since every tree is known by the fruit, the culprit behind these events must be the spirit of lawlessness. (Matthew 12:33)

Islamic Invasion of the United States:

The United States avoided the recent Muslim invasion of Europe because it was impossible for the invaders to reach our land by foot, but Islam has successfully infiltrated our nation from within our government, media, businesses, and schools, putting us in just as much danger as the people of Europe. In the same way that European leaders ordered their authorities to stand down while their countries were invaded, United States leaders have shown the same flagrant disregard for our national security, even putting dangerous Islamic militants who openly seek our destruction into powerful government positions where they are not only influencing, but controlling the policies and direction of our nation, as shown by the following evidence.

In the largest terrorism-financing trial ever successfully prosecuted in American history, the US vs Holy Land Foundation (HLF) in 2008, in Dallas, Texas, a federal court reviewed extensive evidence and concluded a massive network of Islamic terrorists are operating inside the United States under the direction of an Egyptian based organization called the Muslim Brotherhood (MB). (20.24) The MB's own documents and statements reveal the serious threat they pose to our nation. It was created in Egypt in 1928 with the same two goals as ISIS and Al Qaeda, to implement Islamic Law worldwide and to re-establish the Islamic state (caliphate), which had collapsed four years earlier in 1924 after the fall of the Ottoman Empire. (20.20, 20.26) In the 1950's, their leader, Sayyid Qutb, said their aim was to "establish Islamic rule" wherever it was possible and by "any means available". (20.27) Their own by-laws identify their goals are to wage "Civilization Jihad" to "destroy Western civilization" and overthrow our government to impose Sharia Law and establish an Islamic state. (20.28) Their creed is, "God is our objective; the Koran is our law; the Prophet is our leader; jihad is our way; and death for the sake of Allah is the highest of our aspirations." (20.29) Their own documents identify their organization as "the nucleus for the Islamic Movement in North America." (20.30) Speaking under oath during the HLF trial, one of the MB members confessed, "The Muslim Brotherhood understands that their work in America is a kind of grand jihad… eliminating and destroying America from within." (20.31) Although these facts are well documented and irrefutable, anyone daring to share them is viciously attacked, which has effectively silenced nearly all voices of opposition, but ignoring the facts is putting the lives of many innocent people in danger, which shows this is a spiritual battle with the future of our nation hanging in the balance. (Ephesians 6:12)

Remnant: Lawlessness

The Holy Land Foundation was started in 1989, claiming to be a charitable organization to avoid scrutiny by law enforcement officials. (20.32) Eventually, it became the largest Muslim charity in the United States. (20.33) Five HLF leaders were convicted of 10 counts of conspiracy to provide support for foreign terrorist organizations and were sentenced to prison terms ranging from 15 to 65 years, but their convictions were only the tip of the iceberg. (20.34) The court found 246 co-conspirators, including 208 individuals and 38 organizations, which include the best-known Islamic organizations in the United States, such as the Council on Islamic American Relations (CAIR), the North American Islamic Trust (NAIT), and the Islamic Society of North America (ISNA). (20.35) The complete list of the 38 co-conspirator organizations is shown in Exhibit 26.

The co-conspirators were just as guilty as HLF, as shown by the following statement from the Prosecutorial Memo to the court, "ISNA and NAIT, in fact, shared more with HLF than just a parent organization (MB). They were intimately connected with the HLF and its' assigned task of providing financial support to Hamas." (20.36)

By exposing these organizations as co-conspirators, their leaders were also exposed as part of the conspiracy, which should have prompted more arrests, indictments, convictions and sentencing. Texas Congressman Louie Gohmert confirmed,

> "There were a number of the co-conspirators that asked that their names be stricken from the pleadings. The judge refused to strike ISNA and others because he says there's a prima facie case against them...I've seen documentation – deposit slips, journals, ledgers and things. They have a tremendous amount of evidence that could have been used to prosecute ISNA." (20.37)

The HLF case exposed the MB's deceptive tactics with a vast network of front groups operating under a wide variety of stated purposes while ultimately sharing the goals stated above, including funding terrorist activities and waging stealth jihad with the goal of sabotaging our nation from within. Their despicable actions supporting terrorist organizations, murdering innocent people in the name of God and openly teaching their followers to continue doing so based on the teachings of the Koran prove Islam is a dangerous militant ideology and not a "religion of peace" because no true religion does those things. (see Exhibit 25) Like the front groups exposed by the HLF case, Islam is just a front group for the spirit of lawlessness, which has practiced deception from the beginning, even transforming himself into an angel of light. (2 Corinthians 11:14, Colossians 1:13) By operating under the guise of Islam, this spirit is taking advantage of our religious liberties and must be stopped to protect the innocent.

The illegal activities exposed by the HLF case confirmed what the U.S. State Department already knew back in 2002 when they designated Hamas as a terrorist organization because Hamas is just the Gaza branch of the MB. (20.38) MB should have been designated as a terrorist organization back then, but they weren't. Federal prosecutors should have taken legal action against the 246 co-conspirators in the HLF case, but they didn't. Instead, top MB leaders and co-conspirators in the HLF case have been promoted into positions of great influence where they are advising and training leaders of our federal agencies, including the CIA, FBI, NSA, DHS, the Justice Department, and the White House. The same people seeking our destruction are advising, training, and significantly influencing U.S. foreign policy and domestic counterterrorism strategies, revealing the spirit of lawlessness has a stronghold at the highest levels of the United States government.

For example, in July 2012, the CIA hosted a 2-day training program at its headquarters in Langley, Virginia entitled, "Countering Violent Extremism Workshop for the National Capitol Region." This conference was attended by local, state, and federal officials from nearly every law enforcement, military, and intelligence organization around the Washington DC metropolitan area. Members of the Muslim Brotherhood led the training alongside senior CIA, FBI, and DHS officials, including Imam Mohamed Magid, president of ISNA, a co-conspirator in the HLF case. (20.39)

Imam Mohamed Magid was invited to the White House so many times, he was called Obama's Shariah Czar. (20.40) He has frequently met with top officials at the Department of Justice, including Tom Perez, Assistant Attorney General for Civil Rights, advising them of ways to advance the interests of the MB, such as changing the rules governing investigations of terrorist activities, granting more private meetings with other top officials within the Justice Department, and criminalizing the defamation of Islam, which Magid called "religious bigotry and hate." (20.41) Magid also advises the U.S. State Department and made two trips overseas working for them, all paid for by U.S. taxpayers. (20.42)

DHS Circle of Insanity:

In another example, the Department of Homeland Security appointed six members of the MB to the Homeland Security Advisory Council (HSAC) where they have defined new standards for training federal agents in all federal agencies to ensure the standards protect and promote Islamic interests. These individuals are listed below. (20.43-20.45)

- Imam Mohamed Magid is president of Islamic Society of North America (ISNA) and Executive Director of the All Dulles Area Muslim Society (ADAMS) mosque complex in Northern Virginia, one of the most Sharia-adherent and jihadist in the country, which financially supports the terrorist organization Hamas. (20.46)

- Omar Alomari is a member of Muslim American Society (MAS) and several other MB-linked front groups, Community Engagement Officer, Ohio Homeland Security.

- Mohamed Elibiary is the former leader of the Holy Land Foundation and co-founder, President and CEO of The Freedom and Justice Foundation. He has close associations with Islamic Association of North Texas which operates the Dallas Central Mosque (DCM), which is one of the most active centers of Hamas activity in the United States. (20.47)

- Dahlia Mogahed is a member of CAIR, ISNA, Muslim American Society (MAS) and Muslim Public Affairs Council (MPAC), Senior Analyst and Executive Director, Gallop Center for Muslim Studies, former director and Imam of the Islamic Center of Madison (ICM).

- Nadia Roumani is co-founder and Director of the American Muslim Civic Leadership Institute (AMCLI).

- Arif Alikhan is a member of Muslim Public Affairs Council (MPAC) and the Islamic Shura Council of Southern California (ISCSC).

With the MB controlling both sides of the battle, what could possibly go wrong? These violations of our national security are so flagrant, it's enough to outrage any patriotic American citizen, but apparently not enough to outrage our elected representatives in the U.S. Congress because for the most part, they've done nothing to stop it. However, there were signs of life in the House of Representatives in June 2012 when a whopping total of 5 of the 435 members joined together and sent letters to the Inspectors General of the Departments of Defense, Homeland Security, Department of Justice, State Department and the Office of the Director of National Security, requesting an investigation of Muslim Brotherhood influence within those agencies, but instead of explanations, they received an overwhelming onslaught of criticism. (20.48)

Just as their concerns were dismissed, so were all the facts warning about the MB as a potential security threat. The circle of insanity was completed when DHS made up their own extremist culprits based on no evidence whatsoever, targeting the following groups:

- Anyone opposing federal government policies
- Anyone who believes in end time prophecies
- Anyone who believes in their Constitutional right to bear arms
- White supremacist lone wolves

The above list comes from the following two statements in a 2009 DHS document called "Rightwing Extremism: Current Economic and Political Climate Fueling Resurgence in Radicalization and Recruitment." (20.49)

> "Antigovernment conspiracy theories and "end times" prophecies could motivate extremist individuals and groups to stockpile food, ammunition, and weapons. These teachings also have been linked with the radicalization of domestic extremist individuals and groups in the past, such as violent Christian Identity organizations and extremist members of the militia movement."

> "DHS has concluded that white supremacist lone wolves pose the most significant domestic terrorist threat because of their low profile and autonomy."

Lumping together anyone who believes in end time prophecies and anyone who opposes federal government policies with white supremacists, referring to all of them as "extremist individuals," is a smear campaign against Christians and patriots. It's another example of the spirit of lawlessness ruling over our government leaders.

Islamic Training Camps in United States:

While MB leaders are advising and training America's top leaders, evidence shows Islamic militants are being trained in our land. MB documents and tapes discovered in a 2004 FBI raid in Annandale, Virginia confirmed they have been operating weapons training camps on our soil since at least 1981. (20.50)

A documentary called "Homegrown Jihad: Terrorist Training Camps Around the U.S." provides convincing video evidence of how a group called Muslims of America (MOA) operates 35 terrorist training camps in 22 states with impunity. (20.51) Claims made in the video have been verified by law enforcement reports. (20.52)

In the video, producers visited some camps and interviewed neighbors and local police officials. It also includes excerpts from a MOA recruitment video showing American converts to Islam being instructed in the operation of AK-47 rifles, rocket launchers, machine guns, C4 explosives, hand-to-hand combat, and trained how to kidnap

Americans, kill them, and conduct sabotage operations. The recruitment video also shows the leader, Sheikh Mubarak Gilani (aka Imam El Sheikh Syed Mubarak Ali Shah Gillani Hashimi), saying, "We are fighting to destroy the enemy. We are dealing with evil at its roots and its roots are America." Gilani also claims to have between 10,000 to 15,000 followers within the United States and boasts of having "the most advanced training courses in Islamic military warfare."

MOA formerly operated under the name Jamaat ul-Fuqra and has close ties with the MB. (20.53, 20.54) In 1998, the State Department said Jamaat ul-Fuqra is an "Islamic sect that seeks to purify Islam through violence." (20.55) Gilani changed their name to Muslims of America to distance themselves from their violent history. (20.56) They have a public website, but it presents a completely different story than their own recruitment video, as shown by this statement,

> "The Muslims of America's aims to raise communities with a focus on love for the Almighty Creator and His Commandments, to follow the way of the Holy Last Messenger (peace be upon him) and to preserve a long-lasting relationship with our Christian brethren in the U.S." (20.57)

Their website also has a video section, but the recruitment video is not even mentioned. Instead, they have a video called, "Muslim Christian Jesus Unity Program." (20.58) The inconsistency between their own recruitment video and the public image presented on their website shows the same deceptive practices as the 38 front groups exposed in the HLF case.

United States law enforcement officials are more than capable of removing Islamic military training camps from our land, so their continued existence here shows someone wants them to stay.

Conclusion:

The increased lawlessness that began with the countercultural revolution of the sixties has accelerated in recent years, especially since 2015. The list of examples keeps growing:

- Widespread rebellion against parental authority
- Widespread support for sex outside of marriage
- Widespread support for homosexuality
- Increasing hostilities between the American people

- Exponential increase in violent terrorist attacks on innocent people
- European leaders standing down to allow Islamic invasion
- U.S. government failing to prosecute the HLF co-conspirators
- U.S. government failing to designate the MB as a terrorist organization
- U.S. government promoting MB leaders to high-level positions inside many federal agencies
- U.S. elected representatives standing down to allow MB infiltration in our government agencies
- DHS claiming the real extremists posing the greatest threat of domestic violence are Christians and patriots
- U.S. government allowing Islamic military training camps to operate inside the United States

These are just a few examples and many more could be cited, including the large number of people now crossing our southern border illegally, which could easily be stopped if the ruling authorities wanted to stop it. All these events show a significant increase in lawlessness since the Jewish people reclaimed Jerusalem, making it the prevailing spirit over the United States and Europe. It's another prophetic sign of the times, setting the stage for the fulfillment of many other prophecies.

ENDNOTES

20.01: 1960's counterculture revolution, https://en.wikipedia.org/wiki/Counterculture_of_the_1960s

20.02: Anti-establishment movement, https://en.wikipedia.org/wiki/Anti-establishment#1960s

20.03: Church of Satan established in 1966, https://en.wikipedia.org/wiki/Church_of_Satan

20.04: Donald Trump announces campaign for presidency, https://en.m.wikipedia.org/wiki/Donald_Trump_2016_presidential_campaign

20.05: Terrorist incidents 1970-2018, https://en.wikipedia.org/wiki/List_of_terrorist_incidents#1970.E2.80.93present

20.06: Dr. James Maloney, https://www.doveontherise.com/index.html

20.07: Loren, Julia. Beyond 2012: What the Real Prophets are Saying. Tharseo Publishing. Kindle Edition, Location 450.

Remnant: Lawlessness

20.08: Islamic invasion of Europe, http://www.pewresearch.org/fact-tank/2017/11/29/5-facts-about-the-muslim-population-in-europe/

20.09: Violent attacks by Muslim migrants, https://www.youtube.com/watch?v=QRlFqQ0AXAI

20.10: Violent attacks by Muslim migrants, http://www.wnd.com/2017/04/germany-migrant-crime-drastically-increased-in-2016/

20.11: Violent attacks by Muslim migrants, http://www.israelnationalnews.com/News/News.aspx/250534

20.12: 61 no-go zones in Sweden, https://www.gatestoneinstitute.org/14209/sweden-self-inflicted-mess

20.13: Islamic invasion of Denmark, https://www.gatestoneinstitute.org/13521/denmark-immigration-transformation

20.14: Denmark population 5.7 million, https://www.gatestoneinstitute.org/13876/denmark-collapse

20.15: Germany refuses to deport Islamic invaders, https://www.gatestoneinstitute.org/12723/germany-deportation-system

20.16: Germany news media hiding Islamic attacks, https://www.gatestoneinstitute.org/12618/germany-press-freedom

20.17: Islamic invaders raping Swedish women, https://www.gatestoneinstitute.org/13332/sweden-rapes-police

20.18: Islamic invasion of Germany, http://www.reuters.com/article/us-europe-migrants-germany-idUSKBN1771IP

20.19: Pope Francis claims Islam opposes violence, http://w2.vatican.va/content/francesco/en/apost_exhortations/documents/papa-francesco_esortazione-ap_20131124_evangelii-gaudium.html

20.20: Pope Francis claims Islam is religion of peace, https://w2.vatican.va/content/francesco/en/letters/2014/documents/papa-francesco_20141221_lettera-cristiani-medio-oriente.html

20.21: Pope claims Islamic terrorists do not exist, http://www.catholicnewsagency.com/news/pope-francis-encourages-meeting-of-popular-movements-in-california-89704/

20.22: Marine LePen ordered to take psychiatric exams, Reuters, https://www.reuters.com/article/us-france-politics-le-pen/french-court-orders-le-pen-to-submit-to-psychiatric-evaluation-idUSKCN1M01U1

Remnant: Lawlessness

20.23: Growing support for Germany's anti-immigration party, https://www.gatestoneinstitute.org/12973/germany-anti-immigration-party

20.24: HLF and Leaders Convicted on Providing Material Support to Hamas Terrorist Organization, United States vs Holy Land Foundation, U.S. Department of Justice, May 27, 2009, James T. Jacks, Acting United States Attorney, Northern District of Texas, www.usdoj.gov/usao/txn

20.25: History and goals of the Muslim Brotherhood, Understanding the Threat, https://www.understandingthethreat.com/wp-content/uploads/2015/11/TrueNature_of_the_Threat.pdf

20.26: Fall of the Ottoman Empire, https://en.wikipedia.org/wiki/Caliphate#Abolition_of_the_Caliphate_(1924)

20.27: MB statement from Sayyid Qutb, Gatestone Institute, November 1, 2018, https://www.gatestoneinstitute.org/13206/jihad-threat

20.28: Muslim Brotherhood seeks to destroy western civilization, Understanding the Threat, https://www.understandingthethreat.com/research/

20.29: Muslim Brotherhood Creed, Understanding the Threat, https://www.understandingthethreat.com/wp-content/uploads/2015/11/TrueNature_of_the_Threat.pdf

20.30: Muslim Brotherhood is the nucleus, John Guandolo https://www.breitbart.com/national-security/2011/05/26/US-Congressman-Says-The-Obama-Administration-Materially-Supporting-Terrorists/

20.31: Court statement describing Muslim Brotherhood, Citizens for National Security, https://cfns.us/textbooks-and-terrorists/ and https://www.youtube.com/watch?v=E_sKc5fgjdE

20.32: HLF charitable front group, United States vs Holy Land Foundation, Indictment filed July 26, 2004 in United States District Court for the Northern District of Texas, Dallas Division.

20.33: HLF once the largest Muslim charity in United States, https://en.wikipedia.org/wiki/Holy_Land_Foundation_for_Relief_and_Development

20.34: United States vs Holy Land Foundation, U.S. Department of Justice, James T. Jacks, Acting United States Attorney, Northern District of Texas, Federal Judge Hands Down Sentences in Holy Land Foundation (HLF) Case, www.usdoj.gov/usao/txn, May 27, 2009

20.35: United States vs Holy Land Foundation, Attachment A in the United States District Court for the Northern District of Texas, Dallas Division, CR NO. 3:04-CR-240-G, List of Unindicted Co-conspirators and/or Joint Venturers.

20.36: United States vs Holy Land Foundation, United States District Court for the Northern District of Texas, Dallas Division, CR NO. 3:04-CR-240-P, Government's Amended Memorandum in Opposition To Petitioners Islamic Society Of North America And North American Islamic Trust's Motion For Equitable Relief.

20.37: Comment from Texas Congressman Louie Gohmert, Chuck Guandolo, https://www.breitbart.com/national-security/2011/05/26/US-Congressman-Says-The-Obama-Administration-Materially-Supporting-Terrorists/

20.38: Hamas is Gaza branch of MB and designated as terrorist organization, https://en.wikipedia.org/wiki/Hamas#International_designations_as_a_terrorist_organization

20.39: Muslim Brotherhood led CIA training program, John Guandolo, https://www.breitbart.com/national-security/2012/10/24/cia-hosts-training-by-muslim-brotherhood-leader-and-hamas-supporter/

20.40: Obama's Sharia Czar, PJ Media, July 5, 2012, https://pjmedia.com/blog/obamas-shariah-czar-mohamed-magid-hands-diversity-award-to-jew-hater-dawud-walid/

20.41: Imam Mohamed Magid meeting with officials from Department of Justice, The Daily Caller, October 21, 2011, https://dailycaller.com/2011/10/21/progressives-islamists-huddle-at-justice-department/

20.42: Imam Mohammed Magid traveling overseas working for State Department, https://www.investigativeproject.org/2082/cair-suspected-and-supported-by-the-federal

20.43: Muslim Brotherhood led DHS training program, "Countering Violent Extremism (CVE) Working Group Homeland Security Advisory Council, Spring 2010." http://www.dhs.gov/xlibrary/assets/hsac_cve_working_group_recommendations.pdf

20.44: Six members of Muslim Brotherhood appointed to DHS Advisory Council, Center for Security Policy, https://www.centerforsecuritypolicy.org/2017/01/21/faith-leaders-for-america-denounce-imam-mohamed-magid-call-on-president-trump-to-designate-magids-terrorist-muslim-brotherhood/

20.45: MB defines federal agent training program, John Guandolo, https://www.breitbart.com/national-security/2011/11/20/Assault-on-the-Truth--Part-2--How-the-Muslim-Brotherhood-Censors-Federal-Counterterrorism-Training/

20.46: ADAMS mosque complex supporting Hamas terrorists, John Guandolo, "CIA Hosts Training by Muslim Brotherhood Leader and HAMAS Supporter," Breitbart Big Peace, 24 October 2012. https://www.breitbart.com/national-security/2012/10/24/cia-hosts-training-by-muslim-brotherhood-leader-and-hamas-supporter/

20.47: Mohamed Elibiary, https://www.globalmbwatch.com/mohamed-elibiary/

20.48: Five U.S. Congressmen raise objections to MB influence, (Michele Bachmann, Trent Franks, Louie Gohmert, Tom Rooney, and Lynn Westmoreland) https://www.gatestoneinstitute.org/3672/muslim-brotherhood-us-government

20.49: US DHS Office of Intelligence and Analysis, Rightwing Extremism: Current Economic and Political Climate Fueling Resurgence in Radicalization and Recruitment, April 7 2009, https://fas.org/irp/eprint/rightwing.pdf

20.50: 2004 FBI raid reveals MB weapons training camps, John Guandolo, https://www.breitbart.com/national-security/2011/05/26/US-Congressman-Says-The-Obama-Administration-Materially-Supporting-Terrorists/

20.51: Terrorist training camps within United States, PRB Films, "Homegrown Jihad: Terrorist Training Camps Around the U.S." Directed by Martin Mawyer, Christian Action Network, https://www.youtube.com/watch?v=o3EpagC51mA

20.52: "Jamaat ul-Fuqra: Gilani Followers Conducting Paramilitary Training in U.S.," Regional Organized Crime Information Center (dissemination limited to law enforcement), 2006. http://info.publicintelligence.net/ROCICjamaatulfuqra.pdf

20.53: Muslims of America operated under the name Jamaat ul-Fuqra, https://clarionproject.org/muslims-americas-moa/

20.54: Muslims of America ties to Muslim Brotherhood, https://www.fuqrafiles.com/knowledgebase/muslim-brotherhoodhamas/

20.55: U.S. State Department identifies ul-Fuqra as violent, "Patterns of Global Terrorism Report," U.S. State Department, 1998, http://web.archive.org/web/20081015073850/http://www.terrorisminfo.mipt.org/pdf/1998pogt.pdf.

20.56: Reasons why Muslims of America changed name from Jamaat ul-Fuqra, https://clarionproject.org/muslims-americas-moa/

20.57: Statement from Muslims of America website, http://www.tmoamerica.org/about/

20.58: Muslims of America video of Muslim Christian Jesus Unity Program, http://www.tmoamerica.org/videos2/457-video-umcf-unity

21
Deception and Apostasy

Before the Lord returns, a time of great shaking will come upon the whole earth and heaven too, shaking everything that can be shaken, separating the righteous from the unrighteous, the remnant from those who abandon their faith. (Isaiah 24:1-6, Daniel 7:19-27, 8:22-25, 9:27, 12:1, Zechariah 12:8-9, 14:2-5, 14:12-15, Matthew 24:4-34, Luke 21:26, 2 Thessalonians 1:4-10, 2 Timothy 3:1-8, Hebrews 12:25-27, Jude 1:17-23, Revelation 6:1-17, 8-19) In those days of trouble, a false prophet will arise and deceive multitudes, everyone whose name is not written in the book of life, by performing great signs, even causing fire to come down from heaven and putting to death those who refuse to bow down and worship his false god, which will bring severe persecution upon all true Christians. (Revelation 13:12-15, 17:1-6)

Those who submit to this harlot will receive the same spirit of deception and harlotry, causing them to perform similar acts, speaking lies, abandoning their faith in God and betraying their brothers and sisters. (2 Thessalonians 2:3-4, 1 Timothy 4:1-5, 2 Timothy 4:3-4, 2 Peter 2:20-22, Jude 1:17-23) Fathers will betray their children and children will report their parents to government authorities who will hunt them down and arrest them for execution, often by beheading. (Matthew 24:9-10, Mark 13:12-13, Revelation 6:9-11, 13:15, 20:4)

No one in their right mind would do those things, but multitudes won't be in their right mind because of the great deception coming upon the world. This chapter presents evidence showing large-scale deception started at about the same time the Jewish people reclaimed Jerusalem, beginning with two landmark rulings by the U.S. Supreme Court, which overturned nearly two centuries of legal precedent to ban praying to God and reading the Bible in public school classrooms. Prayer was first to go in June 1962, followed by Bible reading the following year in June 1963. (21.01, 21.02) Those rulings could not have stood without the consent of the people. We could have risen up in mass protests, but instead, we quietly submitted and many even agreed with the deception as the correct interpretation of our Constitution.

By publicly declaring our nation no longer allowed our children to pray to God and was no longer willing to teach them the truth of God's word, we not only banned the truth, but invited the only alternative, which is deception. By 1968, deception was officially embraced by another Supreme Court ruling, Epperson v. Arkansas, banning states from preventing the teaching of evolution in public school classrooms, claiming such actions were establishing a religion. (21.03) Ironically, their ruling established evolution as the new religion taught in our public schools. Although it is taught in the name of science, it's based purely on blind faith in a theory that has no scientific evidence supporting it and volumes of evidence proving it's false. (21.04-21.06) So, the void created by outlawing the truth of the Bible was quickly filled with the lies of evolution.

Deception has also filled our history textbooks as they have been revised to remove the knowledge of God, hiding the true meaning of past events and leaving only a series of seemingly random unrelated events, which makes it nearly impossible to understand our past and therefore robs us of our understanding of current and future events. (Ecclesiastes 1:9) For example, America's public schools taught history for decades using the textbook, "The Story of Liberty," by Charles Coffin, published in 1878, which includes many historical examples of great faith in God demonstrated by previous generations as they prevailed against overwhelming odds, stories we should all know, but have never heard because they were removed from our modern textbooks. For example, Coffin's textbook devotes a chapter to the story of Bohemian martyr John Huss and the Hussite wars that followed his death, in which God repeatedly helped a small number of Bohemian Christians defeat much larger armies, like David killing Goliath. It's just one of many examples showing how thoroughly our history books have been revised, which is why Charles Coffin warned that if we fail to see the divine hand working in our history, it becomes an "incomprehensible enigma." (21.10)

Once again, it was the 1960's when this major shift occurred in our history textbooks, the same decade we removed the Bible and prayer from our schools and opened wide the doors for teaching evolution. Historian David Barton studied decades of history textbooks and concluded that's when the focus shifted away from God to replace Him with money as the central focus. From that time on, history was redefined from a purely economic perspective. He explained, "Since the 1960's, we've only taught an economic view of history and that cuts out 95% of what happens in history."

For example, since the American Declaration of Independence included an economic grievance against Great Britain, "taxation without representation," as one of the reasons why we sought independence, our history textbooks were revised in the 1960's to make this the only grievance we've learned about, causing many Americans to wrongly believe it was the primary reason for the American Revolution, but the Declaration of Independence identifies a "long train of abuses and usurpations" that includes 27 reasons why we separated from Great Britain. Taxation without representation was number 17 on the list, not even close to the top, and it was only mentioned once while other issues were listed multiple times. (21.11) Revising our history to make it all about money has created a distorted view that ignores the fact that the Declaration repeatedly identifies the basis for our rights is "Nature's God", "the Supreme Judge of the world", and our "firm reliance on the protection of Divine Providence". (21.12)

Confirming the significant impact of those changes in our schools, a Gallup poll conducted in April 2017 shows the light of truth in America has been greatly dimmed since the poll started in the mid-seventies. During all that time, the percentage of Americans who believe the Bible is the literal word of God has been dropping steadily. By 2017, the poll found for the first time, more Americans believed the Bible is just a book of fables and legends (26%) than those who believed it's the literal Word of God (24%). (21.07)

As our knowledge of the scriptures has decreased, all sorts of deception has increased in our public school lessons, as shown in the following 2019 school health curriculum standards published by the California Department of Education, which promote gender confusion starting at the preschool and kindergarten levels, as shown by this quote from their guidelines for transitional kindergarten to grade three.

> When providing instruction on sexual and reproductive organs, teachers can introduce the concept that gender does not always match the sexual and reproductive organs described. For example, teachers may share, "In the classroom, we may use the term 'female reproductive organs' but some people who identify as male have these organs. The actual anatomical name for organs is utilized." (21.08)

More confusion is being forced upon children in grades 4-6, as shown in the following statements from California's 2019 health curriculum guidelines:

> Instruction on sexual health content must affirm diverse sexual orientations and include examples of same-sex relationships when discussing relationships.

> When the topic of masturbation is introduced or arises, teachers explain what masturbation is and that it is safe and not mentally or physically harmful.

> Fifth-grade students will have an opportunity to learn that gender is not strictly defined by physical anatomy or sex assigned at birth. Rather, students understand that gender refers to attitudes, feelings, characteristics, and

> behaviors that a given culture associates with being male or female, sometimes labeled "masculine" and "feminine."
>
> Teachers should be mindful of personal biases and use gender neutral language when discussing peer and romantic relationships to be inclusive of all students in terms of gender identity, gender expression, and sexual attraction. For example, use "they" instead of using "he/she." (21.09)

Deception is also prevailing in many churches with a growing number of them making compromises with unrighteousness and replacing the true gospel message with one that requires no repentance from sins, but the truth of God's word has never changed. It's still the same message of repentance proclaimed by John the Baptist, Jesus Christ, and all His disciples. (Mark 1:4, 1:15, Luke 10:13, 11:32, 13:3, 15:7, 17:3, 17:4, Acts 2:38, 2 Peter 3:9, Romans 2:4, 2 Corinthians 7:10, Hebrews 6:4-6, James 2:24, 5:19-20, 1 John 1:6-10, Revelation 2:5,16,21,22, 3:3,19)

Although America is just one nation, it's strategically important due to our spiritual, economic and military leadership position in the world. For example, since the founding of our nation, most missionaries around the world have either been Americans or financially supported by Americans. Despite our many failures, we still have one of the highest concentrations of Christians in the world, which makes us a significant preserving influence in the world, the salt of the earth. (Matthew 5:13) So, when America publicly banned the truth of God's word and invited deception to come upon our children, the rest of the world was also impacted.

Greatest Danger:

When the disciples asked Jesus to tell them the signs identifying the season of His return, the very first sign He gave them was a warning about imposters coming in His name to deceive us. (Matthew 24:4-5, Luke 21:8)

> 4 And Jesus answered and said to them: "Take heed that no one deceives you. 5 For many will come in My name, saying, 'I am the Christ,' and will deceive many. (Matthew 24:4-5 NKJV)

In the above passage, He mentions deception twice. Later in the same passage, He mentioned it twice more. (Matthew 24:11, 24:23-26) Of all the things He could have warned about, this was the first one He mentioned and He repeated it three times, so it must have been His number one concern, the greatest danger facing the final generation. If He only said it once, it would be important, but saying it four times makes it super important. It's so easy to quickly read on past His warnings and miss the significance, as I've done many times, but I believe this is so important, it's worth parking here and staying for a long time to think about what it means for us today and ask God to expose this very dark demonic scheme so we can understand what Jesus clearly wanted us to understand.

Right between His first two mentions of deception in verses 4 and 5, Jesus identified those who come in His name, like a sandwich with poison placed between two pieces of bread. By the outward appearance, it looks safe to eat because the bread hides the poison, but it's deadly poisonous because it's not what it appears to be. Since the poison is coming from those who come in His name, His warning ironically reveals those whom we trust the most, the ones we feel the safest listening to, are the ones we should guard against the most because they're putting us in the greatest danger, which makes sense because we tend to let our guards down and trust whatever they say, making us more vulnerable.

Jesus warned that the imposters who come in His name will say, "I am the Christ." By saying this, they are claiming they alone have the way of salvation because Christ means messiah, the anointed one, the one with the touch of God to save us. In some cases, imposters have claimed to be Jesus Christ, but more often this claim is made by religious cults as a fear tactic to gain control over their prey, terrorizing them by threatening, "Join us and follow our instructions or be forever damned." Sadly, multitudes have fallen for this deception.

True Christians selflessly point their followers to a personal relationship with Jesus Christ, but these imposters selfishly make themselves the essential requirement for receiving salvation by requiring membership in their church or submission to their leader. They come in the name of Jesus Christ only to hide their true agenda of making themselves a substitute for Him. This is the spirit of antichrist, which has been operating in the world since the beginning. (1 John 4:3)

Satan is using his same old plays from his same old playbook, just as he's been doing from the beginning, disguising himself as an angel of light, misquoting scriptures to twist the meaning for the advancement of his kingdom, just as he cleverly deceived Eve in the Garden of Eden by misquoting what God said. (Genesis 3:1-6, 2 Corinthians 11:13-15) Later, he misquoted scriptures to Jesus when He was in the wilderness. (Matthew 4:5-6) Satan not only knows the scriptures, but he also knows the language of Christians, the kinds of phrases often used by true Christians, such as the "strong presence of the Holy Spirit" and the "powerful anointing." So, just because someone quotes scriptures or claims to be a Christian or uses all the right phrases doesn't mean they're a true follower. Just because someone calls their group a Christian church doesn't mean it has anything to do with the true Church. For the final generation, more than any other generation, things will not be what they appear to be, but the good news is God has given us the scriptures and the inner witness of His Holy Spirit to expose Satan's schemes so we can avoid getting deceived.

By coming in the name of Jesus, Satan is pulling the dirtiest trick imaginable because he's striking in our most sacred, most trusted, most important relationship in our life, our relationship with God, which effects every other relationship and every choice we make, so if we get it right, every area of our life comes into right alignment, but if we get it wrong, we can be lured into the deepest darkness imaginable, committing the most despicable evil deeds while justifying it in our darkened mind, mistakenly thinking it's for the greater good, for the glory of God, with eternal rewards, which is why Satan's followers will do anything he tells them to do. (Matthew 6:33) It's the ultimate deception.

The imposters coming in His name are traitors, betraying God and their followers for their own evil purposes. They're harlots, hirelings, and deceivers, practicing all sorts of abominations and filthiness while causing their followers to do the same. They were revealed to the Apostle John as a woman sitting on a scarlet beast, the mother of all harlots. (Revelation 17:1-6) She disguises herself with the appearance of the Lamb of God, having two horns like a lamb, and like the Messiah riding on a white horse, imitating the Lord Jesus Christ, but everything about her is deceptive, the opposite of what she appears to be, all designed to hide her true purpose of getting drunk with the blood of the saints. (John 1:36, Revelation 6:1-2, 13:11, 19:11)

And since she is the mother of all harlots, she must have many daughters practicing the same deception and harlotry, operating under cover to betray their followers, just like their mother. (Revelation 17:5) Her daughters are like front groups whose purpose is to secretly extend her influence while hiding their connection to her, so they operate under different names and wear different disguises, enabling her to deceive many more victims. Since their mother comes in the name of Jesus, they're more likely to come in some other name, perhaps as a secular organization or in the name of another religion, anything to throw us off her trail.

So, this deceptive scheme has many layers built upon many lies, but it's all instigated by the ones who come in His name. To understand what's really happening requires seeing beyond the layers of deception to expose the ones behind it all. Otherwise, the mother proceeds with her schemes unhindered, simply by shifting her plans to another daughter if necessary. Unfortunately, all the deceptive schemes have succeeded in creating lots of confusion, causing many people to follow the wrong trails while encouraging others to do the same, placing all the blame on the daughters, with many possible suspects, including the big bankers, the deep state, politicians, evil corporations, communists, the Illuminati, the Muslims, and of course, the world's all-time favorite villains, the Jews, but none of them are the ones Jesus warned about because none of them come in His name. They might be daughter harlots serving the mother harlot, but they cannot be the true culprits. Simply by paying close attention to the words of Jesus, we can avoid wasting our time and energy exploring the wrong rabbit holes, which frees us up to explore the right rabbit hole where we can learn things that truly matter, so we can be well informed, striking at the heart of the deception to help others avoid falling into Satan's traps. He hates the light, so why not shine it on him extra bright? (Acts 26:18, Colossians 1:13, 2 Thessalonians 2:9)

Large Scale Deception:

Since the whole world will be required to worship the beast, the scale of the deception coming upon our generation will be global. Previous generations did not have the ability to unite the whole world, but it is now possible in our generation due to advanced technology, enabling us to transmit messages to a global audience, which explains why Jesus repeatedly described it as "many" coming in His name to deceive "many". (Matthew 24:4-5, 24:11, 24:23-26, Revelation 13:8, 13:12, 13:15-18)

A scheme to deceive the whole world would require large numbers of people to orchestrate it and secrecy would be essential for its' success, so it's a large scale secret conspiracy, which makes everyone watching for it a conspiracy theorist, which is something the world mocks and ridicules, but since Jesus warned us about it and instructed us to watch for it, that makes Him the first conspiracy theorist, so we can safely do the same, regardless of what anyone else says about it. (Matthew 24:4-5)

Since this scheme is all about deception, even examining the evidence is challenging because everything about it is designed to deceive and nothing is what it appears to be on the surface. Due to the layers of deception and secrecy, connecting all the dots goes way beyond the scope of this book, but this point can be illustrated by examining any evidence of large-scale deception operating today. To that end, we have a great example coming into our homes daily on our favorite news programs, as shown by the following evidence.

Soon after their formation in 1947, the United States Central Intelligence Agency (CIA) launched Operation Mockingbird for the purpose of manipulating public opinion by infiltrating the mainstream news media with hundreds of agents working undercover as journalists. (21.13, 21.14) Back in 1977, journalist Carl Bernstein identified dozens of news organizations with CIA agents on their staffs. He shared the following summary of the CIA's internal program to train their journalist agents for assignments within news organizations:

> The CIA even ran a formal training program in the 1950's to teach its agents to be journalists. Intelligence officers were "taught to make noises like reporters," explained a high CIA official, and were then placed in major news organizations with help from management. "These were the guys who went through the ranks and were told 'You're going to be a journalist,'" the CIA official said. Relatively few of the 400-some relationships described in Agency files followed that pattern, however; most involved persons who were already bona fide journalists when they began undertaking tasks for the Agency. (21.15)

Way back in 1977, Bernstein reported that the CIA manipulates, censors and even creates news stories for all major US media organizations, including ABC, NBC, CBS, the AP, UPI, the New York Times, Newsweek, Time Inc, Hearst newspapers, the Miami Herald, the Saturday Evening Post, and the New York Herald-Tribune. (21.16) His list did not include CNN or Fox News because those organizations did not exist at that time.

Confirming Bernstein's claim, Congressional investigations in the 1970's exposed the CIA's systematic media manipulation, beginning in the 1950's. Not only did CIA Director Allen Dulles and his top staff regularly dine and drink with leaders of the news media in New York and Washington, but the investigations confirmed the CIA had hundreds of paid staffers working as journalists in the U.S. and foreign nations. So, the very same news organizations the American people rely on for honest reporting have a long history of presenting bogus news stories, claiming to be the originators and investigators who uncovered the stories when all along it was a deceptive scheme, written by CIA agents, intentionally using our tax dollars to deceive us and manipulate our opinions for their own purposes. (21.17)

Some news reports have claimed the CIA stopped their media manipulation after being caught red-handed, but these reports appear to be nothing more than CIA damage-control as the evidence shows their control is stronger now than ever. For example, Douglas Valentine, author of "The CIA and Organized Crime", spent the past 30 years researching the CIA and summarized his conclusion here:

> "It's pretty much a fallacy to think of the CIA as different from the media. They are the same thing. And I try to show how they are basically the same people. They went to the same schools. They go to the same parties, the publishers and

the top editors and the people who run the CIA and the military and basically the highest-ranking people in every part of the bureaucracy, and the executive branch, and certainly the judicial branch in terms of the Department of Justice. But all these people at the highest level are basically the same group and any distinctions between them are really artificial. And they have the same objectives and they put the same management and organizational systems in place to weed out anybody who they can't assimilate ideologically." (21.18)

Another recent finding, based on 4,000 pages of formerly classified archived documents obtained through the Freedom of Information Act, revealed the CIA's media manipulation has expanded from the news media and now includes many other media sources, such as movies, TV shows, books, magazines, websites, and podcasts. For example, the CIA and Pentagon have worked behind the scenes on at least 800 major movies and more than 1,000 TV titles, and those are just the ones we know about. (21.19) These findings reveal a well-funded, centralized, coordinated effort to control our thoughts, shape our opinions, and prevent us from knowing the truth about what's happening in the world. It's so sinister and so devious, it's hard to believe it's actually happening, but the evidence is well documented and confirmed repeatedly. And advanced technology has empowered this scheme to operate on an unprecedented scale, far greater than what was possible in previous generations.

We are being bombarded with a never-ending flow of false narratives presented in fake news stories designed to engage us in heated debates, mostly warning about the dangers of the evils of every other villain under the sun, the same worn out list of suspects shown above, leading us down all the wrong rabbit holes. This deceptive scheme seeks not only to control us, but also to divide us in any way possible by pushing us into all sorts of false choices, left or right, liberal or conservative, black or white, rich or poor, CNN or Fox News, Democrat or Republican, and many other issues, all filled with deceptions and distractions designed to cause us to lose sight of the real culprits and the most important choice, Christ or antichrist.

This scheme is not limited to the mainstream news but also includes alternative news sources. Even though the motives behind the alternative sources might not be as devious as the CIA, the result is the same if they're wasting our time exploring the wrong rabbit holes, which most of them are. However, given the CIA's long term investment in manipulating public opinion, it seems likely they've also infiltrated some of the alternative news sources, including books, websites, magazines and videos.

Technological advances have not only expanded the scale of the deception, but also produced new ways to deceive us. For example, advanced facial recognition software now exists allowing virtually anyone to create 3D models to produce videos showing someone doing things they never did and saying things they never said, even in real time. The software, commonly called Deepfakes, only requires 15 seconds of video of the real person to replicate their face in any setting, saying anything they want them to say. (21.20) This software is already being used to make celebrities appear in movies, including pornographic videos. Using this capability, anyone could create a smear campaign to discredit any Christian by showing them in a detestable setting, performing shameful acts, or saying hateful things. (21.21) The old saying, "Seeing is believing," is no longer true for our generation, requiring us to rely on the inner witness of the Holy Spirit more than ever before. It's another example of the unprecedented level of deception threatening to destroy our generation.

The evidence of CIA media manipulation should be enough to disturb anyone interested in truth and liberty. Such a long-term operation transcends many presidential administrations, both Republican and Democrat, so it goes beyond the political spectrum. Such a large-scale operation requires a massive commitment of funding and manpower, which requires oversight and direction from a central source, but their involvement must be kept secret, always maintaining with what the CIA calls "plausible deniability", to protect themselves from public scrutiny.

These facts raise many questions about these people at the highest level whom investigator Douglas Valentine discovered were "basically the same group". Given the evidence of large-scale deception, what is the connection with those who come in His name? It's a deep rabbit hole, but I believe it's the right one. In the past, we've relied upon a free press to investigate those kinds of questions, but since they're part of the scheme, the responsibility falls on individual citizens to investigate and share their findings, especially Christians since deception was the number one thing Jesus warned about. With His help, we should be the most informed people on the planet, exposing Satan's schemes with hard evidence, but if we remain in darkness, how will unbelievers have any chance to know the truth?

We have been warned to watch for these things, specifically regarding the coming deception, which will cause many to perish. (Matthew 24:4-5, Luke 21:36, Ephesians 6:18, 1 Thessalonians 5:5-6, 2 Thessalonians 2:9-10) Surely God wants us to know and sound the alarms.

Take the Red Pill:

I can't rant too much about the deception in our land because I've spent most of my life just as deceived as anyone. Back in 2010 when a friend of mine was sharing some things happening in the world, I was concerned, but not about the world. I was concerned about him because I thought he'd been watching too many YouTube videos, listening to too many conspiracy theories. I was too in the dark to even know I was in the dark.

We've all been misled, taught half-truths and even outright lies. We weren't taught things we should have been taught in school. We weren't warned about things we should have been warned about in church. So, we've been living our whole life thinking things are one way, but now God is revealing it's not that way at all. After so many years of being filled with so many lies, we wouldn't know the truth if it slapped us upside the head. It reminds me of a scene from the movie, The Matrix, when Morpheus offered Neo a choice between the blue pill and the red pill, as shown here:

> Morpheus: "The matrix is everywhere. It is all around us. You can see it when you look out your window or when you turn on your television. You can feel it when you go to work, when you go to church, when you pay your taxes. It is the world that has been pulled over your eyes to blind you from the truth."
>
> Neo: "What truth?"
>
> Morpheus: "That you are a slave Neo. Like everyone else, you were born into bondage, born into a prison that you cannot smell or taste or touch. A prison for your mind. Unfortunately, no one can be told what the matrix is. You have to see it for yourself. This is your last chance. After this, there is no turning back. If you take the blue pill, the story ends, you wake up in your bed and believe whatever you want to believe. If you take the red pill, you stay in wonderland and I show you how deep the rabbit hole goes. Remember, all I'm offering is the truth, nothing more." (21.22)

Taking the red pill is like pursuing righteousness. Not only is it the same color as the redeeming blood of Jesus that paid the price for our righteousness, but they also both start with the letter R. In both cases, the instructions are simple and clear, just pursue righteousness. Otherwise, we'll wake up in our bed and believe whatever we want to believe, seeing only blue sky ahead.

After Neo took the red pill, his training started right away. He quickly mastered topics he previously knew nothing about because his trainers downloaded programs into his brain in a few minutes that normally would have taken years of study. After one download completed, he said, "I know Kung Fu."

Okay, so that's not happening, but righteousness causes us to accelerate in the direction

God wants us to go by enabling us to quickly grow in knowledge and understanding, faster than we ever thought possible because it brings us into alignment with His plans and purposes for our life, causing us to hunger for what He wants us to have, which is like rocket fuel for our blast off.

Like Neo, I chose the red pill and God has been showing me how deep the rabbit hole goes, which has completely blown my mind because I found out how deceived I've been. Like Morpheus told Neo, I have discovered, "It is the world that has been pulled over your eyes to blind you from the truth."

As I shared in Part 1, Chapter 14, when I started pursuing righteousness more diligently, God completely transformed my worldview in a relatively short time. It didn't happen overnight, but within a few years, I started understanding things I never understood before. Things that made no sense before finally started making sense as I was able to connect the dots.

Taking the red pill was the key to receiving almost all the dreams and insights I've shared in this book, plus an entirely new understanding of world events that aligns with what God has revealed in His word and in the prophetic dreams He has given me. The learning curve has been steep and fast, but I am eager to learn more. Coming out from the deception after so many years has been quite an experience, causing me to marvel at what's happening.

Sure, taking the red pill is a little freaky, but it's okay because like Morpheus said, "It's the truth." Without the truth, our effectiveness is severely limited. How can we enlighten others when we're deceived? By taking the red pill, we can take back what's been stolen from us, so we're no longer misinformed, but fully informed about what's happening in the world, so we can expose Satan's schemes like bright shining lights, attracting the lost with answers that make sense. (Isaiah 60:1-5) And our light gets brighter and brighter as we continue growing in the truth. (Proverbs 4:18)

God is warning us to prepare now, so we are not deceived and so our faith holds firm until the end. Those who are unwilling to hear the warnings will be unable to bear the news of what's coming upon the world. Our only hope is good old-fashioned righteousness, turning away from all unrighteousness, like the instructions John heard in a voice from heaven: (Proverbs 14:34, Matthew 6:33, Revelation 3:1-6, 14-22)

> 4 And I heard another voice from heaven saying, "Come out of her, My people, lest you share in her sins, and lest you receive of her plagues.

5 For her sins have reached to heaven, and God has remembered her iniquities." (Revelation 18:4-5 NKJV)

ENDNOTES

21.01: Supreme Court bans prayer in public school classrooms, June 1962, https://en.wikipedia.org/wiki/Engel_v._Vitale

21.02: Supreme Court bans Bible reading in public school classrooms, June 1963, https://en.wikipedia.org/wiki/Abington_School_District_v._Schempp

21.03: Supreme Court prevents states from banning teaching evolution, https://en.wikipedia.org/wiki/Epperson_v._Arkansas

21.04: Scientific evidence showing evolution is a lie, "It's a Young World After All, Exciting Evidences for Recent Creation, by Paul D. Ackerman, Baker Book House, 1986.

21.05: Scientific evidence showing evolution is a lie, "The Lie: Evolution/Millions of Years, by Ken Ham, Master Books, 1987.

21.06: Scientific evidence showing evolution is a lie, "Glass House, Shattering the Myth of Evolution," by Ken Ham, Master Books, 2018.

21.07: Gallup poll, April 2017, https://news.gallup.com/poll/210704/record-few-americans-believe-bible-literal-word-god.aspx

21.08: Gender confusion in California public schools, Grades K-3, CA Department of Education Health Education Framework, https://www.cde.ca.gov/ci/he/cf/hefwch3tk-3.docx

21.09: Gender confusion in California public schools, Grades 4-6, CA Department of Education Health Education Framework, https://www.cde.ca.gov/ci/he/cf/hefwch4gr4-6.docx

21.10 History without God is an incomprehensible enigma, The Story of Liberty, by Charles Carleton Coffin, (Harper & Brothers, 1878), p. 3.

21.11 1960's shift in public school history textbooks, American Heritage Series, Episode one, by David Barton, (Bridgestone, 2009)

21.12 Faith in God listed repeatedly in United States Declaration of Independence.

21.13: CIA history, https://en.wikipedia.org/wiki/Central_Intelligence_Agency#History

21.14: CIA control over media, https://en.wikipedia.org/wiki/Operation_Mockingbird

21.15: Carl Bernstein, CIA Journalists, http://www.carlbernstein.com/magazine_cia_and_media.php

21.16: Carl Bernstein report on CIA influence in major news organizations, "The CIA and the Media: How America's Most Powerful News Media Worked Hand in Glove with the Central Intelligence Agency and Why the Church Committee Covered it Up," by Carl Bernstein, (Rolling Stone, 1977)

21.17: The Atlantic, How the CIA Manipulates Hollywood, https://www.theatlantic.com/entertainment/archive/2016/07/operation-tinseltown-how-the-cia-manipulates-hollywood/491138/

21.18: Douglas Valentine, author of "The CIA as Organized Crime", quote from his comments in an interview published by American Freedom Radio, starting at the 7:15-minute mark in this video: https://www.youtube.com/watch?v=xH_veJbpkbI

21.19: Zero Hedge, Here Are 410 Movies Made Under the Direct Influence and Supervision Of The Pentagon, https://www.zerohedge.com/news/2018-08-04/heres-410-movies-made-under-direct-influence-and-supervision-department-defense

21.20: Facial recognition software, https://www.youtube.com/watch?v=SYVExWwmRlI

21.21: Celebrity face swaps in pornographic videos, https://www.theverge.com/2017/12/12/16766596/ai-fake-porn-celebrities-machine-learning

21.22: Transcript of dialogue between Morpheus and Neo, The Matrix, Warner Brothers, 1999.

22

Wars

Jesus warned the generation that sees His return will hear of wars and rumors of wars with nation rising against nation and kingdom against kingdom. (Matthew 24:6-7) The Apostle John received confirming prophetic visions starting with a rider on a white horse going forth "conquering and to conquer." Then he saw a rider on a red horse removing peace from the earth, causing people to kill each other. This rider was followed by a rider on a pale horse given power over a fourth of the earth, to kill with the sword, with hunger, and by the beasts of the earth. This rider's name is Death and Hades followed behind him. (Revelation 6:1-8)

These warnings reveal a rapid escalation of wars, ending with catastrophic events covering large areas and incurring many casualties. The magnitude of those events will make them impossible to miss, but by then it will be too late to avoid them. The smaller events preceding them can provide us with early warnings, but require paying closer attention because they're more likely to be a series of isolated events in various places around the world as part of the ongoing campaign of the rider on the white horse as he goes forth conquering, forcing others to submit.

This chapter presents evidence showing the initial fulfillment of these prophecies started at about the same time the Jewish people reclaimed Jerusalem in 1967. At that time, a significant shift and acceleration in warfare occurred as restraining influences were removed and a new kind of warfare began, confirming the start of the season of the Lord's return.

Unprecedented Power

Historically, wars have been restrained by various factors, including daylight, weather, distance and money. For example, during the eleventh and twelfth century crusades, it took six months for militias fighting for the Roman Catholic Pope to travel from France to the Middle East. During the American Revolution, it took two months for sailing ships to cross the Atlantic Ocean from Great Britain to the United States. Battles usually ended at sunset to be resumed the next day since soldiers couldn't see their targets in the dark. However, the first three of these restraints were removed by advances in technology which have given soldiers the ability to see at night, new ways to bypass and even control adverse weather conditions and new transportation methods to cover great distances rapidly. Removing those restraints expanded the possibilities for warfare, but the last one still remained, the lack of money, which has been the biggest restraint throughout history due to the enormous cost to pay for the military's food, clothing, lodging, weapons, ammunition, transportation and personal compensation. Without sufficient funds, new wars cannot be started and the delays can be significant because it takes time to accumulate large amounts of money. However, this restraint was removed in 1971, just four years after the Jewish people reclaimed Jerusalem, when the U.S. dollar was taken off the gold standard, making it a fiat currency. (22.01)

Although fiat currencies have been around for over a thousand years, the U.S. dollar's status as the world's reserve currency made this an unprecedented situation because it was the first time the world's financial system has relied on a single fiat currency, backed by absolutely nothing. (22.02) Since the Federal Reserve Bank controls the supply of U.S. dollars, this change gave them the ability to create unlimited amounts of dollars since they were no longer required to back them with gold or anything else.

Normally, sovereign nations must carefully control their money supply to avoid devaluing their currency and hyper-inflating prices of everything else, but since the dollar is the world's reserve currency, there's a worldwide demand for them because all nations are required to hold them on reserve to conduct International trade, so the strong demand allows the Fed to create more without causing inflation in the United States. And just in case that wasn't enough already, their power was increased even more in 1978 by the passage of the Federal Banking Agency Audit Act, which made it illegal for the Government Accountability Office (GAO) to audit the Fed's transactions with foreign central banks, foreign governments and any transactions made by the Federal Open Market Committee. (22.03, 22.04) By removing all accountability, this law positioned the Fed above the law, allowing them to operate lawlessly, so it only served their interests while putting everyone else at greater risk of holding potentially worthless paper, including every American citizen and every sovereign government, so it's another example of the spirit of lawlessness prevailing over our federal government.

The inability to audit the Fed's transactions gives them a cloak of darkness, enabling them to move funds wherever they want, anywhere in the world, with no one else having any way of knowing what they're doing. Although they share monthly reports on the money supply, the reports are meaningless because they don't include all the money and no one is allowed to audit the amounts not reported. (22.05, 22.06) For example, after the 2008 financial crisis, they created $3 trillion in bank reserves simply by making electronic entries. As explained in a speech by Fed Chairman Ben Bernanke in

2012 regarding their creation of $3 trillion in shady dollars, "They're not part of any broad measure of the money supply." (22.07)

With just a few electronic entries, without even printing any new dollars and without even including it in the money supply, they created a mind boggling amount of money, $3 trillion. Wouldn't that be nice? They shared those entries with the public to help calm nervous investors, but they can just as easily do the same thing or even larger amounts without telling anyone because no one is allowed to know what they're doing and they're not required to tell us.

This is truly an unprecedented situation, giving the Fed access to unprecedented wealth and therefore unprecedented power to do whatever they want without answering to anyone, which raises the question, who are they? Although they've cleverly disguised themselves as a federal government agency, by calling themselves "Federal" and by using a .gov website extension, which is supposed to be available only to government agencies, they are not part of our government. They are a private bank pursuing their own private interests, not the interests of the American people. Our founding fathers warned us to avoid allowing any private bank to control our currency, but we didn't heed their warning. (22.08)

Our Unseen Enemy:

Although we don't have access to the Fed's backroom meetings to know all their secret schemes, God has given us the prophetic warnings listed at the start of this chapter, including the warning of a rider on a white horse going forth conquering, setting the stage for other riders following him. (Revelation 6:1-11) And we have another prophetic warning that restraints will be removed before the Lord returns, as shown here.

> For the mystery of lawlessness is already at work; only He who now restrains will do so until He is taken out of the way. (2 Thessalonians 2:7)

These warnings reveal our true enemy, which is not human, but unseen evil spiritual beings. Therefore, we can move beyond the lowly stooges carrying out their plans to focus on the real culprits, the demonic spirits operating behind the scenes, the rider on the white horse, which is the spirit of antichrist. This spirit has been given what he has always wanted, unlimited power to operate under cover of total darkness, purchasing anything he wants and waging war in any sphere he wants, including manipulating world markets, governments, politicians, corporations, judges, news media organizations, and anything else. He can also afford unlimited research, development and production of the most advanced weapons systems the world has ever seen.

If this rider is now doing these things, there should be evidence of it, and there's plenty. From 1965 to 2018, the United States military and paramilitary forces fought in at least 40 known conflicts around the world, as shown in Exhibit 27. It's been essentially nonstop warfare, but the total number of conflicts is likely much higher for the following three reasons:

1. First, these 40 conflicts only include ones involving U.S. forces, but since the rider has access to unlimited unaudited money, he can fund military activities of other nations without involvement from the U.S. military, either through direct military aid or covert funding directly to a foreign government.
2. Second, these 40 conflicts only include military conflicts, but military force is usually the last resort in any war, used only after all other measures have failed, including manipulation of financial markets, economic events, assassinations, intervening in foreign elections, and implementing hostile government policies.
3. Third, these 40 conflicts only include publicly reported, overt operations, with only a few covert operations that were later declassified. Adding all covert operations is not possible, but it would likely increase the total significantly. For example, a 2016 study by Carnegie Mellon University professor Dov Levin found that the United States intervened in 81 foreign elections between 1946 and 2000, with most of those being through covert actions. (22.09) Since his study ended in 2000, the total is likely much higher by now.

One final restrainer could have stopped all this, protests from the American people. We have more than enough evidence to justify huge public protests, but instead, there have been hardly any objections, which shows how effectively public opinion is being manipulated by the CIA controlled media, as shared in the previous chapter.

The removal of all these restraints has coincided with rapid increases in knowledge and lawlessness, as shown in the previous two chapters, making the perfect storm and setting the stage for the next two riders to bring forth a new kind of warfare, waged by an exceedingly dreadful beast who will soon devour the whole earth, trampling it and breaking it to pieces. (Daniel 7:19, 7:23) Thank God He is coming to deliver His people, everyone whose name is found written in the book of life, and cut short those days. (Daniel 12:1, Matthew 24:22)

The Phoenix Program:

In 1967, the United States was looking for a way to hand over the military campaign against North Vietnam to the South Vietnamese government, but it wasn't possible because South Vietnam was deeply divided by religious and ideological beliefs. The deep divide also required the United States to fight two wars at the same time, a military campaign against the north and a new kind of war against the civilian resistors in the south, who were commonly lumped together under one derogatory name, Viet Cong. It was for this war against the civilian population that the Phoenix Program was launched in June 1967, the same month the Jewish people reclaimed Jerusalem. (22.101)

It marked a significant shift because instead of fighting a sovereign state, the enemy was redefined as anyone suspected of not supporting the regime, which required waging war against the civilian population to weed out the "bad guys". So, the target shifted from military assets to individual suspects and their loosely defined network of associates, which justified violating the rights of civilians that previously had been protected under the Internationally accepted Geneva Conventions. (22.102) And with no sovereign state to conquer and a never ending threat of more bad guys out there somewhere, this new kind of war could continue forever, making it the perfect excuse for waging endless wars. (22.103)

Since anyone could be a potential threat, the program attempted to covertly gather a massive amount of intelligence data about every citizen, which required recruiting civilians to receive CIA training to work as informants, secretly reporting activities of other civilians by infiltrating the population, posing as teachers, pharmacists, doctors, and other positions, all working together to spy on and report anyone the CIA identified as "national security offenders." (22.104) And they brought in managers who also understood the importance of informants and knew how to organize this complex campaign, such as CIA officer Nelson Brickham who once said, "All counterinsurgency depends in the first instance on informants; without them you're dead, and with them you can do all sorts of things." (22.105)

Since the program's success depended on recruiting a large network of civilian informants, they needed public support, so they deceptively claimed to be all about national security, protecting civilians from terrorist attacks, and promoted it to the public as a war on terror, but it was the opposite of what it claimed to be as it relied heavily on terrorist tactics to wage psychological warfare against the entire civilian population, routinely violating and terrorizing the same civilian population they claimed to be protecting. (22.106) The true goal was to bring as many of South Vietnam's 15,000 hamlets under government control as fast as possible by organizing a massive nationwide manhunt to identify individuals resisting the regime and terrorize then into submission, imprison them or kill them. (22.107)

The suspects captured in the manhunts were granted no due process, no way to defend themselves, no rights whatsoever. No evidence was required to add their name to a blacklist, just the word of an anonymous informant, which was all part of the program's design to produce a climate of fear that was so pervasive, every citizen had to watch every word they said because no one knew who to trust. At the height of the program, Phoenix managers assigned CIA officers and soldiers in the field with quotas of eighteen hundred "neutralizations" per month. The enormous manhunts packed South Vietnam's prisons, jails, and detention centers to overflowing. (22.108)

To manage their secret network of informants, the program joined many agencies together to establish a highly bureaucratized system of Gestapo-style secret police forces, coordinating their efforts with Military Assistance Command, Vietnam (MACV), Central Intelligence Agency (CIA), Civil Operations and Revolutionary Development (CORDS), and special operations forces. They all came together in a nationwide network of CIA centers, at the region, province, and district levels. The centers were called Intelligence and Operations Coordinating Centers (IOCCs) and were used primarily for intelligence gathering, interrogations, and analyzing data. (22.109)

In addition to the large number of civilian informants, the program used the latest technology to monitor the civilian population, including starlight scopes, ground surveillance radar, remote listening devices, and infrared and radio transmission detection devices. All findings were reported to the Phoenix Directorate in Saigon where attempts were made to enter every citizen's biographical data into a computer, marking the start of the era of the computerized blacklist. (22.110) By July 1970, Vietnamese citizens could report resistors by entering data directly into the computer at the National Police Interrogation Center. (22.111) The data was then analyzed to identify top-ranking suspects so they could be pursued and arrested.

Once the suspect's name was on the blacklist, they were hunted down, harassed, falsely accused, arrested, interrogated, often tortured to get their confessions, and detained for two years without trial, or even murdered. Attempts were often made to turn them into informants. (22.112)

A surviving Vietnamese suspect, Tran Van Truong, shared his encounter with the Phoenix Program in a book, A Vietcong Memoir. On June 16, 1967, he was driving home from work to have lunch with his wife. Suddenly, a car cut him off and two men jumped out and took him captive to an interrogation center where an interrogator informed him he had the right to beat him to death because there were no laws to protect him. He described this secret interrogation center like something from a horror movie. He saw a hallway filled with suspects sitting on the floor chained together by their ankles. Their faces were bloody and swollen. Some of them had broken limbs sticking out in abnormal ways. They were groaning and weeping in agony. Along the hallway, doors led to interrogation rooms where he heard people cursing and screaming in pain, like medieval torture chambers. In these rooms, he saw iron hooks, ropes and chains with ankle and wrist rings hanging from the ceiling. The prisoners knew about these devices and referred to them as the Airplane. (22.113)

The Phoenix Program was a significant turning point because it was the start of using the U.S. military to target innocent civilians, killing anyone who got in the way. Prior to that, our military was only allowed to target civilians in very rare instances, like if a guerilla force of civilians was attacking a military base. (22.114) Under the Phoenix Program, those restraints were removed to allow the most severe tactics to be used against the civilian population, including bombing raids of their villages, spraying their fields with toxic Agent Orange, sending hunter-killer teams of American soldiers wearing black uniforms, sending battalion-sized "cordon and search" operations, death squads, and brutally massacring large numbers of civilians, including women, children and elderly, like the My Lai massacre in March 1968 in which an estimated 347 to 504 civilians were killed and many women were gang raped and mutilated. (22.115) That was just one example of many horrible massacres and other war crimes against the Vietnamese people, which were reported by concerned American soldiers to their superior officers in other parts of Vietnam, but their reports were kept hidden from the American public by the CIA-controlled news media until American soldiers eventually returned home and shared their stories as first-hand eyewitnesses.

Despite these atrocities and subsequent cover-ups, only one man was ever convicted of any crimes, Lieutenant William Calley Jr, with a mere three years under house arrest. Although Lieutenant Calley repeatedly claimed he was obeying orders from his superior officers, no higher-level officers were ever convicted. (22.115) On the contrary, the man overseeing this devilish program, William Colby, was rewarded with a big promotion to CIA director in 1973. (22.116, 22.117)

Ironically, soon after the U.S. military started targeting innocent civilians in Vietnam, they also started killing innocent civilians in the United States. On May 4, 1970, four unarmed college students were shot and killed and nine others wounded by the Ohio National Guard during anti-war protests at Kent State University. (22.118) Since the nation was already deeply divided by the war, the shootings ignited violent protests across the land. Ten days later, on May 14, 1970, it happened again when police opened fire on unarmed college students at Jackson State University in Jackson, Mississippi, killing two students and injuring twelve. (22.119) Amazingly, none of the killers in either incident were arrested or charged with any crimes. They were given a free pass to continue, just like those who massacred innocent civilians in Vietnam, showing the same spirit ruling over both places.

Phoenix Arises from the Ashes:

Although the United States lost the Vietnam war, the CIA considers the Phoenix Program as the war's silver lining and adopted it as the model for waging war against the civilian populations of other nations, including the United States.

The Phoenix was resurrected from the ashes to take on a new life on a much larger scale than before, in response to the tragic attacks on the World Trade Towers and the Pentagon on September 11, 2001. Very few people even questioned the stories we were told about who was behind those attacks or our government's response to them because our compromises with unrighteousness have severely damaged our spiritual radar systems, blinding us from seeing the spirit of antichrist ruling over our land, but overwhelming scientific evidence proves the 9/11 attacks were planned and orchestrated by our own government agencies. (22.201) The attacks were false flag events designed to manipulate public opinion to support launching a new Phoenix-type war and to convince us to voluntarily surrender many of our personal liberties.

Less than one month later, the U.S. government launched the global war on terror, selling it to the American people the same way the Phoenix Program was sold to the Vietnamese, as a necessary national security measure to protect us from terrorist attacks, while in reality, it was the exact opposite, authorizing our government to terrorize and murder innocent civilians throughout the world, just like they terrorized and murdered tens of thousands of Vietnamese citizens and over three thousand American civilians on 9/11.

The so-called war on terror began with a campaign called Operation Enduring Freedom, which started in Afghanistan in October 2001 with a nationwide manhunt to capture or kill members of al Qaeda and Taliban insurgents, including Osama bin Laden. (22.202) Many prisoners were detained indefinitely at Bagram Theater Internment Facility where many were tortured and executed without any legal rights to due process. Innocent civilians were massacred at events like the Kandahar massacre on March 11, 2012. Suspected dissidents were assassinated by drone strikes, airstrikes, and other ways, including many innocent civilians. Afterwards, the U.S. government refused to cooperate with prosecution of any U.S. soldiers for war crimes. (22.203)

From 2002 to 2004, the manhunts were extended into Saudi Arabia, Yemen, Pakistan and Algeria. Many of the captured suspects were transferred to the Guantánamo Bay detention camp in Cuba, operated by the CIA and U.S. military personnel. Like the detention center at Bagram, suspects were detained indefinitely without any rights to a trial and reported being interrogated hundreds of times, subjected to ongoing torture, pepper spray, sexual assaults, sleep deprivation, and forced drug injections. (22.204)

From 2004 to 2006, similar kinds of manhunts were conducted in Iraq where thousands of suspected dissidents were detained and interrogated by CIA and U.S. military soldiers at Abu Ghraib prison. Many of them were tortured physically with beatings, bindings, sleep deprivation, starvation, waterboarding, confined in small coffin-like boxes, sexually raped and sodomized, and others were murdered. In addition, threats were made to harm suspects' children and sexually abuse or kill their mothers. (22.205, 22.206)

Similar manhunts were launched in many other nations, including the Philippines, from 2002 to 2015, to capture or kill members of various jihadist groups, and in seven nations of northern Africa, including Sudan, Somalia, Djibouti, Ethiopia, Eritrea, Seychelles and Kenya, to capture or kill members of the Al-Shabaab jihadist group starting in 2005 and still continuing as of 2019. (22.207, 22.208) In 2007, a campaign that later became known as Operation Juniper Shield was launched in the Sahara/Sahel region of Africa and continued until 2016, seeking traffickers of weapons and drugs in Algeria, Chad, Mali, Mauritania, Niger, Senegal, Nigeria, and Morocco. (22.209) In addition to all these, investigative journalist Douglas Valentine claims the Phoenix Program has been used as a model for other CIA black sites, secret operations, around the world. (22.210)

The global war on terror resurrected all the terror of the Phoenix Program on a much larger scale, but it was still limited to specific hotspots, so it did not literally include the whole world, but at least one top-level U.S. government advisor has called for a truly global Phoenix Program. In 2004, Australian author and counterinsurgency expert, David Kilcullen, published a 72-page document called "Countering Global Insurgency" in which he proposed a global program that would "target the insurgent infrastructure that would resemble the unfairly maligned (but highly effective) Vietnam-era Phoenix program." (22.211)

The Phoenix Program's numerous massacres, kidnapping, tortures and murders of innocent civilians were so horrible that anyone describing it as "unfairly maligned" is nothing short of a psychopathic monster and a dangerous threat to humanity. This is the same kind of insanity that led to the horrible massacres of the holocaust of World War 2, ultimately murdering over six million Jews and millions of Christians too. (22.212)

David Kilcullen's proposed Global Phoenix Program should be enough to have him blacklisted from any influential positions, but instead, he was promoted the next year to Chief Strategist in the Office of the Coordinator for Counterterrorism at the U.S. State

Department where he served from 2005 to 2006. Then in 2007, he became the senior counter-insurgency advisor to General David Petraeus and special advisor for counter-insurgency to Secretary of State Condoleezza Rice. (22.213)

When the most powerful leaders of the U.S. government are not alarmed by the idea of a global Phoenix Program, it reveals the prevailing spirit over our government is not the Spirit of God, but the spirit of antichrist, which should be enough to alarm all of us due to the long history of violent atrocities committed by this spirit, especially against Christians and Jews. Instead, we have remained silent while our government has proceeded with forming a nationwide network of fusion centers in the United States, modeled after the Phoenix Program.

Fusion Centers:

The same way the Phoenix Program fused together all levels of society with one common goal, the United States Department of Homeland Security did the same thing with the creation of fusion centers, initially established in 2003 and completed by 2007, fusing together federal, state, and local government military, police and intelligence agencies with nongovernmental private sector partners, including colleges, universities, nonprofit groups, and other partners. (22.214) These agencies include the Federal Bureau of Investigation (FBI), the U.S. Department of Homeland Security (DHS), the U.S. Department of Justice, Customs and Border Protection, Drug Enforcement Administration (DEA), Coast Guard, National Guard, Highway Patrol, and state-level Departments of Corrections. (22.215)

The same way the Phoenix Program established centers in each province and district in South Vietnam, the Department of Homeland Security established primary fusion centers in every state in the nation, plus Washington DC, Puerto Rico, Guam and the U.S. Virgin Islands, making a total of 54. Each primary center focuses on their state or territory. In addition, there are 25 recognized fusion centers targeting specific large urban areas, making a total of 79. (22.216)

The same way the Phoenix Program gathered intelligence data on every individual in the civilian population, the fusion centers do the same thing within their designated territory, which has prompted complaints from concerned citizens claiming the scope of the surveillance poses an unprecedented threat to our privacy because it goes way beyond criminal intelligence to include all public and private sector activities. And while they're gathering all sorts of data about us, we're not allowed to know anything about them because they purposely hide their operations under a cover of secrecy, making it impossible to hold them accountable, like the Phoenix Program and the Federal Reserve Bank, as discussed in chapter 20. (22.217)

However, advances in technology have made it possible for the fusion centers to gather far more data than the Phoenix Program ever could and without the help of an army of secret informants. They can now spy on us remotely through the Internet, eavesdropping through our electronic devices like smart phones, tablets and computers, which are always listening to every word we say, and even watching us through our device cameras. They can also monitor our phone calls, emails and text messages to identify our network of friends and family and the topics we're discussing with them, which can now be stored in data files without any data entry work required.

Public awareness of these kinds of surveillance tactics is growing as more people are realizing someone out there is listening to our conversations. For example, a friend recently shared this story, "Yesterday, my daughter and I were laughing about how my neighbor had questioned the sex of her beautiful baby girl. Suddenly, Siri chimed in on my iPhone, 'That is a personal decision that should be left up to the individual.' I hadn't touched my device."

Another friend shared this, "My tablet heard me praying. There were ads on there, pertaining to what I was praying about. It was very disturbing. So, no more electronic devices when I pray."

The fusion of all intelligence agencies gives the fusion centers access to whatever surveillance data they need to keep track of us, empowering them in ways that were not possible just a few years ago to know virtually everything about us. Even our car tires now contain microchips, secretly tracking everywhere we drive. The data collected is being sold to whoever wants to pay for it with the market size currently estimated at $8-9 billion and expected to double by 2026. (22.218)

Sharing intelligence data between agencies makes sense, but there is a downside risk of centralizing control over organizations that were previously controlled at the local or state level where there is generally greater accountability. For example, a local community can hold their local police chief accountable since he's well known and local, but they have no control over an unknown shadow figure operating inside their state fusion center, so there's a growing danger of combining increased power with decreased accountability.

While fusion centers have been empowered with new ways to gather unprecedented amounts of personal data about us, our local law enforcement agencies have been empowered with far more lethal military weapons than ever before, such as armored vehicles, machine guns, grenade launchers, bayonets, and military aircraft while also training local police officers to use military tactics, such as SWAT teams, paramilitary-style teams, and no-knock raids on private residences. (22.219) All these changes have been justified as necessary to fight terror, but ironically have the opposite effect, terrifying the civilian population with concerns that these weapons could be used to force us to consent to even greater restrictions on our civil liberties, giving even greater power to our government.

Meanwhile, our federal government continues to grow more powerful with far more lethal and more easily deniable high tech weapons, such as directed-energy weapons, liquid lasers, sonic and ultrasonic weapons, microwave weapons, psychotronic weapons, robot soldiers, exoskeleton robotic suits, and much more, including nuclear bombs at least 80 times more powerful than the atomic bombs used against Japan in 1945. (22.220-22.226)

Government Abuses:

With all these developments, private citizens need more safeguards than ever before to protect us from our government, but exactly the opposite is happening. Safeguards are being removed, not added. For example, the 2012 Patriot Act, signed into law on December 31, 2011, by President Obama, combined with a series of executive orders, legalized the indefinite detention of American citizens without any charges filed and without any rights of citizenship whatsoever, making it legal to treat American citizens the same way innocent civilians in other nations have been treated by the Phoenix Program and the global war on terror. (22.227)

Although our government claims they needed these new powers for national security purposes, to protect us from terrorists, evidence shows they've been grossly abusing these powers by conducting ongoing surveillance of every American citizen, not just those suspected of criminal activity or being part of a terrorist organization. In 2013, a former contract worker for the National Security Agency (NSA), named Edward Snowden, leaked an estimated 1.7 million classified documents exposing the NSA's crimes of illegally spying on Americans. He also shared tens of thousands of documents revealing the same kinds of practices by intelligence agencies in Australia, the UK, and Canada. (22.228)

Regarding the NSA, Snowden said, "They are intent on making every conversation and every form of behavior in the world known to them." (22.229) In his first interview with The Guardian's Glenn Greenwald, Snowden explained the severity of the danger.

"There is an infrastructure in place in the United States and worldwide that NSA has built, in cooperation with other governments as well, that intercepts basically every digital communication, every radio communication, every analog communication that it has sensors in place to detect, and with these capabilities basically the vast majority of human and computer to computer communications, device-based communications, which sort of form the relationships between humans, are automatically ingested without targeting and that allows individuals to retroactively search your communications based on self-certifications. So, for example, if I wanted to see the content of your emails or your wife's phone calls or anything like that, all I have to do is use what is called a selector, any kind of thing in the communications chain that might uniquely or almost uniquely identify you as an individual, and I am talking about things like email addresses, IP addresses, phone numbers, credit cards, even passwords that are unique to you that aren't used by anyone else, I can input those into the system and it will not only go back through the database and go, "Have I seen this anywhere in the past?" It will basically put an additional level of scrutiny on it moving into the future that says, if this is detected now or at any time in the future, I want this to go to me immediately and alert me in real time that you are communicating with someone." (22.230)

Snowden also revealed a secret NSA program called Prism, which proved the NSA was granted access to gather data directly from the servers of giant Internet corporations including Microsoft, Apple, Google, YouTube (owned by Google), Facebook, Skype (owned by Microsoft), and a growing list of others starting in 2007. This data allows the NSA to record every Internet search, every video we watch, the contents of every email we send, every chat conversation and every file we transfer. By participating in this program, these corporations are directly contradicting their own public claims. For example, Google has publicly stated, "Google cares deeply about the security of our users' data." Microsoft uses the following advertising slogan, "Your privacy is our priority." A spokesman from Apple denied any knowledge of Prism, but NSA files show they joined the program in 2012. (22.231)

Snowden's documents also revealed the Federal Bureau of Investigation (FBI) was granted blanket access to every Verizon customer's phone records on a daily basis, including every call made, who they talked with, and how long they talked. Similar access was granted separately to other telecom companies to effectively include every American. (22.232) The evidence exposes President Barack Obama for lying to the American public on national television in August 2013 saying, "There is no spying on Americans" and "We don't have a domestic spying program." (22.233) It also exposes top NSA officials, such as former Director of National Intelligence James Clapper, for lying under oath during Congressional hearings by repeatedly denying the NSA was doing these things. (22.234)

Government surveillance has continued increasing under President Trump with no evidence of any attempts to curtail it. (22.235) In January 2019, he signed into law a bill that extends Section 702 of the Foreign Intelligence Surveillance Act (FISA) until the end of 2023, allowing the NSA to conduct searches of foreigners' communications without any warrant. The process also collects private information from American citizens inside the United States. (22.236)

Since we've already lost our privacy, our freedoms are in great danger because we can no longer feel safe expressing our views, especially if we disagree with government policies. Their unlimited surveillance gives them unlimited power to use the information against us however they choose, including targeting dissidents the same way the Phoenix Program did in Vietnam. It's a real threat considering this is the same government that has already identified as extremist threats anyone opposing federal government policies, anyone who believes in end time prophecies, and anyone who believes in the Constitutional right to bear arms, as shown in the 2009 Department of Homeland Security (DHS) document, which was presented in chapter 20.

Another ominous sign showing how much things have changed came in 2013 when former Attorney General Eric Holder openly admitted, "It is possible, I suppose, to imagine an extraordinary circumstance in which it would be necessary and appropriate under the Constitution and applicable laws of the United States for the president to authorize the military to use lethal force within the territory of the United States." (22.237)

Conclusion:

In summary, the restraining influence of the lack of money, which has limited warfare in all previous generations, has been removed in our generation. The empowerment of a private entity to produce unlimited wealth without any accountability has coincided with the U.S. military engaging in at least 40 conflicts from 1965 to 2018. During that same time, the Phoenix Program arose as a new kind of warfare, using U.S. military forces to target the civilian population for the first time ever, and relying on terrorist tactics to control them, exactly the opposite of what it claimed to be. This most dreadful program was resurrected on a global scale by the staged events on September 11, 2001, to justify launching the global "war on terror," including a nationwide network of fusion centers.

Remnant: Wars

Like the Phoenix Program, the global war on terror has targeted civilians and relied on intelligence data which was often based on the words of anonymous informants to direct massive manhunts to arrest and indefinitely detain suspects. Both campaigns massacred many innocent civilians. Both granted suspects no rights whatsoever, no due process, which resulted in many reports of barbaric torture tactics to extract confessions and the names of new suspects. Both campaigns were created and implemented by the same government that is now using far more powerful surveillance methods aimed at a far larger civilian population.

Our government's past crimes are horrific, their current power is unprecedented, and their future intentions are suspect since they've been caught lying to us. Although the fusion centers have yet to begin large scale manhunts, U.S. laws have already been changed to remove our personal rights to legally defend ourselves and our police forces have already been militarized and centralized, making them effective forces for waging war against the civilian population. For all these reasons, I believe the so-called "war on terror" is the opposite of what it claims to be, like the Phoenix Program was in Vietnam, and is being orchestrated by deceived followers of the spirit of antichrist, which the Bible exposes as the world's greatest terrorist threat. (Revelation 6:1-11, 13)

So, our struggle is not against human beings, but against evil spiritual powers in the unseen realm who seek to enslave and destroy us. (Ephesians 6:12) Likewise, we do not look to any man for our victory, but to God through our pursuit of righteousness because that is what qualifies us for all His promises, including His promise to exalt any nation who walks uprightly before Him. (Proverbs 14:34)

I believe all these events are fulfilling end time prophetic warnings of wars and rumors of wars as another sign of the times. Combining these with the fulfillment of other prophetic signs presented in previous chapters shows the return of the Lord is close, especially since the fulfillment of even one sign indicates our generation will see them all fulfilled. (Matthew 24:33-34) In addition, these events repeatedly trace back to the same time period when the Jewish people reclaimed their land and specifically their city of Jerusalem, confirming the significance of that event as the start of the Messianic end times. Since His return is close, the rise of His army of forerunners is also close.

Despite all the dangers we face, the righteous have nothing to fear because the terrible judgment coming upon the world is not aimed at us. Righteousness qualifies us for God's protection from every storm, making it our best safety plan. (Exhibit 12) Since He is with us, no matter what trouble lies ahead, we always overwhelmingly prevail in every situation. (Matthew 16:18, Romans 8:37)

Remnant: Wars

Even if it appears all hope is gone, we can hold onto His promise that in a moment, in the twinkling of an eye, our corruptible mortal bodies will put on immortality as death is swallowed up in victory. (Matthew 24:29-31, 1 Corinthians 15:51-54) Everyone whose name is found written in the book of life will be delivered and caught up together with the angels to meet the Lord in the air and we will shine like the brightness of the stars, always with the Lord forever and ever. (Daniel 12:1-3, 1 Thessalonians 4:17) Glory to God!

ENDNOTES

22.01: U.S. dollar taken off gold standard, https://en.wikipedia.org/wiki/Nixon_shock

22.02: Fiat currencies are not new, https://en.wikipedia.org/wiki/Fiat_money

22.03: Federal Banking Audit Act, https://www.govinfo.gov/content/pkg/STATUTE-92/pdf/STATUTE-92-Pg391.pdf

22.04: Restrictions on auditing the Federal Reserve Bank, https://en.wikipedia.org/wiki/Federal_Reserve

22.05: Federal Reserve reports money supply, https://www.federalreserve.gov/releases/h6/current/default.htm

22.06: Dollars in circulation, https://www.federalreserve.gov/faqs/currency_12773.htm

22.07: Fed creates money with electronic entries, https://neweconomicperspectives.org/2012/03/where-did-the-federal-reserve-get-all-that-money.html

22.08: Warnings about the banking system, Extract from Thomas Jefferson's letter to Richard Rush, Monticello, June 22, 1819, http://tjrs.monticello.org/letter/2259

22.09: United States interventions in foreign elections, Levin, Dov H. (June 2016). "When the Great Power Gets a Vote: The Effects of Great Power Electoral Interventions on Election Results". International Studies Quarterly. 60 (2): 189–202.

22.101: Phoenix Program launched in 1967, The Phoenix Program: America's Use of Terror in Vietnam, by Douglas Valentine, (Open Road Media, 2014) Kindle Edition.

22.102: Phoenix violated Geneva Conventions, The Phoenix Program: America's Use of Terror in Vietnam, by Douglas Valentine, (Open Road Media, 2014) Kindle Edition, location 264.

22.103: Phoenix relied on anonymous informants, The Phoenix Program: America's Use of Terror in Vietnam, by Douglas Valentine, (Open Road Media, 2014) Kindle Edition, location 4977.

22.104: Civilian spies in Phoenix Program, The Phoenix Program: America's Use of Terror in Vietnam, by Douglas Valentine, (Open Road Media, 2014) Kindle Edition, location 92.

22.105: Nelson Brickham comment on informants, The Phoenix Program: America's Use of Terror in Vietnam, by Douglas Valentine, (Open Road Media, 2014) Kindle Edition, locations 2008 and 2138.

22.106: Phoenix Program claimed to be about national security, The Phoenix Program: America's Use of Terror in Vietnam, by Douglas Valentine, (Open Road Media, 2014) Kindle Edition, location 6702.

22.107: Phoenix brings hamlets under government control, The Phoenix Program: America's Use of Terror in Vietnam, by Douglas Valentine, (Open Road Media, 2014) Kindle Edition, locations 5010.

22.108: Phoenix quotas per month, The Phoenix Program: America's Use of Terror in Vietnam, by Douglas Valentine, (Open Road Media, 2014) Kindle Edition, location 116.

22.109: Phoenix joins agencies together, The Phoenix Program: America's Use of Terror in Vietnam, by Douglas Valentine, (Open Road Media, 2014) Kindle Edition, location 2333.

22.110: Findings reported to Phoenix Directorate in Saigon, The Phoenix Program: America's Use of Terror in Vietnam, by Douglas Valentine, (Open Road Media, 2014) Kindle Edition, location 114.

22.111: National Police Interrogation Center, The Phoenix Program: America's Use of Terror in Vietnam, by Douglas Valentine, (Open Road Media, 2014) Kindle Edition, location 4998.

22.112: National Police Interrogation Center, The Phoenix Program: America's Use of Terror in Vietnam, by Douglas Valentine, (Open Road Media, 2014) Kindle Edition, location 7596.

22.113: Testimony of Phoenix torture chamber, The Phoenix Program: America's Use of Terror in Vietnam, by Douglas Valentine, (Open Road Media, 2014) Kindle Edition, location 3224.

22.114: U.S. military force against civilians, Valentine, Douglas. The CIA as Organized Crime: How Illegal Operations Corrupt America and the World (p. 25). Clarity Press, Inc. Kindle Edition.

22.115: My Lai Massacre, https://en.wikipedia.org/wiki/My_Lai_Massacre

22.116: William Colby head of Phoenix Program, Valentine, Douglas. The CIA as Organized Crime: How Illegal Operations Corrupt America and the World (p. 59). Clarity Press, Inc.. Kindle Edition.

22.117: Phoenix Program CEO, William Colby https://en.wikipedia.org/wiki/William_Colby

22.118: Kent State shootings, https://en.wikipedia.org/wiki/Kent_State_shootings

22.119: Jackson State shootings, https://en.wikipedia.org/wiki/Jackson_State_killings

22.201: 2001 9/11 CIA false flag attack on World Trade Towers and Pentagon, https://www.youtube.com/watch?v=Ja67D0vKh6U

22.202: War on terror launched with Operation Enduring Freedom, https://en.wikipedia.org/wiki/Operation_Enduring_Freedom

22.203: Operation Enduring Freedom in Afghanistan, https://en.wikipedia.org/wiki/War_in_Afghanistan_(2001–present)

22.204: Manhunts in Saudi Arabia, Yemen, Pakistan and Algeria, https://en.wikipedia.org/wiki/Guantanamo_Bay_detention_camp

22.205: Suspected terrorists in Iraq tortured and murdered, https://en.wikipedia.org/wiki/Abu_Ghraib_torture_and_prisoner_abuse

22.206: Torture interrogation techniques at Abu Ghraib, https://en.wikipedia.org/wiki/Enhanced_interrogation_techniques#U.S._government

22.207: Operation Enduring Freedom in Philippines, https://en.wikipedia.org/wiki/Operation_Enduring_Freedom_–_Philippines

22.208: Operation Enduring Freedom in Horn of Africa, https://en.wikipedia.org/wiki/Operation_Enduring_Freedom_–_Horn_of_Africa

22.209: Operation Juniper Shield in Africa, https://en.wikipedia.org/wiki/Operation_Juniper_Shield

22.210: CIA established "black sites" around the world, The Phoenix Program: America's Use of Terror in Vietnam, by Douglas Valentine, (Open Road Media, 2014) Kindle Edition, location 127.

22.211: U.S. government advisor calls for global Phoenix, Countering Global Insurgency, by David Kilcullen, 2004, page 40.

22.212: Millions of Jews and Christians murdered in holocaust, https://en.wikipedia.org/wiki/Holocaust_victims

22.213: David Kilcullen promoted to top level advisor, https://en.wikipedia.org/wiki/David_Kilcullen

22.214: Fusion centers fuse together many groups, https://www.dhs.gov/state-and-major-urban-area-fusion-centers

22.215: Fusion center agencies, https://en.wikipedia.org/wiki/Fusion_center

22.216: Fusion centers located in every state, territory and major urban area, https://www.dhs.gov/fusion-center-locations-and-contact-information

22.217: Complaints about fusion center surveillance, https://www.aclu.org/report/whats-wrong-fusion-centers-executive-summary

22.218: Car tires track our drives with microchips, https://www.ericpetersautos.com/2018/07/13/chipped-tires/

22.219: Militarization of Police Forces, https://www.charleskochinstitute.org/issue-areas/criminal-justice-policing-reform/militarization-of-police/

22.220: Directed energy weapons, https://en.wikipedia.org/wiki/Directed-energy_weapon

22.221: Liquid laser weapons, https://en.m.wikipedia.org/wiki/High_Energy_Liquid_Laser_Area_Defense_System

22.222: Sonic and ultrasonic weapons, https://en.m.wikipedia.org/wiki/Sonic_weaponry

22.223: Military robot soldiers, https://en.m.wikipedia.org/wiki/Sarcos

22.224: Exoskeleton Robotic Suits, https://en.m.wikipedia.org/wiki/Sarcos#Powered_exoskeleton

22.225: Nuclear bombs 80 times more powerful today, https://www.popularmechanics.com/military/a23306/nuclear-bombs-powerful-today/

22.226: US Air Force using microwave weapons, https://www.washingtonpost.com/archive/lifestyle/magazine/2007/01/14/mind-games-span-classbankheadnew-on-the-internet-a-community-of-people-who-believe-the-government-is-beaming-voices-into-their-minds-they-may-be-crazy-but-the-pentagon-has-pursued-a-weapon-that-can-do-just-that-span/a0d09db6-d7aa-4fcd-a829-2a3ebc56df9d/?utm_term=.b93a6924390d

22.227: 2012 Patriot Act legalized indefinite detention of American citizens, https://www.aclu.org/press-releases/president-obama-signs-indefinite-detention-bill-law

22.228: Edward Snowden reveals classified documents, https://en.wikipedia.org/wiki/Global_surveillance_disclosures_(2013–present)

22.229: Edward Snowden comments on NSA, "How Edward Snowden went from loyal NSA contractor to whistleblower" by Luke Harding, (The Guardian, February 1, 2014) https://www.theguardian.com/world/2014/feb/01/edward-snowden-intelligence-leak-nsa-contractor-extract

22.230: Snowden describes NSA infrastructure, CitizenFour, (documentary film produced by Praxis Films, distributed by RADIUS TWC, 2014)

22.231: NSA Prism program collaborating with Internet giants, "NSA Prism program taps in to user data of Apple, Google and others," by Glenn Greenwald and Ewen MacAskill, (The Guardian, June 7, 2013) https://www.theguardian.com/world/2013/jun/06/us-tech-giants-nsa-data

22.232: FBI access to Verizon's phone records, "NSA collecting phone records of millions of Verizon customers daily" by Glenn Greenwald, (The Guardian, June 6, 2013) https://www.theguardian.com/world/2013/jun/06/nsa-phone-records-verizon-court-order

22.233: Obama caught lying to American people, "Obama to Leno: 'There is No Spying on Americans' by Greg Henderson, (NPR, August 7 2013) https://www.npr.org/sections/thetwo-way/2013/08/06/209692380/obama-to-leno-there-is-no-spying-on-americans

22.234: James Clapper lied to Congress, CitizenFour, (documentary film produced by Praxis Films, distributed by RADIUS TWC, 2014)

22.235: Government surveillance is increasing under President Trump, "Administration Ups Data Collection and General Surveillance, (The National Law Review, June 19, 2019) https://www.natlawreview.com/article/administration-ups-data-collection-and-general-surveillance

22.236: Trump extends NSA FISA until 2023, https://en.wikipedia.org/wiki/Presidency_of_Donald_Trump#Surveillance

22.237: Eric Holder defends legality of murdering American citizens, John Swaine, "Barack Obama 'has authority to use drone strikes to kill Americans on US soil'", The Telegraph, 6 March 2013. https://www.telegraph.co.uk/news/worldnews/barackobama/9913615/Barack-Obama-has-authority-to-use-drone-strikes-to-kill-Americans-on-US-soil.html

Exhibits

Exhibit 1: Reasons Why Elijah is One of the Two Witnesses

Here are five reasons why Elijah is well qualified for the witness assignment.

1. Elijah is one of only two people who departed earth without dying, so by returning as one of the witnesses, he would fulfill the prophecy that it is appointed to man once to die because both witnesses will be killed by the beast. (Genesis 5:24, 2 Kings 2:11, Hebrews 9:27, Revelation 11:7)
2. The two witnesses will minister as prophets, like Elijah did during his first ministry. (2 Kings 1:17, Revelation 11:3)
3. The two witnesses will shut the heavens so no rain falls for one thousand two hundred and sixty days, which is three and a half years, the same amount of time Elijah shut the heavens from raining during his first ministry. (1 Kings 17:1, Luke 4:25, Revelation 11:3-6) So, he is an ideal candidate.
4. The two witnesses will have power to devour their enemies by fire, like Elijah did when he destroyed the false prophets after calling down fire from heaven. (1 Kings 18:20-40, Revelation 11:5)
5. The two witnesses will come back to life after it appears their lives have ended, like Elijah returned to earth and was seen by the disciples, speaking with Jesus during His transfiguration. (Luke 9:27-31, Revelation 11:11)

Exhibit 2: 41 Proofs God is Not Finished with the Jewish People

There is a lot of confusion regarding God's end time plans for the Jewish people, the flesh and blood descendants of Abraham, Isaac, and Jacob. God has not forgotten them, but has amazing plans to bring a remnant of them to salvation. Even before they rebelled against Him, He had already revealed to them His plans to restore them back to Himself in the end, a message He repeated many times through His prophets, including Moses, Isaiah, Daniel, Ezekiel, Amos, Paul, and the Lord Jesus.

1) Israel will Mourn with Regret

If God is done with the Jewish people, why did He prophesy of a day coming when they look upon the one they pierced and mourn for Him like one would mourn for their only son and they will weep bitterly over Him like the bitter weeping over a firstborn. (Zechariah 12:10-14) This prophecy can only be fulfilled by physical Israel and makes no sense when applied to spiritual Israel.

Israel will mourn and repent for three days; on the third day, they will live. (Hosea 6:2)

> 10 "And I will pour on the house of David and on the inhabitants of Jerusalem the Spirit of grace and supplication; then they will look on Me whom they pierced. Yes, they will mourn for Him as one mourns for his only son, and grieve for Him as one grieves for a firstborn.
> 11 In that day there shall be a great mourning in Jerusalem, like the mourning at Hadad Rimmon in the plain of Megiddo.
> 12 And the land shall mourn, every family by itself: the family of the house of David by itself, and their wives by themselves; the family of the house of Nathan by itself, and their wives by themselves;
> 13 the family of the house of Levi by itself, and their wives by themselves; the family of Shimei by itself, and their wives by themselves;
> 14 all the families that remain, every family by itself, and their wives by themselves. (Zechariah 12:10-14 NKJV)

2) God Promises to Make Jerusalem a Praise in the Earth

If God is finished with the Jewish people, then why did God say He would have no rest, He would not keep silent, He would not remain still until He does all the following things for Jerusalem and the people of Israel?

- He establishes and makes Jerusalem a praise in the earth.
- Her salvation will be like a burning torch.

Exhibit 2: 41 Proofs God is Not Finished with the Jewish People

- Until all nations see the righteousness of the people of Israel shining brightly.
- Until kings see the glory of Israel
- Until He makes Israel a crown of beauty in His hand
- Until He makes Israel a royal diadem in His hand
- Until they are no longer called Forsaken or Desolate
- Until they are called "My delight is in her."
- Until the nations call them, "The holy people, the redeemed of the Lord."

All these promises were recorded by the Prophet Isaiah (Isaiah 62), but they have not yet been fulfilled, which proves God's plans for the Jewish people are not done yet. The best is yet to come.

3) Jesus Prophesied the Times of the Gentiles Will End

God's plans for the Jewish people will be fulfilled when the times of the Gentiles are completed, which clearly has not happened yet, proving God still has unfulfilled plans for the Jewish people:

> 20 "But when you see Jerusalem surrounded by armies, then know that its desolation is near.
> 21 Then let those who are in Judea flee to the mountains, let those who are in the midst of her depart, and let not those who are in the country enter her.
> 22 For these are the days of vengeance, that all things which are written may be fulfilled.
> 23 But woe to those who are pregnant and to those who are nursing babies in those days! For there will be great distress in the land and wrath upon this people.
> 24 And they will fall by the edge of the sword, and be led away captive into all nations. And Jerusalem will be trampled by Gentiles until the times of the Gentiles are fulfilled. (Luke 21:20-24 NKJV)

In this prophecy, Jesus warned about the coming destruction of Jerusalem and the second temple, which was fulfilled when Roman armies conquered Jerusalem in 70 AD, but He also revealed hope for the future by revealing Israel's trouble will come to an end after the times of the Gentiles are fulfilled. Until then, Satan will continue seeking to advance his plans by establishing his throne in the reconstructed temple, which was foretold by the Prophet Daniel. (Daniel 9:26-27) But Satan's schemes will backfire when Jesus returns to fight in behalf of the inhabitants of Jerusalem and Satan will be cast down into the pit. (Isaiah 14:15)

4) Jesus Promises to Restore the Kingdom to Israel

If God is finished with the Jewish people, then why did Jesus promise to restore the kingdom to Israel? When His disciples asked if He was going to restore the kingdom of Israel at that time, He could have said He had no plans to do so, but instead He told them it was not for them to know when He would do it, so it was only a question of when it would happen, not if it would happen.

> 6 Therefore, when they had come together, they asked Him, saying, "Lord, will You at this time restore the kingdom to Israel?"
> 7 And He said to them, "It is not for you to know times or seasons which the Father has put in His own authority.
> 8 But you shall receive power when the Holy Spirit has come upon you; and you shall be witnesses to Me in Jerusalem, and in all Judea and Samaria, and to the end of the earth." (Acts 1:6-8 NKJV)

Webster's Dictionary defines 'restore' as "to bring back into existence or put back into a former or original state", so restoring the kingdom to Israel makes no sense if it does not include the original people of Israel, the Jewish people. (Acts 1:6-8) Although Israel was reborn as a nation in 1948, it has not yet been restored to its' former state, like it was in the days of King Solomon, so these prophecies remain unfulfilled and refer to future events.

5) God Will Gather All Nations Against Jerusalem

If God is finished with the Jewish people, then why has He promised to gather all nations in the Valley of Jehoshaphat where He will judge them in behalf of His people Israel? This place is also called the Valley of Decision and Valley of Judgment. God plans to judge the nations for their crimes of scattering His people among the nations, dividing up His land, and casting lots for His people. (Joel 3:2-3)

> 2 I will also gather all nations, and bring them down to the Valley of Jehoshaphat; and I will enter into judgment with them there on account of My people, My heritage Israel, whom they have scattered among the nations; they have also divided up My land.
> 3 They have cast lots for My people, have given a boy as payment for a harlot, and sold a girl for wine, that they may drink. (Joel 3:2-3 NKJV)

Exhibit 2: 41 Proofs God is Not Finished with the Jewish People

> 2 For I will gather all the nations to battle against Jerusalem; the city shall be taken, the houses rifled, and the women ravished. Half of the city shall go into captivity, but the remnant of the people shall not be cut off from the city. (Zechariah 14:2 NKJV)

6) God Will Fight for the Inhabitants of Jerusalem

If God is finished with the Jewish people, then why is He planning to fight against all nations in behalf of Jerusalem? He coming back to fight for the inhabitants of their holy city of Jerusalem. Both are at the center of His end time plans.

The Prophet Zechariah saw Him returning in the last days, standing on the Mount of Olives, which is in front of Jerusalem on the east. He was not referring to the Lord's first visit to earth because all nations were not gathered to fight against Jerusalem and He did not fight against the nations. Before the Lord returns, Jerusalem will be surrounded and captured by the Gentile nations with their houses plundered, their women ravished and half the city in exile. (Zechariah 14:2-7)

> 2 For I will gather all the nations to battle against Jerusalem; the city shall be taken, the houses rifled, and the women ravished. Half of the city shall go into captivity, but the remnant of the people shall not be cut off from the city.
> 3 Then the Lord will go forth and fight against those nations, as He fights in the day of battle.
> 4 And in that day His feet will stand on the Mount of Olives, which faces Jerusalem on the east. And the Mount of Olives shall be split in two, from east to west, making a very large valley; half of the mountain shall move toward the north and half of it toward the south.
> 5 Then you shall flee through My mountain valley, for the mountain valley shall reach to Azal. Yes, you shall flee as you fled from the earthquake in the days of Uzziah king of Judah. Thus the Lord my God will come, and all the saints with You.
> 6 It shall come to pass in that day that there will be no light; the lights will diminish.
> 7 It shall be one day which is known to the Lord— neither day nor night. But at evening time it shall happen that it will be light. (Zechariah 14:2-7 NKJV)

God will fight for Jerusalem by sending a terrible plague against their enemies.

> 12 And this shall be the plague with which the Lord will strike all the people who fought against Jerusalem: their flesh shall dissolve while they stand on their feet,

Exhibit 2: 41 Proofs God is Not Finished with the Jewish People

> their eyes shall dissolve in their sockets, and their tongues shall dissolve in their mouths.
> 13 It shall come to pass in that day that a great panic from the Lord will be among them. Everyone will seize the hand of his neighbor, and raise his hand against his neighbor's hand; (Zechariah 14:12-13 NKJV)

When the Lord fights for Jerusalem, He will also watch over the house of Judah and defend the inhabitants of Jerusalem, so it is not just the city He will defend, but also the inhabitants, the Jewish people. (Zechariah 12:3-7)

> 3 And it shall happen in that day that I will make Jerusalem a very heavy stone for all peoples; all who would heave it away will surely be cut in pieces, though all nations of the earth are gathered against it.
> 4 In that day," says the Lord, "I will strike every horse with confusion, and its rider with madness; I will open My eyes on the house of Judah, and will strike every horse of the peoples with blindness.
> 5 And the governors of Judah shall say in their heart, 'The inhabitants of Jerusalem are my strength in the Lord of hosts, their God.'
> 6 In that day I will make the governors of Judah like a firepan in the woodpile, and like a fiery torch in the sheaves; they shall devour all the surrounding peoples on the right hand and on the left, but Jerusalem shall be inhabited again in her own place—Jerusalem.
> 7 "The Lord will save the tents of Judah first, so that the glory of the house of David and the glory of the inhabitants of Jerusalem shall not become greater than that of Judah. (Zechariah 12:3-7 NKJV)

Not only is God going to defend the inhabitants of Jerusalem, but He is also going to empower them to join in the battle, fighting alongside of Him, making the one who is feeble among them like David, and the house of David like God, like the angel of the Lord before them. (Zechariah 12:8)

The same prophecy was given to the Prophet Obadiah. He saw the Lord fighting in behalf of His people, Jacob, on the day of Yahweh, and He also saw the Lord empowering the people of Israel to fight and destroy their enemies, making the house of Jacob a fire and the house of Joseph a flame, setting on fire the house of Esau, causing them to be consumed until there are no survivors in the house of Esau. (Obadiah 1:18)

Why will God fight for the Jewish people? It is His judgment coming upon the nations for

Exhibit 2: 41 Proofs God is Not Finished with the Jewish People

what they have done to His people, the Jewish people, specifically for scattering them among the nations, dividing His land, and mistreating them.

> 1 "For behold, in those days and at that time, when I bring back the captives of Judah and Jerusalem,
> 2 I will also gather all nations, and bring them down to the Valley of Jehoshaphat; and I will enter into judgment with them there on account of My people, My heritage Israel, whom they have scattered among the nations; they have also divided up My land.
> 3 They have cast lots for My people, have given a boy as payment for a harlot, and sold a girl for wine, that they may drink. (Joel 3:1-3 NKJV)

Although some have claimed the Church, spiritual Israel, will fulfill all prophecies regarding Israel, Joel's prophecy can only be fulfilled by physical Israel, the Jewish people, because the nations have never scattered the Church among the nations, nor divided up the Church's land, nor sold the Church into captivity, but all these things happened to the Jewish people after Jerusalem was conquered in 70 AD. So all these signs reveal it is for the sake of the Jewish people that God enters into judgment against the nations, which is amazing because the Jewish people who endured all these terrible events are the same people who rejected Him, which is why these things came upon them. Yet, God still calls them His people and His inheritance, demonstrating His grace, mercy, and faithfulness. If God was ever going to give up on them, He had every opportunity to do so after they rejected their Messiah and were sold into captivity, but instead, He entered into judgment against everyone who mistreated them. He remains committed to fulfilling His promises to their forefathers no matter what they do, but the consequences of their disobedience have been severe.

Why would God fight in behalf of such undeserving people? Perhaps the answer was given to Zechariah when God told him whoever touches Israel touches the apple of His eye and vowed to fight against the nations who plundered Israel. (Zechariah 2:8-9)

When God fights for Israel, He is fighting against Satan, so this is another reason why He plans to fight for them.

> 8 And then the lawless one will be revealed, whom the Lord will consume with the breath of His mouth and destroy with the brightness of His coming.
> 9 The coming of the lawless one is according to the working of Satan, with all power, signs, and lying wonders,

Exhibit 2: 41 Proofs God is Not Finished with the Jewish People

> 10 and with all unrighteous deception among those who perish, because they did not receive the love of the truth, that they might be saved. (2 Thessalonians 2:8-10 NKJV)

7) Israel Saved at the End of this Age

If God is finished with the Jewish people, then why has God revealed a remnant of Israel will be saved at the end of this age? This event was prophesied by Moses, as presented in chapter 17, including an explanation of why it could only be fulfilled by physical Israel. (Deuteronomy 4:25-31) The following prophecies confirm what Moses saw, including words from Isaiah, Jeremiah, Ezekiel, Daniel, Zechariah, Obadiah, and Jesus.

Confirmed by Isaiah: The Prophet Isaiah saw a day coming when a remnant of His people would consider God as their most valued possession, like a beautiful crown and a glorious diadem, which could apply to both physical and spiritual Israel.

> In that day the Lord of hosts will be for a crown of glory and a diadem of beauty to the remnant of His people. (Isaiah 28:5 NKJV)

Confirmed by Jeremiah: The Prophet Jeremiah saw the sins of Israel and Judah pardoned after a remnant returns to the same land where their fathers lived, specifically including Carmel, Bashan, and the hill country of Ephraim and Gilead.

> 19 But I will bring back Israel to his home, and he shall feed on Carmel and Bashan; his soul shall be satisfied on Mount Ephraim and Gilead.
> 20 In those days and in that time," says the Lord, "The iniquity of Israel shall be sought, but there shall be none; and the sins of Judah, but they shall not be found; for I will pardon those whom I preserve. (Jeremiah 50:19-20 NKJV)

This prophecy remains unfulfilled since we can still find the iniquity of Israel and the sins of Judah. I believe Jeremiah saw events coming at the end of this age when the Lord returns.

> Alas! For that day is great, so that none is like it; and it is the time of Jacob's trouble, but he shall be saved out of it. (Jeremiah 30:7 NKJV)

Confirmed by Ezekiel: The Prophet Ezekiel saw a time when God would hide His face from His people because of their unrighteousness, giving them into the hand of their enemies, but Ezekiel saw afterwards God would restore their fortunes, have mercy on them, forget their sins against Him, bring them out of the lands of their enemies, gather

Exhibit 2: 41 Proofs God is Not Finished with the Jewish People

them into their own land, cause them to live securely in their land with no one to make them afraid, stop hiding His face from them, and pour out His Spirit on them. (Ezekiel 39:23-29)

> 25 "Therefore thus says the Lord God: 'Now I will bring back the captives of Jacob, and have mercy on the whole house of Israel; and I will be jealous for My holy name—
> 26 after they have borne their shame, and all their unfaithfulness in which they were unfaithful to Me, when they dwelt safely in their own land and no one made them afraid.
> 27 When I have brought them back from the peoples and gathered them out of their enemies' lands, and I am hallowed in them in the sight of many nations,
> 28 then they shall know that I am the Lord their God, who sent them into captivity among the nations, but also brought them back to their land, and left none of them captive any longer.
> 29 And I will not hide My face from them anymore; for I shall have poured out My Spirit on the house of Israel,' says the Lord God." (Ezekiel 39:25-29 NKJV)

The first part of Ezekiel's prophecy was fulfilled when Israel turned away from God, was given into the hand of their adversaries, and fell by the sword, not just once, but twice. They were defeated by King Nebuchadnezzar of Babylon in 597 BC and again by Roman armies in 70 AD. Ezekiel's prophecy was not fulfilled when they returned home from exile in Babylon because they did not live securely in their land with no one to make them afraid. Instead, they were exiled a second time, so the fulfillment of this prophecy must be in the future, during the thousand-year reign of the Lord. Only the flesh and blood descendants of Jacob could fulfill this prophecy because they're the only ones who were conquered, exiled, scattered among the nations, and returned to the land of their fathers. No one else meets all those requirements.

Confirmed by Daniel: The angel Gabriel also confirmed God's plans to deliver a remnant of Daniel's people on the day of Yahweh, telling Daniel, "And at that time your people shall be delivered, everyone who is found written in the book." (Daniel 12:1b NKJV) Gabriel referred to them as Daniel's people, the people of Israel, but then narrowed it down further by identifying "everyone who is found written in the book." So a remnant of the Jewish people will be delivered, the ones whose names are found in the book.

> Note: The Hebrew word sepher is translated as book, but the same word is translated as scroll in other scriptures. I believe this is the same scroll sealed with seven seals, broken only by the Lamb of God before His return. (Revelation 6)

Exhibit 2: 41 Proofs God is Not Finished with the Jewish People

Confirmed by Zechariah: The Prophet Zechariah also saw a day coming when God will save a remnant of His people and they will be His people and He will be their God in truth and righteousness. (Zechariah 8:6-8) God also showed Zechariah His reasons for saving them is because they are like precious stones in a crown, sparkling in His land. In those days, they will be beautiful and will flourish with grain and wine. (Zechariah 9:16-17)

> "So I will strengthen them in the Lord, and they shall walk up and down in His name," says the Lord. (Zechariah 10:12 NKJV)
>
> I will say, 'This is My people'; and each one will say, 'The Lord is my God.' (Zechariah 13:9b NKJV)

Confirmed by Obadiah: The Prophet Obadiah saw a remnant of God's people escaping on Mount Zion on the day of Yahweh, describing it as a holy event. (Obadiah 1:17) This prophecy has not yet been fulfilled because the day of Yahweh has not yet happened. Since he specifically identified Mount Zion as the area where these people will escape, it is another confirmation God plans to deliver the Jewish people and even though these events happen in the future, on the day of Yahweh, God still refers to them as "My people." (Obadiah 1:13)

Confirmed by Jesus: Jesus prophesied of a day coming when Jerusalem would be made desolate, but then afterwards, a day would come when they would see Him again and would recognize He comes in the name of the Lord.

> 37 "O Jerusalem, Jerusalem, the one who kills the prophets and stones those who are sent to her! How often I wanted to gather your children together, as a hen gathers her chicks under her wings, but you were not willing!
> 38 See! Your house is left to you desolate;
> 39 for I say to you, you shall see Me no more till you say, 'Blessed is He who comes in the name of the Lord!'" (Matthew 23:37-39 NKJV)

Jesus spoke this warning specifically to the same people who rejected Him during His first visitation, accusing Him of blaspheme and killing Him by crucifixion. It was those same people, the Jewish people, who endured great hardships when the first part of this prophecy was fulfilled in 70 AD when Roman armies destroyed Jerusalem and made it desolate as the Jewish people were taken into captivity and scattered among the nations. Since it was spoken to them and the first part has already been fulfilled by them, it makes no sense to suggest the second part will be fulfilled by anyone other than their descendants, physical Israel, because this is a message of hope for them, telling them God saw those terrible events coming before they happened and already had a plan to turn it around in the end.

I believe this passage reveals the heart of God for His people because even after they rejected Him, He still wanted to gather them together the way a hen gathers her chicks under her wings, but He couldn't because they were not willing. So, Jesus echoed the same warning given by Moses before they entered the land, with the same hope for a future day when they would see Him again, but then the outcome will be different because they will receive Him saying, "Blessed is He who comes in the name of the Lord!"

8) Israel's Sins Will Be Forgiven

If God is finished with the Jewish people, then why is He planning to forgive their sins at the end of the age? This was revealed to at least four witnesses, including Daniel, Ezekiel, Zechariah and Paul.

Confirmed by Daniel: After seeing a vision of the end times, the Prophet Daniel was troubled because he did not understand what he saw. After he prayed earnestly about it, he was visited by the angel Gabriel who explained significant future events for Daniel's people and his holy city Jerusalem, occurring within seventy periods of seven years each, which he described as seventy sevens.

> "Seventy weeks (sevens) are determined for your people and for your holy city, to finish the transgression, to make an end of sins, to make reconciliation for iniquity, to bring in everlasting righteousness, to seal up vision and prophecy, and to anoint the Most Holy. (Daniel 9:24 NKJV)

Gabriel explained the following seven things would happen during the seventy sevens.

1. Transgression will be finished, completed, finally reaching its' climax when the man of sin establishes his throne in the temple in Jerusalem to rule as God on earth. (Matthew 24:15, 2 Thessalonians 2:1-4)
2. Sin will be brought to an end, meaning it will no longer be tolerated or permitted by the Lord because after He returns, He will rule the earth with a rod of iron, requiring everyone to walk uprightly before God. The rebellion against God will be crushed when He returns with His army of holy ones.
3. Atonement will be made for iniquity, which was fulfilled by the death and resurrection of the Lord Jesus, paying the full price for the sins of everyone willing to receive it by faith.

Exhibit 2: 41 Proofs God is Not Finished with the Jewish People

4. Everlasting righteousness will be brought in, as the Lord establishes His eternal kingdom on earth, ruling from Jerusalem, which will be called the Throne of Yahweh, established upon righteousness.
5. Vision will be sealed up because after the Lord returns, we will no longer see through a glass dimly, but will see all things clearly as mysteries will no longer be hidden from our view.
6. Prophecy will be sealed up because after the Lord returns, we will have access to unlimited knowledge, so there will no longer be any need for prophecy, which only provides limited partial information.
7. The most holy place will be anointed, meaning the dwelling place of the Most High God will be here on earth, ruling from the holy place, the temple in Jerusalem.

Although atonement for our sins was completed during the Lord's earthly ministry, the other events have not yet been fulfilled because sin is still increasing as the world enters greater darkness and Satan advances his agenda, which will continue until the Lord returns. People today are still sinning against God, so everlasting righteousness has not yet begun. We do not yet have all knowledge, so the gifts of visions and prophecy are still needed and still in operation. The holy dwelling place of God, the temple in Jerusalem, has not yet been constructed. Since these specific events for Daniel's people, the Jewish people, and his holy city, have not yet been fulfilled, God still has plans for them, which proves He has not given up on them. At the end of the age, He will forgive the sins of the surviving remnant of Israel.

Confirmed by Ezekiel: The Prophet Ezekiel also saw Israel cleansed from their sins, as shown in this scripture:

> 33 "Thus says the Lord God: 'On the day that I cleanse you from all your iniquities, I will also enable you to dwell in the cities, and the ruins shall be rebuilt.
> 34 The desolate land shall be tilled instead of lying desolate in the sight of all who pass by.
> 35 So they will say, 'This land that was desolate has become like the garden of Eden; and the wasted, desolate, and ruined cities are now fortified and inhabited.'
> 36 Then the nations which are left all around you shall know that I, the Lord, have rebuilt the ruined places and planted what was desolate. I, the Lord, have spoken it, and I will do it." (Ezekiel 36:33-36 NKJV)

Exhibit 2: 41 Proofs God is Not Finished with the Jewish People

Ezekiel also saw the following accompanying signs, which provide us with clues regarding the timing of the fulfillment of his prophecy.

1. The cities of Israel will be inhabited.
2. The waste places of Israel will be rebuilt.
3. The desolate land will be cultivated.
4. The desolate land will become like the garden of Eden.
5. The desolate and ruined cities will be fortified.
6. The nations surrounding Israel will know the Lord has rebuilt the ruined places.

Although some of these things have been fulfilled since Israel regained possession of Jerusalem in 1967, not all of them have happened yet because Israel has not become like the garden of Eden and the surrounding nations have not yet acknowledged God is with Israel, restoring their ruined places. The opposite is still happening; the surrounding nations believe Allah is god and that he wants to destroy the people and cities of Israel. Therefore, the fulfillment of Ezekiel's prophecy remains in the future as another confirmation that God is not done with the Jewish people.

Confirmed by Zechariah: Zechariah saw God will remove iniquity from the land of Israel in one day.

> 8 'Hear, O Joshua, the high priest, you and your companions who sit before you, for they are a wondrous sign; for behold, I am bringing forth My Servant the BRANCH.
> 9 For behold, the stone that I have laid before Joshua: upon the stone are seven eyes.
> Behold, I will engrave its inscription,' says the Lord of hosts, and I will remove the iniquity of that land in one day.
> 10 In that day,' says the Lord of hosts, 'Everyone will invite his neighbor under his vine and under his fig tree.'" (Zechariah 3:8-10 NKJV)

Zechariah saw it will be like a fountain opened for the inhabitants of Jerusalem to wash away their sins and removing the unclean spirit from the land. Their past idols will be cut off and remembered no more. (Zechariah 13:1-2)

Confirmed by Paul: The Apostle Paul saw Israel's sins will be taken away, as shown in the following scripture.

Exhibit 2: 41 Proofs God is Not Finished with the Jewish People

25 For I do not desire, brethren, that you should be ignorant of this mystery, lest you should be wise in your own opinion, that blindness in part has happened to Israel until the fullness of the Gentiles has come in.
26 And so all Israel will be saved, as it is written: "The Deliverer will come out of Zion, and He will turn away ungodliness from Jacob;
27 For this is My covenant with them, when I take away their sins." (Romans 11:25-27 NKJV)

Paul's prophecy confirms this event has not yet happened because the accompanying sign, the fullness or completion of the Gentiles entering God's kingdom, has not happened yet and will not happen until the end of the age when the Lord returns.

9) Israel will Possess the Lands of their Enemies

If God is done with the Jewish people, then why did the Prophet Obadiah see a future day when the Jewish people will take possession of lands and cities now belonging to Jordan, Lebanon, and the Palestinian West Bank. Only the Jewish people can fulfill this prophecy because they are the only ones who meet all the requirements revealed to Obadiah, identifying them as the remnant of survivors who were previously attacked violently by the descendants of Esau (Arabs), sold into captivity, and eventually delivered when the Lord returns on the day of Yahweh to fight for them, enabling them to inhabit Mount Zion and govern from there. These lands and cities are listed below. (Obadiah 1:19-21)

- The mountain of Esau, also called Mount Seir, a mountainous region stretching between the Dead Sea and the Gulf of Aqaba, demarcating the southeastern border of Edom with Judah. These mountains were part of ancient Israel, but today they are possessed by Jordan, near their western border with southern Israel.
- Shephelah, also called Shfela, are the lowland plains located in modern Israel between the West Bank and the Coastal Plains region.
- The territory of Ephraim, which is the land allotted to the tribe of Ephraim. This area is located north of Jerusalem in the area designated as the West Bank, which currently belongs to the Palestinians and includes the city of Ramallah, which is currently the headquarters for the Palestinian Authority.
- Samaria – The ancient city of Samaria was once the capital of the northern kingdom of Israel. The territory of Samaria is located just north of Tel Aviv (formerly called Jaffa), reaching to the Mediterranean Sea between the Sea of Galilee and the Dead Sea. Samaria today is divided between Israel and the Palestinian Authority.

Exhibit 2: 41 Proofs God is Not Finished with the Jewish People

- The region of Gilead is located in modern Jordan, east of the Jordan River and extending from the Sea of Galilee in the north to the Dead Sea in the south.
- Zarephath, also called Sarepta, was an ancient Phoenician city located on the Mediterranean coast of modern Lebanon, between Sidon and Tyre.
- The Negev is a rocky desert region located in southern Israel, extending south to the Gulf of Aqaba and accounting for 55% of modern Israel's total land. Beersheba is the current capital city of the Negev.

Since Obadiah saw these lands becoming part of Israel after the Lord fights for them on the day of Yahweh (Obadiah 1:15), this prophecy remains unfulfilled, so it is another confirmation God has not abandoned the Jewish people.

10) Israel Will Not be Exiled Again

If God is finished with the Jewish people, then why did the Prophet Amos see Israel will be restored, the captive people will return and rebuild their ruined cities and God will plant them on their land, and they will never again be rooted out from their land?

This prophecy was not fulfilled by Israel's first exile and return from Babylonian captivity because afterwards they were again uprooted out from their land. It cannot be fulfilled by the Church because we're not the fallen house of David. So, it remains unfulfilled and can only be fulfilled by physical Israel.

Already today we see the partial fulfillment as Israel has repossessed the land, rebuilt the ruined cities, and made gardens for growing fruit. Based on this prophecy, Israel will never again be rooted out from their land. The people of Israel will not be exiled and scattered among the nations again because the Lord Himself will return to fight in their behalf. (Amos 9:11-15)

> 11 "On that day I will raise up the tabernacle of David, which has fallen down, and repair its damages; I will raise up its ruins, and rebuild it as in the days of old;
> 12 That they may possess the remnant of Edom, and all the Gentiles who are called by My name," says the Lord who does this thing.
> 13 "Behold, the days are coming," says the Lord, "When the plowman shall overtake the reaper, and the treader of grapes him who sows seed; the mountains shall drip with sweet wine, and all the hills shall flow with it.
> 14 I will bring back the captives of My people Israel; they shall build the waste cities and inhabit them; they shall plant vineyards and drink wine from them; they shall also make gardens and eat fruit from them.

15 I will plant them in their land, and no longer shall they be pulled up from the land I have given them," says the Lord your God. (Amos 9:11-15 NKJV)

11) Israel will Blossom and Fill the Whole World with Fruit

God promises to restore the fortunes of Israel, which we are starting to see in modern Israel as they are already a major exporter of physical fruit but I believe the following prophecies reveal Israel will have a much greater impact on the world in the future when it fills the whole world with the fruit of the Spirit after it becomes a place of holiness and deliverance. So these prophecies refer to future events when they will be fulfilled by the descendants of the captives of Judah and Jerusalem returning to their land, which could only be the Jewish people.

> Those who come He shall cause to take root in Jacob; Israel shall blossom and bud, and fill the face of the world with fruit. (Isaiah 27:6 NKJV)

> "But on Mount Zion there shall be deliverance, and there shall be holiness; the house of Jacob shall possess their possessions. (Obadiah 1:17 NKJV)

12) God Promised to Reign and Dwell in Jerusalem

If God is done with the Jewish people, why did He promise Jerusalem will one day be called the Throne of Jehovah? (Jeremiah 3:17-18) By identifying Jerusalem, He also identified the Jewish people because it is their capital city. God plans to dwell in the midst of Jerusalem.

> 3 "Thus says the Lord: 'I will return to Zion, and dwell in the midst of Jerusalem. Jerusalem shall be called the City of Truth, the Mountain of the Lord of hosts, the Holy Mountain.' (Zechariah 8:3 NKJV)

In that day when the Lord dwells in the midst of Jerusalem, many other nations will join themselves to the Lord, which indicates a great end time harvest of souls entering God's Kingdom. The combination of those two events has not happened yet. It was not fulfilled by the earthly ministry of the Lord Jesus because it was not preceded by a time when many nations joined themselves to the Lord and the Lord Jesus did not possess Judah during His earthly ministry, but was rejected and put to death by them.

> 10 "Sing and rejoice, O daughter of Zion! For behold, I am coming and I will dwell in your midst," says the Lord.

Exhibit 2: 41 Proofs God is Not Finished with the Jewish People

> 11 "Many nations shall be joined to the Lord in that day, and they shall become My people. And I will dwell in your midst. Then you will know that the Lord of hosts has sent Me to you.
> 12 And the Lord will take possession of Judah as His inheritance in the Holy Land, and will again choose Jerusalem. (Zechariah 2:10-12 NKJV)

Other scriptures help identify the timing of this great revival, which happens near the end of the age, just before the Lord returns, including Isaiah 60:1-5, Joel 3:18, Amos 9:13-15, Matthew 13:24-30, Mark 16:15-18, John 4:35-36. Other scriptures give us more insights into the Lord's end-time plans to dwell in Jerusalem, referring to the heavenly Jerusalem, which will come down out of heaven to Mount Zion. (Hebrews 12:22) Jesus called it "the city of My God, which comes down out of heaven from My God." (Revelation 3:12, 21:2, 21:10) Paul described the Jerusalem above as the free woman, as opposed to the slave woman. She is our mother because we are children of promise, born according to the Spirit as children of Jerusalem. (Galatians 4:21-31) These events will be fulfilled after the Lord returns and establishes His thousand-year reign from Jerusalem. God has not revealed any such plans for any other city, but He has many unfulfilled plans for Jerusalem.

13) He is called the God and King of Israel and King of the Jews

If God is finished with the Jewish people, why is He called the God of Israel 186 times in the scriptures? He is also called the God of Jerusalem, the King of Israel, and the King of the Jews.

- God of Israel (186 times, 2 in the New Testament)
- God of Jerusalem (2 times)
- God and Jesus both called King of Israel (4 times, 3 in the New Testament, all referring to Jesus)
- Jesus is called King of the Jews 8 times (all New Testament)

> "Thus says the Lord, the King of Israel, and his Redeemer, the Lord of hosts: 'I am the First and I am the Last; besides Me there is no God. (Isaiah 44:6 NKJV)

Jesus was called the King of Israel three times, twice respectfully by his disciple Nathaniel and by the crowds praising Him as He entered Jerusalem and a third time disrespectfully by the religious leaders while he hung on the cross.

> 49 Nathanael answered and said to Him, "Rabbi, You are the Son of God! You are the King of Israel!" (John 1:49 NKJV)

Exhibit 2: 41 Proofs God is Not Finished with the Jewish People

12 The next day a great multitude that had come to the feast, when they heard that Jesus was coming to Jerusalem,
13 took branches of palm trees and went out to meet Him, and cried out: "Hosanna! 'Blessed is He who comes in the name of the Lord!'
The King of Israel!" (John 12:12-13 NKJV)

42 "He saved others; Himself He cannot save. If He is the King of Israel, let Him now come down from the cross, and we will believe Him. (Matthew 27:42 NKJV, confirmed by Mark 15:32)

19 And they spoke against the God of Jerusalem, as against the gods of the people of the earth—the work of men's hands. (2 Chronicles 32:19 NKJV)

19 Also the articles that are given to you for the service of the house of your God, deliver in full before the God of Jerusalem. (Ezra 7:19 NKJV)

In the same way, Jesus was called King of the Jews 8 times, all in the New Testament.

2 saying, "Where is He who has been born King of the Jews? For we have seen His star in the East and have come to worship Him." (Matthew 2:2 NKJV)

29 When they had twisted a crown of thorns, they put it on His head, and a reed in His right hand. And they bowed the knee before Him and mocked Him, saying, "Hail, King of the Jews!" (Matthew 27:29 NKJV)

2 Then Pilate asked Him, "Are You the King of the Jews?" He answered and said to him, "It is as you say." (Mark 15:2 NKJV, confirmed by Luke 23:3 and John 18:33)

9 But Pilate answered them, saying, "Do you want me to release to you the King of the Jews?" (Mark 15:9 NKJV, confirmed by John 18:39)

3 Then they said, "Hail, King of the Jews!" And they struck Him with their hands. (John 19:3 NKJV)

37 and saying, "If You are the King of the Jews, save Yourself." (Luke 23:37 NKJV)

26 And the inscription of His accusation was written above: THE KING OF THE JEWS. (Mark 15:26 NKJV, confirmed by Luke 23:38 and John 19:19)

21 Therefore the chief priests of the Jews said to Pilate, "Do not write, 'The King of the Jews,' but, 'He said, "I am the King of the Jews."'" (John 19:21 NKJV)

14) Their Mistakes Were an Essential Part of God's Plan All Along

Amplifying the point presented in chapter 17, mistakes made by the Jewish people did not cause God to abandon His plans for them. He was not caught off guard by their failures. Their mistakes were an essential part of His plan all along, which is why it is so foolish to claim His plans were somehow derailed. Hundreds of years ahead of time, He told them they would reject their Messiah, scourging Him like a lamb led to the slaughter, sneering at Him, pulling His bones out of joint, piercing His hands and feet, killing Him and casting lots for His garments. Their betrayal and murder of the Messiah was necessary to pay the price for the sins of the world, which is why it pleased God when they struck Him and bruised Him because His wounds paid the price for the sins of the whole world. (Psalm 22:7-18, Isaiah 53:4-10)

He also warned them ahead of time that the consequences for their mistakes would be severe. Their land would be divided, their sons and daughters would be killed by the sword, and their survivors would be taken captive and exiled in a foreign land, which was fulfilled in 70 AD when Jerusalem was conquered by Roman armies. (Amos 7:15-17)

15) Jesus is Returning to Jerusalem

If God is finished with the Jewish people, why is Jesus returning to Jerusalem rather than Rome or New York or London or any other city?

> 4 And in that day His feet will stand on the Mount of Olives, which faces Jerusalem on the east. And the Mount of Olives shall be split in two, from east to west, making a very large valley; half of the mountain shall move toward the north and half of it toward the south. (Zechariah 14:4 NKJV)

Jerusalem, the capital city of the Jewish state of Israel, remains at the center of God's plans even until the end.

16) Israel Will be a Curse and Then a Blessing to the Nations

If God is finished with the Jewish people, why has He promised to first make them a curse to the nations and afterwards make them a blessing to the nations. The Prophet Zechariah received both prophecies, as shown below:

Exhibit 2: 41 Proofs God is Not Finished with the Jewish People

13 And it shall come to pass that just as you were a curse among the nations, O house of Judah and house of Israel, so I will save you, and you shall be a blessing. Do not fear, let your hands be strong.' (Zechariah 8:13 NKJV)

3 And it shall happen in that day that I will make Jerusalem a very heavy stone for all peoples; all who would heave it away will surely be cut in pieces, though all nations of the earth are gathered against it. (Zechariah 12:3 NKJV)

11 The people shall dwell in it; and no longer shall there be utter destruction, but Jerusalem shall be safely inhabited. (Zechariah 14:11 NKJV)

These prophecies were not fulfilled in ancient Israel, but it began when modern Israel was established and immediately became a heavy stone for all nations. After they were established, they were attacked the next day by a coalition of Arab nations in 1948 and have been attacked repeatedly since then. Just as Zechariah saw, God's judgment came upon Israel's enemies each time they came against Israel. Even Israel's friends, like the United States, received severe judgment each time they came against Israel, such as Hurricane Katrina striking the United States within 24 hours after U.S. President George W Bush forced Israel to permanently evacuate from Gaza in 2005.

Zechariah saw another time coming afterwards when God would rescue, save, and deliver Israel, referring to a time after the Lord Jesus returns when He fights against the armies of the nations gathered around Jerusalem, defeats them, and establishes His throne in Jerusalem. In those days, He will also bring eternal salvation to a remnant of Israel, causing them to become a blessing to all nations.

17) Israel and Judah Reunited in their Land Forever

If God is finished with the Jewish people, why did the Prophet Ezekiel see the two kingdoms of Israel and Judah reunited and living in the land given to Jacob forever?

This prophecy was not fulfilled by their return home after being exiled to Babylon because they were scattered again in 70 AD, and it cannot be fulfilled by Gentile disciples because this prophecy says God will take the sons of Israel from among the nations where they have gone and will gather them from every side and bring them into their own land; and He will make them one nation in the land, on the mountains of Israel; and one king will be king for all of them, which can only be fulfilled by the Jewish people living in the same land promised to their father Jacob. One king ruling over them, making an everlasting covenant of peace with them and dwelling in their midst forever

Exhibit 2: 41 Proofs God is Not Finished with the Jewish People

can only be fulfilled by the King of Kings, who has promised to return and fight for them. (Ezekiel 37:19-28)

> 19 say to them, 'Thus says the Lord God: "Surely I will take the stick of Joseph, which is in the hand of Ephraim, and the tribes of Israel, his companions; and I will join them with it, with the stick of Judah, and make them one stick, and they will be one in My hand."'
> 20 And the sticks on which you write will be in your hand before their eyes.
> 21 "Then say to them, "Thus says the Lord God: 'Surely I will take the children of Israel from among the nations, wherever they have gone, and will gather them from every side and bring them into their own land;
> 22 and I will make them one nation in the land, on the mountains of Israel; and one king shall be king over them all; they shall no longer be two nations, nor shall they ever be divided into two kingdoms again.
> 23 They shall not defile themselves anymore with their idols, nor with their detestable things, nor with any of their transgressions; but I will deliver them from all their dwelling places in which they have sinned, and will cleanse them. Then they shall be My people, and I will be their God.
> 24 "David My servant shall be king over them, and they shall all have one shepherd; they shall also walk in My judgments and observe My statutes, and do them.
> 25 Then they shall dwell in the land that I have given to Jacob My servant, where your fathers dwelt; and they shall dwell there, they, their children, and their children's children, forever; and My servant David shall be their prince forever.
> 26 Moreover I will make a covenant of peace with them, and it shall be an everlasting covenant with them; I will establish them and multiply them, and I will set My sanctuary in their midst forevermore.
> 27 My tabernacle also shall be with them; indeed I will be their God, and they shall be My people.
> 28 The nations also will know that I, the Lord, sanctify Israel, when My sanctuary is in their midst forevermore." (Ezekiel 37:19-28 NKJV)

18) Gentiles Saved to Make Jews Jealous

If God is finished with the Jewish people, why did the Apostle Paul say the end result of their turning away from God is not for them to fall, but by their rejecting God, salvation came to the Gentiles to make them jealous, confirming God's plans for their salvation? Instead of giving up on them, God has gone to extraordinary great lengths to bring them back into right relationship with Him again.

Exhibit 2: 41 Proofs God is Not Finished with the Jewish People

> 11 I say then, have they stumbled that they should fall? Certainly not! But through their fall, to provoke them to jealousy, salvation has come to the Gentiles. (Romans 11:11 NKJV)

19) God's Promises Still Belong to the Jews

If God is finished with the Jewish people, then why was the Apostle Paul claim adoption as sons and the glory and the covenants still belong to them, not in the past tense, but in the present tense? (Romans 9:3-5, Romans 11:14) Paul believed this so strongly, he was even willing to forfeit his own eternal life for the sake of his unsaved Jewish kinsmen. I believe Paul's heart for his fellow Jewish people reveals God's heart for them.

> 3 For I could wish that I myself were accursed from Christ for my brethren, my countrymen according to the flesh,
> 4 who are Israelites, to whom pertain the adoption, the glory, the covenants, the giving of the law, the service of God, and the promises;
> 5 of whom are the fathers and from whom, according to the flesh, Christ came, who is over all, the eternally blessed God. Amen. (Romans 9:3-5 NKJV)

> 14 if by any means I may provoke to jealousy those who are my flesh and save some of them. (Romans 11:14 NKJV)

20) Partial Hardening Will Be Removed at the End of this Age

If God is finished with the Jewish people, then why did the Apostle Paul prophesy the hardening of their hearts would be removed after the fullness of the Gentiles comes in?

The Apostle Paul identified one of the consequences suffered by the Jewish people for rejecting their Messiah was a partial hardening came upon them, but this would not be a permanent condition. It would only last until the fullness of the Gentiles has come in. Once that happens, the partial hardening would be removed, resulting in salvation for all of Israel. This shows God has not forgotten them or given up on them. He has a plan to restore them into a right relationship with Him after a specific period, after the time of salvation coming upon the Gentiles.

> 25 For I do not desire, brethren, that you should be ignorant of this mystery, lest you should be wise in your own opinion, that blindness in part has happened to Israel until the fullness of the Gentiles has come in.
> 26 And so all Israel will be saved, as it is written: "The Deliverer will come out of Zion, and He will turn away ungodliness from Jacob;

Exhibit 2: 41 Proofs God is Not Finished with the Jewish People

> 27 For this is My covenant with them, when I take away their sins."
> 28 Concerning the gospel they are enemies for your sake, but concerning the election they are beloved for the sake of the fathers.
> 29 For the gifts and the calling of God are irrevocable. (Romans 11:25-29 NKJV)

Paul acknowledged the Jewish people became enemies of the gospel because they rejected God's plan for their salvation. Although they suffered terribly for their rebellion, Paul still calls them beloved for the sake of their fathers, explaining the gifts and the calling of God are irrevocable, totally contradicting all claims that God has no more plans for the Jewish people. He has not forgotten them or given up on them. He has a plan to restore them into a right relationship with Him at a specific time, after the time of the Gentiles is completed. No wonder Paul described this as a mystery, but since he explained it, we can now understand it.

21) Third Temple Will be Built in Jerusalem

If God is finished with the Jewish people, then why do we find ancient prophecies still unfulfilled regarding a temple in Jerusalem? The Prophet Daniel, the Lord Jesus, and the Apostle Paul all warned about a terrible event that would happen in the temple in Jerusalem, known as the abomination that brings desolation, when the man of sin, the antichrist, would one day enter the temple and seek to establish His throne there. That event cannot happen unless the temple is first rebuilt, as shown in these scriptures.

> 27 Then he shall confirm a covenant with many for one week; but in the middle of the week he shall bring an end to sacrifice and offering. And on the wing of abominations shall be one who makes desolate, even until the consummation, which is determined, is poured out on the desolate." (Daniel 9:27 NKJV)

> 15 "Therefore when you see the 'abomination of desolation,' spoken of by Daniel the prophet, standing in the holy place" (whoever reads, let him understand), (Matthew 24:15 NKJV)

> 3 Let no one deceive you by any means; for that Day will not come unless the falling away comes first, and the man of sin is revealed, the son of perdition, 4 who opposes and exalts himself above all that is called God or that is worshiped, so that he sits as God in the temple of God, showing himself that he is God. (2 Thessalonians 2:3-4 NKJV)

The Apostle John also saw this temple and wrote about it after the second temple was destroyed in 70 AD. (Revelation 11:1-2)

Exhibit 2: 41 Proofs God is Not Finished with the Jewish People

> 1 Then I was given a reed like a measuring rod. And the angel stood, saying, "Rise and measure the temple of God, the altar, and those who worship there.
> 2 But leave out the court which is outside the temple, and do not measure it, for it has been given to the Gentiles. And they will tread the holy city underfoot for forty-two months. (Revelation 11:1-2 NKJV)

22) Future Assignments Given to 144,000 Jewish Bond Servants

If God is finished with the Jewish people, why do His end-time plans include 144,000 bond servants with 12,000 coming from each tribe of Israel? These bond servants are clearly Jewish because they come from each of the twelve tribes of Israel, but they are also followers of Yeshua. These 144,000 bond servants will be used by God during the coming great tribulation. (Revelation 7:2-8, Revelation 14:1-5)

> 2 Then I saw another angel ascending from the east, having the seal of the living God. And he cried with a loud voice to the four angels to whom it was granted to harm the earth and the sea,
> 3 saying, "Do not harm the earth, the sea, or the trees till we have sealed the servants of our God on their foreheads."
> 4 And I heard the number of those who were sealed. One hundred and forty-four thousand of all the tribes of the children of Israel were sealed:
> 5 of the tribe of Judah twelve thousand were sealed; of the tribe of Reuben twelve thousand were sealed; of the tribe of Gad twelve thousand were sealed;
> 6 of the tribe of Asher twelve thousand were sealed; of the tribe of Naphtali twelve thousand were sealed; of the tribe of Manasseh twelve thousand were sealed;
> 7 of the tribe of Simeon twelve thousand were sealed; of the tribe of Levi twelve thousand were sealed; of the tribe of Issachar twelve thousand were sealed;
> 8 of the tribe of Zebulun twelve thousand were sealed; of the tribe of Joseph twelve thousand were sealed; of the tribe of Benjamin twelve thousand were sealed. (Revelation 7:2-8 NKJV)

> 1 Then I looked, and behold, a Lamb standing on Mount Zion, and with Him one hundred and forty-four thousand, having His Father's name written on their foreheads.
> 2 And I heard a voice from heaven, like the voice of many waters, and like the voice of loud thunder. And I heard the sound of harpists playing their harps.

> 3 They sang as it were a new song before the throne, before the four living creatures, and the elders; and no one could learn that song except the hundred and forty-four thousand who were redeemed from the earth.
> 4 These are the ones who were not defiled with women, for they are virgins. These are the ones who follow the Lamb wherever He goes. These were redeemed from among men, being firstfruits to God and to the Lamb.
> 5 And in their mouth was found no deceit, for they are without fault before the throne of God. (Revelation 14:1-5 NKJV)

23) Being Jewish is a Great Advantage during Church Age

If God is finished with the Jewish people, why did the Apostle Paul claim being Jewish is a great advantage in every respect? He explained their unbelief will not nullify the faithfulness of God. If God was done with them, being Jewish would offer no advantage. (Romans 3:1-4)

> 1 What advantage then has the Jew, or what is the profit of circumcision?
> 2 Much in every way! Chiefly because to them were committed the oracles of God.
> 3 For what if some did not believe? Will their unbelief make the faithfulness of God without effect?
> 4 Certainly not! Indeed, let God be true but every man a liar. As it is written: "That You may be justified in Your words, and may overcome when You are judged." (Romans 3:1-4 NKJV)

24) Paul Claimed God Has Not Rejected His People

If God is finished with the Jewish people, why did the Apostle Paul say God has not and would never reject His people? Paul clarifies he was referring to the Israelites by identifying himself as one of them, not based on his faith, but solely based on being a descendant of Abraham, of the tribe of Benjamin. (Romans 11:1).

> 1 I say then, has God cast away His people? Certainly not! For I also am an Israelite, of the seed of Abraham, of the tribe of Benjamin.
> 2 God has not cast away His people whom He foreknew. Or do you not know what the Scripture says of Elijah, how he pleads with God against Israel, saying, (Romans 11:1-2 NKJV)

25) Sons of Israel Return from Assyria and Egypt to Worship God

Exhibit 2: 41 Proofs God is Not Finished with the Jewish People

If God is finished with the Jewish people, why has He promised to gather the sons of Israel from Assyria and Egypt and bring them back to His holy mountain at Jerusalem where they will worship the Lord? Although they have twice returned to their land after being exiled among the nations, this prophecy has never been fulfilled because it begins with the blast of a great trumpet, which has not yet happened. Many Bible scholars believe this trumpet blast is the same one marking the rapture. (Matthew 24:31) So, this is another proof that God is not done with the Jewish people.

> 12 And it shall come to pass in that day that the Lord will thresh, from the channel of the River to the Brook of Egypt; and you will be gathered one by one, O you children of Israel.
> 13 So it shall be in that day: the great trumpet will be blown; they will come, who are about to perish in the land of Assyria, and they who are outcasts in the land of Egypt, and shall worship the Lord in the holy mount at Jerusalem. (Isaiah 27:12-13 NKJV)

26) Jerusalem Will be Called the Throne of Jehovah

If God is finished with the Jewish people, why has He promised Jerusalem will one day be called the Throne of the Lord and all nations will be gathered to it? The prophecy shown below has never been fulfilled because Jerusalem is not yet called the Throne of the Lord and the nations are still walking after the stubbornness of their evil heart. Only the Jewish people living in the land of their fathers can fulfill this prophecy because it requires Judah and Israel being rejoined in the same land given to their fathers as an inheritance.

> 17 At that time Jerusalem shall be called The Throne of the Lord, and all the nations shall be gathered to it, to the name of the Lord, to Jerusalem. No more shall they follow the dictates of their evil hearts.
> 18 In those days the house of Judah shall walk with the house of Israel, and they shall come together out of the land of the north to the land that I have given as an inheritance to your fathers. (Jeremiah 3:17-18 NKJV)

27) Enemies of Israel Cut off forever

If God is finished with the Jewish people, why did the Prophet Obadiah see their enemies put to shame and cut off forever. This prophecy remains unfulfilled since modern Israel still has many enemies. They have not yet been cut off.

Exhibit 2: 41 Proofs God is Not Finished with the Jewish People

> 8 "Will I not in that day," says the Lord, "Even destroy the wise men from Edom, and understanding from the mountains of Esau?
> 9 Then your mighty men, O Teman, shall be dismayed, to the end that everyone from the mountains of Esau may be cut off by slaughter.
> 10 "For violence against your brother Jacob, shame shall cover you, and you shall be cut off forever. (Obadiah 1:8-10 NKJV)

This prophecy will not be fulfilled until the day of Yahweh when all the nations who fought against Israel and looted their wealth and imprisoned their survivors will become as if they had never existed. (Obadiah 1:13-16) The Prophet Jeremiah also saw God's plans to deliver Israel from their enemies on the day of Yahweh, breaking off the yoke from their necks, bursting their bonds, and promising their enemies would never again sell them into captivity. (Jeremiah 30:8)

28) Ezekiel's Prophecy of Gog and Magog

If God is finished with the Jewish people, why has He promised to set Himself apart in the eyes of all nations in the last days through His mighty deliverance of His people Israel from an attack by Gog of the land of Magog? Ezekiel specifically identified the people of Israel as the ones who will be brought back from the sword and gathered from many nations to live in the hills of Israel. (Ezekiel 38:8-9)

> 8 After many days you will be visited. In the latter years you will come into the land of those brought back from the sword and gathered from many people on the mountains of Israel, which had long been desolate; they were brought out of the nations, and now all of them dwell safely.
> 9 You will ascend, coming like a storm, covering the land like a cloud, you and all your troops and many peoples with you." (Ezekiel 38:8-9 NKJV)

The context of Ezekiel 38 refers to an attack on Israel from Gog and Magog, which will be fulfilled at the end of the thousand-year reign of the Lord, marking the devil's final attack on God's people, showing God's plans for Israel extend far into the future.

> 7 Now when the thousand years have expired, Satan will be released from his prison
> 8 and will go out to deceive the nations which are in the four corners of the earth, Gog and Magog, to gather them together to battle, whose number is as the sand of the sea.

Exhibit 2: 41 Proofs God is Not Finished with the Jewish People

> 9 They went up on the breadth of the earth and surrounded the camp of the saints and the beloved city. And fire came down from God out of heaven and devoured them.
> 10 The devil, who deceived them, was cast into the lake of fire and brimstone where the beast and the false prophet are. And they will be tormented day and night forever and ever. (Revelation 20:7-10 NKJV)

Many people claim the Gog and Magog attacks happen prior to the return of the Lord, but if so, there must be two separate attacks, but the scriptures only identify one attack happening at the end of the thousand years. Among those claiming it happens prior to the return of the Lord, many claim it will not come against Israel, but against the United States, but that claim contradicts the scriptures shown below, which prove Israel is the one attacked because the people live in the hills of Israel and specifically the cities of Sheba, Dedan, and Tarshish.

> 13 Sheba, Dedan, the merchants of Tarshish, and all their young lions will say to you, 'Have you come to take plunder? Have you gathered your army to take booty, to carry away silver and gold, to take away livestock and goods, to take great plunder?'
> 14 "Therefore, son of man, prophesy and say to Gog, "Thus says the Lord God: "On that day when My people Israel dwell safely, will you not know it?
> 15 Then you will come from your place out of the far north, you and many peoples with you, all of them riding on horses, a great company and a mighty army.
> 16 You will come up against My people Israel like a cloud, to cover the land. It will be in the latter days that I will bring you against My land, so that the nations may know Me, when I am hallowed in you, O Gog, before their eyes." (Ezekiel 38:13-16 NKJV)

29) Jerusalem Will Dwell in Security

If God is finished with the Jewish people, why did the Prophet Zechariah see a day coming when the Lord will be king over all the earth and in that day, Jerusalem will dwell in security? This prophecy confirms Jerusalem is at the center of God's plans, making it unique among all the cities of the earth. It remains unfulfilled because Satan is still the god of this world (2 Corinthians 4:4) and the Lord has not yet returned to rule over all the earth and people living in Jerusalem still don't dwell in security. (Zechariah 14:9-11)

Exhibit 2: 41 Proofs God is Not Finished with the Jewish People

> 9 And the Lord shall be King over all the earth. In that day it shall be— "The Lord is one,"
> And His name one.
> 10 All the land shall be turned into a plain from Geba to Rimmon south of Jerusalem. Jerusalem shall be raised up and inhabited in her place from Benjamin's Gate to the place of the First Gate and the Corner Gate, and from the Tower of Hananel to the king's winepresses.
> 11 The people shall dwell in it; and no longer shall there be utter destruction, but Jerusalem shall be safely inhabited. (Zechariah 14:9-11 NKJV)

30) The Antichrist Will Divide Israel's Land for Gain

If God is done with the Jewish people, why does He warn about the schemes of the future antichrist to appoint rulers over them and divide their land for a price?

> 39 Thus he shall act against the strongest fortresses with a foreign god, which he shall acknowledge, and advance its glory; and he shall cause them to rule over many, and divide the land for gain. (Daniel 11:39 NKJV)

By warning them about these schemes, He shows He still cares about them and has plans for them that remain unfulfilled.

31) Antichrist Will Establish His Throne in the Temple in Jerusalem

If God is done with the Jewish people, why is Satan still bent on taking possession of Jerusalem? If God was done with them, Satan would have no reason to seek to make Jerusalem his headquarters, specifically establishing his throne in the temple on Mount Zion, but he will have his demon possessed man of sin plant the tents of his palace there.

> 45 And he shall plant the tents of his palace between the seas and the glorious holy mountain; yet he shall come to his end, and no one will help him. (Daniel 11:45 NKJV)

Satan plans to do these things because he desires to be like the Most High, exalting himself as God, seeking to be worshiped as God. So Satan's unfulfilled plans confirm God's unfulfilled plans for the Jewish people.

> 12 "How you are fallen from heaven, O Lucifer, son of the morning! How you are cut down to the ground, you who weakened the nations!

Exhibit 2: 41 Proofs God is Not Finished with the Jewish People

> 13 For you have said in your heart: 'I will ascend into heaven, I will exalt my throne above the stars of God; I will also sit on the mount of the congregation on the farthest sides of the north;
> 14 I will ascend above the heights of the clouds, I will be like the Most High.'
> 15 Yet you shall be brought down to Sheol, to the lowest depths of the Pit. (Isaiah 14:12-15 NKJV)

> 1 Now, brethren, concerning the coming of our Lord Jesus Christ and our gathering together to Him, we ask you,
> 2 not to be soon shaken in mind or troubled, either by spirit or by word or by letter, as if from us, as though the day of Christ had come.
> 3 Let no one deceive you by any means; for that Day will not come unless the falling away comes first, and the man of sin is revealed, the son of perdition,
> 4 who opposes and exalts himself above all that is called God or that is worshiped, so that he sits as God in the temple of God, showing himself that he is God. (2 Thessalonians 2:1-4 NKJV)

32) Jesus Already Forgave Them

If God is rejected the Jewish people after they rejected their Messiah, then why did Jesus ask the Father to forgive them while He was still hanging on the cross? I believe His prayer reveals God's heart for them.

> 33 And when they had come to the place called Calvary, there they crucified Him, and the criminals, one on the right hand and the other on the left.
> 34 Then Jesus said, "Father, forgive them, for they do not know what they do." And they divided His garments and cast lots. (Luke 23:33-34 NKJV)

He had every reason to condemn them, curse them, and be forever done with them, but instead, His great love for them was not shaken or diminished. Since He did not give up on them in that dark hour, even when He was suffering in great pain, which they wrongly inflicted upon Him, it makes no sense to claim He later changed His mind and gave up on them.

33) God's Promise to Remain Faithful to a Thousandth Generation

If God is done with the Jewish people, why did He promise to remain faithful to keep His promises, which He made to their forefathers, to a thousand generations after them?

Exhibit 2: 41 Proofs God is Not Finished with the Jewish People

> 7 The Lord did not set His love on you nor choose you because you were more in number than any other people, for you were the least of all peoples;
> 8 but because the Lord loves you, and because He would keep the oath which He swore to your fathers, the Lord has brought you out with a mighty hand, and redeemed you from the house of bondage, from the hand of Pharaoh king of Egypt.
> 9 "Therefore know that the Lord your God, He is God, the faithful God who keeps covenant and mercy for a thousand generations with those who love Him and keep His commandments; (Deuteronomy 7:7-9 NKJV)

God has not abandoned His plans for the Jewish people and He never will. Every promise He ever made to them is still just as true and valid today as it ever was, not because they deserve it, but because of the oath He swore to their fathers.

34) Israel's Oppressors Will Serve them as Slaves

If God is done with the Jewish people, why did He promise they will take captive their captors and rule over the same people who once oppressed them?

> 1 When the Lord will have compassion on Jacob and again choose Israel, and settle them in their own land, then foreigners will join them and attach themselves to the house of Jacob.
> 2 The peoples will take them along and bring them to their place, and the house of Israel will possess them as an inheritance in the land of the Lord as male servants and female servants; and they will take their captors captive and will rule over their oppressors. (Isaiah 14:1-2)

In this prophecy, Isaiah saw the favor of God coming upon the nation of Israel as He would again choose them and have compassion on them, allowing them to return and settle in their land after being exiled. At that time, foreigners would join them and attach themselves to them as part of their inheritance, and not just any foreigners, but from the same people who had once been Israel's captors. Isaiah saw Israel taking them captive and ruling over them, making them their servants in Jehovah's land, the land of Israel. There are only two possible times when this prophecy could be fulfilled because Isaiah saw them returning from exile to settle in their land, which has only happened twice in history. The first time was when they returned from exile in Babylon in 538 BC. The second time was after they were scattered into many nations in 70 AD and returned to their land in 1948 AD. It was not fulfilled when they returned from exile in Babylon because they did not rule over their oppressors and did not become a conquering power. They managed to rebuild their temple in 516 BC, but enjoyed only 237 years of

Exhibit 2: 41 Proofs God is Not Finished with the Jewish People

freedom before they were again oppressed by foreign powers, starting with the Ptolemaic Empire in 301 BC, then the Seleucid Empire in 200 BC, and finally the Roman Empire, starting in 63 BC and continuing until they were exiled again in 70 AD. So, the fulfillment of Isaiah's prophecy must still be in the future, to be fulfilled by modern Israel, which means God's not done with the Jewish people.

35) Tribulation, Glory, Honor and Peace are to the Jew First

If God is done with the Jewish people, why did Paul make a distinction between Jews and Greeks, putting the Jews first when it comes to the most important topic of all, the salvation of our eternal souls.

> 16 For I am not ashamed of the gospel of Christ, for it is the power of God to salvation for everyone who believes, for the Jew first and also for the Greek. (Romans 1:16 NKJV)

Since the gospel goes to the Jew first, God still makes a distinction between Jewish and non-Jewish people, which proves has not abandoned or forgotten them. Not only salvation, but also all rewards for good and evil deeds will go to the Jew first and then the Greek.

> 9 tribulation and anguish, on every soul of man who does evil, of the Jew first and also of the Greek;
> 10 but glory, honor, and peace to everyone who works what is good, to the Jew first and also to the Greek.
> 11 For there is no partiality with God. (Romans 2:9-11 NKJV)

Paul warned the Jewish people not to make the mistake of trusting in their Jewish heritage or their knowledge of God's commandments, because their knowledge will not deliver them in the coming judgment. Only their obedience will deliver them. Instead of giving them a free pass, God will hold them accountable at a higher level because of their knowledge of His commandments. Each of us will be judged based on what we did with what we knew we should do.

36) Jesus Rules Forever on the Throne of David over the House of Jacob

If God is done with the Jewish people, why is Jesus planning to rule forever on the throne of David over the house of Jacob?

> 32 He will be great, and will be called the Son of the Highest; and the Lord God will give Him the throne of His father David.
> 33 And He will reign over the house of Jacob forever, and of His kingdom there will be no end." (Luke 1:32-33 NKJV)

Since this plan is forever, it has not ended and is not changing or going away.

37) God Promises Israel will not be Oppressed Again

If God is done with the Jewish people, why has He promised to camp around His house so they will never again be oppressed.

> 8 I will camp around My house because of the army, because of him who passes by and him who returns. No more shall an oppressor pass through them, for now I have seen with My eyes. (Zechariah 9:8 NKJV)

This prophecy remains unfulfilled, but will be fulfilled after the Lord returns to fight for the Jewish people.

38) God Promises to Refine and Test One-third of Them

If God is done with the Jewish people, why has He promised to refine and test one-third of them?

> 8 And in that day it shall be that living waters shall flow from Jerusalem, half of them toward the eastern sea and half of them toward the western sea; in both summer and winter it shall occur.
> 9 And the Lord shall be King over all the earth. In that day it shall be— "The Lord is one," and His name one. (Zechariah 13:8-9 NKJV)

This prophecy remains unfulfilled, so will be fulfilled in the last days during the tribulation and great tribulation.

39) God Promises to Give Them Great Abundance and Wealth

If God was finished with the Jewish people, why did He promise to give them the wealth and spoils that were stolen from them?

> 1 Behold, the day of the Lord is coming, and your spoil will be divided in your midst. (Zechariah 14:1 NKJV)

> 14 Judah also will fight at Jerusalem. And the wealth of all the surrounding nations shall be gathered together: gold, silver, and apparel in great abundance. (Zechariah 14:14 NKJV)

Obadiah saw Israel's fortunes restored on the day of Yahweh when the house of Jacob will possess the possessions of those who previously looted them, divided their land, and sold them into captivity. (Obadiah 1:10-17) These prophecies were not fulfilled after their return from Babylon since they did not receive the wealth of all the surrounding nations. They only controlled their nation for a relatively brief time of about 237 years before they were conquered and eventually sold into captivity and exiled again.

40) Living Waters Will Flow Out of Jerusalem

If God was finished with the Jewish people, why did He promise a day is coming when living waters will flow out of Jerusalem? This has not yet been fulfilled, so the fulfillment must be in the future.

> And in that day it shall be that living waters shall flow from Jerusalem, half of them toward the eastern sea and half of them toward the western sea; in both summer and winter it shall occur. (Zechariah 14:8 NKJV)

41) All Nations Required to Worship at Jerusalem

If God is done with the Jewish people, why is He planning to require all nations to worship Him in Jerusalem? Even those nations that fought against Him will be required to go to Jerusalem to worship the Lord of hosts. Those who refuse will have no rain.

> 16 And it shall come to pass that everyone who is left of all the nations which came against Jerusalem shall go up from year to year to worship the King, the Lord of hosts, and to keep the Feast of Tabernacles.
> 17 And it shall be that whichever of the families of the earth do not come up to Jerusalem to worship the King, the Lord of hosts, on them there will be no rain. (Zechariah 14:16-17 NKJV)

This promise shows God's plans for Jerusalem, the capital city of the Jewish state, continue long into the future, even after His return. Why Jerusalem? If God has abandoned His plans for the Jewish people, why not establish His temple in some other city? All these unfulfilled prophecies reveal God's plans have not changed, not for Jerusalem and not for the flesh and blood descendants of Abraham, Isaac and Jacob.

Exhibit 3: Satan's 5 Favorite Lies About the Jewish People

Satan twists the meaning of scriptures to deceive people with his favorite lies to stir up the world's hatred for the Jewish people, as shown in this list.

Lie #1: God is done with the Jewish people because their deeds are unrighteous.

Since this point was already explained in chapter 17, the following provides only an additional example of God's faithfulness to the Jewish people after they turned away from Him.

In 586 BC, God removed His protection from Israel and gave them into the hands of King Nebuchadnezzar of Babylon because of their rebelliousness and stubbornness, using Babylon like a rod of discipline in hopes of driving them back to Him. About 150 years before Jerusalem was conquered by Nebuchadnezzar, God gave a prophetic warning to the Prophet Hosea regarding the coming disaster, but like Moses, Hosea's warning included a promise it would turn out well for them in the end, saying, "In the place where it is said to them, 'You are not My people, it will be said to them, 'You are the sons of the living God.'" (Hosea 1:10) So, He not only warned them about the terrible things ahead, but He also gave them hope and encouragement to get through it, showing more evidence He was not caught off guard by any of it and never abandoned them or forgot His promises to them afterwards. Although they suffered terribly for turning away from Him, His plans and purposes for them were not changed.

Then about 20 years after they returned home from their exile in Babylon, He spoke to the Prophet Zechariah, calling them the apple of His eye, showing His love for them was not diminished, even after they had rejected Him. (Ezra 1:1, Zechariah 1:1 and 2:8) Since His plans were not moved by their first exile, why should we expect any different from their second exile? The gifts and the calling of God are irrevocable. (Romans 11:24-29)

Lie #2: God is done with the Jewish people because there is no longer Jew nor Greek.

Satan uses the following scriptures out of context to claim it makes no difference to God whether someone is Jewish or Greek or any other nationality, but it's a lie because these scriptures are specifically referring to those who are in Christ Jesus, not to those who are unbelievers, outside of Christ, which is why it says, "you are all one in Christ Jesus" and "Christ is all and in all."

Exhibit 3: Satan's 5 Favorite Lies About the Jewish People

> 26 For you are all sons of God through faith in Christ Jesus.
> 27 For as many of you as were baptized into Christ have put on Christ.
> 28 There is neither Jew nor Greek, there is neither slave nor free, there is neither male nor female; for you are all one in Christ Jesus.
> 29 And if you are Christ's, then you are Abraham's seed, and heirs according to the promise. (Galatians 3:26-29 NKJV)
>
> 9 Do not lie to one another, since you have put off the old man with his deeds,
> 10 and have put on the new man who is renewed in knowledge according to the image of Him who created him,
> 11 where there is neither Greek nor Jew, circumcised nor uncircumcised, barbarian, Scythian, slave nor free, but Christ is all and in all. (Colossians 3:9-11 NKJV)

These scriptures don't reveal anything about the way God views unbelieving Jews or unbelieving Gentiles, which is why it makes no sense to use these as the basis for any claims that God has no plans for the unbelieving Jewish people today. Nothing could be further from the truth. Many other scriptures reveal His plans to bring salvation to a remnant of the Jewish people, as shown in Exhibit 2, proving He still makes a clear distinction between the unbelieving Jews and unbelieving Gentiles. (Joel 3:1-3, Zechariah 12:10)

Prior to the Messiah, there was a barrier between Jews and Gentiles, a dividing wall, which was put there by God to bring forth His plan of salvation through the Jews, but this wall of separation was removed through Jesus Christ, so when Jews or Gentiles receive salvation in the Messiah, both groups come together in Him to form one new man. (Ephesians 2:11-16) Jewish disciples are given no special favoritism over Gentile disciples, but that does not change or cancel any of God's plans for unsaved Jewish people.

Lie #3: God is done with the Jewish people because they are not true Jews, merely children of the flesh.

Satan misquotes Romans 9:6-8 out of context to claim the Jewish people today don't qualify to be called Jewish because they are only Jewish by birth, falsely claiming to be children of God based only on to their flesh.

> 6 But it is not that the word of God has taken no effect. For they are not all Israel who are of Israel,

Exhibit 3: Satan's 5 Favorite Lies About the Jewish People

> 7 nor are they all children because they are the seed of Abraham; but, "In Isaac your seed shall be called."
> 8 That is, those who are the children of the flesh, these are not the children of God; but the children of the promise are counted as the seed. (Romans 9:6-8 NKJV)

Based on many other scriptures, this passage refers to spiritual Israel, not physical Israel, so it can only be properly understood in that context. The flesh and blood descendants of Abraham, Isaac, and Jacob are physical Israel, but they are not part of spiritual Israel unless they obey the instructions given by Messiah Jesus, as shown in the following passage when Jesus explained this mystery to Nicodemus, a Jewish religious leader.

> 3 Jesus answered and said to him, "Most assuredly, I say to you, unless one is born again, he cannot see the kingdom of God."
> 4 Nicodemus said to Him, "How can a man be born when he is old? Can he enter a second time into his mother's womb and be born?"
> 5 Jesus answered, "Most assuredly, I say to you, unless one is born of water and the Spirit, he cannot enter the kingdom of God.
> 6 That which is born of the flesh is flesh, and that which is born of the Spirit is spirit. (John 3:3-6 NKJV)

By this definition, everyone who is born again is a child of God and part of spiritual Israel, and everyone who is not born again is not a child of God and not part of spiritual Israel, which is why Romans 9:6-8 explained being a flesh and blood descendant of Abraham and Isaac does not make anyone a child of God. For this reason, the Apostle Paul put no confidence in his flesh, although some might say he had good reason for it because he was "circumcised the eighth day, of the nation of Israel, of the tribe of Benjamin, a Hebrew of Hebrews; as to the Law, a Pharisee; as to zeal, a persecutor of the church; as to the righteousness which is in the Law, found blameless." (Philippians 3:5-6) Although fleshly ancestry does not qualify anyone for salvation, other scriptures reveal there are great benefits of being a flesh and blood descendant of Abraham, Isaac, and Jacob because they qualify as heirs for other promises, which God will fulfill in these last days. (Romans 3:2)

Lie #4: God is done with the Jewish people because they're not really Jews because they are not from the tribe of Judah.

Since the tribe of Judah separated from the other tribes of ancient Israel, Satan has used this separation to claim most Jewish people today are not Jewish because only the tribe of Judah qualifies as truly Jewish. Once we believe this lie, it's easy for us to turn against the Jewish people. Any lie works for him if it achieves his goal of turning us against them, but Satan has a big flaw in his argument because the Apostle Paul referred to himself as a Jew from the tribe of Benjamin. (Acts 22:3, Romans 11:1) Since the tribe of Benjamin qualifies as Jewish, being Jewish is not limited to the tribe of Judah and all twelve tribes qualify on the same basis.

The separation between Judah and Israel was only temporary. The Prophet Jeremiah saw the house of Judah will come together with the house of Israel and walk side by side in the land God gave their fathers as an inheritance. (Jeremiah 3:17-18) The Jewish people living in the land of Israel today are fulfilling this ancient prophecy.

In another example, the 144,000 bond servants who will serve the Lord on earth during the great tribulation come from all twelve tribes, not just Judah, showing God's plans for the Jewish people include all twelve tribes. (Revelation 7)

Lie #5: God is done with the Jewish people because they are the synagogue of Satan.

Satan claims the Jewish people are not Jews by twisting the words of Jesus when He referred to "those who say they are Jews and are not, but are a synagogue of Satan," (Revelation 2:8-9, 3:7-10), but Jesus never called the flesh and blood descendants of Abraham, Isaac, and Jacob a synagogue of Satan. He was speaking to the Christian churches in Smyrna and Philadelphia, speaking in spiritual terms to those who had been born of His spirit, so when He used the term Jews, He was referring to those who were claiming to be spiritual Jews, but were failing to meet the requirements because of practicing unrighteousness, so He exposed them as disciples of Satan. By exposing the hypocrisy of those who claimed to be spiritual Jews, Jesus did not nullify any of God's promises to the natural Jews. It's another example of taking scriptures out of context, applying scriptures to physical Israel that were intended for spiritual Israel.

Jesus identified His true disciples as spiritual Jews the same way Paul did, based on the inward circumcision of the heart, by the Spirit, not based on outward evidence of the flesh. (Romans 2:28-29) True children of God, the spiritual Jews, are the children of the promise, regardless of their ancestry, because it is received by faith which is backed up by deeds. (Romans 9:6-8, James 2:24, Revelation 3:10) By contrast, the qualifications for being a natural Jew are not based on deeds, but only on ancestry.

Exhibit 4: New Testament Commandment Scriptures

19 Whoever therefore breaks one of the least of these commandments, and teaches men so, shall be called least in the kingdom of heaven; but whoever does and teaches them, he shall be called great in the kingdom of heaven. (Matthew 5:19 NKJV)

14 "For if you forgive men their trespasses, your heavenly Father will also forgive you. 15 But if you do not forgive men their trespasses, neither will your Father forgive your trespasses. (Matthew 6:14-15 NKJV)

17 So He said to him, "Why do you call Me good? No one is good but One, that is, God. But if you want to enter into life, keep the commandments." (Matthew 19:17 NKJV)

18 He said to Him, "Which ones?" Jesus said, "'You shall not murder,' 'You shall not commit adultery,' 'You shall not steal,' 'You shall not bear false witness,'
19 'Honor your father and your mother,' and, 'You shall love your neighbor as yourself.'
20 The young man said to Him, "All these things I have kept from my youth. What do I still lack?"
21 Jesus said to him, "If you want to be perfect, go, sell what you have and give to the poor, and you will have treasure in heaven; and come, follow Me." (Matthew 19:18-21 NKJV)

36 "Teacher, which is the great commandment in the law?"
37 Jesus said to him, " 'You shall love the Lord your God with all your heart, with all your soul, and with all your mind.'
38 This is the first and great commandment.
39 And the second is like it: 'You shall love your neighbor as yourself.' (Matthew 22:36-39 NKJV)

19 You know the commandments: 'Do not commit adultery,' 'Do not murder,' 'Do not steal,' 'Do not bear false witness,' 'Do not defraud,' 'Honor your father and your mother.'
20 And he answered and said to Him, "Teacher, all these things I have kept from my youth."
21 Then Jesus, looking at him, loved him, and said to him, "One thing you lack: Go your way, sell whatever you have and give to the poor, and you will have treasure in heaven; and come, take up the cross, and follow Me." (Mark 10:19-21 NKJV)

Exhibit 4: New Testament Commandment Scriptures

36 He who believes in the Son has everlasting life; and he who does not believe the Son shall not see life, but the wrath of God abides on him." (John 3:36 NKJV)

15 "If you love Me, keep My commandments. (John 14:15 NKJV)

23 Jesus answered and said to him, "If anyone loves Me, he will keep My word; and My Father will love him, and We will come to him and make Our home with him.
24 He who does not love Me does not keep My words; and the word which you hear is not Mine but the Father's who sent Me. (John 14:23-24 NKJV)

19 Circumcision is nothing and uncircumcision is nothing, but keeping the commandments of God is what matters. (1 Corinthians 7:19 NKJV)
14 For He Himself is our peace, who has made both one, and has broken down the middle wall of separation,
15 having abolished in His flesh the enmity, that is, the law of commandments contained in ordinances, so as to create in Himself one new man from the two, thus making peace,
16 and that He might reconcile them both to God in one body through the cross, thereby putting to death the enmity. (Ephesians 2:14-16 NKJV)

1 Therefore, when we could no longer endure it, we thought it good to be left in Athens alone, 2 and sent Timothy, our brother and minister of God, and our fellow laborer in the gospel of Christ, to establish you and encourage you concerning your faith,
3 that no one should be shaken by these afflictions; for you yourselves know that we are appointed to this.
4 For, in fact, we told you before when we were with you that we would suffer tribulation, just as it happened, and you know.
5 For this reason, when I could no longer endure it, I sent to know your faith, lest by some means the tempter had tempted you, and our labor might be in vain.
6 But now that Timothy has come to us from you, and brought us good news of your faith and love, and that you always have good remembrance of us, greatly desiring to see us, as we also to see you—
7 therefore, brethren, in all our affliction and distress we were comforted concerning you by your faith. (1 Thessalonians 3:1-7 NKJV)

3 Now by this we know that we know Him, if we keep His commandments.
4 He who says, "I know Him," and does not keep His commandments, is a liar, and the truth is not in him.
5 But whoever keeps His word, truly the love of God is perfected in him. By this we know that we are in Him.

Exhibit 4: New Testament Commandment Scriptures

6 He who says he abides in Him ought himself also to walk just as He walked.
7 Brethren, I write no new commandment to you, but an old commandment which you have had from the beginning. The old commandment is the word which you heard from the beginning.
8 Again, a new commandment I write to you, which thing is true in Him and in you, because the darkness is passing away, and the true light is already shining.
9 He who says he is in the light, and hates his brother, is in darkness until now.
10 He who loves his brother abides in the light, and there is no cause for stumbling in him.
11 But he who hates his brother is in darkness and walks in darkness, and does not know where he is going, because the darkness has blinded his eyes. (1 John 2:3-11 NKJV)

21 I have not written to you because you do not know the truth, but because you know it, and that no lie is of the truth.
22 Who is a liar but he who denies that Jesus is the Christ? He is antichrist who denies the Father and the Son.
23 Whoever denies the Son does not have the Father either; he who acknowledges the Son has the Father also.
24 Therefore let that abide in you which you heard from the beginning. If what you heard from the beginning abides in you, you also will abide in the Son and in the Father. (1 John 3:21-24 NKJV)

2 By this we know that we love the children of God, when we love God and keep His commandments.
3 For this is the love of God, that we keep His commandments. And His commandments are not burdensome. (1 John 5:2-3 NKJV)

4 I rejoiced greatly that I have found some of your children walking in truth, as we received commandment from the Father.
5 And now I plead with you, lady, not as though I wrote a new commandment to you, but that which we have had from the beginning: that we love one another.
6 This is love, that we walk according to His commandments. This is the commandment, that as you have heard from the beginning, you should walk in it. (2 John 1:4-6 NKJV)

17 And the dragon was enraged with the woman, and he went to make war with the rest of her offspring, who keep the commandments of God and have the testimony of Jesus Christ. (Revelation 12:17 NKJV)

12 Here is the patience of the saints; here are those who keep the commandments of God and the faith of Jesus. (Revelation 14:12 NKJV)

Exhibit 5: 445 Laws of Moses

In addition to the Ten Commandments, Moses received an additional 435 laws from God, making a total of 445. These include 3,435 separate commands, but there is some overlap between them so the total number is slightly less. Anyone seeking to obey the Law of Moses must follow all 445 laws and all the commands included, which is impossible to do perfectly because if any of them are violated even once, the whole law is violated. The references are listed here to show the futility of pursuing right standing with God by obedience to the Law.

Laws to Keep God first (23 commands): Exodus 20:3, 22:20, 23:13, 23:24, 23:32-33, 34:14-16, Leviticus 22:32, Deuteronomy 6:5, 6:13-18, 11:1, 11:14-15, 18:13

Laws Forbidding Idolatry (38 commands): Exodus 20:4-5, 20:23, 34:17, Leviticus 18:21, 19:4, 26:1, Deuteronomy 4:15-19, 5:8-10, 7:16, 11:16, 12:30, 13:1-11, 16:21-22, 17:2-7, 27:15

Laws Forbidding Blasphemy (12 commands): Exodus 20:7, 22:28, Leviticus 19:12, 19:14, 24:10-16, Deuteronomy 5:11

Laws for Practicing Weekly Sabbath (62 commands): Exodus 16:23, 16:29, 20:8, 20:10, 31:13-17, 34:21, 35:2-3, Leviticus 23:3, 23:12, 24:8, 26:2, Numbers 15:32-36, 28:9-10, Deuteronomy 5:12, 5:14-15, Ezekiel 20:12, 20:20, 46:1-4, 46:12

Laws for Practicing Year-long Sabbath (34 commands): Exodus 23:10-11, Leviticus 25:1-7, 25:18-24, Deuteronomy 15:1-4

Laws for 2-year-long Sabbath (35 commands): Leviticus 25:8-10, 25:11-17, 25:25-34

Laws for Practicing Special Yearly Sabbath (138 commands): Leviticus 16:31, 23:7-8, 23:21, 23:24-44

Laws for Sacrifices and Offerings (21 commands): Exodus 20:24-25, 23:18-19, 34:25-26, Leviticus 1:1-8, 1:10-17, 2:1-3, 2:11, 2:13, 2:15, 5:7-10, 6:8-13, 9:3-4, 12:8, Deuteronomy 14:21

Laws for Practicing Baked offerings (9 commands): Leviticus 2:6, 6:14-23

Laws for Practicing Fried offerings (6 commands): Leviticus 2:7-9, 3:1-17, 7:11-21

Laws for Practicing Sin offerings (75 commands): Leviticus 4:1-35, 6:24-30

Exhibit 5: 445 Laws of Moses

Laws for Practicing Trespass offerings (45 commands): Leviticus 5:1-19, 6:1-7, 7:1-10

Laws for Practicing Day of Atonement (78 commands): Leviticus 16:5-22, 16:26-34, Numbers 7

Laws for Practicing General Offerings (26 commands): Numbers 15:1-12, 15:17-29

Laws for Practicing Red-heifer Offering (65 commands): Numbers 19:1-21

Laws for Showbread Offerings (10 commands): Leviticus 19:5-8, 24:5-9, Numbers 28:1-29:40

Laws for Kinds of sacrifices (30 commands): Leviticus 22:17-30, Deuteronomy 17:1

Place of sacrifices (60 commands): Leviticus 17:1-9); (Deuteronomy 12:5-28)

Tabernacle laws (329 commands): Exodus 25:1-40, 26:1-37, 27:1-10, 27:16-17, 27:20-21, 30:1-1-38, 31:1-11, 35:4, 35:21, 36:7-38, 37:1-28, 37:29, 38:1-20, 38:31, 40, Leviticus 16:1-3, 19:30, 24:1-9, 26:2

Laws for Priesthood Services (628 commands): Exodus 20:26, 28, 29:1-25, Leviticus 2:16, 5:12-18, 6:19, 7:21, 8:1-29, 8:30, 8:33-36, 9:1-2, 10:8-11, 16:4, 16:23-25, 17:8-13, 21:1-24, 22:1-9, Numbers 1:47-54, 3:5-13, 3:21-38, 3:40-43, 4:1-33, 8:1-26, 18:20-24, Deuteronomy 22:12

Laws for Rewarding Service (64 commands): Leviticus 2:10, 7:28-38, 8:31-32, 10:12-15, 22:10-13, Numbers 18:8-24, Deuteronomy 14:22-29, 18:1-8

Laws for Practicing Eight Feasts of Jehovah (242 commands): Exodus 12, 23:15-16, 34:18, 34:22, 34:26, Leviticus 23:1-44, Numbers 9:1-14, 10:1-16, 16:1-8, 28:16-31, 29:1-38, Deuteronomy 16:1-15, 26:1-11

National Laws (35 commands): Exodus 23:14-17, 23:25, 34:18-24, Leviticus 23:4-21, 23:33-44, Deuteronomy 14:22-29, 16:16-17

Laws Requiring Separation from Foreigners (15 commands): (Exodus 23:32-33, Deuteronomy 7:1-6, 23:1-5)

Laws Forbidding Unclean Things (153 commands): Leviticus 11:1-43, 14:33-53, Numbers 5:1-4, Deuteronomy 14:1-21, 23:10-11

Exhibit 5: 445 Laws of Moses

Tithing Laws (43 commands): Leviticus 27:30-34, Numbers 18:21-28, Deuteronomy 14:22-29, 26:12-15

Laws for Making and Enforcing Vows (113 commands): Leviticus 27:1-25, 27:28, Numbers 6:1-21, 30:2-6, 30:9-16, Deuteronomy 23:21-23

Laws Requiring Obedience (306 commands):
Exodus 23:20-23, Leviticus 11:44-47, 18, 19:35-36, 20, 22, Numbers 15:38-41, Deuteronomy 4:1, 4:2, 4:9-24, 6, 8, 9, 10:12-22, 11:1, 11:8, 11:13-20, 12:19, 12:29-32, 17:14-20, 18:9-12, 18:15-19, 22:12, 29:9, 30:15-20, 31:10-13, 40

Laws Forbidding False Religions (33 commands): Leviticus 18:24-30, 19:26-28, 19:31, 20:1-6, 20:26-27, Deuteronomy 13:1-18, 16:21-22, 17:2-5, 18:9-14, 18:20-22

Miscellaneous Laws (84 commands): Exodus 22:18, 23:2-5, 29:1, 29:12-15, 30:11-16, 34:19-20, Leviticus 19:31, 20:6, 20:27, 21:9, 22:1-16, Numbers 3:40-51, 6:22-27, 18:15-18, Deuteronomy 14:1-2, 15:19-23, 21:15-17, 26:16-19, 27:1-13

Family Laws (61 commands): Exodus 20:12, 21:8-11, 21:15, 21:17, Leviticus 19:3, 19:32, 20:9, 22:22, Deuteronomy 5:16, 6:6-9, 6:20-25, 21:10-17, 22:5, 24:1-5, 25:5-10, 27:16

Laws Forbidding Murder (61 commands): Exodus 20:13, 21:12-15, 21:20, 21:23-25, 21:29, Leviticus 24:17, 24:22, Numbers 35:16-34, Deuteronomy 5:17, 21:1-9

Sexual Activity Laws (96 commands): Exodus 20:14, 22:16-17, 22:19, Leviticus 18:6-8, 18:19-20, 18:22-23, 19:29, 20:10-21, Numbers 5:11-30, Deuteronomy 5:18, 22:13-23, 22:25-26, 22:28-30, 23:17-18, 27:20-23

Laws Forbidding Stealing (12 commands): Exodus 20:15, 22:1-5, 22:7-12, Leviticus 19:11, 19:13, Deuteronomy 5:19, 24:7

Laws Forbidding Lying (25 commands): Exodus 20:16, 23:1-2, 23:6-7, Leviticus 19:11, 19:16, Deuteronomy 5:20, 17:6-7; 19:15-21

Laws Forbidding Covetousness (21 commands): Exodus 20:17, 22:29-30, Deuteronomy 5:21

Treatment of Neighbor Laws (75 commands): Exodus 22:21-27, 23:9, Leviticus 19:9-14, 19:16-18, 19:33-34, 24:18, 24:19-22, 25:14, 25:17, 25:35, 25:39, 25:43, Numbers 5:5-8,

Exhibit 5: 445 Laws of Moses

15:15-16, Deuteronomy 15:7-11, 15:12-15, 21:15-17, 23:6-8, 23:24-25, 24:14-15, 24:19-22, 27:24

Health and Nutrition Laws (436 commands): Exodus 22:31, Leviticus 7:23-25, 7:27, 11:1-40, 11:26-27, 11:29-31, 11:41-47, 12:1-8, 13:1-3, 13:4-15, 13:16-23, 13:24-59, 14:1-57, 15:1-30, 17:10-14, 17:15-16, 19:26, 22:8, Deuteronomy 14:3-21, 23:10-14, 24:8-9

Laws Forbidding Rebellion (6 commands): Numbers 15:30-31, Deuteronomy 17:12-13, 21:18-21, 27:26

Animal Treatment Laws (26 comands): Exodus 23:4-5, 23:19, Leviticus 22:27-28, Deuteronomy 14:21, 22:1-4, 22:6-7, 22:10, 25:4

Conquest laws (107 commands): Numbers 31:17-24, 31:26-30, Deuteronomy 7:1-6, 7:18-24, 7:25-26, 12:1-4, 20:1-14, 20:15-20, 21:10-14, 23:9, 25:17-19

Slave laws (50 commands): Exodus 21:1-11, Leviticus 19:20-22, 25:39-55, Deuteronomy 15:12-18, 23:15-16

Property Laws (42 commands): Exodus 21:28-36, 22:6-15, Leviticus 19:23-25, 24:18, 24:21, Numbers 27:6-11, 36:5-9, Deuteronomy 19:14, 22:1-3, 22:8, 27:17

Business Laws (14 commands): Exodus 22:25-26, 23:8, Leviticus 25:14, 25:35-37, Deuteronomy 16:19, 23:19-20, 24:6, 24:10-13

Justice Laws (60 commands): Exodus 21:18-27, 23:2, 23:6-7, Leviticus 19:15, 19:35-36, 25:35-37, Deuteronomy 1:16-17, 16: 18-20, 24:16-18, 25:1-3, 25:11-12, 25:14-16, 27:19

Source: Dake Study Bible Notes, by Finis Jennings Dake.

Exhibit 6: Unrighteous Deeds of Lawlessness

Unrighteous lawless deeds are usually easy to identify because they're listed in many scriptures including these:

- Worshiping and serving the creature rather than the creator (Romans 1:25)
- Exchanging the natural sexual functions for the unnatural (Romans 1:26)
- People of the same sex burning in their desire for one another (Romans 1:27)
- Wickedness (Romans 1:29)
- Greed (Romans 1:29)
- Being full of envy (Romans 1:29)
- Murder (Romans 1:29, Revelation 21:8)
- Strife (Romans 1:29, Romans 13:13, 2 Corinthians 12:20, Galatians 5:20)
- Deceit (Romans 1:29)
- Malice (Romans 1:29)
- Gossip (Romans 1:29, 2 Corinthians 12:20)
- Slander (Romans 1:30, 2 Corinthians 12:20)
- Hating God (Romans 1:30)
- Insolent (Romans 1:30)
- Arrogance (Romans 1:30, 2 Corinthians 12:20)
- Boastful (Romans 1:30)
- Inventing evil schemes (Romans 1:30)
- Disobedience to parents (Romans 1:30)
- Being untrustworthy (Romans 1:31)
- Being unloving (Romans 1:31)
- Being unmerciful (Romans 1:31)
- Giving approval of others breaking God's commandments (Romans 1:32)
- Fornicating - Google defines it as "sexual intercourse between two people not married to each other," but it goes way beyond that. The Greek word translated as fornication is porneia, which is where we get the word pornography and the shorter form, porno. It literally means harlotry, which is a violation of our relationship with God for the purpose of indulging our lust for another person, which would include looking at pornography, looking at people who are fully clothed but indulging our imagination in sexual fantasies and sexual dreams, masturbation, and giving ourselves over to any kind of unlawful sexual acts. Fornication takes away our spirit and is practiced by those who do not know God. (Hosea 4:11, Hosea 5:3-4, 1 Corinthians 6:9)
- Idolatry - It is defined as "worship, admiration, adoration, devotion, or obsession with anything or anyone" (other than God). Anything or anyone can be an idol to us, including celebrities, cars, money, alcohol, drugs, sports, movies, hobbies, etc. None of those things are wrong in themselves, but they become wrong if we

Exhibit 6: Unrighteous Deeds of Lawlessness

- adore them too much. We are instructed to turn away from all idols because our God is a jealous God. The second of the Ten Commandments forbids idolatry. (Exodus 20:4-6, 23:23, Deuteronomy 12:2-3, Jonah 2:8-9, 1 Corinthians 6:9, Galatians 5:20)
- Adultery - Google defines adultery as "voluntary sexual intercourse between a married person and a person who is not his or her spouse," but Jesus set the standard much higher when He said, "Everyone who looks at a woman with lust for her has already committed adultery with her in his heart." Adultery is not just a physical act and is not limited to sexual intercourse, but includes our willingness to entertain the strong sexual desire in our heart for anyone other than our spouse. This includes looking at anyone other than our spouse and longing for them, imagining ourselves engaging with them in a romantic or sexual relationship. The seventh of the ten commandments tells us not to commit adultery. (Exodus 20:14, 1 Corinthians 6:9)
- Effeminate - For a man, this means having or showing characteristics regarded as typical of a woman. For a woman, it means having or showing characteristics regarded as typical of a man. This is gender confusion, which is now being promoted by our government, business leaders, schools and even some so-called churches. (Deuteronomy 22:5, 1 Corinthians 6:9)
- Homosexuality (1 Corinthians 6:9) – Although our society has embraced homosexuality, even putting it on the same level as our ethnic background, which implies people who practice homosexuality are born that way and have no choice in the matter, God still calls it an abomination and an act of unrighteousness throughout the Bible (Leviticus 18:22, Leviticus 20:13, Romans 1:18-32, 1 Timothy 8-11, and Revelation 22:14-15).
- Stealing - Google defines stealing as "taking another person's property without permission or legal right and without intending to return it." Even this definition is perverted because it says it is okay to steal as long as you intend to return it. Employers often have a hard time finding employees who will not steal from them. Increasing numbers of retail businesses are refusing to accept payments in cash because of so many problems with employee theft. Our consciences have become so hardened, we routinely steal e-books, music, and movies by downloading them without paying for them and without anyone's permission. The eighth of the ten commandments tells us not to steal (Exodus 20:15, 1 Corinthians 6:10).
- Covetousness - Google defines covetous as "having a great desire to possess something, typically something belonging to someone else." The Bible gives us specific examples of things we should not covet, including our neighbor's house, wife, servants, animals, or anything else belonging to our neighbor. The tenth of the ten commandments tells us not to covet (Exodus 20:17, 1 Corinthians 5:11, 1

Exhibit 6: Unrighteous Deeds of Lawlessness

Corinthians 6:10)
- Drunkenness (Romans 13:13, 1 Corinthians 5:11, 1 Corinthians 6:10) - Google defines a drunkard as "a person who is habitually drunk." We tend to limit this to alcoholics, but it applies to any form of substance abuse including illegal drugs and prescription drugs because these are all used for the same purpose, seeking a substitute for the comfort and peace that comes from a right relationship with God. God commanded the Israelites not to drink wine or strong drink as a perpetual statute throughout their generations, but the real problem is that we love the substance more than we love God. (Leviticus 10:8-11)
- Reviling - Google defines reviling, "to assail with contemptuous language, to speak abusively." Examples include insulting others, condemning them, scorning them, abusing them, or berating them. Reviling can happen face to face, but more often it is done behind the person's back by saying things about them to other people that make them sound bad. We are more likely to revile someone after hanging up the phone than talking to them on the phone. We are more likely to revile someone in an email than we would face to face. We might think nothing about it, but the angels who are far greater in might and power than us refuse to speak a reviling word. Even the archangel Michael refused to revile against the devil. (1 Corinthians 5:11, 1 Corinthians 6:10, 2 Peter 2:10-16, Jude 1:9-10)
- Swindling - Dictionary.com defines swindler, "to cheat a person or business out of money or other assets, to put forth plausible schemes or use unscrupulous trickery to defraud others, to cheat." The Apostle Paul instructed us if anyone calls themselves a Christian brother, but acts like a swindler, we should not even eat a meal with them. Instead, we are told to judge those who are within the church and remove them. (1 Corinthians 5:11, 1 Corinthians 6:10)
- Sexual promiscuity (Romans 13:13)
- Sensuality (Romans 13:13, Galatians 5:19)
- Jealousy (Romans 13:13, 2 Corinthians 12:20, Galatians 5:20)
- Angry temper (2 Corinthians 12:20, Galatians 5:20)
- Causing disturbances, disputes, dissensions, and factions (2 Corinthians 12:20, Galatians 5:20)
- Immorality (1 Corinthians 5:11, Galatians 5:19, Revelation 21:8)
- Impurity (Galatians 5:19)
- Sorcery (Galatians 5:20, Revelation 21:8)
- Enmity (Galatians 5:20)
- Cowardly (Revelation 21:8)
- Liars (Revelation 21:8)

Exhibit 7: Word Study - Righteous, Righteousness

Yasar
Language: Hebrew
Strong's Number: h3477
Definition: straight, upright, correct, right, straight, level, right, pleasing, correct, straightforward, just, upright, fitting, proper, uprightness, righteous, upright, that which is upright
Translation Count: right (53), upright (42), righteous (9), straight (3), convenient (2), Jasher (2), equity (1), just (1), meet (1), meetest (1), upright ones (1), uprightly (1), uprightness (1), well (1)

Sadiyq
Language: Hebrew
Strong's Number: h6662
Definition: just, lawful, righteous, just, righteous (in government), just, right (in one's cause), just, righteous (in conduct and character), righteous (as justified and vindicated by God), right, correct, lawful
Translation Count: righteous (163), just (42), lawful (1)

sadaq
Language: Hebrew
Strong's Number: h6663
Definition: to be just, be righteous, Qal - to have a just cause, to be in the right, to be justified, to be just (of God), to be just, be righteous (in conduct and character), Niphal - to be put or made right, to be justified, Piel - justify, make to appear righteous, make someone righteous, Hiphil - to do or bring justice (in administering law), to declare righteous, justify, to justify, vindicate the cause of, save, to make righteous, turn to righteousness, Hithpael - to justify oneself
Translation Count: acquit (1), acquitted (1), declare you right (1), do justice (1), give him justice (1), just (2), justified (5), justifies (1), justify (5), justifying (2), lead them to righteousness (1), made you appear righteous (2), properly restored (1), proved right (1), proved...righteous (1), right (4), righteous (9), vindicated (1), vindicates (1)

sedeq
Language: Hebrew
Strong's Number: h6664
Definition: justice, rightness, righteousness (what is right or just or normal, rightness, justness of weights and measures), righteousness (in government), righteousness of judges, righteousness of rulers, righteousness of kings, righteousness of law, righteousness of Davidic king, righteousness of Messiah, righteousness of Jerusalem as

Exhibit 7: Word Study - Righteous, Righteousness

seat of just government, righteousness of God's attribute, righteousness, justice (in case or cause), rightness (in speech), righteousness (as ethically right), righteousness (as vindicated), justification (in controversy), deliverance, victory, prosperity, righteousness of God as covenant-keeping in redemption, righteousness in name of Messianic king, righteousness of people enjoying salvation, righteousness of Cyrus
Translation Count: accurate (1), fairly (1), just (10), just cause (1), justice (3), righteous (15), righteously (6), righteousness (76), righteousness (1), rightly (1), vindication (1), what is right (3)

Sidqa
Language: Hebrew
Strong's Number: h6665
Definition: right doing, doing right, righteousness
Translation Count: righteousness (1)

sedaqa
Language: Hebrew
Strong's Number: h6666
Definition: justice, righteousness in government, righteousness of judge, righteousness of ruler, righteousness of king, righteousness of law, righteousness of Davidic king Messiah, righteousness (of God's attribute), righteousness (in a case or cause), righteousness, truthfulness, righteousness (as ethically right), righteousness (as vindicated), justification, salvation of God, prosperity (of people), righteous acts
Translation Count: honesty (1), justice (1), merits (1), right (2), righteous (1), righteous acts (3), righteous deeds (7), righteously (1), righteousness (136), rights (1), vindication (3)

Dikaios
Language: Greek
Strong's Number: g1342
Definition: righteous, observing divine laws, in a wide sense, upright, righteous, virtuous, keeping the commands of God, of those who seem to themselves to be righteous, who pride themselves to be righteous, who pride themselves in their virtues, whether real or imagined, innocent, faultless, guiltless, used of him whose way of thinking, feeling, and acting is wholly conformed to the will of God, and who therefore needs no rectification in the heart or life, only Christ truly, approved of or acceptable of God, in a narrower sense, rendering to each his due and that in a judicial sense, passing just judgment on others, whether expressed in words or shown by the manner of dealing with them
Translation Count: righteous (41), just (33), right (5), meet (2)

Exhibit 7: Word Study - Righteous, Righteousness

Dikaiosyne
Language: Greek
Strong's Number: g1343
Definition: in a broad sense: state of him who is as he ought to be, righteousness, the condition acceptable to God, the doctrine concerning the way in which man may attain a state approved of God, integrity, virtue, purity of life, rightness, correctness of thinking feeling, and acting, in a narrower sense, justice or the virtue which gives each his due
Translation Count: righteousness (92)

Cumulative Counts:
Righteous (238): Yasar (9), Sadiyq (163), Sadaq (9), Sedeq (15), Sedaqa (1), Dikaios (41)

Upright (42): Yasar (42)

Just (85): Sadiyq (42), sedeq (10), Dikaios (33)

Exhibit 8: 19 Promises for Provision

Note: Each promise includes the scripture verse (NKJV translation) plus a summary or amplified definition of key words from the original Hebrew or Greek.

Every place on which the soles of your feet tread will be given to you. (summarized from Deuteronomy 11:24)

> Every place on which the sole of your foot treads shall be yours: from the wilderness and Lebanon, from the river, the River Euphrates, even to the Western Sea, shall be your territory. (Deuteronomy 11:24 NKJV)

The offspring of your animals will be blessed. (summarized from Deuteronomy 28:4)

> Blessed shall be the fruit of your body, the produce of your ground and the increase of your herds, the increase of your cattle and the offspring of your flocks. (Deuteronomy 28:4 NKJV)

Yahweh will command the blessing upon you in your barns. (summarized from Deuteronomy 28:8)

> The Lord will command the blessing on you in your storehouses and in all to which you set your hand, and He will bless you in the land which the Lord your God is giving you. (Deuteronomy 28:8 NKJV)

Yahweh will make you have more than enough in good things in the fruit of your animals. (amplified from Hebrew word yather in Deuteronomy 28:11)

> And the Lord will grant you plenty of goods, in the fruit of your body, in the increase of your livestock, and in the produce of your ground, in the land of which the Lord swore to your fathers to give you. (Deuteronomy 28:11 NKJV)

You shall lend to many people, but you shall not borrow. (summarized from Deuteronomy 28:12)

> The Lord will open to you His good treasure, the heavens, to give the rain to your land in its season, and to bless all the work of your hand. You shall lend to many nations, but you shall not borrow. (Deuteronomy 28:12 NKJV)

You will have no need to borrow from others because you will have enough to lend to them. (amplified from Hebrew word lavah in Psalm 37:26)

Exhibit 8: 19 Promises for Provision

> 25 I have been young, and now am old; yet I have not seen the righteous forsaken, nor his descendants begging bread.
> 26 He is ever merciful, and lends; and his descendants are blessed. (Psalm 37:25-26 NKJV)

Yahweh God will give you good things and will not withhold any good thing from you. (summarized from Psalm 84:11 and 85:12)

> For the Lord God is a sun and shield; the Lord will give grace and glory; no good thing will He withhold from those who walk uprightly. (Psalm 84:11 NKJV)

> Yes, the Lord will give what is good; and our land will yield its increase. (Psalm 85:12 NKJV)

Wealth and riches will be in your house. (summarized from Psalm 112:3 and Proverbs 15:6)

> 1 Praise the Lord! Blessed is the man who fears the Lord, who delights greatly in His commandments.
> 2 His descendants will be mighty on earth; the generation of the upright will be blessed.
> 3 Wealth and riches will be in his house, and his righteousness endures forever. (Psalm 112:1-3 NKJV)

> In the house of the righteous there is much treasure, but in the revenue of the wicked is trouble. (Proverbs 15:6 NKJV)

Yahweh will not allow you to be hungry. (summarized from Proverbs 10:3)

> The Lord will not allow the righteous soul to famish, but He casts away the desire of the wicked. (Proverbs 10:3 NKJV)

You will be completed and paid in full in the earth. (summarized from Proverbs 11:31)

> If the righteous will be recompensed on the earth, how much more the ungodly and the sinner. (Proverbs 11:31 NKJV)

You will be rewarded with things that are good and beneficial. (amplified from Hebrew words shalem and tob in Proverbs 13:21)

Exhibit 8: 19 Promises for Provision

> Evil pursues sinners, but to the righteous, good shall be repaid. (Proverbs 13:21 NKJV)

You will increase in abundance. (amplified from Hebrew word rabah in Proverbs 29:2)

> When the righteous are in authority, the people rejoice; but when a wicked man rules, the people groan. (Proverbs 29:2 NKJV)

The desires of your soul will be satisfied by what you consume. (amplified from Hebrew words akal, soba and nephesh in Proverbs 13:25) You will be more satisfied than people who have very large incomes. (amplified from Hebrew words meat, rob, and tebuah in Proverbs 16:8)

> Better is a little with righteousness, than vast revenues without justice. (Proverbs 16:8 NKJV)

You will have fullness, abundance, enough to satisfy you. (amplified from Hebrew word osba in Proverbs 13:25)

> The righteous eats to the satisfying of his soul, but the stomach of the wicked shall be in want. (Proverbs 13:25 NKJV)

When wicked people are perishing, you will become great. (amplified from Hebrew word rabah in Proverbs 28:28)

> When the wicked arise, men hide themselves; but when they perish, the righteous increase. (Proverbs 28:28 NKJV)

He will teach you to profit and lead you in the way if you pay attention to His commandments. (summarized from Isaiah 48:17-18)

> Thus says the Lord, your Redeemer, the Holy One of Israel: "I am the Lord your God, who teaches you to profit, who leads you by the way you should go. (Isaiah 48:17 NKJV)

Your well-being will flow like a river. (summarized from Isaiah 48:18)

> Oh, that you had heeded My commandments! Then your peace would have been like a river, and your righteousness like the waves of the sea. (Isaiah 48:18 NKJV)

Exhibit 8: 19 Promises for Provision

All the things you need, including food, drink and clothing, will be added to you without you having to seek after it. (summarized from Matthew 6:33)

> But seek first the kingdom of God and His righteousness, and all these things shall be added to you. (Matthew 6:33 NKJV)

You will receive a hundred times as much in this life as you give up to follow Him. (summarized from Mark 10:28-30)

> 28 Then Peter began to say to Him, "See, we have left all and followed You."
> 29 So Jesus answered and said, "Assuredly, I say to you, there is no one who has left house or brothers or sisters or father or mother or wife or children or lands, for My sake and the gospel's,
> 30 who shall not receive a hundredfold now in this time—houses and brothers and sisters and mothers and children and lands, with persecutions—and in the age to come, eternal life. (Mark 10:28-30 NKJV)

Exhibit 9: 5 Promises for Answered Prayers

Note: Each promise includes the scripture verse (NKJV translation) plus a summary or amplified definition of key words from the original Hebrew or Greek.

The eyes and ears of Yahweh will be on you. (summarized from Psalm 34:15)

> The eyes of the Lord are on the righteous, and His ears are open to their cry. (Psalm 34:15 NKJV)

Whatever your heart desires and longs for, whatever pleases you, will be added to you, given to you. (amplified from Hebrew words taawah and natan in Proverbs 10:24)

> The fear of the wicked will come upon him, and the desire of the righteous will be granted. (Proverbs 10:24 NKJV)

The ears of Yahweh will be attentive to your cries and prayers. (summarized from Psalm 34:15 and 34:17, Proverbs 15:29, 1 Peter 3:12)

> The eyes of the Lord are on the righteous, and His ears are open to their cry. (Psalm 34:15 NKJV)

> The righteous cry out, and the Lord hears, and delivers them out of all their troubles. (Psalm 34:17 NKJV)

> The Lord is far from the wicked, but He hears the prayer of the righteous. (Proverbs 15:29 NKJV)

> For the eyes of the Lord are on the righteous, and His ears are open to their prayers; but the face of the Lord is against those who do evil." (1 Peter 3:12 NKJV)

Your prayers will accomplish much. (summarized from James 5:16)

> Confess your trespasses to one another, and pray for one another, that you may be healed. The effective, fervent prayer of a righteous man avails much. (James 5:16 NKJV)

You can ask whatever you desire and it will be done for you. (amplified from Greek word thelo in John 15:7-10, which means to determine, so in this context, this is an invitation to ask whatever we determine, whatever we wish, whatever we choose, whatever we prefer, whatever pleases us)

Exhibit 9: 5 Promises for Answered Prayers

7 "If you abide in Me, and My words abide in you, you will ask what you desire, and it shall be done for you.
8 By this My Father is glorified, that you bear much fruit; so you will be My disciples.
9 As the Father loved Me, I also have loved you; abide in My love.
10 If you keep My commandments, you will abide in My love, just as I have kept My Father's commandments and abide in His love." (John 15: 7-10 NKJV)

Exhibit 10: 22 Promises for More of God

Note: Each promise includes the scripture verse (NKJV translation) plus a summary or amplified definition of key words from the original Hebrew or Greek.

God will show you His goodness, kindness and faithfulness. (amplified from Hebrew word hesed in 1 Kings 3:6)

> And Solomon said: "You have shown great mercy to Your servant David my father, because he walked before You in truth, in righteousness, and in uprightness of heart with You; You have continued this great kindness for him, and You have given him a son to sit on his throne, as it is this day. (1 Kings 3:6 NKJV)

You will perceive and behold God's presence. (amplified from Hebrew words haza and paniym in Psalm 11:7)

> For the Lord is righteous, He loves righteousness; His countenance beholds the upright. (Psalm 11:7 NKJV)

God will be with you. (summarized from Psalm 14:5)

> There they are in great fear, for God is with the generation of the righteous. (Psalm 14:5 NKJV)

You will gaze upon the face of Yahweh. (amplified from Hebrew words haza and paniym in Psalm 11:7, Psalm 17:15)

> As for me, I will see Your face in righteousness; (Psalm 17:15a NKJV)

> For the Lord is righteous, He loves righteousness; His countenance beholds the upright. (Psalm 11:7 NKJV)

When you awake, you will be saturated with the presence of God, which will bring you great contentment and satisfaction. (amplified from Hebrew word temunah in Psalm 17:15)

> I shall be satisfied when I awake in Your likeness. (Psalm 17:15b NKJV)

Yahweh will love you. (amplified from Hebrew word ahab in Psalm 11:7, Psalm 146:8, Proverbs 15:9)

Exhibit 10: 22 Promises for More of God

> For the Lord is righteous, He loves righteousness; His countenance beholds the upright. (Psalm 11:7 NKJV)

> The Lord loves the righteous. (Psalm 146:8 NKJV)

> The way of the wicked is an abomination to the Lord, but He loves him who follows righteousness. (Proverbs 15:9 NKJV)

God will never leave you or forsake you. (amplified from Hebrew word azab in Psalm 37:25)

> 25 I have been young, and now am old; yet I have not seen the righteous forsaken, nor his descendants begging bread.
> 26 He is ever merciful, and lends; and his descendants are blessed. (Psalm 37:25-26 NKJV)

You will have a reason to give praise to God, even something to boast about what He has done. (summarized from Psalm 64:10)

> The righteous shall be glad in the Lord, and trust in Him. And all the upright in heart shall glory. (Psalm 64:10 NKJV)

The presence of God will settle upon you and stay with you, so you will live in His presence. (amplified from Hebrew word yashab from Psalm 140:13)

> Surely the righteous shall give thanks to Your name; the upright shall dwell in Your presence. (Psalm 140:13 NKJV)

Yahweh will all you into His inner council. (amplified from Hebrew word sod in Proverbs 3:32)

> For the perverse person is an abomination to the Lord, but His secret counsel is with the upright. (Proverbs 3:32 NKJV)

You will please Yahweh by your righteousness more than by making sacrifices. (summarized from Proverbs 21:3)

> To do righteousness and justice is more acceptable to the Lord than sacrifice. (Proverbs 21:3 NKJV)

Exhibit 10: 22 Promises for More of God

You will come near to Him, minister to Him, stand before Him, enter His holy presence, and watch over His work while others are not allowed. (summarized from Ezekiel 44:15-16)

> 15 "But the priests, the Levites, the sons of Zadok, who kept charge of My sanctuary when the children of Israel went astray from Me, they shall come near Me to minister to Me; and they shall stand before Me to offer to Me the fat and the blood," says the Lord God.
> 16 "They shall enter My sanctuary, and they shall come near My table to minister to Me, and they shall keep My charge. (Ezekiel 44:15-16 NKJV)

Your pursuit of righteousness will produce a harvest of God's mercy and kindness and a rain, an outpouring, of His righteousness. (summarized from Hosea 10:12)

> Sow for yourselves righteousness; reap in mercy; break up your fallow ground, for it is time to seek the Lord, till He comes and rains righteousness on you. (Hosea 10:12 NKJV)

The words of Yahweh will do good to you. (summarized from Micah 2:7)

> You who are named the house of Jacob: "Is the Spirit of the Lord restricted? Are these His doings? Do not My words do good to him who walks uprightly? (Micah 2:7 NKJV)

I will grant you free access among the Lord and the angel of the Lord. (summarized from Zechariah 3:7)

> "Thus says the Lord of hosts: "If you will walk in My ways, and if you will keep My command, then you shall also judge My house, and likewise have charge of My courts; I will give you places to walk among these who stand here. (Zechariah 3:7 NKJV)

You will be a friend of God. (summarized from John 15:14)

> You are My friends if you do whatever I command you. (John 15:14 NKJV)

You will be born of God. (summarized from 1 John 2:29)

> If you know that He is righteous, you know that everyone who practices righteousness is born of Him. (1 John 2:29 NKJV)

Exhibit 10: 22 Promises for More of God

You will never again leave His holy place, His sanctuary. (amplified from Greek word naos from Revelation 3:12)

God the Father's name will be written on you. (summarized from Revelation 3:12)

The name of the new Jerusalem will be written on you. (summarized from Revelation 3:12)

The Lord Jesus's new name will be written on you. (summarized from Revelation 3:12)

> He who overcomes, I will make him a pillar in the temple of My God, and he shall go out no more. I will write on him the name of My God and the name of the city of My God, the New Jerusalem, which comes down out of heaven from My God. And I will write on him My new name. (Revelation 3:12 NKJV)

You will be ready to enter the innermost intimate chambers of the Lord in a covenant relationship of marriage, as represented by bright and clean linen clothing. (summarized from Revelation 19:7-8)

> 7 Let us be glad and rejoice and give Him glory, for the marriage of the Lamb has come, and His wife has made herself ready."
> 8 And to her it was granted to be arrayed in fine linen, clean and bright, for the fine linen is the righteous acts of the saints. (Revelation 19:7-8 NKJV)

Exhibit 11: 8 Promises for Your Words

Note: Each promise includes the scripture verse (NKJV translation) plus a summary or amplified definition of key words from the original Hebrew or Greek.

You will speak words of justice and wisdom. (summarized from Psalm 37:30)

> The mouth of the righteous speaks wisdom, and his tongue talks of justice. (Psalm 37:29 NKJV)

Your mouth will be a fountain of life because you continually speak good and wholesome words. (amplified from Hebrew word maqor in Proverbs 10:11)

> The mouth of the righteous is a well of life, but violence covers the mouth of the wicked. (Proverbs 10:11 NKJV)

Your tongue will be like choice silver because you utter words that are precious, pure, pleasant, and profitable. (amplified from Hebrew words bachar and keseph in Proverbs 10:20)

> The tongue of the righteous is choice silver; the heart of the wicked is worth little. (Proverbs 10:20 NKJV)

The words of your mouth will produce the fruit of wisdom. (amplified from Hebrew word nub in Proverbs 10:31)

> The mouth of the righteous brings forth wisdom, but the perverse tongue will be cut out. (Proverbs 10:31 NKJV)

Your lips will bring forth what is good and acceptable. (amplified from Hebrew word ratson in Proverbs 10:32)

> The lips of the righteous know what is acceptable, but the mouth of the wicked what is perverse. (Proverbs 10:32 NKJV)

The words of your mouth will deliver you from harm by stripping it away from you. (amplified from Hebrew word natsal in Proverbs 12:6)

> The words of the wicked are, "Lie in wait for blood," but the mouth of the upright will deliver them. (Proverbs 12:6 NKJV)

Exhibit 11: 8 Promises for Your Words

Your words will cause kings to delight in you. (amplified from Hebrew words saphah and ratson in Proverbs 16:13a)

Your words will be straight and right, causing people to dearly love you. (amplified from Hebrew words yashar and aheb in Proverbs 16:13b)

> Righteous lips are the delight of kings, and they love him who speaks what is right. (Proverbs 16:13 NKJV)

Exhibit 12: 23 Promises for Protection

Note: Each promise includes the scripture verse (NKJV translation) plus a summary or amplified definition of key words from the original Hebrew or Greek.

Yahweh will drive out people from before you, so you take possession from them, even from those who are greater and mightier than you. (summarized from Deuteronomy 11:22-23)

> 22 For if you carefully keep all these commandments which I command you to do—to love the Lord your God, to walk in all His ways, and to hold fast to Him 23 then the Lord will drive out all these nations from before you, and you will dispossess greater and mightier nations than yourselves. (Deuteronomy 11:22-23 NKJV)

Yahweh shall cause your enemies who rise against you to be defeated before you; they will come out against you one way and will flee before you seven ways. (summarized from Deuteronomy 28:7)

> The Lord will cause your enemies who rise against you to be defeated before your face; they shall come out against you one way and flee before you seven ways. (Deuteronomy 28:7 NKJV)

God will make things right with you by cleansing you and clearing you of all charges brought against you. He will justify you and declare you are righteous. (amplified from Hebrew word sadaq from 2 Chronicles 6:22-23)

> 22 "If anyone sins against his neighbor, and is forced to take an oath, and comes and takes an oath before Your altar in this temple,
> 23 then hear from heaven, and act, and judge Your servants, bringing retribution on the wicked by bringing his way on his own head, and justifying the righteous by giving him according to his righteousness. (2 Chronicles 6:22-23 NKJV)

God will deliver you from all misery and distress and strip all of it off you. (amplified from Hebrew words raah, natsal, and tsarah in Psalm 34:17 and 19)

> The righteous cry out, and the Lord hears, and delivers them out of all their troubles. (Psalm 34:17 NKJV)

You will encounter much evil, but Yahweh will plunder all of it and snatch you away from it. (amplified from Hebrew words raah and natsal in Psalm 34:19)

Exhibit 12: 23 Promises for Protection

Many are the afflictions of the righteous, but the Lord delivers him out of them all. (Psalm 34:19 NKJV)

Yahweh will not leave you in the hands of the wicked who seek to kill you. (summarized from Psalm 37:32-33)

When you are judged, Yahweh will not allow you to be condemned. (summarized from Psalm 37:33)

> 32 The wicked watches the righteous, and seeks to slay him.
> 33 The Lord will not leave him in his hand, nor condemn him when he is judged. (Psalm 37:32-33 NKJV)

Yahweh will help you by protecting you and supporting you. (amplified from Hebrew word azar in Psalm 37:40)

Yahweh will make a way of escape for you so you can slip away into a safe place. (amplified from Hebrew word palat in Psalm 37:40)

> And the Lord shall help them and deliver them; He shall deliver them from the wicked, and save them, because they trust in Him. (Psalm 37:40 NKJV)

He will put a hedge of protection around your path like a shield and keep watch over it. (amplified from Hebrew words samar and mginnah in Proverbs 2:7b-8)

> 7 He stores up sound wisdom for the upright; He is a shield to those who walk uprightly;
> 8 He guards the paths of justice, and preserves the way of His saints. (Proverbs 2:7-8 NKJV)

When a storm passes by, you will not perish, but will remain standing because you have a firm foundation that lasts forever. (amplified from Hebrew words yesod and olam in Proverbs 10:25)

> When the whirlwind passes by, the wicked is no more, but the righteous has an everlasting foundation. (Proverbs 10:25 NKJV)

You will be snatched away from trouble so that you are rescued and delivered. (amplified from Hebrew word nasal in Proverbs 11:6)

Exhibit 12: 23 Promises for Protection

The righteousness of the upright will deliver them, but the unfaithful will be caught by their lust. (Proverbs 11:6 NKJV)

You will be drawn away from trouble so it does not come upon you. (amplified from Hebrew word chalats in Proverbs 11:8)

> The righteous is delivered from trouble, and it comes to the wicked instead. (Proverbs 11:8 NKJV)

You will escape from trouble. (summarized from Proverbs 12:13)

> The wicked is ensnared by the transgression of his lips, but the righteous will come through trouble. (Proverbs 12:13 NKJV)

Any evil that comes against you will be rendered powerless to harm you. (amplified from Hebrew words aven and anah in Proverbs 12:21)

> No grave trouble will overtake the righteous, but the wicked shall be filled with evil. (Proverbs 12:21 NKJV)

Righteousness will watch over you, guard you, and protect you. (summarized from Proverbs 13:6)

> Righteousness guards him whose way is blameless, but wickedness overthrows the sinner. (Proverbs 13:6 NKJV)

Anyone who acts wickedly towards you will be an abomination to Yahweh. (amplified from Hebrew words rasha and toebah in Proverbs 17:15)

> He who justifies the wicked, and he who condemns the just, both of them alike are an abomination to the Lord. (Proverbs 17:15 NKJV)

Anyone who imposes fines on you will have to answer to God because He says it is not good to do that to the righteous. (amplified from Hebrew words tob and anash in Proverbs 17:26)

> Also, to punish the righteous is not good, nor to strike princes for their uprightness. (Proverbs 17:26 NKJV)

Exhibit 12: 23 Promises for Protection

Anyone who stretches the truth about you to make a wrong judgment against you must answer to God because He says it is not good to do that to the righteous. (amplified from Hebrew words natah and mishpat in Proverbs 18:5)

> It is not good to show partiality to the wicked, or to overthrow the righteous in judgment. (Proverbs 18:5 NKJV)

The name of Yahweh will be a strong tower for you to run into and whenever you do He will set you on high, out of harm's way. (summarized from Proverbs 18:10)

> The name of the Lord is a strong tower; the righteous run to it and are safe. (Proverbs 18:10 NKJV)

You will be delivered out of trouble and wicked people will take your place as a ransom for your life. (amplified from Hebrew word kopher in Proverbs 21:18) The wicked will be cut off by God's judgments to preserve the righteous (summarized from Genesis 6- 8, Exodus 7- 12, Isaiah 43:3)

> The way of a guilty man is perverse; but as for the pure, his work is right. (Proverbs 21:18 NKJV)

No weapon formed against you shall prosper. (summarized from Isaiah 54:17)

> No weapon formed against you shall prosper, and every tongue which rises against you in judgment you shall condemn. This is the heritage of the servants of the Lord, and their righteousness is from Me," says the Lord. (Isaiah 54:17 NKJV)

Misery and distress will be removed from you. Instead, you will enter peace and rest in your bed. (amplified from Hebrew words asaph and raah in Isaiah 57:1-2)

> 1 The righteous perishes, and no man takes it to heart; merciful men are taken away, while no one considers that the righteous is taken away from evil.
> 2 He shall enter into peace; they shall rest in their beds, each one walking in his uprightness. (Isaiah 57:1-2 NKJV)

Exhibit 13: 11 Promises for More Joy

Note: Each promise includes the scripture verse (NKJV translation) plus a summary or amplified definition of key words from the original Hebrew or Greek.

You will have a reason to be glad, to rejoice, to shout and sing for joy. (summarized from Psalm 32:11 and 33:1)

> Be glad in the Lord and rejoice, you righteous; and shout for joy, all you upright in heart! (Psalm 32:11 NKJV)

> Rejoice in the Lord, O you righteous! For praise from the upright is beautiful. (Psalm 33:1 NKJV)

God will anoint you with the oil of joy above your companions. (summarized from Psalm 45:7)

> You love righteousness and hate wickedness; therefore God, Your God, has anointed you with the oil of gladness more than Your companions. (Psalm 45:7 NKJV)

You will rejoice when you see the vengeance of God. (summarized from Psalm 58:10)

> The righteous shall rejoice when he sees the vengeance; he shall wash his feet in the blood of the wicked. (Psalm 58:10 NKJV)

You will rejoice and be glad in Yahweh. (summarized from Psalm 64:10)

> The righteous shall be glad in the Lord, and trust in Him. And all the upright in heart shall glory. (Psalm 64:10 NKJV)

His joy will be sown into you like seed, with the power to produce a harvest of much more joy, reproducing after its kind like every other seed, if it is properly received into an upright heart and nurtured. (amplified from Hebrew words simchah and zara in Psalm 97:11)

> Light is sown for the righteous, and gladness for the upright in heart. (Psalm 97:11 NKJV)

Shouts of joy will be in your house. (summarized from Psalms 118:15)

Exhibit 13: 11 Promises for More Joy

>The voice of rejoicing and salvation is in the tents of the righteous; the right hand of the Lord does valiantly. (Psalms 118:15 NKJV)

You will have hope for joy and gladness in the days ahead. (amplified from Hebrew words tocheleth and simchah in Proverbs 10:28)

>The hope of the righteous will be gladness, but the expectation of the wicked will perish. (Proverbs 10:28 NKJV)

The light of God will shine forth in you joyfully because He is an eternal source of joy. (amplified from Hebrew words or and samach in Proverbs 13:9)

>The light of the righteous rejoices, but the lamp of the wicked will be put out. (Proverbs 13:9 NKJV)

God will be glorified when you rejoice. It will be a beautiful and glorious thing. (amplified from Hebrew words alats and tipharah in Proverbs 28:12)

>When the righteous rejoice, there is great glory; but when the wicked arise, men hide themselves. (Proverbs 28:12 NKJV)

By turning away from all unrighteousness, your singing and rejoicing will no longer be hindered. (summarized from Proverbs 29:6)

>By transgression an evil man is snared, but the righteous sings and rejoices. (Proverbs 29:6 NKJV)

You will be given the oil of gladness instead of mourning. (summarized from Isaiah 61:3)

>To console those who mourn in Zion, to give them beauty for ashes, the oil of joy for mourning, the garment of praise for the spirit of heaviness; that they may be called trees of righteousness, the planting of the Lord, that He may be glorified." (Isaiah 61:3 NKJV)

Exhibit 14: 13 Promises for Your Children

Note: Each promise includes the scripture verse (NKJV translation) plus a summary or amplified definition of key words from the original Hebrew or Greek.

Your children will be blessed. (summarized from Deuteronomy 28:4)

> Blessed shall be the fruit of your body, the produce of your ground and the increase of your herds, the increase of your cattle and the offspring of your flocks. (Deuteronomy 28:4 NKJV)

Yahweh will make you have more than enough in good things in the fruit of your womb. (amplified from Hebrew word yather in Deuteronomy 28:11)

> And the Lord will grant you plenty of goods, in the fruit of your body, in the increase of your livestock, and in the produce of your ground, in the land of which the Lord swore to your fathers to give you. (Deuteronomy 28:11 NKJV)

Your children will never have to seek for food or beg for bread. (summarized from Psalm 37:25)

> I have been young, and now am old; yet I have not seen the righteous forsaken, nor his descendants begging bread. (Psalm 37:25 NKJV)

Your children will be a blessing. (summarized from Psalm 37:26)

> He is ever merciful, and lends; and his descendants are blessed. (Psalm 37:26 NKJV)

You will have a posterity, a good residual or remnant left behind after you are gone, because you walk uprightly. (amplified from Hebrew word ahariyt from Psalm 37:37)

> Mark the blameless man, and behold the upright; for the man of peace will have a posterity. (Psalm 37:37 NASB)

> Mark the blameless man, and observe the upright; for the future of that man is peace. (Psalm 37:37 NKJV)

God's faithfulness to perform His promises will be extended to your children and grandchildren if they walk uprightly. (summarized from Psalm 103:17-18)

Exhibit 14: 13 Promises for Your Children

> 17 But the mercy of the Lord is from everlasting to everlasting on those who fear Him, and His righteousness to children's children,
> 18 To such as keep His covenant, and to those who remember His commandments to do them. (Psalm 103:17-18 NKJV)

Your children will be strong, mighty and courageous in the earth. (amplified from Hebrew word gibbor in Psalm 112:2)

> His descendants will be mighty on earth; the generation of the upright will be blessed. (Psalm 112:2 NKJV)

Your children will slip away from any harm that comes their way. (amplified from Hebrew word malat in Proverbs 11:21)

> Though they join forces, the wicked will not go unpunished; but the posterity of the righteous will be delivered. (Proverbs 11:21 NKJV)

Your children will be a tree of life. (amplified from Hebrew words peri and chayyim in Proverbs 11:30)

> The fruit of the righteous is a tree of life, and he who wins souls is wise. (Proverbs 11:30 NKJV)

You will receive enough possessions to pass on to your children's children. (amplified from Hebrew words nachal and ben in Proverbs 13:22)

> A good man leaves an inheritance to his children's children, but the wealth of the sinner is stored up for the righteous. (Proverbs 13:22 NKJV)

Your sons after you will be happy. (amplified from Hebrew word esher in Proverbs 20:7)

> The righteous man walks in his integrity; his children are blessed after him. (Proverbs 20:7 NKJV)

Your descendants will be as numerous as the sand. (summarized from Isaiah 48:18-19)

The names of your children will never be cut off or destroyed. (summarized from Isaiah 48:18-19)

Exhibit 14: 13 Promises for Your Children

18 Oh, that you had heeded My commandments! Then your peace would have been like a river, and your righteousness like the waves of the sea.
19 Your descendants also would have been like the sand, and the offspring of your body like the grains of sand; his name would not have been cut off nor destroyed from before Me." (Isaiah 48:18-19 NKJV)

Exhibit 15: 7 Promises for Wisdom

Note: Each promise includes the scripture verse (NKJV translation) plus a summary or amplified definition of key words from the original Hebrew or Greek.

God has hidden away a treasure of wisdom that is most helpful and substantial. (amplified from Hebrew words tsaphan and tushiya from Proverbs 2:7a)

> He stores up sound wisdom for the upright; He is a shield to those who walk uprightly; (Proverbs 2:7 NKJV)

You will be able to discern every good path. (summarized from Proverbs 2:9-10)

> 9 Then you will understand righteousness and justice, equity and every good path.
> 10 When wisdom enters your heart, and knowledge is pleasant to your soul, (Proverbs 2:9-10 NKJV)

You will find wisdom walking along beside you on the same path. (summarized from Proverbs 8:20)

> I traverse the way of righteousness, in the midst of the paths of justice, (Proverbs 8:20 NKJV)

When you are instructed and taught, you will learn wisdom. (summarized from Proverbs 9:9)

> Give instruction to a wise man, and he will be still wiser; teach a just man, and he will increase in learning. (Proverbs 9:9 NKJV)

You will learn to rely on your inner man, carefully meditating on what is in your heart, before you answer other people. (summarized from Proverbs 15:28)

> The heart of the righteous studies how to answer, but the mouth of the wicked pours forth evil. (Proverbs 15:28 NKJV)

You will wisely consider the house of the wicked, not being deceived by their apparent prosperity, but recognizing their ultimate end is destruction. (amplified from Hebrew word sakal in Proverbs 21:12)

> The righteous God wisely considers the house of the wicked, overthrowing the wicked for their wickedness. (Proverbs 21:12 NKJV)

Exhibit 15: 7 Promises for Wisdom

God will give you discernment between the clean and the unclean, the holy and the unholy, and use you to teach these things to His people, just as He did with the sons of Zadok. (righteous) because they faithfully guarded the manifested presence of God in His sanctuary. (summarized from Ezekiel 44:23)

> And they shall teach My people the difference between the holy and the unholy, and cause them to discern between the unclean and the clean. (Ezekiel 44:23 NKJV)

Exhibit 16: 9 Promises for Health and Long Life

Note: Each promise includes the scripture verse (NKJV translation) plus a summary or amplified definition of key words from the original Hebrew or Greek.

Diseases will not come upon your body. (summarized from Exodus 15:26)

> And said, "If you diligently heed the voice of the Lord your God and do what is right in His sight, give ear to His commandments and keep all His statutes, I will put none of the diseases on you which I have brought on the Egyptians. For I am the Lord who heals you." (Exodus 15:26 NKJV)

Yahweh will be your strength in times of trouble. (summarized from Psalm 37:39)

> But the salvation of the righteous is from the Lord; He is their strength in the time of trouble. (Psalm 37:39 NKJV)

Your strength will be increased. (amplified from Hebrew words qeren and rum in Psalm 75:10)

> All the horns of the wicked I will also cut off, but the horns of the righteous shall be exalted. (Psalm 75:10 NKJV)

In your old age, you will still bear fruit and continue to prosper and be full of sap and thriving with abundance so you can declare the righteousness of Yahweh. (amplified from Hebrew words nub, dashen, and raanan in Psalm 92:14-15)

> 14 They shall still bear fruit in old age; they shall be fresh and flourishing,
> 15 To declare that the Lord is upright; He is my rock, and there is no unrighteousness in Him. (Psalm 92:14-15 NKJV)

Length of days and long life will be added to you. (summarized from Proverbs 3:1-2)

> 1 My son, do not forget my law, but let your heart keep my commands;
> 2 For length of days and long life and peace they will add to you. (Proverbs 3:1-2 NKJV)

You will live long enough to attain a gray head of hair, which is a crown of glory. (amplified from Hebrew words atarah and tipharah in Proverbs 16:31)

> The silver-haired head is a crown of glory, if it is found in the way of righteousness. (Proverbs 16:31 NKJV)

Exhibit 16: 9 Promises for Health and Long Life

You will find life and honor. (summarized from Proverbs 21:21)

> He who follows righteousness and mercy finds life, righteousness and honor. (Proverbs 21:21 NKJV)

Even if you fall seven times, you will rise again each time. (summarized from Proverbs 24:16)

> For a righteous man may fall seven times and rise again, but the wicked shall fall by calamity. (Proverbs 24:16 NKJV)

You will surely live. (summarized from Ezekiel 18:9)

> If he has walked in My statutes and kept My judgments faithfully, he is just; He shall surely live!" Says the Lord God. (Ezekiel 18:9 NKJV)

Exhibit 17: 17 Promises for Your Position

Note: Each promise includes the scripture verse (NKJV translation) plus a summary or amplified definition of key words from the original Hebrew or Greek.

Yahweh will raise you up into a position of holiness, setting you apart from all others for His service. (summarized from Deuteronomy 28:9)

> The Lord will establish you as a holy people to Himself, just as He has sworn to you, if you keep the commandments of the Lord your God and walk in His ways. (Deuteronomy 28:9 NKJV)

Yahweh will make you the head and not the tail. (summarized from Deuteronomy 28:13)

You only will be above, and you will not be underneath. (summarized from Deuteronomy 28:13)

> 13 And the Lord will make you the head and not the tail; you shall be above only, and not be beneath, if you heed the commandments of the Lord your God, which I command you today, and are careful to observe them.
> 14 So you shall not turn aside from any of the words which I command you this day, to the right or the left, to go after other gods to serve them. (Deuteronomy 28:13-14 NKJV)

God will act in your behalf to restore you to your rightful place. (summarized from Job 8:5-6)

> 5 If you would earnestly seek God and make your supplication to the Almighty,
> 6 If you were pure and upright, surely now He would awake for you, and prosper your rightful dwelling place. (Job 8:5-6 NKJV)

Yahweh will surround you with favor and encircle you with kindness. (amplified from Hebrew word rason in Psalm 5:12)

> For You, O Lord, will bless the righteous; with favor, you will surround him as with a shield. (Psalm 5:12 NKJV)

You will be given authority to rule over the foolish who are appointed for Sheol (summarized from Psalm 49:13-14)

Exhibit 17: 17 Promises for Your Position

> 13 This is the way of those who are foolish, and of their posterity who approve their sayings. Selah
> 14 Like sheep they are laid in the grave; death shall feed on them; the upright shall have dominion over them in the morning; and their beauty shall be consumed in the grave, far from their dwelling. (Psalm 49:13-14 NKJV)

You will be like a green olive tree in the house of God. (summarized from Psalm 52:8)

> But I am like a green olive tree in the house of God; I trust in the mercy of God forever and ever. (Psalm 52:8 NKJV)

God will never allow you to slip or be shaken. (summarized from Psalm 55:22)

> Cast your burden on the Lord, and He shall sustain you; He shall never permit the righteous to be moved. (Psalm 55:22 NKJV)

You will be raised up and promoted in your position. (amplified from Hebrew words qeren and rum in Psalm 75:10)

> All the horns of the wicked I will also cut off, but the horns of the righteous shall be exalted. (Psalm 75:10 NKJV)

You will be planted and flourish in the house of Yahweh. (summarized from Psalm 92:12-13)

> 12 The righteous shall flourish like a palm tree, he shall grow like a cedar in Lebanon.
> 13 Those who are planted in the house of the Lord shall flourish in the courts of our God. (Psalm 92:12-13 NKJV)

You will never stumble or stagger or be shaken. (amplified from Hebrew word mot in Psalm 112:6)

> Surely he will never be shaken; the righteous will be in everlasting remembrance. (Psalm 112:6 NKJV)

You will never slip or be shaken. (amplified from Hebrew word mot in Proverbs 10:30)

> The righteous will never be removed, but the wicked will not inhabit the earth. (Proverbs 10:30 NKJV)

Exhibit 17: 17 Promises for Your Position

You will not be moved, but will stand fast like a well rooted tree. (amplified from Hebrew words shoresh and mot in Proverbs 12:3)

> A man is not established by wickedness, but the root of the righteous cannot be moved. (Proverbs 12:3 NKJV)

You will govern in God's house and have charge over His courts. (summarized from Zechariah 3:7)

> Thus says the Lord of hosts: "If you will walk in My ways, and if you will keep My command, then you shall also judge My house, and likewise have charge of My courts; I will give you places to walk among these who stand here. (Zechariah 3:7 NKJV)

I will give you authority over the nations. (summarized from Revelation 2:26)

You shall rule the nations with a rod of iron. (summarized from Revelation 2:27)

> 26 And he who overcomes, and keeps My works until the end, to him I will give power over the nations,
> 27 "He shall rule them with a rod of iron; they shall be dashed to pieces like the potter's vessels'—as I also have received from My Father; (Revelation 2:26-27 NKJV)

You will be a pillar in the temple of God. (summarized from Revelation 3:12)

> He who overcomes, I will make him a pillar in the temple of My God, and he shall go out no more. I will write on him the name of My God and the name of the city of My God, the New Jerusalem, which comes down out of heaven from My God. And I will write on him My new name. (Revelation 3:12 NKJV)

Exhibit 18: 10 Promises for Your Path

Note: Each promise includes the scripture verse (NKJV translation) plus a summary or amplified definition of key words from the original Hebrew or Greek.

You will be blessed when you come in. (summarized from Deuteronomy 28:6)

You will be blessed when you go out. (summarized from Deuteronomy 28:6)

> Blessed shall you be when you come in, and blessed shall you be when you go out. (Deuteronomy 28:6 NKJV)

Yahweh will know your way, He will see your path and consider your journey. He will discern and detect the right direction for your life. He will be well acquainted with the course of your life. (amplified from Hebrew words yada and derek in Psalm 1:6)

> For the Lord knows the way of the righteous, but the way of the ungodly shall perish. (Psalm 1:6 NKJV)

Righteousness will go before you and prepare the path for your feet to walk. It will guide your steps to help you walk in the right way. It will set your feet on the right path so you can follow it. (amplified from Hebrew words sum, paam, and derek in Psalm 85:13)

> Righteousness will go before Him, and shall make His footsteps our pathway. (Psalm 85:13 NKJV)

Your path will grow brighter and brighter like the rising of the sun until the full day. (summarized from Proverbs 4:18)

> But the path of the just is like the shining sun, that shines ever brighter unto the perfect day. (Proverbs 4:18 NKJV)

The path of Yahweh will be a place of safety and protection to you. (amplified from Hebrew word maoz in Proverbs 10:29)

> The way of the Lord is strength for the upright, but destruction will come to the workers of iniquity. (Proverbs 10:29 NKJV)

Righteousness will keep you on the right path, following the straight way. (amplified from Hebrew word yashar in Proverbs 11:5)

Exhibit 18: 10 Promises for Your Path

The righteousness of the blameless will direct his way aright, but the wicked will fall by his own wickedness. (Proverbs 11:5 NKJV)

You will walk in the path of life. (summarized from Proverbs 12:28)

In the way of righteousness is life, and in its pathway there is no death. (Proverbs 12:28 NKJV)

Your path will be even and smooth because God will make it level. (amplified from Hebrew words meshar and palas in Isaiah 26:7)

The way of the just is uprightness; O Most Upright, you weigh the path of the just. (Isaiah 26:7 NKJV)

You will walk in the ways of Yahweh. (summarized from Hosea 14:9)

Who is wise? Let him understand these things. Who is prudent? Let him know them. For the ways of the Lord are right; the righteous walk in them, but transgressors stumble in them. (Hosea 14:9 NKJV)

Exhibit 19: 20 Promises for Your Character

Note: Each promise includes the scripture verse (NKJV translation) plus a summary or amplified definition of key words from the original Hebrew or Greek.

You will fear no evil when you walk through the valley of the shadow of death.

> 3 He restores my soul; He leads me in the paths of righteousness for His name's sake.
> 4 Yea, though I walk through the valley of the shadow of death, I will fear no evil; for You are with me; Your rod and Your staff, they comfort me. (Psalm 23:3-4 NKJV)

All day long you will be gracious to others and show favor to them. (summarized from Psalm 37:26)

> 25 I have been young, and now am old; yet I have not seen the righteous forsaken, nor his descendants begging bread.
> 26 He is ever merciful, and lends; and his descendants are blessed. (Psalm 37:25-26 NKJV)

You will be a man of peace. (summarized from Psalm 37:37)

> Mark the blameless man, and observe the upright; for the future of that man is peace. (Psalm 37:37 NKJV)

You will see and be glad when God sets the needy securely on high away from affliction, and makes his families like a flock. (summarized from Psalm 107:41-42)

> 41 Yet He sets the poor on high, far from affliction, and makes their families like a flock.
> 42 The righteous see it and rejoice, and all iniquity stops its mouth. (Psalm 107:41-42 NKJV)

You will be gracious and compassionate. (summarized from Psalm 112:4)

> Unto the upright there arises light in the darkness; he is gracious, and full of compassion, and righteous. (Psalm 112:4 NKJV)

You will have no fear of bad news or any kind of evil report. (amplified from Hebrew words ra and shemuah in Psalm 112:7)

Exhibit 19: 20 Promises for Your Character

> He will not be afraid of evil tidings; his heart is steadfast, trusting in the Lord. (Psalm 112:7 NKJV)

Your inner man will remain firm and steady, trusting in Yahweh. (summarized from Psalm 112:8)

Your inner man is upheld because you have support to lean on. (amplified from Hebrew word samak in Psalm 112:8)

> His heart is established; he will not be afraid, until he sees his desire upon his enemies. (Psalm 112:8 NKJV)

You will give freely to the needy. (summarized from Psalm 112:9)

> He has dispersed abroad, he has given to the poor; his righteousness endures forever; his horn will be exalted with honor. (Psalm 112:9 NKJV)

You will an attitude of gratitude, giving thanks to the name of God. (summarized from Psalm 140:13)

> Surely the righteous shall give thanks to Your name; the upright shall dwell in Your presence. (Psalm 140:13 NKJV)

Your desires will change so you desire only things that are surely good and beneficial. (amplified from Hebrew words ak and tob in Proverbs 11:23)

> The desire of the righteous is only good, but the expectation of the wicked is wrath. (Proverbs 11:23 NKJV)

You will think right thoughts. (summarized from Proverbs 12:5)

> The thoughts of the righteous are right, but the counsels of the wicked are deceitful. (Proverbs 12:5 NKJV)

You will hate lies and any kind of deception, so you will want no part in it. (amplified from Hebrew word sheqer in Proverbs 13:5)

> A righteous man hates lying, but a wicked man is loathsome and comes to shame. (Proverbs 13:5 NKJV)

Exhibit 19: 20 Promises for Your Character

You will have the right foundation for ruling from a seat of honor. (amplified from Hebrew words kisse and kun in Proverbs 16:12)

> It is an abomination for kings to commit wickedness, for a throne is established by righteousness. (Proverbs 16:12 NKJV)

You will be glad when wrong things are made right. (amplified from Hebrew word mishpat in Proverbs 21:15)

> It is a joy for the just to do justice, but destruction will come to the workers of iniquity. (Proverbs 21:15 NKJV)

You will freely give of yourself without holding anything back. (amplified from Hebrew words nathan and chasak in Proverbs 21:25-26)

> 25 The desire of the lazy man kills him, for his hands refuse to labor.
> 26 He covets greedily all day long, but the righteous gives and does not spare. (Proverbs 21:25-26 NKJV)

You will be bold as a lion, feeling safe and secure because of your trust and confidence in God. (amplified from Hebrew word batah in Proverbs 28:1)

> The wicked flee when no one pursues, but the righteous are bold as a lion. (Proverbs 28:1 NKJV)

You will be concerned for the rights of the poor. (summarized from Proverbs 29:7)

> The righteous considers the cause of the poor, but the wicked does not understand such knowledge. (Proverbs 29:7 NKJV)

You will find the behavior of unrighteous people to be abominable, you will want no part in their deeds. (amplified from Hebrew word toebah in Proverbs 29:27)

> An unjust man is an abomination to the righteous, and he who is upright in the way is an abomination to the wicked. (Proverbs 29:27 NKJV)

You will be given the mantle of praise instead of a dim, faint spirit. (amplified from Hebrew word keheh in Isaiah 61:3)

Exhibit 19: 20 Promises for Your Character

To console those who mourn in Zion, to give them beauty for ashes, the oil of joy for mourning, the garment of praise for the spirit of heaviness; that they may be called trees of righteousness, the planting of the Lord, that He may be glorified. (Isaiah 61:3 NKJV)

Exhibit 20: 13 Promises for Eternity

Note: Each promise includes the scripture verse (NKJV translation) plus a summary or amplified definition of key words from the original Hebrew or Greek.

You will inherit the land and dwell in it forever. (summarized from Psalm 37:29)

> The righteous shall inherit the land, and dwell in it forever. (Psalm 37:29 NKJV)

You will trust in the lovingkindness of God forever and ever. (summarized from Psalm 52:8)

> But I am like a green olive tree in the house of God; I trust in the mercy of God forever and ever. (Psalm 52:8 NKJV)

Your name will be recorded in the book of life. (summarized from Psalm 69:28)

> Let them be blotted out of the book of the living, and not be written with the righteous. (Psalm 69:28 NKJV)

The goodness and kindness of Yahweh will be upon you forever and ever. (summarized from Psalm 103:17-18)

> 17 But the mercy of the Lord is from everlasting to everlasting on those who fear Him, and His righteousness to children's children,
> 18 To such as keep His covenant, and to those who remember His commandments to do them. (Psalm 103:17-18 NKJV)

Your righteousness will endure forever. (summarized from Psalm 112:3b and 112:9)

> Wealth and riches will be in his house, and his righteousness endures forever. (Psalm 112:3 NKJV)

> He has dispersed abroad, He has given to the poor; His righteousness endures forever; His horn will be exalted with honor. (Psalm 112:9 NKJV)

You will be remembered forever. (summarized from Psalm 112:6b)

> Surely he will never be shaken; the righteous will be in everlasting remembrance. (Psalm 112:6 NKJV)

The voice of salvation will be in your house. (summarized from Psalms 118:15)

Exhibit 20: 13 Promises for Eternity

The voice of rejoicing and salvation is in the tents of the righteous; the right hand of the Lord does valiantly. (Psalms 118:15 NKJV)

You will be delivered from death. (summarized from Proverbs 10:2b, 11:4)

Treasures of wickedness profit nothing, but righteousness delivers from death. (Proverbs 10:2 NKJV)

Riches do not profit in the day of wrath, but righteousness delivers from death. (Proverbs 11:4 NKJV)

You will be rewarded with life. (summarized from Proverbs 10:16a, 11:19)

The labor of the righteous leads to life, the wages of the wicked to sin. (Proverbs 10:16 NKJV)

The hypocrite with his mouth destroys his neighbor, but through knowledge the righteous will be delivered. (Proverbs 11:19 NKJV)

You will get a sure reward that will never be taken away from you. (amplified from Hebrew words emeth and seker in Proverbs 11:18)

The wicked man does deceptive work, but he who sows righteousness will have a sure reward. (Proverbs 11:18 NKJV)

You will find a refuge to protect you from death. (summarized from Proverbs 14:32)

The wicked is banished in his wickedness, but the righteous has a refuge in his death. (Proverbs 14:32 NKJV)

You will shine forth like the sun in the kingdom of your Father. (summarized from Matthew 13:43)

Then the righteous will shine forth as the sun in the kingdom of their Father. He who has ears to hear, let him hear! (Matthew 13:43 NKJV)

You will go into eternal life. (summarized from Matthew 25:46)

"And these will go away into everlasting punishment, but the righteous into eternal life." (Matthew 25:46 NKJV)

Exhibit 21: 8 Promises for Your Land

Note: Each promise includes the scripture verse (NKJV translation) plus a summary or amplified definition of key words from the original Hebrew or Greek.

Yahweh will cause the early and late rain to fall upon your land, so you have a harvest of grain, wine, and oil. (summarized from Deuteronomy 11:13-14)

> 13 And it shall be that if you earnestly obey My commandments which I command you today, to love the Lord your God and serve Him with all your heart and with all your soul,
> 14 then I will give you the rain for your land in its season, the early rain and the latter rain, that you may gather in your grain, your new wine, and your oil. (Deuteronomy 11:13-14 NKJV)

The fruit of your ground will be blessed. (summarized from Deuteronomy 28:4)

> Blessed shall be the fruit of your body, the produce of your ground and the increase of your herds, the increase of your cattle and the offspring of your flocks. (Deuteronomy 28:4 NKJV)

Yahweh will bless you in the land which He gives you. (summarized from Deuteronomy 28:8)

> The Lord will command the blessing on you in your storehouses and in all to which you set your hand, and He will bless you in the land which the Lord your God is giving you. (Deuteronomy 28:8 NKJV)

Yahweh will make you have more than enough in good things in the fruit of your land. (amplified from Hebrew word yather in Deuteronomy 28:11)

> And the Lord will grant you plenty of goods, in the fruit of your body, in the increase of your livestock, and in the produce of your ground, in the land of which the Lord swore to your fathers to give you. (Deuteronomy 28:11 NKJV)

Yahweh will open for you His good storehouse, the heavens, to give rain to your land in its season. (summarized from Deuteronomy 28:12)

> The Lord will open to you His good treasure, the heavens, to give the rain to your land in its season, and to bless all the work of your hand. You shall lend to many nations, but you shall not borrow. (Deuteronomy 28:12 NKJV)

Exhibit 21: 8 Promises for Your Land

Your fields will produce crops and fruit and give you an increase. (summarized from Psalm 85:12)

> Yes, the Lord will give what is good; and our land will yield its increase. (Psalm 85:12 NKJV)

The authority of wickedness will have no dominion over your land. (amplified from Hebrew words shebet and nuach in Psalm 125:3)

> For the scepter of wickedness shall not rest on the land allotted to the righteous, lest the righteous reach out their hands to iniquity. (Psalm 125:3 NKJV)

You will live in the land and remain in it. (summarized from Proverbs 2:21)

> For the upright will dwell in the land, and the blameless will remain in it; (Proverbs 2:21 NKJV)

Exhibit 22: 12 Promises for Honor

Note: Each promise includes the scripture verse (NKJV translation) plus a summary or amplified definition of key words from the original Hebrew or Greek.

No man will be able to stand before you because Yahweh God will lay the dread of you and the fear of you on all the land on which you set your foot. (summarized from Deuteronomy 11:25)

> No man shall be able to stand against you; the Lord your God will put the dread of you and the fear of you upon all the land where you tread, just as He has said to you. (Deuteronomy 11:25 NKJV)

All the peoples of the earth will see that you are called by the name of Yahweh and they will fear you. (summarized from Deuteronomy 28:10)

> Then all peoples of the earth shall see that you are called by the name of the Lord, and they shall be afraid of you. (Deuteronomy 28:10 NKJV)

Other people will see His rewards upon you and acknowledge God has done it. (summarized from Psalm 58:11)

> So that men will say, "Surely there is a reward for the righteous; surely He is God who judges in the earth." (Psalm 58:11 NKJV)

Your strength will be exalted with honor. (amplified from Hebrew word qeren in Psalm 112:9)

> He has dispersed abroad, he has given to the poor; his righteousness endures forever; his horn will be exalted with honor. (Psalm 112:9 NKJV)

Your name will be so highly honored, other people will be blessed by the mention of it or whenever they remember you. (amplified from Hebrew word zeker in Proverbs 10:7)

> The memory of the righteous is blessed, but the name of the wicked will rot. (Proverbs 10:7 NKJV)

The good things in your roots will come forth. (amplified from Hebrew words shoresh and Nathan in Proverbs 12:12)

> The wicked covet the catch of evil men, but the root of the righteous yields fruit. (Proverbs 12:12 NKJV)

Exhibit 22: 12 Promises for Honor

Wicked people will bow their faces at your gates to give honor to that which is good and agreeable and pleasant. (amplified from Hebrew words shachach, shaar and tob in Proverbs 14:19)

> The evil will bow before the good, and the wicked at the gates of the righteous. (Proverbs 14:19 NKJV)

Your people and nation will be exalted to a higher place. (amplified from Hebrew words rum and goy in Proverbs 14:34)

> Righteousness exalts a nation, but sin is a reproach to any people. (Proverbs 14:34 NKJV)

You will find honor. (summarized from Proverbs 21:21)

> He who follows righteousness and mercy finds life, righteousness and honor. (Proverbs 21:21 NKJV)

Your earthly father will greatly rejoice because of you. (amplified from Hebrew word ab in Proverbs 23:24-25)

> 24 The father of the righteous will greatly rejoice, and he who begets a wise child will delight in him.
> 25 Let your father and your mother be glad, and let her who bore you rejoice. (Proverbs 23:24-25 NKJV)

Other people will rejoice when you increase in authority and abundance. (amplified from Hebrew word rabah in Proverbs 29:2)

> When the righteous are in authority, the people rejoice; but when a wicked man rules, the people groan. (Proverbs 29:2 NKJV)

God will distinguish between you and the wicked who do not serve Him. (summarized from Malachi 3:18)

> Then you shall again discern between the righteous and the wicked, between one who serves God and one who does not serve Him. (Malachi 3:18 NKJV)

Exhibit 23: 25 Promises for Blessings

Note: Each promise includes the scripture verse (NKJV translation) plus a summary or amplified definition of key words from the original Hebrew or Greek.

You will be blessed in the city. (summarized from Deuteronomy 28:3a)

You will be blessed in the country. (summarized from Deuteronomy 28:3b)

> Blessed shall you be in the city, and blessed shall you be in the country. (Deuteronomy 28:3 NKJV)

Your basket and your storehouse will be blessed. (summarized from Deuteronomy 28:5)

> Blessed shall be your basket and your kneading bowl. (Deuteronomy 28:5 NKJV)

Yahweh will command the blessing upon all that you put your hand to. (summarized from Deuteronomy 28:8 and 28:12)

> The Lord will command the blessing on you in your storehouses and in all to which you set your hand, and He will bless you in the land which the Lord your God is giving you. (Deuteronomy 28:8 NKJV)

> The Lord will open to you His good treasure, the heavens, to give the rain to your land in its season, and to bless all the work of your hand. You shall lend to many nations, but you shall not borrow. (Deuteronomy 28:12 NKJV)

Yahweh will reward you according to your righteousness. (summarized from 1 Samuel 26:23, 2 Samuel 22:21-25, 2 Chronicles 6:22-23)

> May the Lord repay every man for his righteousness and his faithfulness; for the Lord delivered you into my hand today, but I would not stretch out my hand against the Lord's anointed. (1 Samuel 26:23 NKJV)

Yahweh will bless you, praise you, congratulate you, and salute you. (amplified from Hebrew word barak in Psalm 5:12)

> For You, O Lord, will bless the righteous; with favor, You will surround him as with a shield. (Psalm 5:12 NKJV)

Songs of praise will be becoming to you. (summarized from Psalm 33:1)

Exhibit 23: 25 Promises for Blessings

> Rejoice in the Lord, O you righteous! For praise from the upright is beautiful. (Psalm 33:1 NKJV)

You will see and laugh at the man who would not make God his refuge. (summarized from Psalm 52:6-7)

> 6 The righteous also shall see and fear, and shall laugh at him, saying,
> 7 "Here is the man who did not make God his strength, but trusted in the abundance of his riches, and strengthened himself in his wickedness." (Psalm 52:6-7 NKJV)

You will wash your feet in the blood of the wicked. (summarized from Psalm 58:10)

> The righteous shall rejoice when he sees the vengeance; He shall wash his feet in the blood of the wicked, (Psalm 58:10 NKJV)

You will blossom and sprout, shooting up like a palm tree. (amplified from Hebrew word parach in Psalm 92:12a)

You will grow like a cedar in Lebanon. (summarized from Psalm 92:12b)

> The righteous shall flourish like a palm tree, he shall grow like a cedar in Lebanon. (Psalm 92:12a NKJV)

You will blossom and flourish in the courts of your God. (summarized from Psalm 92:13)

> Those who are planted in the house of the Lord shall flourish in the courts of our God. (Psalm 92:13 NKJV)

The light of God will be sown into you like seed, which means it has the power to produce a harvest of more light the same way any seed reproduces after its kind, if it is properly received and nurtured. (amplified from Hebrew words or and zara in Psalm 97:11)

> Light is sown for the righteous, and gladness for the upright in heart. (Psalm 97:11 NKJV)

You will be happy. (amplified from Hebrew word eser in Psalm 106:3)

Exhibit 23: 25 Promises for Blessings

> Blessed are those who keep justice, and he who does righteousness at all times! (Psalm 106:3 NKJV)

Your generation will be blessed because of your righteousness. (summarized from Psalm 112:2)

> His descendants will be mighty on earth; the generation of the upright will be blessed. (Psalm 112:2 NKJV)

Light will arise in the darkness for you. Even in dark times light breaks forth to help you see what others cannot see. (amplified from Hebrew words zarach and choshek in Psalm 112:4)

> Unto the upright there arises light in the darkness; he is gracious, and full of compassion, and righteous. (Psalm 112:4 NKJV)

You will look with satisfaction upon your enemies. (summarized from Psalm 112:8)

> His heart is established; he will not be afraid, until he sees his desire upon his enemies. (Psalm 112:8 NKJV)

Peace will be added to you. (summarized from Proverbs 3:1-2)

> 1 My son, do not forget my law, but let your heart keep my commands;
> 2 For length of days and long life and peace they will add to you. (Proverbs 3:1-2 NKJV)

Blessings will be upon your head. (summarized from Proverbs 10:6)

> Blessings are on the head of the righteous, but violence covers the mouth of the wicked. (Proverbs 10:6 NKJV)

You will blossom like a budding leaf. (amplified from Hebrew words parech and aleh in Proverbs 11:28)

> He who trusts in his riches will fall, but the righteous will flourish like foliage. (Proverbs 11:28 NKJV)

The fruit of your life will produce a tree of life. (amplified from Hebrew words peri and chayyim in Proverbs 11:30)

Exhibit 23: 25 Promises for Blessings

The fruit of the righteous is a tree of life, and he who wins souls is wise. (Proverbs 11:30 NKJV)

You will see the ultimate destruction of the wicked. (amplified from Hebrew word mappeleth in Proverbs 29:16)

When the wicked are multiplied, transgression increases; but the righteous will see their fall. (Proverbs 29:16 NKJV)

A ransom will be paid for your life. (amplified from Hebrew word padah in Isaiah 1:27)

Zion shall be redeemed with justice, and her penitents with righteousness. (Isaiah 1:27 NKJV)

It will go well with you because you will eat the fruit of your own actions. (summarized from Isaiah 3:10)

Say to the righteous that it shall be well with them, for they shall eat the fruit of their doings. (Isaiah 3:10 NKJV)

I will give you the morning star. (summarized from Revelation 2:28)

And I will give him the morning star. (Revelation 2:28 NKJV)

Exhibit 24: 38 Things that Must Happen Before the Lord Returns

11 Birth Pang Events:

1. There must first be a time of birth pangs, causing intense pain and suffering for many people, but like birth pangs, these contractions will be separated by times of relief. (Matthew 24:8) I believe this has already started and will accelerate in coming years.
2. There must be a transfer of great wealth from the unrighteous to the righteous, filling the house of God with glory. The latter glory of this house will be greater than the former. (Proverbs 13:22, Isaiah 60:4-5, Haggai 2:6-9, Mark 10:29-30)
3. The good news of the kingdom of God must be proclaimed in the whole world as a testimony to all people. (Matthew 24:14)
4. There must be a great harvest of souls (Isaiah 60:1-5, Amos 9:13-15, Zechariah 2:10-12, Matthew 13:24-30, Mark 16:15-18, John 12:32-33, Acts 1:7-8).
5. Nation will rise against nation and kingdom against kingdom. (Matthew 24:7)
6. Many will come in my name saying I am the messiah, and will mislead many. (Matthew 24:5)
7. God will make Jerusalem a heavy stone for all nations. Anyone who tries to lift it will be severely injured. (Zechariah 12:3)
8. Increased famines will mark the beginning of birth pangs. (Matthew 24:7) I don't believe this has been fulfilled yet.
9. The second seal on the book of life must be broken, releasing the rider on the red horse, taking peace from the earth, resulting in men killing one another in war. (Revelation 6:3-4)
10. The third seal on the book of life must be broken, releasing the rider on the black horse, causing a global economic collapse and hyper-inflation. This sounds like a collapse of national currencies, setting the stage for a global currency. (Revelation 6:5-6)
11. The fourth seal on the book of life must be broken, releasing the rider on the pale green horse, bringing death and hell upon a fourth of the earth, killing through war, famine, pestilence, and by attacks from wild animals. (Revelation 6:7-8)

27 Tribulation Events:

1. The tribulation must happen first. (Matthew 24:29-31)
2. The fifth seal must be broken, releasing great persecution and many righteous people killed for their faith. (Matthew 24:9, Revelation 6:9-11)
3. There must first be a great falling away from the faith. (Matthew 24:9-10, 2 Thessalonians 2:3-4)

Exhibit 24: 38 Things that Must Happen Before the Lord Returns

4. The beast kingdom, called the fourth beast, must be established in the earth. It will be dreadful and terrifying and extremely strong with teeth of iron and claws of bronze. It will be different from all other kingdoms preceding it. It will devour the whole earth and tread it down and crush it. (Daniel 7:7 and 7:23)
5. Within this kingdom called the fourth beast, ten kings must arise. (Daniel 7:24) They will receive authority as kings with the beast for one hour. They will have a common purpose, giving their power and authority and their kingdom to the beast. (Revelation 17:12-17)
6. The ten kings will hate the harlot and make her desolate and naked and will eat her flesh and burn her with fire. (Revelation 17:16) The harlot is the great city, which reigns over the kings of the earth. (Revelation 17:18)
7. Three of those ten kings will be subdued by one who arises after them. This is the little horn who arises among the ten horns, replacing three of the ten kings. (Daniel 7:8 and 7:24)
8. An evil king, the antichrist, must take action against the strongest of fortresses with the help of a foreign god. (Daniel 11:39)
9. The first beast, which is the antichrist, must be given authority over every tribe and people and tongue and nation. (Revelation 13:7)
10. All who dwell on earth will worship the beast. (Revelation 13:8)
11. The one who now restrains lawlessness must be taken out of the way. (Daniel 12:1, 2 Thessalonians 2:6-8) The restrainer cannot be the Church because the restrainer is removed prior to the revealing of the man of lawlessness, and his revealing happens prior to the rapture of the Church. (2 Thessalonians 2:1-8) The restrainer cannot be the Holy Spirit because He has promised He would never leave us or forsake us. (Hebrews 13:5)
12. The man of lawlessness must be revealed. (2 Thessalonians 2:6-8)
13. The antichrist must make a seven-year covenant with the many. (Daniel 9:27)
14. The third temple must be rebuilt. (Isaiah 66:6, Daniel 8:13-14 and 9:27, Zechariah 1:16-17, 2 Thessalonians 2:3-4, Revelation 11:1-2)
15. In the middle of the week, the antichrist violates his seven-year covenant and establishes his throne in the temple in Jerusalem. (Daniel 9:27, Matthew 24:15)
16. The little horn, which replaces the three kings, also called the antichrist, must make war against the holy ones. They will be given into his hand and overcome by him for 42 months, (Daniel 7:21, 7:25 and 8:24, Revelation 13:7) until their power is shattered. (Daniel 7:25 and 12:6-7)
17. The little horn, the antichrist, will make changes in times and in laws. (Daniel 7:25) This might include changes to the calendar, holidays, and laws, especially regarding religious practices, as he attempts to sever all ties to our historical heritage, eliminating all references to the true messiah, all designed to bring everyone under his control.

Exhibit 24: 38 Things that Must Happen Before the Lord Returns

18. The sanctuary of the third temple must be thrown down. (Daniel 8:11)
19. The holy place of the temple must be trampled for 2,300 evenings and mornings. (Daniel 8:13-14)
20. A remnant of God's people must be made holy and blameless, having no spot or wrinkle or any such thing. (Ephesians 5:27)
21. God's people must do greater works than Jesus did in His earthly ministry. (John 14:12)
22. The ministry of the apostles and prophets must become the foundation of the Church, no longer outcasts, no longer a freak show. (Ephesians 2:20, Revelation 12:14)
23. The second beast, the false prophet, must make fire come down out of heaven to the earth in the presence of men. (Revelation 13:13)
24. The second beast, the false prophet, must require everyone to be given a mark on their right hand or on their forehead. (Revelation 13:16)
25. All the nations of the earth must be gathered around Jerusalem to make war against her. (Psalm 83:1-5, Joel 3:2-3, Zechariah 12:3)
26. Damascus, the capital city of Syria, must be removed from being a city and become a fallen ruin. (Isaiah 17:1, Jeremiah 49:23-27)
27. Sin must be completed, brought to full maturity, before it is brought to an end. (Daniel 7:24) This will be fulfilled with the abomination that brings desolation.

Exhibit 25: Koran Teaches Terror and Murder of Non-Muslims

Note: This is just a small sample of verses from the Koran teaching Muslims to terrorize and murder non-Muslims. There are many other similar verses proving it is not a religion of peace.

Soon shall We cast terror into the hearts of the Unbelievers, for that they joined companions with Allah, for which He had sent no authority. (Koran 3:151)

The punishment of those who wage war against Allah and His messenger and strive to make mischief in the land is only this, that they should be murdered or crucified or their hands and their feet should be cut off on opposite sides or they should be imprisoned; this shall be as a disgrace for them in this world, and in the hereafter they shall have a grievous chastisement. (Koran 5:33)

If you encounter those who disbelieve, strike their necks... behead them. (Koran 7:4)

Give firmness to the believers: I will instill terror into the hearts of the unbelievers. You smite them above their necks and smite all their fingertips off them. (Koran 8:12)

Strike terror into the hearts of the enemies of God (Allah) and your enemies and others. (Koran 8:60)

When the sacred months are over, slay the idolaters wherever you find them. Arrest them, besiege them, and lie in ambush everywhere for them. (Koran 9:5)

And the Jews say: Ezra is the son of Allah; and the Christians say: The Messiah is the son of Allah; these are the words of their mouths; they imitate the saying of those who disbelieved before; may Allah destroy them; how they are turned away! (Koran 9:30)

O Prophet! Make war on the unbelievers and the hypocrites. Be harsh with them. Their ultimate abode is hell, a hapless journey's end. (Koran 9:73)

Believers! Make war on the infidels who dwell around you. Let them find harshness in you. (Koran 9:123)

When you meet the unbelievers, smite their necks (cut off their heads), then when you have made wide slaughter among them, tie fast the bonds, then set them free, either by grace or ransom, until the war lays down its burdens. (Koran 47:4)

Prophet! Make war on the unbelievers and the hypocrites and deal sternly with them. Hell shall be their home, evil their fate. (Koran 66:9)

Exhibit 26: 38 Islamic Co-conspirator Organizations Names in Federal Court Case, US vs Holy Land Foundation, 2008

1. Al Anwar Al Ibrahimi Library
2. Al Aqsa Educational Fund
3. Al Aqsa Society
4. Al Razi Hospital
5. Al Salah Society
6. American Middle Eastern League, aka AMEL
7. Association de Secours Palestinians
8. Bethlehem Orphans Society
9. Commiti De Bienfaisance et de Secours aux Palestinians, aka CBSP
10. Council on American Islamic Relations, aka CAIR
11. HAMAS
12. IAP Information Office
13. INFOCOM
14. International Computers and Communications, aka ICC
15. Interpal
16. Islamic Action Front
17. Islamic Association for Palestine in North America, aka IAP
18. Islamic Association for Palestine, aka IAP
19. Islamic Center of Gaza, aka Islamic Complex, aka Al Mojamma Al Islami
20. Islamic Charitable Society of Hebron
21. Islamic Heritage Committee
22. Islamic Relief Committee
23. Islamic Science and Culture Committee
24. Islamic Society of Gaza
25. Islamic Society of North America, aka ISNA
26. Islamic University of Gaza
27. Jersualem Fund, aka IRFAN
28. K & A Overseas Trading
29. Muslim Arab Youth Association, aka MAYA
30. Muslim Womens' Society
31. North American Islamic Trust, aka NAIT
32. Palestine and Lebanon Relief Fund
33. Palestine Relief and Development Fund
34. Palestinian Association of Austria
35. Patients Friends Society
36. Sanabil Foundation for Relief and Development
37. United Association for Studies and Research, aka UASR
38. Young Mens' Muslim Society

Source: HLF and Leaders Convicted on Providing Material Support to Hamas Terrorist Organization, U.S. Department of Justice, May 27, 2009, James T. Jacks, Acting United States Attorney, Northern District of Texas, www.usdoj.gov/usao/txn

Exhibit 27: 40 U.S. Military & Paramilitary Conflicts 1965-2018

1964-1975 – Vietnam War
U.S. and South Vietnamese forces relied on air superiority and overwhelming firepower to conduct search and destroy operations, involving ground forces, artillery, and airstrikes. The U.S. conducted a large-scale strategic bombing campaign against North Vietnam. (E2701)

1965 US Military Invasion of Dominican Republic
Allegations of foreign support for the rebels led to a United States intervention in the conflict, which later transformed into an Organization of American States occupation of the country. United States overthrow of Dominican Republic President Donald Reid Cabral and defeat of his Loyalist forces, followed by US military occupation until 1966. (E2702)

1966-1967 US Military Assists Bolivian Military Against Rebel Forces (E2703)
U.S. military personnel trained, advised and assisted Bolivian special forces in hunting down and destroying rebel guerilla forces led by Che Guevera.

1970 US Bombing and Military Attach to Overthrow Kingdom of Cambodia
US supported Communist Party of Kampuchea, also known as Khmer Rouge, overthrew the Kingdom of Cambodia in 1970, causing the Cambodian Civil War, which ended in 1975. The US attack included 1969-1970 Operation Menu, which was the codename for a covert United States bombing of eastern Cambodia. Operation Menu bombings were an escalation of what had previously been tactical air attacks. Newly inaugurated President Richard Nixon authorized for the first time use of long range B-52 heavy bombers to carpet bomb Cambodia. (E2704, E2705, E2706)

1971 US Military Operation Lam Son 719 Invasion of Laos
The United States provided logistical, aerial, and artillery support to the operation, but its ground forces were prohibited by law from entering Laotian territory. The objective of the campaign was the disruption of a possible future offensive by the People's Army of Vietnam (PAVN), whose logistical system within Laos was known as the Ho Chi Minh Trail (the Truong Son Road to North Vietnam). (E2707)

1973 Chilean False Flag Attacks and Military Coup
The Nixon Administration laid the groundwork for an overthrow of the Chilean government and covert CIA operatives were inserted into Chile to destabilize the nation through false flag events designed to instigate the overthrow of Salvador Allende's Chilean government in 1973 by military force. (E2708)

Exhibit 27: 40 U.S. Military & Paramilitary Conflicts 1965-2018

1974-1981 US Military Intervention in Ethiopian Civil War
After Soviet backed communists overthrew the government of the Ethiopian Empire and Emperor Haile Selassie in a coup d'état on 12 September 1974, the United States armed, trained and assisted opposition groups to join the Eritrean separatists who were already fighting for liberation from Ethiopian rule. The civil war led to a famine and caused at least 1.4 million deaths, with 1 million of the deaths being related to famine and the remaining 400,000 killed in the war. (E2709)

1975 US Backed Indonesian Invasion of East Timor
American military advisers and mercenaries fought alongside Indonesian soldiers against FRETILIN in two battles. In the meantime, American pilots flew OV-10 Bronco aircraft for the Indonesian Air Force in bombing raids against the liberated areas under FRETILIN control. Using US military weapons and equipment and with the full support of US President Gerald Ford, Indonesia invaded East Timor and subsequently occupied the conquered nation. After the conquest, the United States continued providing military aid to Indonesia. (E2710)

1975 Angolan Civil War
Operation IA Feature, a covert Central Intelligence Agency operation, authorized U.S. military support for Jonas Savimbi's National Union for the Total Independence of Angola (UNITA) and Holden Roberto's National Liberation Front of Angola (FNLA) militants in the Angolan Civil War. (E2711)

1977-1978 US Airforce Repels Congo Forces Invading Zaire
In 1977 and again in May, 1978, 6,500 Congolese rebels invaded Zaire, but military intervention by the United States, France and Belgium beat back the invasion. U.S. Air Force elements involved included a Combat Control Team (air traffic controllers) of the 435th Tactical Airlift Wing, the 445th Military Airlift Wing, and other airlift wings. (E2712)

1979-1989 – CIA Operation Cyclone in Afghanistan
United States CIA armed, trained, and financed Mujahideen in Afghanistan to fight USSR through Operation Cyclone. (E2713)

1979-1990 US Military Attempts to Overthrow Nicaraguan Government
The U.S. played a very large role in financing, training, arming, and advising a militant rebel group called the Nicaraguan Contras from 1979-1990. The Contras only became capable of carrying out significant military operations because of this support. By 1987, virtually all contra organizations were united, at least nominally, into the Nicaraguan Resistance. (E2714)

Exhibit 27: 40 U.S. Military & Paramilitary Conflicts 1965-2018

1981 Gulf of Sidra Conflict with Libya

In August 1981, Reagan authorized a large naval force led by a pair of aircraft carriers, USS Forrestal and USS Nimitz, to deploy to the disputed Gulf of Sidra, which Libya claimed as part of its territorial waters. Two Russian made Libyan Su-22 Fitter fired upon and were subsequently shot down by two U.S. F-14 Tomcats off the Libyan coast. (E2715)

1983 US Military Operation Urgent Fury invasion of Grenada

The invasion, led by the United States, of the Caribbean island nation of Grenada, which has a population of about 91,000 and is located 160 kilometers (99 mi) north of Venezuela, resulted in a U.S. victory within a matter of days. (E2716)

1986 US Military Operation El Dorado Canyon Attacked Libya

The 1986 United States bombing of Libya, code-named Operation El Dorado Canyon, comprised air strikes by the United States against Libya on Tuesday, April 15, 1986. The attack was carried out by the U.S. Air Force, U.S. Navy and U.S. Marine Corps via air strikes, in retaliation for the 1986 West Berlin discotheque bombing. There were 40 reported Libyan casualties, and one U.S. plane was shot down. (E2717)

1987-1988 US Military Operation Praying Mantis Attack on Iran

The Iranian Navy ship Sahand was sunk in Operation Praying Mantis on 18 April 1988. Located by two American A-6E Intruders of Attack Squadron VA-95steaming roughly 16 kilometers (10 mi) southwest of Larak Island, she was hit by two Harpoon missiles and four AGM-123 Skipper II laser-guided missiles. A pair of Rockeye cluster bombs from the aircraft and a single Harpoon from the destroyer USS Joseph Strauss finished off the ship. Left heavily aflame, dead in the water and listing to port, Sahand burned for several hours before fire reached her ammunition magazines and they detonated, sinking the ship in over 660 feet (200 meters) of water southwest of Larak Island, 45 of her crew were killed. (E2718, E2719)

1989-1990 US Military Operation Just Cause Invasion of Panama

This military operation involved 27,684 U.S. troops and over 300 aircraft, including C-130 Hercules tactical transports flown by the 317th Tactical Airlift Wing. During the invasion, de facto Panamanian leader, military general and dictator Manuel Noriega was deposed, president-elect Guillermo Endara sworn into office, and the Panamanian Defense Force dissolved. (E2720)

1990-1991 US Military Operation Desert Storm invasion of Iraq

Coalition forces from 35 nations led by the United States against Iraq in response to Iraq's invasion and annexation of Kuwait arising from oil pricing and production

Exhibit 27: 40 U.S. Military & Paramilitary Conflicts 1965-2018

disputes. The war is also known under other names, such as the Persian Gulf War, First Gulf War, Gulf War I, Kuwait War, First Iraq War. (E2721)

1993 US Military Operation Gothic Serpent Against Somalia
Operation Gothic Serpent was a military operation conducted by United States special operations forces during the Somali Civil War with the primary mission of capturing faction leader Mohamed Farrah Aidid. The operation occurred in Somalia from August to October 1993 and was supervised by the Joint Special Operations Command (JSOC). (E2722)

1994-1995 US Operation Uphold Democracy Invasion of Haiti
United States military invasion of Haiti in September 1994 removed the military regime installed by the 1991 Haitian coup d'état that overthrew the elected Roman Catholic Priest, President Jean-Bertrand Aristide. (E2723)

1994-1997 – US Involvement in Iraqi Kurdish Civil War
The Iraqi Kurdish Civil War was a military conflict that took place between rival Kurdish factions in Iraqi Kurdistan during the mid-1990s, most notably between the Patriotic Union of Kurdistan and the Kurdistan Democratic Party. Over the course of the conflict, Kurdish factions from Iran and Turkey, as well as Iranian, Iraqi and Turkish forces were drawn into the fighting, with additional involvement from American forces. (E2724)

1995 US Military Operation Deliberate Force Against Bosnia
Operation Deliberate Force was a sustained air campaign conducted by the United States and other NATO allies to undermine the military capability of the Bosnian Serbian Army (aka Republika Srpska - VRS). The Bosnian War took place in Bosnia and Herzegovina between 1 April 1992 and 14 December 1995. (E2725)

1996 CIA Coup Attempt to Remove Saddam Hussein from Iraq
The CIA organized military training and supplied lethal weapons to Kurdish National Congress guerillas in northern Iraq and helped them launch an offensive against Saddam Hussein regime, which failed. (E2726)

1998 US Naval Operation Infinite Reach Cruise Missile Strikes Against Sudan
Operation Infinite Reach was the codename for American cruise missile strikes on al-Qaeda bases in Khost, Afghanistan, and the Al-Shifa pharmaceutical factory in Khartoum, Sudan, on August 20, 1998. The attacks were launched by the U.S. Navy. (E2727)

Exhibit 27: 40 U.S. Military & Paramilitary Conflicts 1965-2018

1998 US Military Airstrikes in Republic of Kosovo
United States military airstrikes against the Republic of Kosovo, combined with NATO allies, caused an estimated 1,200 to 5,700 civilian casualties. The Kosovo War was an armed conflict in Kosovo that started in late February 1998 and lasted until 11 June 1999. It was fought by the forces of the Federal Republic of Yugoslavia (by this time, consisting of the Republics of Montenegro and Serbia), which controlled Kosovo before the war, and the Kosovo Albanian rebel group known as the Kosovo Liberation Army (KLA), with air support from the NATO from 24 March 1999, and ground support from the Albanian army. (E2728)

1999 US Military Operation Allied Force against Yugoslavia
The U.S. was the dominant member of the coalition against Yugoslavia, although other NATO members were involved. During the ten weeks of the conflict, NATO aircraft flew over 38,000 combat missions by over 1,000 aircraft operating from air bases in Italy and Germany, and the aircraft carrier USS Theodore Roosevelt stationed in the Adriatic Sea. (E2729)

2001 9/11 CIA Attack on World Trade Towers and Pentagon
This 3-hour video explains scientific evidence proving the attack on the World Trade Towers and Pentagon on September 11, 2001, which killed over 3,000 American citizens, were CIA-instigated false flag events. The purpose was to manipulate US public support for the bogus war on terror, justifying unlimited wars throughout the world. (E2730)

2001 Operation Enduring Freedom Afghanistan
The United States military first invaded Afghanistan, then followed up with this Nationwide manhunt in Afghanistan to capture or kill members of al Qaeda and Taliban insurgents, including Osama bin Laden. (E2731)

2002-2006 US Military Intervention in Kingdom of Nepal Civil War
The United States provided extensive military and economic aid to the Nepali government to fight against communist insurgents. On 1 February 2005, in response to the inability of the relatively democratic government to restore order, King Gyanendra seized full control of Nepal to end the insurgency. (E2732)

2003 US Military Operation Iraqi Freedom
Combined military forces from the United States, the United Kingdom, Australia and Poland invaded Iraq. The American-led coalition sent 177,194 troops into Iraq during the initial invasion phase, which lasted from 19 March to 9 April 2003. (E2733)

Exhibit 27: 40 U.S. Military & Paramilitary Conflicts 1965-2018

2004 US Drone Strikes in North-West Pakistan

The War of North-West Pakistan is also known as the War in Khyber Pakhtunkhwa. It is an armed conflict involving Pakistan, and armed militant groups such as the Tehrik-i-Taliban Pakistan (TTP), Jundallah, Lashkar-e-Islam (LeI), TNSM, al-Qaeda, and their Central Asian allies such as the ISIL–Khorasan (ISIL), Islamic Movement of Uzbekistan, East Turkistan Movement, Emirate of Caucasus, and elements of organized crime. U.S. military drone strikes introduced by President George W. Bush[241] and continued by President Barack Obama. As of present, almost 60%–80% of Pakistanis consider the United States as an enemy combatant state. (E2734)

2007-2008 US Military Operation Enduring Freedom Horn of Africa

Nationwide manhunt in seven nations in northern Africa, called the Horn of Africa, to capture or kill members of Al-Shabaab jihadist group. These nations include Sudan, Somalia, Djibouti, Ethiopia, Eritrea, Seychelles and Kenya. This campaign started in 2005 and is still underway as of 2019. On March 3, 2008, the United States launched an air strike on Dhoble, a Somali town. The same area was targeted by U.S. bombers one year earlier. A successful air strike occurred on May 1, 2008 in Dhusamareb. (E2735)

2009 US Military Operation Enduring Freedom Philippines

Operation Enduring Freedom – Philippines (OEF-P) or Operation Freedom Eagle was part of Operation Enduring Freedom and the global War on Terror. The Operation targeted the various Jihadist terror groups operating in the country. By 2009, about 600 U.S. military personnel were advising and assisting the Armed Forces of the Philippines (AFP) in the Southern Philippines. In addition, by 2014, the CIA had sent its elite paramilitary officers from their Special Activities Division to hunt down and kill or capture key terrorist leaders. (E2736)

2011 US Military Attacks on Libya

American involvement in the Libyan Civil War initially consisted of diplomatic initiatives and sanctions. This was followed by the implementation of the UN-mandated no-fly zone, the development of diplomatic relations with the rebels as well as humanitarian aid, bombing missions to destroy Gaddafi's military capabilities, and diplomatic assistance to the rebels. In March 2011, five United States Air Force bombers (three B-2s and two B-1Bs) dropped bombs on at least 100 targets in Libya. American and British naval forces fired over 110 Tomahawk cruise missiles in an overthrow of the Libyan government of Colonel Muammar Gaddafi. The attack was supported by the French Air Force, British Royal Air Force, and Royal Canadian Air Force undertaking sorties across Libya and a naval blockade by Coalition forces. (E2737, E2738)

Exhibit 27: 40 U.S. Military & Paramilitary Conflicts 1965-2018

2013 US Military Operation Juniper Shield in Niger

American military and CIA deployed special forces and armed drones in support of the Niger's government against militant groups in Niger, Libya and Mali. Between 2015 through 2017 American personal had been involved in at least 10 firefights while operating with partner Niger military. On October 4, 2017 a joint American and Nigerien force of 46 personal and eight vehicles was ambushed outside the village of Tongo Tongo by an estimated force of over 50 militants with around 20 motorcycles and 12 technical fighters from the Islamic State in the Greater Sahara (ISGS). During the firefight which lasted for more than three hours, four American, four Nigerien and at least 21 ISGS militants died and eight Nigerien and two Americans including the teams commander were wounded. On December 6, 2017 two months after the October ambush a joint force of American Green Berets and Nigerien soldiers were attacked by ISIL-West Africa militants in the Chad Lake basin Region. During the firefight 11 militants died including two wearing suicide vests, one weapons cache was also destroyed during the operation. (E2739)

2011-2107 US Military Operation Observant Compass in Uganda

Operation Observant Compass is the name of the deployment of US forces to Uganda and other countries in central Africa to counter the Lord's Resistance Army (C-LRA). The force provider to the operation's US Africa Command (AFRICOM) C-LRA Control Element (ACCE) for the operation is the Special Operations Command and Control Element - Horn of Africa (SOCCE-HOA), the special operations forces component of AFRICOM's Combined Joint Task Force - Horn of Africa (CJTF-HOA). On 30 March 2017, the United States Military announced it was ending this operation. (E2740)

2012 Mali Tuareg Rebellion in Mali

The Tuareg Rebellion of 2012 was an early stage of the Northern Mali conflict; from January to April 2012, a war was waged against the Malian government by rebels with the goal of attaining independence for the northern region of Mali, known as Azawad. The United States Air Force air-dropped supplies via C-130 Hercules aircraft in support of the besieged Malian soldiers.[153] The C-130's most likely came from either Ouagadougou, Burkina Faso, or Mauritania, both of which are known to have been used by the United States military. (E2741)

2014-2019 US Attempted Overthrow of Syrian Government

The United States first supplied the rebels of the Free Syrian Army with non-lethal aid (including food rations and pickup trucks), but quickly began providing training by U.S. military personnel, money, and intelligence to selected Syrian rebel commanders. Two U.S. programs attempted to assist the Syrian rebels. One was a 2014 Pentagon program that planned to train and equip 15,000 rebels, which was canceled in 2015 after spending $500 million and producing only a few dozen fighters. A simultaneous $1 billion covert program ran by the Central Intelligence Agency (CIA) was more successful, but was decimated by Russian bombing and canceled in mid-2017 by the Trump administration. (E2742)

2015 US-Saudi Arabian Attack Against Yemen

U.S. forces supported the Saudis in their military intervention in Yemen, establishing a "Joint Planning Cell" with Saudi Arabia, including numerous drone strikes and a US Navy Seal raid on Yakla Yemen on January 29, 2017. The Yemeni Civil War is an ongoing conflict that began in 2015 between two factions: the internationally recognized Yemeni government, led by Abdrabbuh Mansur Hadi, and the Houthi armed movement, along with their supporters and allies. (E2743)

2017-2018 US Missile Strikes Against Syria

On the morning of 7 April 2017, the United States launched 59 Tomahawk cruise missiles from the Mediterranean Sea into Syria, aimed at Shayrat Airbase controlled by the Syrian government. Like all these other unconstitutional wars, the US Congress was never given any opportunity to vote on this act of war, but a select group of more than two dozen Congressmen were notified of the plans by President Trump the night before. On 14 April 2018, beginning at 04:00 Syrian time, the United States, France, and the United Kingdom carried out a series of military strikes involving aircraft and ship-based missiles against multiple government sites in Syria. (E2744, E2745)

ENDNOTES

E2701: 1964-1975 – Vietnam War - https://en.wikipedia.org/wiki/Vietnam_War

E2702: 1965 US Military Invasion of Dominican Republic, https://en.wikipedia.org/wiki/Dominican_Civil_War#U.S._intervention

E2703: 1966-1967 CIA Arms Militant Groups in Bolivia, https://en.wikipedia.org/wiki/Ñancahuazú_Guerrilla

E2704: 1970 Coup Overthrow of Kingdom of Cambodia, https://en.wikipedia.org/wiki/Cambodian_coup_of_1970

E2705: 1970 Coup Overthrow of Kingdom of Cambodia, https://en.wikipedia.org/wiki/Operation_Menu

Exhibit 27: 40 U.S. Military & Paramilitary Conflicts 1965-2018

E2706: 1970 Coup Overthrow of Kingdom of Cambodia, https://en.wikipedia.org/wiki/Cambodian_Civil_War

E2707: 1971 US Military Operation Lam Son 719 Invasion of Laos, https://en.wikipedia.org/wiki/Operation_Lam_Son_719

E2708: 1973 Chilean Coup, https://en.wikipedia.org/wiki/1973_Chilean_coup_d%27état

E2709: 1974-1981 US Military Intervention in Ethiopian Civil War, https://en.wikipedia.org/wiki/Ethiopian_Civil_War

E2710: 1975 US Backed Indonesian Invasion of East Timor, https://en.wikipedia.org/wiki/Indonesian_occupation_of_East_Timor#United_States

E2711: 1975 Angolan Civil War, https://en.wikipedia.org/wiki/Operation_IA_Feature

E2712: 1977-1978 US Airforce Repels Congo Forces Invading Zaire, https://en.wikipedia.org/wiki/Shaba_II

E2713: 1979-1989 – CIA Operation Cyclone in Afghanistan, https://en.wikipedia.org/wiki/Operation_Cyclone

E2714: 1979-1990 US Military Attempts to Overthrow Nicaraguan Government, https://en.wikipedia.org/wiki/Contras#U.S._military_and_financial_assistance

E2715: 1981 Gulf of Sidra Conflict with Libya, https://en.wikipedia.org/wiki/Gulf_of_Sidra_incident_(1981)

E2716: 1983 US Military Operation Urgent Fury invasion of Grenada, https://en.wikipedia.org/wiki/United_States_invasion_of_Grenada

E2717: 1986 US Military Operation El Dorado Canyon Attacked Libya, https://en.wikipedia.org/wiki/1986_United_States_bombing_of_Libya

E2718: 1987-1988 US Military Operation Praying Mantis Attack on Iran, https://en.wikipedia.org/wiki/Operation_Praying_Mantis

E2719: 1987-1988 US Military Operation Praying Mantis Attack on Iran, https://en.wikipedia.org/wiki/Iranian_frigate_Sahand

E2720: 1989-1990 US Military Operation Just Cause Invasion of Panama, https://en.wikipedia.org/wiki/United_States_invasion_of_Panama#Invasion

E2721: 1990-1991 US Military Operation Desert Storm invasion of Iraq, https://en.wikipedia.org/wiki/Gulf_War

E2722: 1993 US Military Operation Gothic Serpent Against Somalia, https://en.wikipedia.org/wiki/Operation_Gothic_Serpent

Exhibit 27: 40 U.S. Military & Paramilitary Conflicts 1965-2018

E2723: 1994-1995 US Operation Uphold Democracy Invasion of Haiti, https://en.wikipedia.org/wiki/Operation_Uphold_Democracy

E2724: 1994-1997 – US Involvement in Iraqi Kurdish Civil War, https://en.wikipedia.org/wiki/Iraqi_Kurdish_Civil_War

E2725: 1995 US Military Operation Deliberate Force Against Bosnia, https://en.wikipedia.org/wiki/Operation_Deliberate_Force

E2726: 1996 CIA Coup Attempt to Remove Saddam Hussein from Iraq, Association of Former Intelligence Officers (19 May 2003), US Coup Plotting in Iraq, Weekly Intelligence Notes 19-03, https://www.washingtonpost.com/archive/politics/1997/06/26/how-cias-secret-war-on-saddam-collapsed/b83592cb-0117-4c3c-a101-9550e29c94a3/?utm_term=.f1bad22dcd47

E2727: 1998 US Naval Operation Infinite Reach Cruise Missile Strikes Against Sudan, https://en.wikipedia.org/wiki/Operation_Infinite_Reach

E2728: 1998 US Military Airstrikes in Republic of Kosovo, https://en.wikipedia.org/wiki/Kosovo_War

E2729: 1999 US Military Operation Allied Force against Yugoslavia, https://en.wikipedia.org/wiki/NATO_bombing_of_Yugoslavia

E2730: 2001 9/11 CIA Attack on World Trade Towers and Pentagon, https://www.youtube.com/watch?v=Ja67D0vKh6U

E2731: Operation Enduring Freedom in Afghanistan, https://en.wikipedia.org/wiki/War_in_Afghanistan_(2001–present)

E2732: 2002-2006 US Military Intervention in Kingdom of Nepal Civil War, https://en.wikipedia.org/wiki/Nepalese_Civil_War

E2733: 2003 US Military Operation Iraqi Freedom, https://en.wikipedia.org/wiki/2003_invasion_of_Iraq

E2734: 2004 US Drone Strikes in North-West Pakistan, https://en.wikipedia.org/wiki/War_in_North-West_Pakistan#United_States_role

E2735: 2007-2008 US Military Airstrikes on Somalia, https://en.wikipedia.org/wiki/Somali_Civil_War_(2006–2009)

E2736: 2009 US Military Operation Enduring Freedom Philippines, https://en.wikipedia.org/wiki/Operation_Enduring_Freedom_-_Philippines

E2737: 2011 US Military Attacks on Libya, https://en.wikipedia.org/wiki/2011_military_intervention_in_Libya

Exhibit 27: 40 U.S. Military & Paramilitary Conflicts 1965-2018

E2738: 2011 US Military Attacks on Libya, https://en.wikipedia.org/wiki/Libyan_Civil_War_(2011)

E2739: 2013 US Military Operation Juniper Shield in Niger, https://en.wikipedia.org/wiki/Operation_Juniper_Shield_-_Niger

E2740: 2011-2107 US Military Operation Observant Compass in Uganda, https://www.globalsecurity.org/military/ops/observant-compass.htm

E2741: 2012 Mali Tuareg Rebellion in Mali, https://en.wikipedia.org/wiki/Tuareg_rebellion_(2012)

E2742: 2014-2019 Attempted Overthrow of Syrian Government, https://en.wikipedia.org/wiki/American-led_intervention_in_the_Syrian_Civil_War

E2743: 2015 US-Saudi Arabian Attack Against Yemen, https://en.wikipedia.org/wiki/Yemeni_Civil_War_(2015–present)

E2744: 2017 US Missile Strikes Against Syria, https://en.wikipedia.org/wiki/2017_Shayrat_missile_strike

E2745: 2018 US Missile Strikes Against Syria, https://en.wikipedia.org/wiki/2018_missile_strikes_against_Syria

CPSIA information can be obtained
at www.ICGtesting.com
Printed in the USA
FSHW021043130721
83189FS